W9-ASD-610

Credit Reporting Systems and the International Economy

Credit Reporting Systems and the International Economy

edited by
Margaret J. Miller

The MIT Press
Cambridge, Massachusetts
London, England

© 2003 Massachusetts Institute of Technology

All rights reserved. No part of this book may be reproduced in any form by any electronic or mechanical means (including photocopying, recording, or information storage and retrieval) without permission in writing from the publisher.

This book was set in Palatino on 3B2 by Asco Typesetters, Hong Kong. Printed and bound in the United States of America.

Library of Congress Cataloging-in-Publication Data

Credit reporting systems and the international economy / edited by Margaret J. Miller.
    p.   cm.
Many of the papers included here were first presented at the International Conference on Credit Reporting Systems, held in Miami, Florida, in June 2000.—Foreword.
Includes bibliographical references and index.
ISBN 0-262-13422-5 (hc. : alk. paper)
    1. Credit bureaus—Congresses. 2. Consumer credit—Congresses. 3. Credit bureaus—Directories. I. Miller, Margaret J., 1963–
HG3751.5 .C73   2003
332.3—dc21   2002026344

Contents

Foreword

The institutional aspects of development have received increasing attention in recent years and rightly so. Credit reporting is one of the most important institutions in a modern financial system; however, it has been largely ignored until recently. This book is the culmination of a multiyear international research project sponsored by the World Bank Group to better understand how credit reporting works in financial systems around the world, to provide empirical evidence of the value of credit reporting data for credit analysis, and to identify appropriate public policy recommendations.

There are several reasons for the interest of policymakers and private sector agents in credit reporting—in both developing and developed economies. First, credit reporting systems can be instrumental in expanding the breadth and depth of the financial sector, by providing opportunities for new financial products in existing consumer segments (such as e-finance) or by enabling financial institutions to successfully serve consumers who were previously ignored or underserved. Of particular interest for policymakers and development specialists, as well as for many private sector lenders, is the role that credit reporting can play in reaching marginal borrowers such as micro, small, and medium enterprises and low-income consumers. Since these borrowers often lack physical collateral that can be used as a loan guarantee, credit reporting can help them create "reputation collateral," which can be more valuable in the credit market. In this way, credit reporting can be seen as part of a strategy to "democratize" financial systems, increasing opportunities for poorer borrowers to participate and contributing to more equitable economic growth.

A second reason for interest in credit reporting is the contribution it can make to strengthening financial systems by reducing transaction costs, improving portfolio quality, increasing competition, and facilitating transactions at a distance from bank offices. Credit reporting can also promote the stability of financial systems and enhanced supervision. Financial institutions that have access to accurate and timely credit reports on potential borrowers can use this information to more precisely assess risk, which reduces opportunities for making loans not supported by sound business criteria and results in improved portfolio quality. Use of credit reports and related decision tools, such as credit scoring, can also facilitate supervision of financial institutions by providing standardized and objective criteria for credit analysis. In countries where there are public credit registries operated by the central bank or bank supervisor, this data can also be helpful in identifying questionable or poorly performing loans to be reviewed during on-site examinations as well as for monitoring the portfolio quality of institutions and detecting economy-wide trends. Credit reports are most closely associated with their role in supporting credit markets; however, their value in an economy extends to other private transactions, including employment screening, insurance contracts, commercial transactions, and property rentals.

While some developed countries have a long tradition of credit reporting, in many developing countries it is a relatively new activity as documented by the chapters in this book. The public policy environment in a country is a critical determinant of whether, and how, credit reporting will develop. Many countries, both developed and developing, have bank secrecy laws that unduly restrict information sharing. Another common problem is lack of an appropriate regulatory framework for this activity, so that basic consumer rights are protected in a cost-efficient manner and regulations contribute to rather than detract from the credibility and soundness of the industry. In many countries competition policy must also be addressed in order for credit reporting to develop its full potential; in particular, credit reporting may be less likely to develop in financial systems where assets are concentrated in only a few institutions, a typical problem in developing countries.

The research presented in this book provides convincing evidence of the importance of credit reporting in financial systems, in both developed and developing countries. In the World Bank, we view credit reporting as a key part of our strategy to strengthen financial systems and assist small businesses with their credit needs. We have found that countries in every region of the world are interested in developing credit reporting, and the World Bank and its sister organization, the International Finance Corporation (IFC), hope to contribute to realizing the potential this industry has to offer. Finally, we hope that this book, by providing a common knowledge base previously lacking regarding credit reporting, will not only help our dialogue with our client countries, but also contribute to a stronger dialogue on this topic within developing countries between the public and private sectors, as well as inspire further research on this important and evolving topic.

Cesare Calari
Vice President
Financial Sector Network
World Bank

Acknowledgments

The research presented in this book was inspired by observing the rapid growth of both public and private sector credit reporting in Latin America in the 1990s. I would first like to thank the many public-sector officials, especially from central banks throughout the region, for their willingness to discuss their policies on credit reporting. Officials of the Argentine and Brazilian central banks were especially helpful in this process. In the Argentine Central Bank, Andrew Powell, Oscar del Rio and Guillermo Escudé contributed greatly to this work. Roberto Fatorelli provided generous assistance in the Brazilian Central Bank.

Individuals in the private sector made themselves equally available and executives of many credit reporting firms provided significant assistance to the research effort. There are too many to name them all individually, but I would like to recognize Barry Connelly and Norm Magnuson of the Consumer Data Industry Association; O. D. Nelson, formerly of Fair Isaac; Carlo Gerardi of CRIF and ACCIS; Alfredo Vicens of Veraz; and John Ford of Equifax.

In the World Bank, I was fortunate to find support from several managers to take on this new topic. I would like to thank the finance team from the Latin America Region including Danny Leipziger, Augusto de la Torre, Fernando Montes-Negret, and Stefan Alber-Glanstaetten for their contributions and support of this work. The Finance Sector Vice Presidency also encouraged and funded this work, including specific support from Cesare Calari, Manuel Conthe, Patrick Conroy, Jerry Caprio, Robert Keppler, Giovanni Majnoni, and Jimmy Olazo. Others at the World Bank who have contributed to this work include Hany Assaad, Peer Stein, and Makanda Kioko in the IFC and Joseph Pegues, Laurence Hart, and John Saville in the World Bank Institute. I would also like to thank Paul Meo,

Hemant Shah, and Luis Serven for their early encouragement of this work. Micky Ananth was flawless in her handling of the administrative aspects of this research endeavor. Nataliya Mylenko provided excellent research assistance, including help in preparing the final manuscript. Gwendolyn Alexander provided valuable research assistance in the initial phase of the research project. I was also fortunate to have excellent editorial assistance from Elizabeth Murry, Jane Macdonald, and Kathleen Caruso at The MIT Press.

I would like to thank the contributors to this volume for the energy they put into original research on this topic and their sustained enthusiasm, which helped in getting the final manuscript to print. I would also like to thank the participants of the International Conference on Credit Reporting Systems, held in Miami, Florida, in June 2000, where many of the papers included in this book were first presented. I would like to extend special thanks to Robert Clarke, former chair of the Federal Deposit Insurance Corporation, for his contributions to the research project and the Miami conference.

The research presented in this book was initially funded by the Regional Studies Program of the Latin America Region of the World Bank. Additional funding for the project was provided by the World Bank Financial Sector Board. My sincere thanks go to both sources of funding. Researchers at several central banks also contributed their time to this project, including officials from the Argentine and Mexican central banks and from the U.S. Federal Reserve Board, and I thank them for their cooperation.

Finally, I would like to thank the members of my family for their support and encouragement, especially my husband, Ernesto Stein, our daughters Katherine and Emily, and my mother, Marjorie Miller.

Introduction

Margaret J. Miller

Credit reporting firms and other types of public credit information registries are critical elements of the institutional framework necessary to support a well-functioning and modern financial system. They provide rapid access to accurate and reliable standardized information on potential borrowers, be they individuals or firms. Credit reports are becoming increasingly important throughout the world, fueled by demand for the data they contain from banks and other financial intermediaries as well as by demand from private firms, retailers, employers, and others. Bank supervisors and regulators are also increasing their demand for high-quality credit data to more effectively monitor credit risks in supervised financial institutions. Technological advances in data processing and analysis have improved the accuracy and cost-effectiveness of decision and application tools, such as credit scoring, that increase the value of access to information for agents in both the private and public sector. The Internet and e-commerce are creating yet more opportunities for the beneficial use of credit data and other consumer and business information for a range of commercial purposes, where lenders are only one among many potential users.

Credit reporting addresses a fundamental problem of credit markets: asymmetric information between borrowers and lenders that leads to adverse selection and moral hazard. The heart of a credit report is the record it provides of a consumer or firm's payment history. Since one of the best predictors of future behavior is past behavior, data on how a potential borrower has met obligations in the past enable lenders to more accurately evaluate credit risk, easing adverse selection problems. At the same time, credit reports strengthen borrower discipline and reduce moral hazard, since late or nonpayment with one institution can result in sanctions by many others. Credit reports that include both positive and negative information, so that responsible borrowers can document good credit histories, also help to build "reputation collateral." A borrower's "good name" (reputation collateral) provides an incentive to meet commitments much the same way as does a pledge of physical collateral, thus reducing moral hazard. In segments of the credit market where physical assets are limited—such as consumer lending (especially for lower income consumers), microenterprise, and small business lending—reputation collateral is particularly important.

Credit reporting can also play a key role in improving the efficiency of financial institutions by reducing loan processing costs as well as the time required to process loan applications. Lenders may also use credit data to monitor their existing portfolios, identify potential problems, and develop and sell new products, thus contributing to their profitability through more accurate pricing and targeting. By providing a standard measure of borrower quality, as in the U.S. mortgage market where Fannie Mae requires a minimum FICO (Fair Isaac Company) credit score, credit data can facilitate the development of secondary markets and securitized portfolios. Since credit registries promote transparency and reduce the information advantage that institutions have over their existing clients, they can also encourage greater competition, which can lead to lower prices and greater access to credit.

The development of credit registries, however, is not without controversy. A major concern is violation of an individual's privacy via transmission of sensitive information among unauthorized third parties. Financial intermediaries in many countries are also loathe to lose their "information rents" from their exclusive knowledge of their customer base, and they invoke bank secrecy laws to discourage the development of credit registries. The reputation of credit registries has also suffered in nations where data quality is poor and consumer protections are either limited or nonexistent; some registries are plagued by inaccuracies, others have a narrow scope so only a partial picture of a person or firm's debt situation is possible, still others are relatively new and have limited historical data on which to base credit ratings. In many nations the credit registry industry is underdeveloped, dominated by a single firm or by nonprofit organizations such as chambers of commerce or bank associations that collect credit data on behalf of their members. In the past ten years, however, foreign investments and alliances by the largest U.S. and

European private credit bureaus have significantly increased, as have local investments in this industry, contributing to a renewed dynamism and market demand brought about by increased understanding of the benefits provided by such services.

The limitations of private credit registries, together with (in some cases) a legal and regulatory framework that discourages information sharing in the private sector, have prompted government officials in many nations to establish publicly operated credit information registries, typically through the central bank or bank supervisor. In such cases, an additional objective of public credit registries (PCRs) is to provide data for use by bank supervisors. Seven of the fifteen member nations of the European Union (EU) have public credit registries, as do most nations in Latin America. The PCR phenomenon is spreading to other regions, including Asia, Eastern Europe, and Africa. In many cases, there are limits on the information provided by PCRs, such as focusing only on large loan sizes or aggregating information so that the exposure of an institution with a given borrower is not disclosed.

The role of public policy in creating reliable credit information registries has thus far been considered almost exclusively a domestic policy topic.[1] This is likely to change, however, since access to credit information may well become an integral part of the new "international financial architecture." Rules, protocols, and minimum performance criteria may also be developed for sharing credit information as part of the emerging standards for financial sector regulation and stability. For example, financial information from ratings firms, which is available on corporate borrowers, including banks, has been included as an element of "The New Basel Capital Accord" (Bank for International Settlements 2001). Moreover, some are suggesting that data on the creditworthiness of consumers and small and medium-sized firms contained in public credit registries could be used to produce a type of proxy rating for use with the new Basel approach for smaller, unrated firms.[2]

The importance of asymmetric information for explaining the behavior of credit markets (and other markets with opaque information) has long been recognized in economic theory. The 2001 Nobel Prize in Economics was awarded to three pioneers in this field, George Akerlof, Michael Spence, and Joseph Stiglitz. Although the work of these three, and many others who followed in their footsteps, discussed the real-world consequences of asymmetric information, such as high borrowing rates in developing countries or screening by lenders to determine risk classes of borrowers, little work has been done to understand the institutional responses to asymmetric information in credit markets, such as information sharing initiatives. Here are a few of the basic questions that the economics literature has not yet addressed:

1. What are the main characteristics of information sharing mechanisms (credit reporting activities) in financial markets?

2. How important are credit reports in determining creditworthiness?

3. What is the role of public policy in the development of credit reporting initiatives, including the role of PCRs managed by central banks, and the role of legal, regulatory and institutional factors in supporting credit reporting?

This book provides at least initial answers to these fundamental questions about how credit reporting institutions can enable markets to overcome problems of asymmetric information. Most of the chapters in this book were written as part of a World Bank research project, which brought together more than twenty academics and policymakers from Latin America, the European Union, and North America, to address these issues.

The research was initiated in the Latin America region of the World Bank, where the 1990s saw an expansion of the PCR policy to nearly every country, as well as a boom in private foreign and domestic investment in this industry. The relative stabilization of previously volatile economies during the 1990s, such as Argentina, Brazil, and Chile, and the corresponding reduction in interest rates—especially evident in Chile—created opportunities for term finance and a demand for credit reports. Latin American countries that experienced financial crises during this time, including most notably Mexico, also looked to the development of credit reporting as part of a comprehensive solution for strengthening credit markets. As the research progressed, however, it quickly became apparent that this was a topic with international relevance, so the project was expanded to include a more global view. The World Bank is now working on this topic, in an advisory capacity or through loan projects, with countries in every region of the world.

Literature Review

Akerlof (1970) was the first economist to recognize the critical role played by asymmetric information in many markets, including the credit market. In his seminal paper, Akerlof used the market for credit in a developing country as one of several examples to describe the problem posed by asymmetric information. Moneylenders in India, he noted, can operate because they have "personal knowledge about the character of the borrower"[3] as well as an ability to enforce contracts. Lenders lacking this information would face adverse selection, since the moneylenders would service the better borrowers, leaving only the poorer risks.

Jaffee and Russell (1976) were among the first to link the problem of asymmetric information to credit rationing. Their theoretical paper suggested that lenders use loan size as a screening device to avoid adverse selection. The theoretical treatment of asymmetric information in credit markets was further advanced by Stiglitz and Weiss (1981), who provided an elegant and thorough treatment of these issues, using a model of the small business credit market. They found that credit rationing was an optimizing behavior for lenders, since high risk projects cannot reasonably be charged the high interest rates that would be necessary for them to be profitable, as a group, for the lender.

Theoretical models of financial intermediation quickly began to incorporate these insights, with papers suggesting that a central feature of banks was their ability to gather information on borrowers about payment history and intangible knowledge regarding honesty and trustworthiness. Leland and Pyle (1977) stated that asymmetric information provides justification for the development of financial intermediaries. Information is a public good, the authors state, that cannot readily be sold; however, this information can be used for supporting profitable lending. Campbell and Kracaw (1980), Diamond (1984, 1991), and Stiglitz and Weiss (1988) are other examples of papers advancing the idea that banks are institutions "specializing in the acquisition and dissemination of information."[4] These papers suggest that monitoring the behavior of customers over time, including repayment of loans and other transactions, provides banks with an information advantage they can use to successfully perform the function of resource allocation in an economy.

The importance of information gathering to financial intermediaries was further advanced in the literature on "relationship
banking." Nakamura (1993) stated that lenders use their information
advantage over their existing or continuing borrowers to increase
their rents, a finding that corroborated earlier work by Sharpe (1989),
suggesting that banks use their information advantage with their
repeat customers to wield monopoly power. Empirical work by
Petersen and Rajan (1994), Berger and Udell (1995), and Peek and
Rosengren (1995) on the U.S. small business loan market, one of the
most informationally opaque segments of the U.S. credit market, also
supported the importance of relationship lending. A recent contribution to this literature by Petersen and Rajan (2000), however, suggests that the importance of the banking relationship is diminishing.
Using data from the 1988 and 1993 National Survey of Small Business Finance, they show that the distance between borrowers and
lenders showed rapid growth over this period, indicating that frequent personal communication or interaction (the banking relationship) was becoming less important. The authors posit that the
reduced importance of the banking relationship may be due, at least
in part, to increasing availability of credit records.

The significant economics literature on the role of asymmetric
information in credit markets has been relatively silent on institutional mechanisms, such as credit bureaus, that banks and other
lenders have developed to mitigate this problem. A series of papers
by Tullio Jappelli, Jorge Padilla, and Marco Pagano over the last
decade, which largely focus on the theoretical rationale for credit
reporting, are the main published contributions in this field.[5] The
1993 Pagano and Jappelli paper in the *Journal of Finance* was the first
article on information sharing in credit markets that was published
in a major journal. Using a model of adverse selection, Pagano and
Jappelli analyze the factors that would encourage information sharing to arise endogenously. They find that information sharing is
more likely to occur when there is greater mobility among economic
agents, borrowers are heterogeneous, the credit market is large, and
the cost of information exchange is low. The results of their model
also suggest that the structure of the credit market will affect information sharing; if the credit market is competitive except for the
information advantage enjoyed by lenders over their clients, then
lenders will not voluntarily share information as this would eliminate their market power and profits. The benefits of sharing infor-

mation should improve the pool of borrowers, reduce defaults, and reduce interest rates; however, the structure of the credit market determines whether the volume of lending is increased.

Jappelli and Pagano's results support those of Klein (1992) who used a model from game theory to discuss how the problems of moral hazard and adverse selection can be reduced by developing a reputation in a credit bureau. Klein's model points to similar conditions that support information sharing—cost of sharing data, size of the market, and mobility of borrowers—and shows that a credit bureau can act as a borrower discipline device. Klein also finds that the absence of a credit bureau in a competitive loan market can be a stable equilibrium.

Papers by Vercammen (1995) and Padilla and Pagano (1997, 2000) are other relevant theoretical contributions to understanding the factors that may encourage or discourage the development of credit reporting in a credit market. Vercammen develops a model with moral hazard and adverse selection where a credit history can reduce the impact of both of these problems and be welfare improving. The author argues, however, that this effect is not sustainable over time; as credit histories lengthen, creditors learn more about their borrowers, reducing the value of each additional piece of negative information, so incentives for compliance are also reduced. The implications of the model are that full information sharing can be an inferior solution to one with limits, such as a limit on the number of years data are maintained.

In their 1997 paper, Padilla and Pagano use a two-period model of the credit market with risk-neutral borrowers and lenders to probe whether information sharing agreements arise endogenously between lenders. They state that information sharing affects bank profits through two channels: (1) profits are increased because credit reporting increases borrower discipline, reducing moral hazard and defaults; (2) profits decrease due to greater competition in the credit market. If the impact of greater borrower discipline on profits exceeds that of greater competition, then information sharing is Pareto improving, since both lenders and borrowers will benefit and this would be a sustainable equilibrium result. They further suggest that interest rates would fall and the volume of credit could increase under plausible credit market conditions where there are a range of borrower types.

In Padilla and Pagano (2000), the authors focus on the type of information shared, positive and negative or strictly negative data, to show that not all information sharing mechanisms are efficient—a finding similar to that by Vercammen. In their model, if only negative information on borrowers is shared, borrowers will have strong incentives to stay off the list so that they do not face higher interest rates. A system where only negative information is shared may induce too much effort on avoiding default, from an efficiency viewpoint. According to this model, if positive and negative information is shared, then this may have the unexpected effect of reducing effort to avoid default, since the impact of negative information is tempered by the borrower's full credit history. A credit sharing arrangement where the mix of positive and negative data is carefully considered could elicit an efficient level of effort to avoid default without unduly reducing incentives for borrower discipline. The authors point out, however, that it may be difficult in practice for lenders to coordinate and establish an appropriate information sharing mechanism and this may help to explain the widespread existence of PCRs.

Empirical work on credit reporting is limited. Until recently, most of the empirical papers related to this topic analyzed the predictive power—or other statistical dimensions—of credit scoring tools and were found in specialized banking or statistical journals. Notable in this literature are articles by Chandler and Parker (1989) and Chandler and Johnson (1992).[6] These papers analyzed the importance of including data from credit reports in credit scoring models compared to using only data from credit applications. They found that the predictive power of credit scoring increased significantly by including credit report data, in particular, the positive information on repayment histories.

Kallberg and Udell (2002) use data from Dun & Bradstreet (D&B) to empirically test the added-value provided by mercantile reports over and above the financial statement data they contain. They find evidence that the trade credit histories contained in D&B credit reports have substantially greater predictive power than data from financial statements alone.

Little empirical work has been done, however, to understand the impact that credit reporting has at the economy-wide level, including issues such as the volume of credit, price of credit, quality of credit portfolios, or access to credit. Jappelli and Pagano, forthcoming in the *Journal of Banking and Finance*, address these questions and find evidence that information sharing is associated with higher levels of lending in relation to GNP as well as lower default rates—although this last result is somewhat weaker due to the data available to determine defaults. Using data from a survey conducted by the authors of both public and private credit sharing arrangements in approximately forty countries, their findings also suggest that PCRs are more likely to be established in countries that lack private credit reporting firms, indicating that the two may serve some of the same functions.

Galindo and Miller (2001) analyze the extent to which credit reporting alleviates credit rationing to firms. Using data from the Worldscope database of firms and from the World Bank survey of credit reporting, they analyze how the quality of credit reporting in a country affects firm-level access to credit. They find that the existence of credit reporting in a country reduces the importance of internal funds for project finance, indicating that firms are less credit constrained when credit reports are available.

The chapters in this volume complement and extend existing research in several important dimensions. First, they provide insights on the institutional dimensions of credit reporting arrangements in many countries of the world. Prior to this book, such information was not readily available in any published material, either in academic or trade publications, especially about PCRs.[7] Second, they offer further theoretical and empirical evidence on the importance of credit reporting for determining creditworthiness, often using data from credit reporting firms or public credit registries that was not previously available for academic research. The empirical contributions in this volume include chapters that explore how the policy environment for credit reporting, such as exclusions on certain types of data or fragmentation of data by source of credit (bank vs. retail, for example), affect the predictive power of the information. Finally, several chapters in this book extend analysis of credit reporting to experiences in developing countries where virtually no prior work has been done.

This book is organized in three parts.

Part I: Institutional Arrangements for Credit Reporting

The chapters in part I provide a comprehensive picture of the different institutional forms that credit reporting arrangements take in countries around the world. The various institutional forms covered include both public credit registries administered by central banks and private credit reporting firms. Private firms specializing in credit data from banks and other financial intermediaries are analyzed as well as firms that specialize in trade credit, typically the most important source of external finance for small businesses.

Before this research was undertaken, the extent of the spread of credit reporting to developing countries was not known, and even in the case of developed countries there was little published information. These chapters demonstrate that credit reporting is now established in some form in all advanced economies as well as in many developing countries, including most of the nations considered to be middle-income or emerging economies. Even the poorest countries in the world increasingly look to credit reporting as a basic element of financial sector development.

In seven of the fifteen EU member countries and in many developing countries, the central bank or bank supervisor administers a public credit registry. The chapters by Miller and by Jappelli and Pagano both discuss how public and private registries differ, but they come to different conclusions about the relationship between these two institutional forms of credit reporting. Based on the World Bank survey, Miller finds that public and private registries are complements rather than substitutes, while Jappelli and Pagano, using their survey data, suggest that public registries usually substitute for the lack of private credit reporting firms. Additional research on this topic is warranted to better understand not only the sequencing of private versus public credit reporting, but also their different roles and objectives, since many developing countries are currently establishing, or considering establishing, credit reporting, and they are debating whether to do this in the public and/or private sector or via joint public-private ventures.

Chapters 1 and 3 also provide insights into the broad role that credit reporting plays in an economy beyond its usefulness for evaluating credit risk of potential borrowers. Olegario (chapter 3) takes a historical perspective on commercial credit reporting in the United States, and she describes the valuable role of this activity in encouraging trade and instilling common business norms and ethics across a diverse and geographically dispersed society. Miller (chapter 1) shows that private credit reports typically include data from a variety of sources, including private businesses and nonbank sources of credit, and they often make this data available to a broad spectrum of financial and nonfinancial businesses as well as to government agencies. This enables credit reporting to support a variety of commercial transactions, such as employment screening and business to business transactions, whether involving credit or not, and government objectives, including tax collection, as well as the more traditional uses for credit risk evaluation. More detailed descriptions of the chapters in part I follow.

Chapter 1 by Margaret Miller provides detailed analysis of this industry internationally. The chapter is based on the most exhaustive survey ever undertaken of credit reporting, distributed by the World Bank in two waves—one in 1999, the second in 2001, covering nearly eighty countries about PCRs and more than forty countries about private registries. The detailed responses to the questionnaires made it possible to identify the key characteristics of both public and private registries, including how they differ in sources of data (public registries only collect data from supervised institutions while private registries have a much broader set of sources, including firms, leasing and finance companies, retail establishments, etc.), types of data collected (public registries focus on data needed to analyze aggregate risk of an institution and therefore often fail to collect specific data on borrowers collected in the private sector such as address or even tax identification numbers), and policies on distribution of data (public registry data is typically limited to those institutions providing the data, private registries sell data to a much wider range of financial and business institutions as well as government agencies). These results suggest that PCRs are not substitutes for private credit reporting firms, but rather complements. The survey research also demonstrates the need for greater consumer protections on this activity as well as the importance of the legal framework in a country for determining how credit reporting will develop.

Tullio Jappelli and Marco Pagano describe in detail how Western European PCRs operate in chapter 2. The earliest PCRs were established in Germany, France, Italy, and Spain. Central bank officials in developing countries often state that they use these established registries as models when designing their own PCRs, yet the specific institutional features of the European PCRs are not always well understood. Jappelli and Pagano also discuss why it may be necessary to establish a PCR based on theoretical models that indicate information sharing does not necessarily develop in the private sector. Looking to the future, the authors suggest that PCRs in the EU member states may be losing relevance since increasingly firms receive finance throughout the region, and in some cases, the world. A region-wide PCR would address this problem; however, they doubt such an institution will be established anytime soon.

Chapter 3, by Rowena Olegario, discusses the development of commercial credit reporting in the United States in the nineteenth century, using data from the R. G. Dun archives. As Olegario states, often the only credit available to small merchants or manufacturers in the frontier United States was credit from their suppliers—a situation replicated today in many developing countries. Early credit reporting agencies, such as the R. G. Dun Company (later merged to create Dun & Bradstreet), did not have access to reliable quantitative data to build a credit report—businesses seldom had formal financial statements much less ones that followed a common accounting practice or were audited—another parallel with current circumstances in many developing countries. In the absence of financial data, credit reports used a type of standardized format to describe relevant character traits, such as honesty, thrift, and work discipline. Since the credit reporting agencies made these reports available to anyone who would pay for them, they encouraged transparency in the economy at the same time they promoted a fairer basis for commerce—one based on measures of business quality rather than membership in a closed group or network.

Part II: The Role of Credit Reporting Data in Financial Systems

There are three main uses for the information from credit reports: (1) to support financial and commercial transactions by assisting in evaluation of risk and by modeling consumer behavior; (2) to enable bank supervisors to accurately evaluate credit risk in supervised financial institutions; and (3) for economic analysis. The chapters included in part II show how credit reports can be valuable in each of these areas. Three of the four chapters in this section involve data from developing countries, two on Argentina and one on Chile, while the fourth focuses on the U.S. credit market. The inclusion of both developed and developing country examples provide evidence of the relevance of credit reporting in financial systems at different stages of development.

In chapter 4, using data from SINACOFI, a private credit reporting firm in Chile, Kevin Cowan and José De Gregorio test the impact that data from the credit report have in predicting defaults. The authors find that both the positive and negative information available in credit reports in Chile significantly contributes to explaining defaults. In addition, Cowan and De Gregorio estimate the consumption function for credit for the economy, including a measure of information sharing in the credit market. Their results suggest that information sharing increases the volume of lending, and that the longer the historical record or the more data in the credit record, the greater is this effect.

In chapter 5, Jarl G. Kallberg and Gregory F. Udell extend recent theoretical work on credit reporting, by developing a model that takes into account the fact that most firms operate with more than one lender. This environment creates incentives for lenders to share information. Using data provided by Dun & Bradstreet, the authors also provide graphical evidence that trade or mercantile data, such as that found in D&B credit reports, has substantially greater predictive power than relying only on financial statement data.

Michael Falkenheim and Andrew Powell address the second use of credit information mentioned above—as a regulatory tool—in chapter 6. Falkenheim and Powell use 1998–1999 data from the public credit registry run by the Argentine Central Bank to estimate economic capital and provisioning requirements for Argentine banks using a simple portfolio model of credit risk. The authors then compare these results with regulatory standards and actual bank levels of capital and provisions. The results indicate that Argentine banks should face higher capital requirements than those set by Basel (based on an 8 percent capital to assets ratio and Basel Accord risk weights), but, on average, slightly lower capital requirements than those imposed by the Argentine Central Bank. Interestingly, the authors also note that the average capital level of Argentine banks was often in excess of even the strict capital standards of the central bank, for example, 19 percent of assets for medium-sized banks when the Argentine requirement was 13.5 percent on average and 24.7 percent for small-sized banks vs. an average 16.1 percent requirement. While the authors include the standard caution that the modeling techniques and data have their limitations, it is clear that these techniques will be a valuable tool for banking supervisors and regulators to use in countries with PCRs.

The use of public credit registry data for economic analysis is explored in chapter 7 by Allen N. Berger, Leora F. Klapper, Margaret

J. Miller, and Gregory F. Udell. Using the same data source as Falkenheim and Powell, public credit registry data from the Argentine Central Bank, the authors explore whether firm size is correlated with the type of bank used by the firm. Since small firms represent one of the most informationally opaque segments of a credit market, they may rely more on relationship banking, where information collected through continuous contact over time by the lender is an important element of the transaction, than do large firms on which more information is available. The data support this hypothesis. Small firms are more likely to work with small banks, which typically have a greater focus on relationship lending, and less likely to work with foreign banks, which are usually at an informational disadvantage vis-à-vis local banks.

Part III: The Impact of Public Policies on Credit Reporting

Public policies can greatly affect whether credit reporting develops in a country, how it develops, and the usefulness of the credit reports for predicting risk. Public policies are also vital in promoting an understanding of credit reporting among citizens, including safeguards, so that consumers can effectively challenge erroneous information and exercise their privacy rights.

Bank secrecy laws in many developing countries effectively prohibit —or drastically limit—the operation of private credit registries. Limits on the data that can be shared, including limits on positive data or sensitive data, or on the period of time that data can be archived and used to determine creditworthiness, greatly affect the predictive power of credit reports. Laws limiting access to data to specific sectors of the economy (only banks, only regulated utilities, etc.) also limit the role that credit reporting can play in a variety of economic transactions.

Chapters 8 and 9 provide strong empirical evidence as to the importance of public policies in credit reporting. Chapter 10 provides a detailed analysis of the Brazilian credit market, where mostly negative information is exchanged, and derives lessons for public policy. Chapter 11 compares the legal, regulatory, and institutional frameworks for credit reporting in the United States, European Union, and Latin America. The results indicate that the public policy environment for this activity is not adequately addressed in many developing countries, including the emerging economies of Latin America.

John M. Barron and Michael Staten provide an important contri- bution to the empirical literature on credit reporting in chapter 8. Barron and Staten obtained data from one of the "big three" U.S. consumer reporting firms, Experian, to study the importance of limits on data included in credit reports. In one test, they included only negative information from the credit reports, then compared these results with those from a model including both positive and negative data. Many countries, including Australia and Brazil, have strict limits on sharing positive data. Barron and Staten show that credit reports that only contain negative data have less predictive power than complete reports with both types of data. Another test divides data by bank credit and retail credit to model countries, such as Chile, where there are separate credit reporting initiatives for differ- ent sectors and data are not exchanged. Again, the complete model, with both bank and retail credit information, performs better than the model relying only on retail data. Their results clearly show that limiting data collection reduces the benefits that can be achieved through credit reporting, likely leading to higher lending costs and reduced volume of credit. Barron and Staten further suggest that credit reports are particularly important for extending credit to low- income and marginal segments of a population, so limits on data that reduce the predictive power of credit reports may have a dis- proportionate impact on these individuals.

Raphael W. Bostic and Paul S. Calem address the sometimes un- intended consequences of public policies in chapter 9. The authors analyze how the restriction on including a borrower's gender in determining credit risk in the United States affects the efficiency of credit scoring models. In response to difficulties women had in access- ing credit, the Equal Credit Opportunity Act (ECOA) was passed in 1974. One provision of this law was to state that lenders could not take gender into account in deciding on a loan, which extended to including gender as a variable in credit scoring models. Bostic and Calem show that while this law was enacted to protect women, now more than twenty-five years later, this same law is prejudicial to women, who are more likely to repay loans than are men. In one test, the authors state that women with a score of 600 in the model were as likely to default as men with a score of 720, and these results were remarkably robust in the data and to different specifications.

Armando Castelar Pinheiro and Alkimar Moura in chapter 10 explore how the structure of the Brazilian credit market may act to limit information sharing among lenders, suggesting a role for public policy. They also discuss the role of the recently established PCR in the Central Bank of Brazil in bank supervision. Castelar and Moura develop a theoretical model where there are three distinct credit market segments: corporate, middle-market, and retail. They assume that there is full information disclosure in the corporate market and no information available (complete asymmetry of information) on the retail market, so the only market where information can be learned over time is the small business or middle-market. Since the information monopoly that banks have on their middle-market customers is the only source of their profits, they will likely only share negative information to enforce repayment discipline, but they will refuse to share positive data. This result reflects the current situation in Brazil. While the authors recognize that limits on information sharing reduce the predictive power of credit reports, and that public policies, such as the PCR, may be necessary to promote wider access to credit data, they also see risks if banks suddenly lose their "information rents." These risks include lower bank charter values and temptations to engage in riskier lending.

Chapter 11, by Rafael del Villar, Alejandro Díaz de León, and Johanna Gil Hubert, provides a detailed look at the legal, regulatory, and institutional frameworks that support credit reporting. Previous chapters in part III, as well as results of the World Bank survey, indicate that the public policy environment for credit reporting can have a significant impact on how this activity develops, the kind of information that is included in reports, and their predictive power. The authors compare the experience of countries in Latin America with the United States and European Union and find that while the laws in Latin America are similar to those in the developed nations, the regulatory and institutional frameworks are much weaker. Basic consumer protections, such as knowing who has accessed your credit report or when an adverse action has been taken based on your credit report (i.e., denial of credit or employment) are lacking throughout the region. The analysis of del Villar, Díaz de León, and Gil Hubert also indicates that nonjudicial means for challenging erroneous data are limited in most Latin American countries, regulators have limited instruments for enforcing codes of conduct, and virtually no attention has been paid to educating consumers as to their rights and responsibilities with respect to credit reporting.

A Comment on Terminology

While the focus of this book is on the information infrastructure critical for credit decisions and other financial transactions, it is important to frame this work in the context of a more broadly based development of consumer and business data in an economy. This is because many types of nonfinancial data are important for evaluating creditworthiness as well as due to the usefulness of credit or consumer reports for providing an objective assessment of the trustworthiness of an individual or business for other types of commercial transactions. In addition, the industry trend in developed countries is toward more comprehensive reporting, rather than fragmentation of data by industry or sector, such as commercial bank-only databases.

For these reasons, there is a trend in the international industry away from referring to these firms as "credit bureaus" in favor of names reflecting the broader range of information they contain and wide range of potential users, such as "consumer data," "business data," "information services" or "advantage network systems." Since there is no single term used to describe these activities, and the most commonly used term, "credit bureau" is now being discarded by the international credit or consumer reporting industry, there has been no attempt to standardize the term used to describe private credit (consumer/business) reporting firms in the different chapters in this book. Many authors use the term "credit bureau"; Olegario, writing about the historical development of business reporting, such as that performed by Dun & Bradstreet, uses the term "credit reporting agency" common in the historical literature. An attempt has been made, however, to standardize the term used to describe credit reporting activities managed by central banks or bank supervisors, which we call public credit registries or PCRs. This is in line with previous scholarship on this topic.

Promising Issues for Future Research

The chapters in this book provide the first comprehensive analysis of credit reporting institutions worldwide, their important role in reducing the impact of asymmetric information in credit markets, and critical public policy issues that must be addressed. These are important contributions, but they represent only the beginning of possible research on this topic and, as is often the case with research and learning, they lead to more questions than they answer. The fast pace of change in computer technology, telecommunications, and decision software, which are key inputs for credit reporting, as well as change in national and global financial markets can only lead to the conclusion that further research on this topic will continue to reveal new insights for some time to come.

There are several lines of inquiry that would clearly benefit from additional research. Microlevel empirical research on the value of credit reports and credit scoring is needed to determine the benefits, as well as the costs, as they relate to bank performance, performance of other financial intermediaries, such as leasing firms, small enterprise access to credit, or access to credit for other marginalized groups, such as low income borrowers. Further research would also be useful on the role played by PCRs, especially in countries that have private credit reporting firms. Questions include the extent to which PCRs assist in supervision and improve the soundness of the financial system, the importance of the data they contain for economic policy analysis, the relative use of PCR data versus data provided by private registries, and the appropriate use of loan classification systems in PCRs.

Additional research would also be helpful on design features of credit reporting systems, whether public or private, including, for example, the scope of information to be included and the length of time data should be maintained. Consideration should also be given to how conditions in a country, such as ease of contract enforcement, would affect these design criteria.

The importance of credit (or consumer/business) reporting data for noncredit transactions has also received little attention. To what extent are these reports facilitating labor market transactions or commercial transactions, including import/export opportunities or access to trade credit? More consideration needs to be given to the economic impact of different public policies, including bank secrecy laws and privacy laws, as well as to how laws and regulations may affect competition in credit markets. Finally, the role of consumers in credit reporting needs to be given greater weight, as they are the ultimate arbiters of quality as well as the main beneficiaries of a responsible and functioning credit reporting system.

Notes

1. The European Union Directive 95/46/EC (also known as the EU Privacy or Data Protection Directive) is an exception, since it creates a regional, and to some extent a de facto international, standard on transmission of data, including credit information.

2. See Andrew Powell's paper, "A Capital Accord for Emerging Economies," July 2001.

3. Akerlof (1970), p. 497.

4. Stiglitz and Weiss (1988), p. 5.

5. Other academic papers that have been written on credit reporting, but which won't be discussed at length here, include the following:

• Laband and Maloney (1994) address the role of credit bureaus in a specialized context—goods markets where seller financing is used as a quality assurance device.

• Van Cayseele, Bouckaert, and Degryse (1995) explore the relationship between credit market structure and the type of information sharing arrangement that is likely to emerge.

6. Other papers on credit scoring include Barry and Ellinger (1989), Avery et al. (1996), Mester (1997), Hand and Henley (1997), Thomas (2000), Bonilla, Casasus, and Sala (2000), and Avery et al. (2000).

7. While the forthcoming paper in the *Journal of Banking and Finance* by Jappelli and Pagano provides some information on the institutional arrangements for credit reporting in a sample of approximately forty-five countries, it is a smaller sample size than that developed by the World Bank—which includes nearly eighty countries— and provides much less detail about how the public registries and private firms work.

References

Akerlof, George A. 1970. "The Market for 'Lemons'." *Quarterly Journal of Economics* 84 (3): 488–500.

Avery, Robert B. et al. 1996. "Credit Risk, Credit Scoring, and the Performance of Home Mortgages." *Federal Reserve Bulletin* 82 (7): 621–648.

Avery, Robert B. et al. 2000. "Credit Scoring: Statistical Issues and Evidence from Credit Bureau Files." *Real Estate Economics* 28 (3): 523–547.

Bank for International Settlements, Basel Committee on Banking Supervision. 2001. "The New Basel Capital Accord." Consultative document, 139 pages.

Barry, Peter J., and Paul N. Ellinger. 1989. "Credit Scoring, Loan Pricing, and Farm Business Performance." *Western Journal of Agricultural Economics* 14 (1): 45–55.

Berger, Allen N., and Gregory F. Udell. 1995. "Relationship Lending and Lines of Credit in Small Firm Finance." Salomon Brothers working paper no. S/95/5.

Bonilla, Maria, Trinidad Casasus, and Ramon Sala, eds. 2000. *Financial Modeling, Contributions to Management Science*. Heidelberg and New York: Physica.

Campbell, Tim S., and William A. Kracaw. 1980. "Information Production, Market Signalling, and the Theory of Financial Intermediation." *Journal of Finance* 35 (4): 863–882.

Chandler, Gary G., and Robert W. Johnson. 1992. "The Benefit to Consumers From Generic Scoring Models Based on Credit Reports." *IMA Journal of Mathematics Applied in Business and Industry* (Oxford University Press) 4: 61–72.

Chandler, Gary G., and Lee E. Parker. 1989. "Predictive Value of Credit Bureau Reports." *Journal of Retail Banking* 11 (4) (winter): 47–54.

Diamond, D. W. 1984. "Financial Intermediation and Delegated Monitoring." *Review of Economic Studies* 51: 393–414.

Diamond, D. W. 1991. "Monitoring and Reputation: The Choice between Bank Loans and Directly Placed Debt." *Journal of Political Economy* 99: 688–721.

Galindo, Arturo, and Margaret J. Miller. 2001. "Can Credit Registries Reduce Credit Constraints? Empirical Evidence on the Role of Credit Registries in Firm Investment Decisions." Paper prepared for the annual meetings of the Inter-American Development Bank, Santiago, Chile, March.

Hand, D. J., and Henley, W. E. 1997. "Statistical Classification Methods in Consumer Credit Scoring: A Review." *Journal of the Royal Statistical Society*, series A, 160 (3): 522–541.

Jaffee, Dwight, and Thomas Russell. 1976. "Imperfect Information, Uncertainty, and Credit Rationing." *Quarterly Journal of Economics* 90 (4): 651–666.

Jappelli, Tullio, and Marco Pagano. 1993. "Information Sharing in Credit Markets." *The Journal of Finance* 43 (5) (December): 1693–1718.

Jappelli, Tullio, and Marco Pagano. 2000. "Information Sharing in Credit Markets: A Survey." CSEF working paper no. 36, University of Salerno.

Jappelli, Tullio, and Marco Pagano. 2001. "Information Sharing, Lending and Defaults: Cross-Country Evidence." *Journal of Banking and Finance*, forthcoming.

Kallberg, Jarl G., and Gregory F. Udell. 2002. "The Value of Private Sector Business Credit Information Sharing: The U.S. Case." *Journal of Banking and Finance*, forthcoming.

Klein, Daniel. 1992. "Promise Keeping in the Great Society: A Model of Credit Information Sharing." *Economics and Politics* 4 (2): 117–136.

Laband, David N., and Michael T. Maloney. 1994. "A Theory of Credit Bureaus." *Public Choice* 80 (3–4): 275–291.

Leland, Hayne E., and David H. Pyle. 1977. "Informational Asymmetries, Financial Structure, and Financial Intermediation." *Journal of Finance* 32 (2): 371–387.

Mester, Loretta J. 1997. "What's the Point of Credit Scoring?" *Federal Reserve Bank of Philadelphia Business Review* (September–October 1997): 3–16.

Nakamura, Leonard I. 1993. "Loan Screening within and Outside of Customer Relations." Federal Reserve Bank of Philadelphia, Economic Research Division, working paper no. 93-15.

Padilla, A. Jorge, and Marco Pagano. 1997. "Endogenous Communication among Lenders and Entrepreneurial Incentives." *The Review of Financial Studies* 10 (1) (winter): 205–236.

Padilla, A. Jorge, and Marco Pagano. 2000. "Sharing Default Information as a Borrower Discipline Device." *European Economic Review* 44 (10): 1951–1980.

Peek, Joe, and Eric S. Rosengren. 1995. "Banks and the Availability of Small Business Loans." Federal Reserve Bank of Boston, working paper no. 95-1, January.

Petersen, Mitchell A., and Raghuram G. Rajan. 1994. "The Benefits of Lending Relationships: Evidence from Small Business Data." *Journal of Finance* 49 (1): 3–37.

Petersen, Mitchell A., and Raghuram G. Rajan. 2000. "Does Distance Still Matter? The Information Revolution in Small Business Lending." University of Chicago, working paper, October.

Powell, Andrew. 2001. "A Capital Accord for Emerging Economies?" World Bank working paper, July.

Sharpe, Steven A. 1989. "Asymmetric Information, Bank Lending and Implicit Contracts: A Stylized Model of Customer Relations." Federal Reserve Board, Finance and Economics Discussion Series, no. 70. Washington, D.C.

Stiglitz, Joseph, and Andrew Weiss. 1981. "Credit Rationing in Markets with Imperfect Information." *American Economic Review* 71: 393–410.

Stiglitz, Joseph, and Andrew Weiss. 1988. "Banks as Social Accountants and Screening Devices for the Allocation of Credit." National Bureau of Economic Research, working paper no. 2710.

Thomas, Lyn C. 2000. "A Survey of Credit and Behavioral Scoring: Forecasting Financial Risk of Lending to Consumers." *International Journal of Forecasting* 16 (2): 149–172.

Van Cayseele, Patrick, Jan Bouckaert, and Hans Degryse. 1995. "Credit Market Structure and Information Sharing Mechanisms." In *Market Evolution: Competition and Cooperation, Studies in Industrial Organization* 20: 129–143. Dordrecht and Boston: Kluwer Academic.

Vercammen, James A. 1995. "Credit Bureau Policy and Sustainable Reputation Effects in Credit Markets." *Economica* 62: 461–478.

I

Institutional
Arrangements for Credit
Reporting

1   Credit Reporting Systems around the Globe: The State of the Art in Public Credit Registries and Private Credit Reporting Firms

Margaret J. Miller

1.1 Introduction

The best predictor of future behavior is past behavior. This basic tenet of psychology explains the power of information contained in credit information registries, which provide detailed information on borrowers' past loan performance. A country may have a credit registry operated by the public or private sector, or both. The data registries contain are critical inputs for credit evaluation and portfolio management by financial institutions in most developed economies and many developing ones. Despite their central role in credit markets, little information exists on these registries or on other related aspects of a nation's credit reporting system, such as the legal and regulatory framework for credit reporting and availability and use of value-added services such as credit scoring.

This chapter presents the results of original surveys conducted by the World Bank on credit reporting systems worldwide between July 1999 and May 2001. The research originally focused on Latin America, where survey information was obtained on virtually all publicly (government) operated credit registries as well as from the largest private credit registries in most nations. The study was later expanded to include countries in other regions of the world, including Eastern and Western Europe, Africa, and Asia, but coverage of these regions is less complete. Still, the research results provide the first detailed empirical data on the worldwide state of credit reporting and allow for some initial comparisons among regions.

The chapter is organized as follows. Section 1.2 is a brief literature review and definition of terms, section 1.3 describes the survey methodology and sample characteristics, section 1.4 analyzes the growth of credit reporting internationally and regionally, section 1.5

describes how public credit registries function, section 1.6 compares private and public registries, section 1.7 provides information from a survey of Latin American banks, and section 1.8 offers concluding remarks.

1.2   Literature Review and Definition of Terms

Economic theorists have long been convinced of the importance of information in credit markets. Akerlof (1970) used the market for credit in a developing country as one of several examples to describe the problem posed by asymmetric information in his seminal article on this topic. Jaffee and Russell (1976) and Stiglitz and Weiss (1981) demonstrated that because credit markets involve a transaction that occurs over time, asymmetric information between the borrower and lender can lead to problems of adverse selection and moral hazard. In this environment, it is impossible for the price of the loan or interest rate to play a market-clearing function, so credit is rationed and some potential borrowers are denied loans. The more severe the problem of asymmetric information is in a credit market, the greater the rationing that is likely to occur. Lenders and good borrowers who pay their loans on time have an incentive to overcome the problem of asymmetric information.

One way that lenders can improve their knowledge of borrowers is through their direct observation of clients over time. Diamond (1991), Petersen and Rajan (1994), Berger and Udell (1995), and Peek and Rosengren (1995) all have written about the importance of information developed over the course of a banking relationship. Proprietary borrower data collected by lenders have several limitations, however, including the limited scope of the information (only from one's own institution), coverage of the population (limited to one's own clients), and the time and cost required for its development. From the borrower's perspective there is another drawback to the information developed with a lender; if not shared with other lenders it can be used to capture rents from high quality borrowers if they cannot otherwise distinguish themselves from lower quality clients.

Credit information registries, commonly known as credit bureaus in many countries, can reduce the extent of asymmetric information by making a borrower's credit history available to potential lenders. Lenders armed with this data can avoid making loans to high risk individuals, with poor repayment histories, defaults, or bankruptcies. Once a lender makes a loan, the borrower knows that their performance will be reported to the credit registry. The information contained in a credit registry becomes part of the borrower's "reputation collateral"; late payments or defaults reduce the value of this collateral, thus providing an additional incentive for timely repayment. At the same time, by reducing the information monopoly that banks have over their existing borrowers, consumers also benefit.

Despite the abundant theoretical literature in economics on the role of information in credit markets, little attention has been paid to the institutional aspects of this issue. There is virtually no source of comparable information on the status of credit information registries in Latin America or elsewhere in the world. As a result, this research project developed a series of on-line surveys to provide empirical data on this topic. Before reviewing the survey methodology and sample characteristics in section 1.3, key terms used in this chapter, which may not be familiar to all readers, will be briefly defined.

The term *credit information registry*, as used in this chapter, refers to a database of information on borrowers in a financial system. Information in these registries is available for individual consumers and/or firms. The core of this data is a borrower's past payment history. The information available may be only negative (information on late payments, defaults, and other irregularities), or it may also contain positive information such as timely repayment of credits and loans. Registries may also contain other types of information, including basic personal information such as address and birth date, as well as information from court records or other public or government sources, which could have a bearing on creditworthiness. Credit registries operated by governments, (usually by bank supervisors), are referred to in the chapter as *public credit registries* (PCRs). Those registries operated outside government, even if they are run by non-profit institutions, are referred to as *private credit registries* or *private credit reporting firms*.

Credit reporting system will be used to describe the broader institutional framework for credit reporting in an economy, including the following: (1) the public credit registry, if one exists; (2) private credit reporting firms, if they exist, including those run by chambers of commerce, bank associations, and any other organized database on borrower performance available in the economy; (3) the legal framework for credit reporting; (4) the legal framework for privacy, as it relates to this activity; (5) the regulatory framework for credit reporting, including the institutional capacity in government to enforce laws and regulations; (6) the characteristics of other pertinent borrower data available in the economy, such as data from court records, utility payments, employment status; (7) the use of credit data in the economy by financial intermediaries and others, for example, the use of credit scoring or use of credit data in creating digital signatures; and (8) the cultural context for credit reporting, including, for example, the society's view on privacy and the importance accorded to reputation collateral. *Credit scoring* refers to the use of an empirically validated statistical model to analyze data from registries, and from other available sources, to make a credit decision.

1.3   Survey Methodology and Sample

The data analyzed in this chapter were collected via three on-line Internet surveys. The first to be circulated was a survey of public credit registries worldwide, in July and August 1999, and which was recirculated in spring 2001 to improve coverage of Eastern and Western Europe and Asia.[1] The survey was sent to ninety-two countries, to the attention of the bank superintendent or director of banking supervision, typically located in the central bank. Responses were received from seventy-seven countries, of which forty-one indicated that they operate a credit registry. The eight member states of the BCEAO are counted as one entry here. Although information was requested from authorities throughout the world, the project prioritized data from Latin America, since the original project design focused on this region. Phone calls were made to bank supervisors or superintendents in virtually all Latin American countries to prompt their responses, resulting in almost full coverage of the region. Of the seventy-seven responses, twenty-nine were from Latin America, including seventeen of the forty-one nations with public registries. Coverage of Western Europe was also high, with all fifteen EU members responding, including all seven EU countries with public credit registries.[2] A more limited response was received from other regions. The response rate to the public registry survey was higher than 80 percent. See table 1.1 for a detailed list of countries that were sent surveys and those that responded.

Table 1.1
Countries invited to respond to the Survey for Central Banks or Bank Supervision Agencies, by region, and if they have a public credit registry

Countries by region	Central bank or superintendency	Existence of PCR
Latin America and the Caribbean		
Argentina	Banco Central de la Republica Argentina	X
Aruba	Centrale Bank Van Aruba	
Bahamas	Central Bank of the Bahamas	
Barbados	Central Bank of Barbados	
Belize	Central Bank of Belize	
Bermuda	Bermuda Monetary Authority	
Bolivia	Superintendencia de Bancos y Entidades Financieras	X
Brazil	Banco Central do Brasil	X
Cayman Islands	Cayman Islands Monetary Authority	
Chile	Superintendencia de Bancos e Institutiones Financieras	X
Colombia	Superbancaria	X
Costa Rica	Superintendencia General de Entidades Financieras de Costa Rica	X
Dominican Republic	Superintendencia de Bancos de la Republica Dominicana	X
Eastern Caribbean	Eastern Caribbean Central Bank	
Ecuador	Superintendencia de Bancos	X
El Salvador	Superintendencia del Sistema Financiero de El Salvador	X
Guatemala	Superintendencia de Bancos	X
Guyana	Bank of Guyana	
Haiti	Banque de la Republique D'Haiti	X
Honduras[a]	Comision Nacional de Bancos y Seguros	
Mexico	Banco de Mexico	X
Netherlands Antilles	Bank van de Nederlandse Antilen	
Nicaragua	Superintendencia de Bancos y de Otras Instituciones Financieras	X
Panama	Superintendencia de Bancos de la Republica de Panama	
Paraguay	Banco Central de Paraguay	X
Peru	Superintendencia de Banca y Seguros del Peru	X
Puerto Rico	Comisionado de Instituciones Financieras	
Trinidad and Tobago	Central Bank of Trinidad & Tobago	
Uruguay	Banco Central del Uruguay	X
Venezuela	Banco Central de Venezuela	X

Table 1.1
(continued)

Countries by region	Central bank or superintendency	Existence of PCR
European Union		
Austria	Oesterreichische Nationalbank	X
Belgium	Commission Bancaire et Financiere	X
Denmark	Danmarks Nationalbank and Finanstilsynet	
Finland	Suomen Pankki	
France	Banque de France	X
Germany	Deutsche Bundesbank	X
Greece	Bank of Greece	
Ireland	Central Bank of Ireland	
Italy	Banca d'Italia	X
Luxembourg	Commission de Surveillance du Secteur Financier	
Netherlands	De Nederlandsche Bank	
Portugal	Banco de Portugal	X
Spain	Banco de Espana	X
Sweden	Financial Supervisory Authority, Sweden	
United Kingdom	Financial Services Authority, UK	
Eastern Europe and the Former Soviet Union		
Armenia[a]	Central Bank of Armenia	
Belarus	Belarussion National Bank	X
Bosnia-Herzigovenia[a]	Bank Supervision Agency for the Federation	
Bulgaria	Bulgarian National Bank	X
Croatia	Croatian National Bank	
Czech Republic	The Czech National Bank	
Estonia	Bank of Estonia	
Hungary	Interbank Informatics Service Ltd.	
Lativa	Bank of Latvia	
Lithuania	Bank of Lithuania	X
Poland[a]	National Bank of Poland	
Romania	National Bank of Romania	X
Russia	Bank of Russia	
Slovak Republic	National Bank of Slovakia	X
Ukraine[a]	National Bank of Ukraine	
Asia		
Hong Kong	Hong Kong Monetary Authority	
India	Reserve Bank of India	
Indonesia	Bank of Indonesia	X

Table 1.1
(continued)

Countries by region	Central bank or superintendency	Existence of PCR
Japan[a]	Financial Supervisory Agency	
Korea[a]	Bank of Korea	
Malaysia	Bank Negara Malaysia	X
Singapore	Monetary Authority of Singapore	
Sri Lanka[a]	Central Bank of Sri Lanka	
Thailand[a]	Bank of Thailand	
Africa		
Angola	Banco Nacional de Angola	X
Benin, Burkina Faso, Cote D'Ivoire, Guinea Bissau, Mali, Niger, Senegal, Togo	Banque Centale des Etats de l'Afrique de l'Ouest (BCEAO)	X
Burundi	Central Bank of Burundi	X
Cameroon[a]	Subregional Banking Commission	
Egypt[a]	Central Bank of Egypt	
Madagascar	Central Bank of Madagascar	X
Malawi	Reserve Bank of Malawi	
Mauritania[a]		
Mozambique	Banco de Mozambique	X
Nigeria	Central Bank of Nigeria and Nigerian Deposit Insurance Corporation	X
Rwanda	Banque Nationale du Rwanda	X
South Africa[a]	South African Reserve Bank	
Tanzania	Bank of Tanzania	
Zambia[a]	Bank of Zambia	
Other		
Australia	Australian Prudential Regulation Authority	
Bahrain	Bahrain Monetary Agency	X
Canada	OSFI Canada	
Cyprus	Central Bank of Cyprus	
Jordan	Central Bank of Jordan	X
Kuwait	Central Bank of Kuwait	
Lebanon[a]	Banque du Liban	
New Zealand	Reserve Bank of New Zealand	
Turkey	Central Bank of the Republic of Turkey	X

[a] Countries that did not respond to the survey.

The second survey, initiated in September 1999, focused on private credit reporting firms. Firms to be included in this survey sample were identified from a variety of sources. Authorities responding to the earlier survey of public credit registries were asked to provide the names of all credit reporting firms they had knowledge of in their country. The World Bank had also developed a list of private registries in Latin America as a result of organizing, in conjunction with the Argentine Central Bank, the December 1997 Workshop on the Role of Timely and Reliable Credit Information in the Development of Stable Financial Markets, held in Buenos Aires. Finally, names were obtained from the First International Consumer Credit Reporting World Conference, held in Rome in October 1998. Emphasis was placed on getting the main credit registries in Latin America to respond. In the spring of 2001, this survey was recirculated to increase the response rate in Eastern and Western Europe and Asia.

The private registry survey was sent to 208 firms and organizations. Included in the list were chambers of commerce known to operate credit registries, usually based on retail credit data, banking associations with registries of loan data provided by their members, and independent private credit reporting firms that collect credit data.[3] Seventy-six firms responded to the survey internationally, including thirty-one based in Latin America and the Caribbean, thirteen in Eastern and fifteen in Western Europe, and eleven from Asia-Pacific, making for an overall response rate of 35 percent. See table 1.2 for a list of countries where private credit registries were contacted for the survey.

The public and private credit information registry surveys were developed in parallel to facilitate comparisons of the data. Both surveys had the following organization:

Section 1. Contact information

Section 2. Basic information about the organization of the registry

Section 3. Description of data collected by the registry

Section 4. Description of how data is disseminated

Section 5. Attention to consumers, legal and public policy issues[4]

The third survey focused on the use of credit data by financial institutions and was circulated only in Latin America. The institu-

Table 1.2
Countries contacted for the survey of private credit registries

Latin America and the Caribbean		Belgium		Japan	X
		Cyprus		Korea	
Antigua and Barbuda*		Denmark		Malaysia	X
Argentina	X	Finland	X	Malta	
Aruba		France		Philippines	X
Bahamas*		Germany	X	Singapore	
Barbados	X	Greece	X	South Korea	
Belize		Ireland	X	Taiwan	
Bermuda*		Italy	X	Thailand	X
Bolivia	X	Netherlands	X	Middle East and Africa	
Brazil	X	Portugal		Bahrain	
Cayman Islands*		Spain	X	Egypt	
Chile	X	Sweden	X	Iran	
Colombia	X	Switzerland		Israel	
Costa Rica	X	UK	X	Jordan	
Dominican Republic	X	Eastern Europe		Kuwait	
Ecuador	X	Bulgaria	X	Lebanon	
El Salvador	X	Croatia	X	Morocco	
Grenada*		Czech Republic	X	Oman	
Guatemala	X	Estonia	X	Qatar	
Haiti		Hungary		Saudi Arabia	
México	X	Latvia	X	Tunisia	
Netherlands Antilles*		Lithuania		Turkey	X
Nicaragua		Poland	X	United Arab Emirates	
Panamá	X	Romania	X	Cote d'Ivoire	
Paraguay		Russia	X	South Africa	X
Peru	X	Slovakia		Other	
Trinidad and Tobago		Slovenia	X	Australia	X
Uruguay	X	Ukraine	X	Canada	
Venezuela		Asia		New Zealand	
Europe		Hong Kong	X	USA	X
Austria	X				

Note: An "X" indicates the country has at least one functioning private credit registry that responded to the survey. In some countries, the Chamber of Commerce responded to our survey and indicated no private credit registry existed—these are marked with an "*."

Many countries have only one operating private credit registry and few have more than two or three, so information presented at the country level could rapidly be linked to specific firms. In order to increase the response rate and accuracy of the answers, surveyed firms were promised their information would be kept confidential with only aggregate data made public. For this reason, there are no detailed tables in the appendix describing the private credit reporting industry internationally, comparable to those for the public credit registries.

tions were selected from the 1998–1999 and 1999–2000 editions of the *Latin Banking Guide & Directory*, published by *Latin Finance* magazine. The top banks in each country were selected, defined as those institutions that cumulatively represented at least 75 percent of a nation's banking assets. The survey was conducted in May 2000 and was sent to the director of credit operations or risk manager of 172 banks and financial institutions in twenty-seven countries throughout Latin America and the Caribbean. Responses were received from forty-three institutions in seventeen countries. The response rate to the bank survey was 25 percent overall.

The survey of financial institutions focused on how lenders use credit registry data, including their view of the relative value and importance of such data in lending decisions. The institutions were also asked to describe the data they provide to credit registries and to give their opinion about relevant public policies, including the adequacy of the legal framework for credit reporting in their country. Although this was a small sample size, there was great uniformity in many of the responses, so these data are presented as indicative, if not statistically significant, of how banks regard credit reporting.

1.4   The Growth of Credit Reporting Worldwide

The credit reporting industry is growing worldwide, spurred by technological innovation and the liberalization of financial markets. Macroeconomic forces, both positive and negative, have also encouraged the development of credit reporting. On the positive side, the relative stabilization of previously volatile economies during the 1990s, such as Argentina, Brazil, and Chile in Latin America, and corresponding reduction of interest rates—especially evident in Chile—created opportunities for term finance that did not exist before. When most lending is short term—thirty to ninety days—the data in a credit registry are less important than a firm's cash flow or person's liquidity; but when terms grow to many months or years, data on past behavior become more important indicators of likely repayment. At the same time, economic crises that have roots in financial sector distress have also encouraged some nations to establish or fortify credit registries. One of the causes of the 1994 Mexican "tequila crisis" was the nonperformance of many loans in the banking sector. As a result, the Mexican government encouraged the development of a private sector credit bureau, which was established in 1995.

The survey results document the growth of credit reporting internationally, with significant recent expansion in both public credit registries and private sector credit reporting firms. In the survey of private reporting firms, approximately half of the sample (thirty-nine of seventy-six respondents) began operations since 1989. This same pattern was observed in the Latin American subsample, where fourteen of thirty-one firms reported beginning their credit reporting activities since 1989. Eastern Europe, not surprisingly, reported the most new credit reporting firms, with all thirteen registries there having been established since 1992. Western Europe has also experienced recent growth in the private sector, with new credit reporting firms established in the 1990s in Germany, Austria, and Spain. There are no doubt other examples of new investments in Western Europe that our survey missed.

In the United States, where credit reporting is almost exclusively handled by private reporting firms, the 1990s were a period of consolidation in the industry. Since the mid-1980s, the number of independent credit bureaus has fallen dramatically, from approximately 2,000 to fewer than 300 today.[5] The U.S. consumer reporting industry is dominated by the "big three" bureaus: Equifax, Experian, and Trans Union, which purchase and unify data from the remaining independent bureaus in addition to collecting information directly. Dun & Bradstreet, which focuses largely on trade credit, maintains its dominance of the U.S. small business credit reporting market.

Mergers and acquisitions are also changing the face of credit reporting in other nations; among the survey sample, twenty-one firms reported that a foreign firm had purchased interest in their company and thirteen since 1994. Equifax has been the most active foreign investor in Latin America, while Experian, based in London, has been more active in Europe. Trans Union's international strategy appears to be based on looking at opportunities in specific markets such as Mexico and South Africa.

There has also been a renewed interest in public credit registries worldwide. Of the seventy-seven countries responding to the survey, forty-one reported having a public credit registry, including seventeen nations in Latin America and the Caribbean and seven nations in the EU.[6] Public credit registers have their genesis in Europe. Germany established the first PCR in 1934, followed by

France in 1946, Italy and Spain in 1962, and Belgium in 1967. Before 1968, only four other nations in the survey had established PCRs: Turkey (1951), Mexico (1964), Burundi (1964), and Jordan (1966). While a handful of nations added PCRs in the 1970s and 1980s, the expansion of this policy internationally occurred in the last decade and appears to have been focused in Latin America.

In the survey, seventeen nations reported that they had established a PCR since 1989 and nine of these were in Latin America: Brazil (1997), Ecuador (1997), Guatemala (1996), Costa Rica (1995), Dominican Republic (1994), El Salvador (1994), Argentina (1991), Colombia (1990), and Bolivia (1989). As a result, Latin America now appears to be the region with the greatest incidence of public credit registries. While all of the largest nations in the region operate a PCR, they are notably absent from small island economies in the Caribbean; only Haiti and the Dominican Republic responded that they operate public credit registries. None of the small, English-speaking countries has a PCR (Aruba, Barbados, Bermuda, Cayman Islands, Guyana, Trinidad, and Tobago), nor does Panama or Puerto Rico, which have economies closely tied to the United States.[7]

The public credit registry phenomenon may be spreading to other regions, such as Asia, Eastern Europe, and Africa. The following countries from these regions reported that they are actively considering creating a PCR: Croatia, the Czech Republic, Hong Kong, India, Singapore, South Africa, and Tanzania. What are the factors contributing to the development of public credit registries in some countries and not in others? Tullio Jappelli and Marco Pagano discuss this question in their paper, "Information Sharing, Lending and Defaults: Cross Country Evidence," forthcoming in the *Journal of Banking and Finance*. They state that "the establishment of public registries has largely been motivated by the 'substitution' role."[8] Using a database they assembled on credit information in forty-six countries, they indicate that private registries only existed in 30 percent of countries with a public registry prior to its establishment, whereas they existed in 65 percent of countries without a public registry. Jappelli and Pagano further suggest that in countries with a legal system based on Napoleonic code, where creditor rights receive less protection, public registries are more likely to evolve. This second finding is consistent with research results here, which indicate a relationship between civil code legal systems and public registries. This chapter's survey results, however, cast doubt upon the idea that public registries are formed in response to an absence of credit reporting by the private sector. Surveys here found that many Latin American nations established their PCR after the private sector registry, including the following cases: Argentina, Brazil, Chile, Colombia, Ecuador, El Salvador, Guatemala, Peru, and Uruguay. Even in Germany, where the first public registry was established, a private sector registry predated it by decades.

Although public registries may be established in some countries to compensate for the lack (or weaknesses) of a private credit reporting industry, what emerges from survey results here are the significant differences between the public and private registries. Rather than being simple substitutes, they appear to be complementary parts of a nation's credit reporting system.

1.5   Public Credit Registries

1.5.1   What Is a Public Credit Registry?
Public credit registries (PCRs) worldwide share a basic framework in their institutional arrangements, the type of data collected, and typical policies about the distribution of credit data to participating financial institutions. Most PCRs are operated by the central bank or bank supervisor, and the financial institutions they supervise are compelled to participate by means of a law or regulation. As a result, the greatest source of data for most PCRs is the commercial banking sector. Institutions are required to report on a regular basis, typically monthly, and usually on both their commercial and consumer borrowers. In most cases, information is requested on borrowers regardless of their standing. Not only is negative data collected on late payments or defaults, but also positive information on credit exposure in good or normal conditions. This information is used as part of the supervision process as well as distributed back to the financial institutions who provided the data. Access to data is typically limited, based on the concept of reciprocity, so only institutions that provide data have access, and they are seldom charged. In response to confidentiality concerns from reporting institutions, the total credit exposure for a borrower is often aggregated, and the names of the lending institutions are omitted, before being distributed. In many countries, the PCR data function as a kind of negative list or enforcement device, since data on defaults or late payments are erased once they have been paid. Also, many nations

only distribute current data, such as data for the previous month, so the PCR does not offer a historical record of a borrower's credit behavior.

Although PCRs share many common characteristics, there are also important differences, especially about the specifics of information collected and the rules on distribution and disclosure. Based on survey results here, these differences are not surprising, as countries have tended to develop their public credit registries independently, with no direct input from PCRs existing in other countries.[9] Moreover, even in Western Europe where public credit registries have the longest tradition and regularly meet in a formal EU working group, there remain significant differences among the models followed by France, Germany, Italy, and Spain. Tables in the appendix to this chapter present detailed results of the survey of public credit registries, providing for the first time an opportunity for an in-depth international comparison and analysis of these policies.

Several key characteristics vary among PCRs, and they can greatly affect the role and impact that the public registry will have in the financial sector. The remainder of this section will focus on the following two critical issues: (1) limitations on data collected and distributed, including whether there is a minimum amount for inclusion in the database, whether positive and/or negative data are collected and distributed, whether reciprocity is required for accessing the data, and the amount of historical data that is made available to lenders; and (2) the nature of the rating policy.

1.5.2   Limitations on PCR Data
The most common exclusion on data provided to the PCRs was for loans below a minimum amount. Twenty-six of the countries with a PCR reported they have set a minimum loan size and only collect information on loans in excess of this amount. These minimum loan sizes vary greatly by country and region as can be seen in figure 1.1. Germany is by far the country with the highest minimum amount: about U.S. $1.5 million. Other countries with high minimum loan amounts (presented in U.S. dollar equivalents) are Austria (U.S. $390,000), Bahrain (U.S. $133,000), Italy (U.S. $83,000), and France (U.S. $82,000). By way of comparison, a large number of countries in Latin America—nine—have no minimum loan size. In these nations, every loan no matter how small must be reported to the public credit registry.

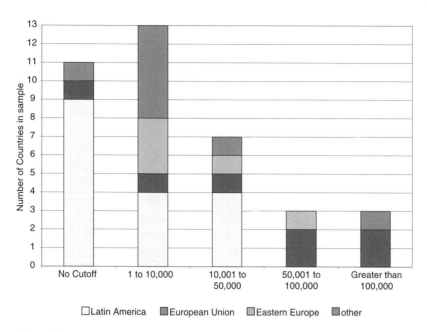

Figure 1.1
Loan size cutoffs, estimated in U.S. dollars

One possible explanation for such different loan sizes could be different primary objectives for PCRs. The survey asked what was the most important reason for starting a PCR and the most common answers were: (1) to assist in bank supervision (46%); and (2) to improve the quality of credit data available to the financial sector (34%). It would be reasonable to assume that PCRs established primarily for supplementing bank supervision would have a higher minimum loan cutoff, since small loans have little impact on system solvency or risk. At the same time, if the goal is to improve the quality of available credit data, supervisors might opt for a low minimum loan size or even none at all. To some extent, the survey results support this analysis.

Of the thirteen PCRs reporting a minimum loan size in excess of U.S. $10,000.00, eight indicated that banking supervision was their primary objective and one more indicated that it was to assist in loan provisioning; only three indicated that their main goal was to increase the availability of credit data. The results are more muddled, however, when analyzing the objectives of PCRs with no minimum loan size. Eleven countries have no minimum loan size, and Argentina has a minimum loan cutoff of only U.S.$50; of these twelve countries, seven indicated they had established the PCR to assist with bank supervision and five indicated that improving credit data was the primary goal.

There are several good reasons for establishing a minimum loan size cutoff for a PCR. First, if banking supervision is the primary goal of the PCR, then information on small loans is not likely to be of significance. Second, by including all loans, or virtually all loans, the number of records in the registry balloons. Consider Germany, for example, one of the largest economies in the world, which collects information from 5,200 institutions for its PCR, but because of the high loan cutoff of over U.S.$1.5 million, only includes records on 96,000 consumers and 170,000 firms. Argentina, by comparison, collects data from only 150 banks, but with a minimum loan size of U.S.$50, includes over 4.5 million consumers and 117,000 firms in its public registry. The greater amount of data complicates management of the PCR and analysis of the data. Data on small loans are also more likely to include errors, reducing the overall quality of the information in the registry, as the following example demonstrates.

In one Latin American country, banks had aggressively marketed credit cards and had sent preapproved cards to customers with the first year's fee waived. Many customers destroyed the cards, never having used them, and then found later that they were being identified as delinquent by the sponsoring banks when they failed to pay the card fee the following year. After complaints, the banks recognized this problem and at least one institution asked to be able to suspend reporting to the PCR on its smallest loans so as not to introduce errors into the system. When told this was not possible, the bank decided to rate all small loans as performing until it could clean its own records, introducing further confusion into the public registry data.

Another reason for establishing a minimum loan size for the public registry is to provide a clear market niche where private registries can develop. Limiting the amount of historical data that public registries make available on an ongoing basis also affects the private market for credit information. In most instances, historical data are not made available to financial institutions via the PCR. For twenty of thirty-five PCRs responding to this question, only the current month of data is available to lenders; another three reported that they provided up to one year of information, and five more stated that they provided up to two years of information. In the total sample, only seven nations provided a historical record beyond two years to financial institutions. In Latin America the tendency to provide only current data was even more pronounced; nine of the thirteen PCRs that responded to this question provide only the current month, and only one nation, Uruguay, provides more than two years of data.

Although public registries are not distributing historical data, they are collecting it. In slightly more than half of the PCRs in the survey that responded to this question (21/40), PCR data are preserved for more than ten years. Only 20 percent of PCRs (8/40) state that they destroy the data after two years or less. These same patterns are observed in the Latin America PCR subsample responding where approximately half report maintaining data more than ten years (9/16) and only three state that they discard the data after two years or less. The complete picture of a borrower's behavior afforded by PCRs is diminished, however, by a common policy of eliminating delinquent credits from the files once they have been resolved. Approximately 55 percent of PCRs (21/39) eliminate outstanding debts from a borrower's files once they have been repaid, including ten of the sixteen Latin American PCRs responding to the survey. Those PCRs that do not erase canceled debts typically preserve the information for an extended period of time—five years or more—and approximately 25 percent of PCRs surveyed indicated negative data were never destroyed.

One of the objectives of public credit registries is to provide a database for supervisors to analyze a financial institution's credit portfolio, either the entire portfolio or a significant segment of the portfolio. PCRs thus typically compel institutions to provide information about their entire universe of borrowers, be they consumer or commercial clients, including those in good standing as well as those with some kind of irregularity, late payment, or default. Of the countries sampled who operate a PCR, a significant majority (31/41) collect both positive and negative data on borrowers and all but three collect data on both firms and individuals.[10] The completeness of the record of bank borrowing that PCRs can amass is unique in many developing nations, and even in some European nations, where institutions are reluctant to share positive information on their better clients and may voluntarily only provide partial reports, primarily of negative information, to private credit information registries. Sharing positive borrower data to create credit histories is more common in Canada and the United States, where banks and other lenders routinely report on all or nearly all their consumer clients, even those in good standing.

Only rarely are either private or public sector users of PCR data charged for accessing the information. Five nations reported charging private sector users: Argentina, Brazil, and Paraguay in Latin America and Belgium and France in the EU.[11] Only Belgium and Paraguay also stated that they charged public sector users of the data.

1.5.3 The Rating Policy

Approximately two-thirds of public registries (28/39) include a rating that is assigned to either loans or to borrowers. In all cases but two (Haiti and Burundi), the rating is assigned by the reporting financial institution, according to written guidelines. Typically there are five or six categories for these ratings, which indicate the level of performance from good standing to default. In many countries these ratings are related to provisioning requirements. Moreover, ratings between institutions for the same borrower are often scrutinized by supervisors to detect cases where default risk may be understated.

The requirement that a rating be assigned on a regular basis to all loans or borrowers can create some potentially undesirable consequences. First, by requiring a broad rating classification—no more than six different categories—the supervisor may be undermining the development of independent borrower ratings by institutions. Credit scoring programs can provide much greater levels of distinction between potential borrowers but may be less likely to be adopted if there is a system-wide rating system. Small financial institutions, in particular, may decide to rely on larger institutions to do the risk management and simply adopt their ratings for common clients. The tendency to rely on the ratings from a PCR would likely be even greater if ratings were linked to provisioning requirements, since banks might decide that greater discrimination between risk categories is not useful if not reflected in provisioning.

Another problem with ratings, if they are communicated back to the financial system, is that they may exacerbate swings in the market. Most PCRs use ratings to identify problem borrowers across institutions and often require that the rating for a borrower be uniform or nearly uniform across the system. This means that if a borrower has a problem in one institution and his or her rating is lowered, then all other institutions where he or she does business must also lower the rating—providing incentives for all the institutions, not only the affected one, to revoke credit. For the same reason, banks may be reluctant to accurately rate their borrowers, since downgrading a customer could have severe consequences. Finally, if ratings are provided by the PCR, they may further implicate the supervisors if there is a bank failure. If a borrower appeared in the PCR as a good credit risk, but was in fact defaulting, bank shareholders might try to hold the PCR, central bank, or supervisors liable in contributing to their poor portfolio with erroneous information. They could also use the PCR as a cover, indicating that if the central bank did not know about a borrower's tenuous position, how could they.

1.6 Comparing Public and Private Credit Information Registries

1.6.1 What Consumer Credit Information Is Collected?
The basic consumer information collected by virtually all public credit registries and private credit reporting firms is limited to a few key items. Only three pieces of consumer data—the name of the borrower, the amount, and type of their loan(s)—were collected by approximately 90 percent of both the public and private credit registries. In two basic information categories, address of the individual and their taxpayer identification number, private registries reported higher levels of coverage than did public ones: 90 percent of private credit reporting firms had address information compared to 39 percent of public registries, and on taxpayer IDs, the figures were 75 percent of the private sample versus 54 percent of the public sample. In general, the private credit registries reported collecting a broader spectrum of information than did public registries, including personal financial data (27% vs. 5%) and other types of personal information such as marital or employment status (60% vs. 12%) and tax information (17% vs. 2%). Both public and private registries are likely to include loan rating data (63% of public and 70% of private) and approximately half of both the public and private registries collect information on the type of collateral used to secure loans. Public registries are more likely to collect data on the value of collateral (37% vs. 22%).

1.6.2.   What Commercial Credit Information Is Collected?

The data collected on commercial loans was similar, in large part, to that collected for consumers. There was, however, more divergence between the public and private sectors concerning the core data collected. The data collected by 90 percent or more of the private reporting firms included name of the firm and address. The data collected by 90 percent or more of the public registries included name of the firm, name of the reporting institution, amount of the loan, and type of the loan.[12] As was the case for consumer data, public registries were more likely to gather data on collateral firms pledged for loans. Private reporting firms were more likely to gather more detailed data on the business, including name of the business owner(s), data on the business group or conglomerate, balance sheet and income statement data, and tax information. Figure 1.2 shows graphically the difference in commercial credit information collected by private and public registries.

The different objectives of the public credit registries and private credit reporting firms are evident in the different types of information they collect. A main goal of public registries is to provide bank supervisors with information on the risk of an institution's credit

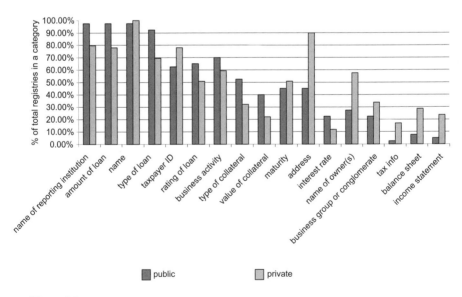

Figure 1.2
Frequency of commercial loan data collected by public and private registries

portfolio. Data useful for this task include the institution's exposure to individual borrowers (amount of loans), loan ratings, and the value of collateral backing loans. Lenders, interested in determining a consumer or firm's creditworthiness, are interested in other information, including address (which is often highly correlated with payment behavior), tax identification number (to ensure that one is following the correct person's credit history), and, for commercial credits, the name of the business owner, since their credit history is highly indicative of firm behavior for small firms. Public entities may also be discouraged from collecting more detailed or personal data on consumers or firms due to political or privacy considerations; governments may believe this would be overstepping their bounds, even if legally possible. Private credit reporting firms, which operate under less public scrutiny, may not be so limited.

There are also some notable differences by region. For example, most public registries in Latin America, Africa, and Eastern Europe collect loan rating data on firms, but only two of the seven PCRs in the EU collect this information. Public registries in Latin America lead in the collection of firm taxpayer identification numbers (15/17) whereas only one of the six African PCRs collects this data. Slightly more than half of the PCRs in Eastern and Western Europe collect taxpayer numbers. All public registries in Eastern Europe collect information on the type of collateral pledged for commercial loans—perhaps reflecting the importance of collateral in these financial systems; in other regions, no more than half of the PCRs collect this data. Data from balance sheets and income statements is only collected by PCRs in Africa.

Most of the private registries responding to the survey collect information on both consumer and commercial loans. Of the sixty-three firms responding to these questions, only twenty-one were dedicated exclusively to either commercial or consumer credit; eleven of these twenty-one firms reported that they collected only commercial credit data. The other forty-two firms stated that they collected both types of credit information.

The dual focus of private credit registries internationally may come as a surprise to those familiar with the U.S. credit reporting industry, where the lines between these businesses are sharply drawn. There are several probable reasons for the different industry structures, beginning with the first-mover advantage gained by Dun & Bradstreet in the U.S. market. Dun & Bradstreet, which is the oldest credit reporting firm in the United States, established over 150 years ago, has such a dominant position in the U.S. market for business credit information that other credit reporting firms have largely decided not to enter this business line. There are other factors, however, which may also contribute to the separation of consumer and credit data in the United States and its combination in other markets.

The core of the data collected by D&B is interfirm credit information, provided on a regular basis by thousands of U.S. corporations, not information from banks. Banks in the United States have traditionally been reluctant to share their small business data with credit reporting firms. One reason for this was their approach to the small business credit market; banks did in-depth analyses of a firm's business prospects and invested significant time and effort in collecting information. They did not have credit scoring models or other decision tools for this market segment that make standardized information particularly valuable. In the 1990s, however, small business credit scoring tools were introduced, increasing the demand for such data. As a result, many of the major U.S. small business lenders established the Small Business Financial Exchange (SBFE) in 2001. This credit reporting service allows members to share information on the basis of reciprocity and with other limitations on access to the database to prevent cherry picking of the best small business customers.

The collection of a broad range of business data in developing countries is especially difficult due to irregular business practices, including tax evasion. For the same reason, there is less confidence in the reliability of basic firm information such as balance sheets, so loans are based on owners' wealth to an even greater extent than in the United States. This blurs the line between the consumer and small business markets and may encourage credit reporting firms in developing countries to collect both types of data.

Public credit registries and private credit reporting firms both collect information from banks. The sources of information are much more diverse, however, for the private firms as figure 1.3 shows. Of the sixty-three firms that provided information about the source of their credit data, fifty stated that it came from commercial banks. The same number of firms reported receiving data on trade credit and forty-three received information from retail merchants. By comparison, the only common sources of credit data for more than 50 percent of the public sample were commercial banks and develop-

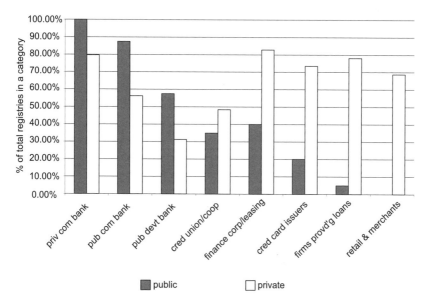

Figure 1.3
Sources of information for credit registries

ment banks. Fewer than 20 percent of PCRs had information on credit card debts and only one had trade credits.

A majority of the private registries (39/57 responding to the question) indicated that they received data from most of the largest banks in their country. Only a few registries indicated that their data came from a restricted group of credit providers or membership; typically these cases were firms focusing on retail credit information and not on bank data.[13]

1.6.3 Data Distributed by Credit Registries

Virtually all of the PCRs in our sample (35/40 responding to the question) distribute at least some of the credit data they collect.[14] The most common recipients of PCR data are financial institutions that provide the data (35/40) and units in the central bank and bank supervisor (33/40). Private credit reporting firms have a broader range of clients for their data, including other private businesses (30% of private vs. 14% of public) and other private credit information providers (48% of private vs. 8% of public). Sixteen percent of the private registries also indicated that they provided data to the public registry in their country. Private registries were also much more likely to provide borrowers with access to their own information; only one-quarter of public registries offered this important service compared with nearly two-thirds of the private registries. Other public sector entities that could be interested in credit data such as that contained in the credit registries are more likely to have access from private registries than public ones: 33 percent of private reporting firms indicated that tax authorities had access to their records compared with only 6 percent of public credit registries; similar figures for other federal government authorities were 17 percent of public versus 28 percent of private and for state or municipal authorities, 11 percent of public versus 41 percent of private.

Access to data in public registries is often limited on the grounds of reciprocity. Thirty-one nations stated that only those financial institutions that contributed data to the PCR had access; exceptions to this rule were Angola, Argentina, Austria, Ecuador, Nigeria, and Rwanda, which allowed other private lenders access to the data.[15] This is in stark comparison to private registries, where 56 percent of the sampled firms stated that they did not require lenders or others to provide data to have some access. Argentina is by far the most open with access, providing some PCR data to the general public via the Internet as well as via CD-ROMs.

Financial institutions that have access to data in the PCR typically see only a restricted portion of the total database. For example, more than half of the PCRs surveyed (20/36) reported that they did not identify which financial institution(s) provided the data when it is distributed. The most common format used for presenting PCR data to financial institutions aggregates all the borrower's loans (14/24) so there is only one entry per person or firm, rather than separate entries for each outstanding loan or for each lender which reported. Private credit reporting firms, on the other hand, are most likely to provide detailed information on each line of credit a borrower has with each reporting institution (60% of the private sample). Another 9 percent of the private sample aggregate information for each institution where a borrower has credit and only 21 percent aggregate all credits across the financial system, as is common with PCRs. Other restrictions on access to public data include requiring a borrower's authorization before their data can be accessed (9/21), limiting access to data on borrowers who are already clients of the financial institution (12/21), limiting access to large borrowers (4/21), commercial clients (4/21), or to borrowers in bad standing (2/21).

The PCR data most commonly distributed to financial institutions includes the amount of loans or debt outstanding for a borrower (30/30), the rating or classification of the borrower or loan (23/30), information on collateral (11/30) and other guarantees (11/30), and information on the borrower's involvement in firms or other loans (11/30). Only ten PCRs provide any data on loan maturities and only three countries provide interest rate information. A similar question was not asked for private registries since they typically sell all the data they collect in some form or another.

PCR data is usually distributed to financial institutions in electronic format via modems or dedicated phone lines (17/37) or via computer disks or CD-Roms (20/37). In Latin America, the most common format was modems or phone lines (7/14), followed by written documents (4/14) and computer disks/CDs (3/14). Only one nation, Lithuania, reported that the Internet was their most common vehicle for distributing PCR data to financial institutions. In the private sector, electronic connection is a must, and 82 percent of the sampled private credit reporting firms indicated they had the capacity to serve real time, on-line spot consultations of their database.

1.6.4 Data Accuracy, Consumer Attention, and Legal Issues

Public and private registries have different approaches for maximizing the accuracy of their data. Data in public registries are required to be provided by law or regulation, so governments have a legal basis for demanding that inaccuracies be remedied or missing data be made available. If banks fail to comply, PCRs have sanctions they can impose, the most common being penalty fees followed by supervisory actions. Most public registries report using these sanctions on a limited basis; only five countries indicated that they had sanctioned twenty-five or more institutions in the last year: four of these were in Latin America and one in Asia.[16] The vast majority, 75 percent, stated that they had sanctioned no more than ten financial institutions in the past year.

Private credit reporting firms, which rely on the voluntary provision of data, also rely on the reporting institutions to voluntarily review and correct erroneous data. Approximately 70 percent of private registries stated that they routinely notified the reporting institution and asked for review when they had a data problem; surprisingly, nearly 30 percent indicated this was not standard practice. Another incentive employed by approximately 30 percent of the private survey sample was to temporarily suspend access to the credit registry for institutions with recurrent data problems.

Other measures that both public and private registries take to ensure and improve their data quality include seeking input from the borrowers listed in the registry and analyzing the data to identify abnormalities. A slim majority of the private firms in the survey (34/60) indicated that they did simple statistical checks, such as comparing debt amounts month-to-month, whereas more than two-thirds of PCRs (26/38) used such checks. Approximately half of the private firms (31/60) stated that they provided consumers with a free copy of their credit report as part of their strategy to identify incorrect data, and twenty-five of the same sample of firms stated that they applied more rigorous computer modeling techniques to identify data problems. When asked about the most common source of inaccurate data, both public registries and private credit reporting firms ranked problems in the data provided by financial institutions first, followed by errors resulting from matching credit data to the wrong individual.

Most of the private reporting firms surveyed had policies in place to deal with consumers. Of the sixty-three firms that responded to the question on how they dealt with consumer complaints, forty-five had a customer relations department, thirty-six handled complaints over the phone, and thirty-two had an established protocol for correcting information. Only eleven firms, however, indicated that they had a toll-free telephone number to take complaints or provide information. Evidently, these policies are working, since fifty-eight of sixty-four firms stated that it took them less than two weeks, on average, to evaluate and correct, if necessary, erroneous data discovered by consumers. It would be interesting to check this rosy self-assessment against information from consumers groups or government agencies, since the ability of consumers to quickly rectify incorrect data has long been a bone of contention in the United States and other developed countries. For example, complaints about problems in one's credit report continue to be one of the most common issues brought before the Federal Trade Commission.

Public credit registries are much less well equipped to deal with consumer complaints or to provide other consumer attention. Fewer than half of the public credit registries indicated they had any policies in place to attend to consumers. Only seven of the forty-one registries indicated they had a telephone number for taking complaints, only eight had an established protocol for correcting information, and only two allowed consumers to place any comments on their records about disputed data. Together with the fact that most public registries do not even allow borrowers access to their records, the lack of attention to consumers, and lack of opportunities to easily correct data, are troubling issues which deserve greater consideration by authorities operating PCRs.

1.7 The Lenders' View of Credit Reporting: The Experiences of Latin American Banks

Forty-three banks responded to the survey on their use of credit information. The vast majority of banks—84 percent—indicated that they used registry data for evaluating consumer loans, an even higher percentage—93 percent—indicated they used such data for commercial loans, and 100 percent of banks responding indicated they used registry data in mortgage lending. Approximately twice as many banks considered private credit registries to be their main source of external credit data compared with those favoring public registries (17 vs. 9). Unfortunately, a large portion of the sample— seventeen banks—did not respond to the questions about whether a public or private registry was their main source of data.

Eighty-eight percent of banks responding to the survey stated that the kind of data they typically receive from credit registries are credit histories containing both positive and negative data. Given that they have both positive and negative data available to them, it is interesting that most banks (76%) stated that any negative information on a person or firm found in a registry would disqualify them from receiving credit. This indicates that many banks still lack more sophisticated credit analysis tools to evaluate borrowers. It may also indicate that positive data are rather limited compared to the negative, and thus a fuller picture of a borrower's credit history does not emerge allowing for more subtle distinctions between borrowers. A surprising 40 percent of banks indicated that they are using bureau scores, obtained directly from the credit registries, however, 28 percent of banks were not familiar with such products. Even more banks—65 percent—use in-house credit scoring programs to evaluate borrowers.

Probably the most interesting part of the survey of financial institutions was their assessment of the importance of credit reporting

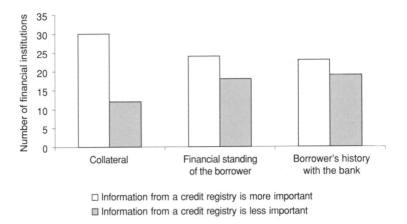

Figure 1.4
Importance of credit registry information relative to other measures of creditworthiness

information to their business operations. Figure 1.4 compares the bankers' assessments of the relative importance of data from credit registries with collateral used to secure a loan, with personal financial data of the borrower, such as wealth or income, and with data the bank might have on a borrower from previous banking accounts, such as checking or payroll services. In each category, bankers indicated that they viewed credit information as relatively more important in their credit review process. This response was particularly strong in the case of collateral, where banks that preferred credit reporting data outnumbered those that preferred collateral by a 2:1 margin.

The importance banks attach to credit information is linked to the savings this type of data can provide in the time and cost of processing loans as well as in improving portfolio quality. Figure 1.5 shows that virtually all banks indicated that without information from credit registries their performance would deteriorate. In the case of the time for loan processing, 31 percent indicated that it would more than double and another third indicated it would rise substantially—between 25 percent and 100 percent. As for cost, the results were similar, with over 60 percent of banks indicating an increase in cost of at least 25 percent. The strongest result, however, was the banks' response to how a lack of credit information would affect defaults—approximately 70 percent of those sampled indicated it would increase defaults by 25 percent or more.

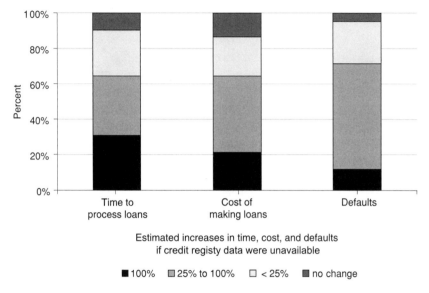

Figure 1.5
Impact of credit registry information on bank lending performance

The bank survey and private credit registry survey both asked respondents to rate the quality of credit information available in their country. The results are presented in figure 1.6. Not surprisingly, the private reporting firms gave themselves higher grades, in most cases, than did their bank clients. Whereas nearly 80 percent of the private bureaus rated the accuracy of information available as "good" or "very good," less than 40 percent of the banks agreed. On timeliness of the data, completeness, and accessibility, the ratings were more similar. The greatest divergence was in rating the price of information; more than 90 percent of private credit reporting firms felt their prices were good, whereas only 20 percent of banks agreed. Most banks indicated that prices were "fair"; however, a sizeable number (9/33) rated prices as "poor."

1.8 Public Policy Considerations

This chapter has presented the results of survey data on public credit registries and private credit reporting firms worldwide as well as the use and evaluation of credit information by financial institutions in Latin America. The following public policy considerations emerge.

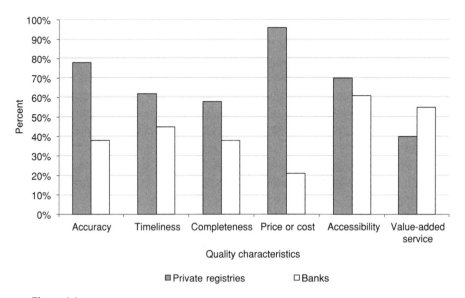

Figure 1.6
Rating the quality of credit information in the respondent's country (percent reporting "good" or "very good" to selected characteristics)

With PCRs, it is clear that they are not a substitute for private sector registries, but rather, a complement. It also appears that, in some cases, there is ambiguity as to whether the registry is to be primarily used to assist in supervision or as a source of additional data for the financial sector. If supervision is the main objective, then a minimum loan size for inclusion in the PCR should be considered. Such a limit should be related to a determination of the size of loans at which systemic risk is likely to become a problem, and it should probably be at least a multiple of per capita income in the country. Even if the PCR is established to improve the quality of data available in the financial system, a minimum loan amount for inclusion may be wise to limit the possibility of errors in the data. Further, especially if the minimum loan size is low, then steps should be taken to provide at least basic consumer attention so that errors can be detected and addressed without undue effort required on the part of consumers.

The distribution of borrower ratings by a PCR should also be reviewed carefully to ensure that they are not encouraging swings in the credit market or discouraging the development of independent risk assessments by financial institutions.

Public or government-owned banks should also be included in this issue, especially in nations where they represent a sizeable share of the banking industry. Public banks should be required to report at least their negative information to both the public and private registries.

Policymakers should also review the legal and regulatory framework for credit reporting to determine if privacy laws, bank secrecy laws, or other legal issues are impeding the development of private sector registries. The regulatory framework should provide a basis for consumer rights and protection and ensure compliance with relevant laws.

A closer public-private dialogue could also be beneficial in this sector. Lenders and private credit reporting firms should be asked for their views on the role of the public registry in the financial sector as well as for needed legal and regulatory reform, as should consumer groups. Further, policymakers may want to consider how they might, together with interested private sector actors, educate the public as to the benefits of a responsibly managed credit reporting system, and of the trade-off between privacy and the cost and access to credit.

Appendix

Table 1A.1
Countries with a public credit register

	Name of registry	Operated by government institution	Year established
Angola	Central de Riscos de Crédito	Banco Nacional de Angola	1998
Argentina	Central de deudores del sistema financiero	Superintendencia de Bancos	1991
Austria	Großkreditevidenz	Oesterreichische Nationalbank	1986
Bahrain	Central Risk Unit	Bahrain Monetary Agency	1979
Belarus		National Bank of the Republic of Belarus	1996
Belgium		Commission Bancaire et Financière	1967
Benin, Burkina Faso, Cote D'Ivoire, Guinea Bissau, Mali, Niger, Senegal, Togo	Centrale des Risques	Banque Centrale des Etats de l'Afrique de l'Ouest (BCEAO)	1979
Bolivia	Central de Información de Riesgo Crediticio	Superintendencia de Bancos y Entidades Financieras	1989
Brazil	Central de Risco de Crédito	Banco Central do Brasil	1997
Bulgaria		Bulgarian National Bank	2000
Burundi		Bank of Republic of Burundi	1964
Chile	Archivo Deudas Generales	Superintendencia de Bancos e Instituciones Financieras (SBIF)	1950
Colombia		Superbancaria	1990
Costa Rica	Central de Deudores	Superintendencia General de Entidades Financieras	1995
Dominican Republic	Sistema de Información de Deudores	Superintendencia de Bancos	1994
Ecuador	Central de Riesgos	Superintendencia del Sistema Financiero de El Salvador	1997

El Salvador	Central de Riesgos	Superintendencia del Sistema Financiero	1994
France	Service Central des Risques	Banque de France	1946
Germany	Evidenzzentrale für Millionenkredite	Deutsche Bundesbank	1934
Guatemala	Sistema de Información Crediticia	Superintendencia de Bancos	1996
Haïti	Centrales des Risques	Banque de la République d'Haïti	1980
Indonesia	Sistem Informasi Debitur	Bank Indonesia	1973
Italy	Centrale dei Rischi	Banca d'Italia	1962
Jordan		Central Bank of Jordan	1966
Lithuania	Loan Risk Data Base	The Bank of Latvia	1996
Madagascar		Banque Centrale de Madagascar	
Malaysia	Central Credit Bureau	Bank Negara Malaysia	1988
Mexico	Servicio Nacional de Información de Crédito Bancario	Banco de Mexico	1964
Mozambique[a]		Banco de Mozambique	
Nicaragua	Sistema de Central de Riesgo	Superintendencia de Bancos y de Otras Instituciones Finanacieras	
Nigeria		Central Bank of Nigeria	1991
Paraguay	Central de Riesgos Crediticio	Superintendencia de Bancos	
Peru	Central de Riesgos	Superintendencia de Banca Y Seguros	1968
Portugal	Serviço de Centralização de Riscos de Crédito	Banco de Portugal	1978
Romania		National Bank of Romania	2000
Rwanda		Banque Nationale du Rwanda	1990
Slovak Republic	Register of Bank Loans and Guarantees	National Bank of Slovakia	1996
Spain	Central de Información de Riesgos.	Banco de España	1962
Turkey		The Central Bank of Turkey	1951
Uruguay	Central de Riesgos Crediticios	Banco Central del Uruguay	1982
Venezuela	Sistema Central de Riesgos	Superintendencia de Bancos	1975

a. Note that data for Mozambique is not included in tables 1A.2 through 1A.8 because very few of the survey questions were answered.

Table 1A.2
Basic statistics on public credit registries

	Number of full-time employees	Number of institutions reporting	Total amount of credits in PCR (billions of US$)	Minimum loan size (US$)
Angola	3	7		0
Argentina		150	97.51	50
Austria	8	1576	296.75	389,936
Bahrain	2	19		132,661
BCEAO		90		
Belarus		27		10,000
Belgium	11	175	200.00	26,602
Bolivia	2	71	5.53	0
Brazil	0	442	168.18	25,905
Bulgaria	2		2.62	4,647
Burundi		15		610
Chile	4	30	50.00	0
Colombia	9	100	30.00	11,000
Costa Rica	2	92	3.21	0
Dominican Republic	5	190	4.00	0
Ecuador	6	103	4.77	0
El Salvador	2	38	6.05	0
France	50	900+	972.16	81,558
Germany		5200	5,618.92	1,646,053
Guatemala		55	2.41	0
Haïti	1	12		4,475
Indonesia		168	45.19	7,326
Italy	34	1063	941.19	83,131
Jordan	6	23	4.90	42,040
Lithuania	1	24	2.20	12,500
Madagascar		9	0.40	7,983
Malaysia	7		62.5	
Mexico	5	119	82.95	21,424
Nigeria	10	94	4.26	8,830
Nicaragua	1	15	1.03	0
Paraguay	2	73	1.93	3,020
Peru	7	133	19.12	3,921
Portugal	7	242	15.17	0
Romania	5	40	4.07	6,664
Rwanda	4	9		
Slovak Republic	3	26	19.14	74,122
Spain	20	435		6,450
Turkey	22	84	76.00	6,371
Uruguay	1	49	7.53	18,000
Venezuela	3	91	10.73	0

Frequency of reporting to PCR	Positive (P) or negative (N) data or both (B)	Is positive data made available?	Reciprocity for access to data?	Consultations available on-line or through modems
as changes occur	B	No	No	
monthly	B	Yes	No	X
monthly	P	Yes	No	
quarterly	P	Yes	Yes	
monthly	P	Yes	Yes	
	B	No	Yes	
monthly	P	Yes	Yes	
monthly	B	Yes	Yes	X
monthly	B		Yes	X
monthly	B	Yes	Yes	
monthly	B	Yes	Yes	
monthly	B	Yes	Yes	
quarterly	B	Yes	Yes	X
monthly	B	No	Yes	
semi-annual	B	No	Yes	
monthly	B	Yes	No	X
monthly	B	Yes	Yes	X
monthly	P		Yes	X
quarterly	N	No	Yes	X
semi-annual	B			
quarterly	B	Yes	Yes	
monthly	B			
monthly	B	Yes	Yes	X
monthly	N	No	Yes	X
	B	Yes	Yes	
monthly	B	Yes	Yes	
monthly	B	Yes	Yes	
monthly	B	Yes	Yes	X
monthly	B		No	X
monthly	B			
monthly	B	Yes	Yes	
monthly	B	Yes	Yes	
monthly	B	Yes	Yes	X
monthly	B	Yes	Yes	
monthly	B	Yes	No	
monthly	B	Yes	Yes	X
daily	P	Yes	Yes	X
monthly	B	Yes	Yes	
quarterly	P	Yes	Yes	X
monthly	B	Yes	Yes	X

Table 1A.3
Consumer data in public credit registries

	PCR contains consumer data	Number of consumers in PCR (thousands)	Coverage of population aged 15–64	Consumer information			
				Name	Address	Taxpayer ID	Reporting institution
Angola	X			X	X	X	X
Argentina	X	4,655	21.0%	X	X		X
Austria	X	59	1.1%	X	X		X
Bahrain	X			X	X		X
BCEAO	X			X	X		X
Belarus	X			X	X		X
Belgium	X	265	3.9%	X	X	X	X
Bolivia	X	780	18.0%	X		X	X
Bulgaria	X	13	0.2%	X	X		X
Burundi	X			X			X
Brazil	X	651	0.6%			X	X
Chile	X	3,024	32.2%	X		X	X
Colombia	X	1,269	5.1%	X		X	X
Costa Rica	X	518	24.2%	X			X
Dominican Rep.	X			X		X	X
Ecuador	X	826	11.5%	X		X	X
El Salvador	X	450	12.9%	X		X	X
France	X						
Germany	X	96	0.2%	X	X		X
Guatemala	X			X		X	X
Haïti	X			X	X	X	X
Indonesia	X			X	X	X	X
Italy	X	5,587	14.2%	X		X	X
Jordan	X			X	X		X
Lithuania	X	8	0.3%	X			X
Madagascar	X			X			
Malaysia	X	473	3.4%	X	X		X
Mexico	X	75	0.1%	X	X	X	X
Nigeria	X			X	X		X
Nicaragua	X			X		X	X
Paraguay	X	81	2.9%	X		X	X
Peru	X	1,120	7.6%	X		X	X
Portugal	X	2,915	44.4%	X		X	X
Romania	X	1	0%	X		X	X
Rwanda	X			X	X		X
Slovak Rep.							
Spain	X	9,370	34.9%	X		X	X
Turkey		379	0.9%				
Uruguay	X	122	6.0%	X		X	X
Venezuela	X	1,560	11.3%	X		X	X

collected in the PCR

Amount of loan	Interest rate	Maturity	Type of loan	Type of collateral	Value of collateral	Rating of loan	Ownership of business	Personal financial data	Other personal info	Tax info
X		X	X	X		X				
X				X	X	X				
X			X				X			
X			X				X			
X		X					X			
X		X	X	X			X			
X			X							
X	X	X	X	X	X	X			X	
X	X	X	X	X		X				
X			X			X				
X		X								
X			X			X				
X			X			X				
X			X			X				
X			X			X				
X			X	X	X	X				
X	X	X	X			X				
X			X				X		X	
X	X		X	X	X	X				
X		X	X			X				
X	X	X	X	X	X	X	X			
X		X	X	X	X	X				
X			X	X			X			
X	X	X	X	X	X	X				
X			X							
X		X	X	X	X	X	X			
X			X			X				
X	X	X	X	X	X	X	X	X		
X	X	X	X	X	X	X				
X					X	X			X	
X			X	X	X	X			X	X
X			X							
X		X	X	X		X				
X	X	X	X	X	X	X	X	X	X	
X		X	X	X		X				
X		X	X	X	X					
X			X	X	X	X				

Table 1A.4
Data on firms in the public credit registry

	PCR contains firm data	Number of firms in PCR (thousands)	Firm information collected in the PCR					
			Name	Address	Taxpayer ID	Name of reporting institution	Amount of loan	Interest rate
Angola	X		X	X	X	X	X	
Argentina	X	118	X		X	X	X	
Austria	X	37	X	X		X	X	
Bahrain	X		X	X		X	X	
BCEAO	X	55	X	X		X	X	
Belarus	X		X	X	X	X	X	
Belgium	X	160	X	X	X	X	X	
Bolivia	X	10	X		X	X	X	X
Brazil	X	230			X	X	X	
Bulgaria	X	18	X	X		X	X	X
Burundi	X		X			X	X	
Chile	X	81	X		X	X	X	
Colombia	X	192	X		X	X	X	
Costa Rica	X	11	X			X	X	
Dominican Rep.	X		X		X	X	X	
Ecuador	X	16	X		X	X	X	
El Salvador	X	150	X		X	X	X	X
France	X	900	X	X		X	X	
Germany	X	170	X	X		X	X	
Guatemala	X		X		X	X	X	X
Haïti	X	6	X	X	X	X	X	
Indonesia	X		X	X	X	X	X	X
Italy	X	1088	X		X	X	X	
Jordan	X	94	X	X		X		
Lithuania	X	7	X	X		X	X	X
Madagascar	X		X				X	
Malaysia	X	67	X	X		X	X	
Mexico	X	120	X	X	X	X	X	
Nigeria	X	15	X	X		X	X	X
Nicaragua	X		X		X	X	X	X
Paraguay	X	38	X		X	X	X	
Peru	X	480	X		X	X	X	
Portugal	X	393	X		X	X	X	
Romania	X	19	X		X	X	X	
Rwanda	X		X	X		X	X	X
Slovak Rep.	X	8	X	X	X	X	X	
Spain	X	622	X		X	X	X	
Turkey	X	1026	X			X	X	
Uruguay	X	51	X		X	X	X	
Venezuela	X	114	X		X	X	X	

Maturity	Type of loan	Type of collateral	Value of collateral	Rating of loan	Name of owner(s)	Business group or conglomerate	Balance sheet	Income statement	Business activity	Tax info
X	X	X		X					X	
		X	X	X						
	X					X			X	
	X				X	X			X	
	X								X	
X	X	X			X				X	
	X									
X	X	X	X	X					X	
X										
X	X	X		X	X					
	X						X		X	
	X			X						
	X			X					X	
	X			X		X			X	
	X			X						
	X	X	X	X					X	
	X			X						
X	X									
	X				X	X			X	
	X	X	X	X						
X	X								X	
X	X	X	X	X	X	X			X	
X	X	X	X	X					X	
	X	X			X				X	
X	X	X	X	X	X					
	X			X					X	
X	X	X	X	X					X	
			X	X					X	
X	X	X	X	X	X		X	X	X	
X	X	X	X	X					X	
			X	X						
	X	X	X	X	X				X	X
	X									
X	X	X		X		X			X	
X	X	X	X	X	X	X	X	X	X	
X	X	X	X	X	X	X			X	
X	X	X		X					X	
	X								X	
X	X	X	X						X	
	X	X	X	X		X			X	

Table 1A.5
Use of PCR for banking sector supervision and making changes of entries in the PCR

	Data used for supervision	Bank supervision named as the most important reason for operating the PCR	Importance of PCR data in strengthening supervision of financial institutions	Groups allowed to	
				PCR staff, after dispute process	Institution providing data
Angola			VI		X
Argentina	X	X	VI		X
Austria	X	X	SI		X
Bahrain	X		SI	X	X
Belgium	X		SI	X	X
BCEAO	X		VI		X
Belarus	X		SI		X
Bolivia	X		VI		X
Brazil	X		VI		X
Bulgaria	X	X			X
Burundi	X		VI		
Chile	X		VI		X
Colombia	X	X	VI		X
Costa Rica	X	X	VI		X
Dominican Rep.	X	X	VI	X	X
Ecuador	X	X	VI		X
El Salvador	X	X	VI		X
France	X	X	VI		X
Germany	X	X	VI	X	
Guatemala	X		SI		
Haïti	X	X	SI		
Indonesia	X	X	SI		X
Italy	X		SI		X
Jordan	X	X	SI	X	X
Lithuania	X	X	VI		
Madagascar	X		SI		X
Malaysia	X	X	VI		X
Mexico	X		OLI		X
Nicaragua	X	X	VI		X
Nigeria	X		VI		X
Paraguay	X		VI		X
Peru	X		VI	X	X
Portugal	X		SI		X
Romania	X		VI		X
Rwanda	X	X	VI	X	
Slovak Rep.	X	X	SI		X
Spain	X		VI	X	X
Turkey	X		VI		X
Uruguay	X	X	VI		X
Venezuela	X	X	VI		X

VI = very important, SI = somewhat important, OLI = of little importance.

| change information | | When data can be deleted | | | | | |
Courts	Individual	At the request of the reporting institution	At the individual or firm's request	After a grievance prodecure	After legal action has been taken	Information cannot be removed, only corrected	Individual can request that entire record be removed from database
X		X				X	
X		X		X	X		
						X	
		X					
X		X			X		
		X					
						X	
						X	
		X			X		
		X					
		X		X			
		X		X			X
						X	
		X				X	
						X	
						X	
		X					
X						X	
		X					
		X					
		X			X		
		X					
						X	
		X		X			
		X					
						X	
		X					
		X					X
		X				X	
X						X	
		X				X	
						X	

Table 1A.6
Measures for consumer attention

	Measures to determine accuracy				Mechanisms for handling complaints	
	Occasional checks with other data provided by financial institutions	Borrower complaints used to identify problems	Statistical Checks	Software program	Staff of PCR follows up	Complainant must go to reporting institution
Angola	X	X		X		X
Argentina	X		X	X		X
Austria		X	X	X	X	
Bahrain	X		X			
BCEAO			X			
Belarus	X			X	X	
Belgium	X	X	X	X	X	
Bolivia			X	X	X	X
Brazil	X	X	X	X		X
Bulgaria	X		X		X	X
Burundi	X		X			
Chile			X	X	X	X
Colombia	X		X	X		X
Costa Rica	X		X	X		X
Dominican Rep.	X	X		X	X	X
Ecuador	X	X			X	X
El Salvador	X				X	X
France			X	X		
Germany		X	X	X	X	
Guatemala						
Haïti	X					
Indonesia	X	X		X	X	X
Italy	X	X	X	X	X	
Jordan					X	X
Lithuania						
Madagascar	X		X			
Malaysia	X		X	X		
Mexico	X	X	X			X
Nicaragua			X	X		X
Nigeria	X	X	X		X	X
Paraguay	X			X		X
Peru		X		X		X
Portugal	X		X		X	X
Romania	X		X	X	X	
Rwanda	X		X			
Slovak Rep.	X	X		X		X
Spain	X	X	X	X	X	X
Turkey		X	X	X		
Uruguay	X		X	X		X
Venezuela	X	X			X	X

	determine accuracy			Procedures to follow up on consumer complaints					
	Written request required	Complaints allowed by telephone	Meeting with staff of PCR required	Consumer relations department	Telephone number	Toll-free telephone number	Standard form	Established protocol	Space for consumer comment on credit report
	X								
	X								
	X				X				
					X				
	X							X	
	X			X	X	X			
	X								
	X			X				X	
				X					
	X	X		X	X				
	X	X							X
			X	X				X	
	X	X	X	X					
	X								
	X								
	X		X						
	X								
	X								
	X	X	X		X		X	X	
	X							X	
	X			X	X				
				X					
	X						X	X	
	X			X				X	
	X								
		X		X	X			X	X

Table 1A.7
Access to data in the public credit registry and future plans for the PCR

	Reporting limited to banks only	Amount of data made available for distribution to financial institutions	Access restricted	
			Borrowers in bad standing	Large borrowers
Angola	Yes	10+ years		
Argentina	No	Current month		
Austria	No	3–5 years		
Bahrain	Yes	Current year		
BCEAO	Yes	Current month		
Belarus	Yes	3–5 years		
Belgium	No	Current month		
Bolivia	No	Current month		
Brazil	No	1–2 years		
Bulgaria	Yes	Current month		
Burundi	Yes	Current month		
Chile	Yes	Current month		
Colombia	No	1–2 years		
Costa Rica	No	Current month		
Dominican Rep.	No		X	X
Ecuador	No	Current month		
El Salvador	Yes	Current month		
France	No	Current year		X
Germany	No	Current month		
Guatemala	Yes			
Haïti	Yes	Current year		
Indonesia	Yes			
Italy	No	1–2 years		
Jordan	No	Current month		
Lithuania	Yes	3–5 years	X	X
Madagascar	No	Current month		
Malaysia	No	3–5 years		
Mexico	Yes			
Nicaragua	Yes			
Nigeria	Yes	1–2 years		
Paraguay	No	Current month		
Peru	No	Current month		
Portugal	No	Current month		
Romania	Yes	1–2 years		
Rwanda	No	Current month		
Slovak Rep.	Yes	Current month		
Spain	No	Current month		
Turkey	Yes	10+ years		
Uruguay	No	3–5 years		X
Venezuela	No	Current month		

to data on specific clients			Future plans of the PCR				
Financial institution's clients	Borrowers authorization required	Commercial clients	Privatizing the PCR	Requiring full or partial cost recovery for PCR	Downsizing the PCR	Expanding the PCR	Eliminating the PCR
	X			X			
						X	
						X	
						X	
						X	
		X					
						X	
	X					X	
X							
X						X	
	X			X		X	
	X					X	
X		X				X	
	X			X		X	
						X	
						X	
X						X	
						X	
						X	
			X				
X						X	
X		X				X	
X						X	
X				X		X	
							X
						X	
				X		X	
	X					X	
		X				X	
X	X					X	
	X					X	
X							
				X		X	
X	X						
						X	
X				X		X	
				X		X	

Table 1A.8
Groups with some access to data in the public credit registry

	Public financial institutions who provide data	Public financial institutions who don't provide data	Private financial institutions who provide data	Private financial institutions who don't provide data	Central Bank and Bank Supervisors
Angola	X		X		X
Argentina	X	X	X	X	X
Austria	X	X	X	X	X
Bahrain	X				X
BCEAO	X		X		X
Belarus			X		X
Belgium					
Bolivia			X		X
Brazil	X		X		X
Bulgaria	X	X	X		X
Burundi	X		X		
Chile	X		X		X
Colombia	X		X		X
Costa Rica	X		X		
Dominican Rep.	X		X		X
Ecuador	X	X	X	X	X
El Salvador	X		X		
France	X	X	X		X
Germany	X		X		X
Guatemala					
Haïti	X		X		
Indonesia					
Italy	X		X		X
Jordan			X		
Lithuania					
Madagascar			X		
Malaysia	X		X		X
Mexico	X		X		X
Nicaragua					
Nigeria	X	X		X	X
Paraguay	X		X		X
Peru	X		X		X
Portugal	X		X		
Romania	X		X		X
Rwanda	X	X	X	X	X
Slovak Rep.			X		
Spain	X		X		X
Turkey	X		X		
Uruguay	X		X		
Venezuela	X		X		X

Unit running the PCR	Office of Tax collection	Law enforcement	Other federal government agencies	State/local or provincial government	Individuals have access to their own data	Private businesses providing loans to clients	Private credit bureaus	Marketing firms
X	X	X	X	X	X	X	X	X
X					X			
X								
		X						
					X			
X		X						
X					X			
X		X						
X								
X						X		
		X	X			X	X	
X		X						
X		X	X	X	X			
X						X		
X								
X					X			
X					X			
X								
X		X			X			
X								
X								
X								
			X					
X			X	X				
X								
	X						X	
X					X			
X								
X								
X		X				X		
X								
X			X	X				

Table 1A.9
Public databases for the financial sector (all countries in sample)

	Government keeps a bad-check list?	Government opperates a collateral registry or registry of liens?	Government operates a public credit registry	Actively considering creation of a PCR	Most important reason for starting or wanting to start a PCR
Angola	Yes	No	X		Improve the quality of credit data available
Argentina	Yes	No	X		Bank Supervision
Aruba	No	Yes		X	Improve the quality of credit data available
Australia	No	No			
Austria	No	No	X		Bank Supervision
Bahrain	Yes	No	X		Improve the quality of credit data available
Barbados	No	No			
BCEAO	Yes	No	X		Borrowing by business groups/ conglomerates
Belarus			X		Control over repayment
Belgium	No	No	X		
Belize	No	No			
Bermuda	No	Yes			
Bolivia	Yes	No	X		Improve the quality of credit data available
Brazil	Yes	No	X		Provisioning for bad debts
Bulgaria	No	No	X		Bank Supervision
Burundi	No	No	X		Improve the quality of credit data available
Canada	No	No			
Cayman Islands	Yes	Yes			Improve the quality of credit data available
Chile	Yes	Yes	X		Improve the quality of credit data available
Colombia	No	No	X		Bank Supervision
Costa Rica	No	Yes	X		Bank Supervision
Croatia	No	No		X	Improve the quality of credit data available
Cyprus	Yes	No			Improve the quality of credit data available

Table 1A.9
(continued)

	Government keeps a bad-check list?	Government opperates a collateral registry or registry of liens?	Government operates a public credit registry	Actively considering creation of a PCR	Most important reason for starting or wanting to start a PCR
Czech Republic	No	No		X	Borrowing by business groups/ conglomerates
Denmark	No	No			
Dominican Republic	No	No	X		Bank Supervision
Eastern Caribbean	No	No			
Ecuador	Yes	Yes	X		Bank Supervision
El Salvador	No	No	X		Bank Supervision
Estonia	No	No		X	
Finland	No	No			
France	No	Yes	X		Bank Supervision
Germany	No	Yes	X		Bank Supervision
Greece	No	No			
Guatemala	No	No	X		Improve the quality of credit data available
Guyana	No	No			Provisioning for bad debts
Haïti	Yes	No	X		Bank Supervision
Hong Kong	No	Yes		X	Improve the quality of credit data available
Hungary	No	Yes			
India	No	No		X	Improve the quality of credit data available
Indonesia	Yes	Yes	X		Bank Supervision
Ireland	No	No			
Italia	Yes	No	X		To allow financial institutions to monitor the borrowers
Jordan	Yes	No	X		Bank Supervision
Latvia	No	No		X	
Lithuania	No	Yes	X		Bank Supervision
Luxembourg	Yes	No			
Madagascar	No	No	X		
Malaysia	Yes	No	X		Bank Supervision
Mexico	No	No	X		Improve the quality of credit data available

Table 1A.9
(continued)

	Government keeps a bad-check list?	Government opperates a collateral registry or registry of liens?	Government operates a public credit registry	Actively considering creation of a PCR	Most important reason for starting or wanting to start a PCR
Mozambique			X		
Netherlands	No	No			
Netherlands Antilles	No	No			Provisioning for bad debts
New Zealand	No	Yes			Improve the quality of credit data available
Nicaragua	No	Yes	X		Bank Supervision
Nigeria	No	No	X		Improve the quality of credit data available
Panama	No	No			Bank Supervision
Paraguay	No	No	X		Improve the quality of credit data available
Peru	Yes	No	X		Improve the quality of credit data available
Portugal	Yes	No	X		Improve the quality of credit data available
Puerto Rico	No	No			Bank Supervision
Romania	No	No	X		
Russia	No	No		X	Improve the quality of credit data available
Rwanda	Yes	No	X		Bank Supervision
Singapore	No	Yes		X	Bank Supervision
Slovak Republic	No	No	X		Bank Supervision
Spain	No	No	X		Improve the quality of credit data available
Sweden	No	No			
Tanzania	No	No		X	Improve the quality of credit data available
Trinidad and Tobago	No	No			Borrowing by business groups/conglomerates
Turkey	Yes	Yes	X		Improve the quality of credit data available
United Kingdom	No	Yes			Improve the quality of credit data available
Uruguay	Yes	No	X		Bank Supervision
Venezuela	No	No	X		Bank Supervision

Table 1A.10
Regulations on credit reporting (all countries in sample)

	No government regulation	Must register with government	Restrictions on entry into the market	Information collected from financial institutions restricted	Information collected from other sources restricted	Distribution of information restricted	Are there legal restrictions that discourage private credit bureaus from forming?
Angola				X		X	Yes
Argentina	X						No
Aruba	X						No
Australia				X	X	X	No
Austria				X	X		Yes
Bahrain		X		X		X	Yes
Barbados	X						No
BCEAO		X					No
Belarus		X					
Belgium							
Belize							
Bermuda							No
Bolivia							No
Brazil	X					X	Yes
Bulgaria	X						No
Burundi		X					No
Canada	X			X			No
Cayman Islands				X		X	Yes
Chile				X		X	Yes
Colombia	X			X			No
Costa Rica						X	Yes
Croatia						X	No
Cyprus	X			X	X		No
Czech Republic							Yes
Denmark							
Dominican Republic		X					No
Eastern Caribbean							No
Ecuador				X			No

Table 1A.10
(continued)

	Regulations affecting private credit information providers						
	No government regulation	Must register with government	Restrictions on entry into the market	Information collected from financial institutions restricted	Information collected from other sources restricted	Distribution of information restricted	Are there legal restrictions that discourage private credit bureaus from forming?
El Salvador					X	X	Yes
Estonia							Yes
Finland							
France		X				X	
Germany	X			X			No
Greece		X		X	X	X	Yes
Guatemala	X						No
Guyana	X			X			No
Haïti	X						No
Hong Kong				X	X	X	No
Hungary		X		X	X	X	Yes
India	X			X	X	X	No
Indonesia	X						No
Ireland							
Italia				X		X	No
Jordan							No
Latvia							
Lithuania	X						No
Luxembourg		X		X		X	No
Madagascar							No
Malaysia				X		X	Yes
Mexico							No
Mozambique							
Netherlands	X						No
Netherlands Antilles	X						No
New Zealand	X						Yes
Nicaragua				X	X		Yes
Nigeria	X						No
Panama		X		X	X	X	No
Paraguay				X		X	Yes
Peru	X						No

Table 1A.10
(continued)

	Regulations affecting private credit information providers						
	No government regulation	Must register with government	Restrictions on entry into the market	Information collected from financial institutions restricted	Information collected from other sources restricted	Distribution of information restricted	Are there legal restrictions that discourage private credit bureaus from forming?
Portugal				X	X	X	Yes
Puerto Rico						X	No
Romania				X			
Russia	X						Yes
Singapore				X			Yes
Slovak Republic		X		X			No
Rwanda	X	X					Yes
Spain		X					No
Sweden			X	X		X	Yes
Tanzania				X	X	X	Yes
Trinidad and Tobago	X			X			No
Turkey				X	X		Yes
United Kingdom							Yes
Uruguay							No
Venezuela	X						No

Acknowledgments

The author would like to thank the officials of the public and private credit registries and financial institutions who made this research possible by taking the time to fill out detailed questionnaires. Valuable research assistance with the survey process and chapter was provided by Nataliya Mylenko and Gwendolyn Alexander. The author would also like to recognize the contributions made by numerous individuals to the surveys and data analysis, including Augusto de la Torre, Marco Pagano, Tullio Jappelli, Alfredo Vicens,

Andrew Powell, Rafael del Villar, John Ford, Peggy Twohig, Armando Castelar, Jerry Caprio, and Leora Klapper. The usual disclaimers apply—any errors or omissions are the sole responsibility of the author, and the chapter represents the author's views, not the official views of the World Bank or any other organization.

Notes

1. Although the survey was extended in spring 2001, the bulk of the data is from 1999. In 1999, questionnaires were sent to eighty-one countries and fifty-nine responses were received. In 2001 the questionnaire was resent to those countries which had not responded in 1999 as well as to twelve additional countries; completed surveys were received from the Central Banks in eighteen more nations. The data discussed in this paper include both the 1999 and 2001 waves.

2. The following EU member countries have a public credit registry: Austria, Belgium, France, Germany, Italy, Portugal, and Spain.

3. The 138 firms sent the private registry survey were distributed among regions as follows: Africa (4), East Asia and the Pacific (19), Eastern Europe (21), Western Europe (37), Latin America and the Caribbean (31), North America (9), and Middle East/Northern Africa (17).

4. Section 5 in the private credit bureau survey was on consumer attention, legal and public policy issues; in the public registry survey, the same type of data was collected in section 7, "Accuracy of Database Information—Attention to Consumers" and in section 8, "Policy Issues." In addition, the public registry survey asked about the use of the data in supervision of financial institutions and the resources that had been devoted to the registry. The private registry survey finished with section 6, which asked the respondents' views of the credit information industry in their country.

5. Figures provided by the Consumer Data Industry Association, the U.S. credit reporting industry association based in Washington, D.C.

6. Jappelli and Pagano (2001) present the results of a separate survey on public credit registries completed in 1998. They report that of forty-six countries responding to their survey, nineteen had a public credit registry and most of the registries established over the last two decades have been concentrated in Latin America.

7. The Netherlands Antilles also reported that it does not operate a PCR.

8. Jappelli and Pagano (2001).

9. Only seven nations stated they received assistance from another country's Central Bank or bank superintendent about PCR policy, including Austria (from Germany), Colombia (from Spain), Costa Rica and the Dominican Republic (in both cases from both Chile and Bolivia), Ecuador (from Colombia), Hong Kong (from Germany and France), and Venezuela (from Chile and Colombia).

10. Surprisingly, seven countries report receiving only positive data, which is unusual given the natural interest supervisors would have in knowing about bad credit risks; these respondents may have misunderstood the question and also be receiving negative data. Only Germany reported receiving purely negative data. In Latin America,

Uruguay reported having only positive data, while all other countries in the region indicated they collected both positive and negative information on borrowers. Only Turkey and the Slovak Republic limit data collected to firms.

11. Chile reported that it charges a fee for borrowers who wish to access their own information, but no fee for consultations by financial institutions.

12. It may seem remarkable that only 80 percent of the private registries collect the name of the reporting institution. One explanation may be the presence of private reporting firms in the survey sample who do direct investigations of firms. Such firms rely on input from a variety of sources and would be less likely to identify specific reporting institutions.

13. Although nine firms answered yes to question 3.5, stating that they received data from only a limited group of credit providers, the follow-up answer to the question indicated that several had misinterpreted the question, so that only four of the nine responses appear to indicate a true case of restricted data.

14. Guatemala, Nicaragua, and Indonesia are the only nations reporting that they have no distribution of PCR data.

15. France reported that only public financial institutions were exempt from the reciprocity rule and could receive some data, even if they had not provided information to the PCR.

16. Argentina, Bolivia, Brazil, the Dominican Republic, and Indonesia indicated they had sanctioned more than twenty-five institutions over the past year.

References

Akerlof, George A. 1970. "The Market for 'Lemons'." *Quarterly Journal of Economics* 84 (3): 488–500.

Berger, Allen N., and Gregory F. Udell. 1995. "Relationship Lending and Lines of Credit in Small Firm Finance." *Journal of Business* 68 (July): 351–381.

Diamond, Douglas W. 1991. "Monitoring and Reputation: The Choice between Bank Loans and Directly Placed Debt." *Journal of Political Economy* 99 (4): 689–721.

Jaffee, Dwight M., and Thomas Russell. 1976. "Imperfect Information, Uncertainty and Credit Rationing." *Quarterly Journal of Economics* 90 (4): 651–666.

Jappelli, Tullio, and Marco Pagano. 2001. "Information Sharing, Lending and Defaults: Cross-Country Evidence." *Journal of Banking and Finance*.

Peek, Joe, and Eric S. Rosengren. 1995. "Banks and the Availability of Small Business Loans." Federal Reserve Bank of Boston, working paper no. 95-1, January.

Peterson, Mitchell A., and Raghuram G. Rajan. 1994. "The Benefits of Lending Relationships: Evidence from Small Business Data." *The Journal of Finance* 49 (1) (March): 3–37.

Stiglitz, Joseph E., and Andrew Weiss. 1981. "Credit Rationing in Markets with Imperfect Information." *American Economic Review* 71 (3) (June): 393–410.

2   Public Credit Information: A European Perspective

Tullio Jappelli and Marco Pagano

2.1 Introduction

The role of institutions in shaping the structure and performance of credit markets has received increasing attention in recent years. The banking literature has analyzed extensively how prudential capital ratios, the separation between banking and industry, and deposit insurance can affect the performance and stability of credit markets. Surprisingly, both theoretical and empirical research has completely neglected one public institution that can deeply affect the operations, incentives, and competitiveness of banks. In many countries central banks require financial institutions under their supervision to supply data about loans and borrowers to a public credit registry (PCR). Data drawn from this public database are then made available automatically or under specific request to each participating institution.

This mandatory exchange of credit information organized by central banks often coexists with private arrangements by which lenders voluntarily share information about their borrowers via information brokers known as credit bureaus or credit reference agencies. The lenders that provide their information to a credit bureau are granted exclusive access to the common database insofar as the data they provide are timely and accurate. Spontaneous arrangements of this type exist, to varying degrees, both in the household credit market and in the corporate lending market.

Due to the variety of its institutions, Europe provides an interesting setting to study the characteristics and effects of information sharing mechanisms. In some countries, information sharing relies almost exclusively on PCRs. In others, mandatory exchange of information coexists with the voluntary exchange carried out by credit bureaus. And in others still, PCRs are absent, but a massive amount of credit information is supplied to credit bureaus voluntarily.

This chapter presents a systematic account of public credit information in Europe. Section 2.2 provides a bird's-eye view of the design and operation of European PCRs, highlighting their common features and the main differences between them (see appendix 2.A for a detailed description of each national PCR). Section 2.3 illustrates the role that PCRs can perform in credit markets, drawing on recent theoretical research. Section 2.4 explores the likely reasons why PCRs are introduced by policymakers, using cross-country data. Section 2.5 concludes by distilling policy implications from the evidence in the previous sections.

2.2 Public Credit Registries in Europe

The Committee of Governors of the European Central Bank defines a PCR as "an information system designed to provide commercial banks, central banks, and other banking supervisory authorities with information about the indebtedness of firms and individuals vis-à-vis the whole banking system."[1] European PCRs are managed by the respective central banks. Access to the PCR is granted only to authorized central bank staff (mainly for surveillance reasons and under tight confidentiality rules) and to the reporting financial institutions.[2] It is the mandatory exchange of information that distinguishes PCRs from private credit bureaus. The credit bureau collects, files, and distributes data voluntarily supplied by lenders on the creditworthiness of the borrowers. Contributing data to the PCR, however, is compulsory for all financial institutions under the supervision of the central bank. The operation of a PCR is similar to that of a private credit bureau; both operate by establishing a two-way flow of data with credit grantors.

2.2.1 Information Provided by PCRs

Generally, the first flow of information is from participating institutions to the PCR; each of them must regularly supply data on individual loans granted. The PCR consolidates data on loans granted to the same borrower by each bank so as to obtain his or her total indebtedness. The return flow of information can take one of two forms. Each bank is automatically informed of the total indebtedness of the borrowers on which it reported loan data. The bank also can obtain the same type of information for new credit applicants but only upon request.[3]

Table 2.1 illustrates the two forms of the return flow of information. The credit report in the example contains data on the borrower's debt and guarantees (positive information) as well as statements on past defaults or arrears (negative information). The example is constructed on the basis of the rules of the Italian PCR, one of the largest and most complete public databases on business loans. Panel A in table 2.1 displays the report on a new applicant who has applied in writing for a loan and is not on file with the bank.

The report contains information on the number of lenders with which the applicant has credit relations and on the standing of the applicant's loans. It also reports aggregate debts (by broad categories of loans) and guarantees. In Italy the crucial distinction is between *credit granted* and *credit used*. Credit granted is the amount of credit that has been authorized and granted, net of past repayments (if any). Credit used automatically exceeds credit granted when there is an overdraft, for instance if the borrower has not paid one installment of a fixed maturity loan. In the example the company has outstanding fixed maturity loans for 550 million lire, but credit used is 600 million lire, implying that there is an overdraft of 50 million lire. The credit report highlights overdrafts for each category of loans. Furthermore, it includes only positive values of overdrafts, so that the total of all overdrafts does not correspond to the difference between total credit used (1,685 million lire) and total credit granted (1,710 million lire), which is actually negative in the example.

If a borrower is already indebted with the bank, the PCR automatically returns the borrower's aggregate position with the entire banking system. The information is similar to that contained in the report for a new applicant, as shown by panel B of table 2.1. Note, however, that the lower panel reports the position of the *group*, rather than of the *bank*. The two would be the same only if the bank was not part of a conglomerate. Conglomerates can therefore use the information contained in the report to check their aggregate exposure toward single borrowers. The company in the example has drawn 5,273 million out of a total credit granted of 7,439. It has overdrafts, however, for 152 million lire (110 in fixed maturity loans, 37 in callable loans and 5 in personal guarantees).

Table 2.1
Example of a credit report by a public credit registry

Panel A: Report a new credit applicant	
ID	
Name	Rossi Inc.
Period	07-1999
Number of lenders	6
New lenders in the period	1
Lenders not giving information in the period	0

	Lender			System		
	Granted	Used	Over-draft	Granted	Used	Over-draft
Self-liquidating debt	0	0	0	200	100	0
Fixed maturity loans	0	0	0	550	600	50
Callable loans	0	0	0	160	180	20
Personal guarantees	0	0	0	800	805	5
Protracted overdrafts	0	0	0	0	0	0
Nonperforming loans	0	0	0	0	0	0
Total				1710	1685	75
Borrowers' guarantees	0	0	0	300	300	0

Note: In the upper panel, the *period* refers to April 1999 (the Italian PCR collects information on a monthly basis). The *number of lenders* is the number of financial institutions reporting information (6 in the example). *New lenders in the period* is the number of lenders that have reported information in July 1999 (1 in the example). *Lenders not giving information in the period* is the number of lenders that do not report information in July 1999 (0 in the example), for instance because the company has repaid its debt or because the loan granted falls below the reporting threshold (150 million lire).

In the lower panel, *lender* refers to the bank requesting information on the company, while *system* refers to the aggregate position of the company towards all participating institutions. The report classifies loans as *self-liquidating debt, fixed maturity loans,* and *callable loans,* and it also gives information on *personal guarantees. Protracted overdrafts* are overdrafts for a period of over six months (for instance, the borrower has not paid on installment for over six months). *Nonperforming loans* are at the discretion of the bank and indicate loans that are considered to be nonrecoverable. These last two items are reported regardless of loan category.

The columns of the table distinguish between *credit granted* and *credit used. Overdraft* is the difference between the two if positive. A positive value indicates that the borrower has not met obligations (for instance, has not paid one installment of fixed maturity loans or has exceeded line of credit). In the example Rossi, Inc. has fixed maturity loans for 550 million lire, but has used 600 million lire, implying an overdraft of 50 million lire with at least one lender. The total overdraft is the sum of the corresponding column. It does not correspond to the difference between total credit used (1685) and total credit granted (1710). For self-liquidating debt, the borrower has used only 100 million lire out of the 200 granted.

Table 2.1
(continued)

Panel B: Return information on an existing borrower

ID	
Name	Bianchi Inc.
Period	07-1999
Number of lenders	8
New lenders in the period	0
Lenders not giving information in the period	0

	Group			System		
	Granted	Used	Over-draft	Granted	Used	Over-draft
Self-liquidating debt	0	0	0	3100	1324	0
Fixed maturity loans	777	887	110	777	887	110
Callable loans	0	0	0	2300	1795	37
Personal guarantees	0	0	0	1262	1267	5
Protracted overdrafts	0	0	0	0	0	0
Nonperforming loans	0	0	0	0	0	0
Total				7439	5273	152
Borrowers' guarantees	0	0	0	238	400	0

Note: This credit report provides an example of the flow of return information that the Italian PCR sends monthly to each lender for each of its clients. The information is similar to that in the report for a new applicant; however, there are two important differences. First, the lower panel reports the position of the *group*, rather than of the *bank*. The two would be the same only if the bank was not part of a group. Second, the first three columns of the lower panel are not blank (i.e., the group has extended fixed maturity loans for 777 million lire to Bianchi Inc.). The aggregate values in the *system* also include the group, so that the same amount of fixed maturity loans are reported in the last three columns of the lower panel. In the example Bianchi, Inc. has used credit for 5273 million lire out of a total granted of 7439 million lire. It has overdrafts, how-ever, for 152 million lire (110 million in fixed maturity loans, 37 in callable loans and 5 in personal guarantees).

The item *protracted overdraft* defines overdrafts for periods of over six months (for instance, an installment is more than six months overdue). The final stage of insolvency is *nonperforming loans*. In Italy, classifying a loan as nonperforming or nonrecoverable is at the discretion of the bank's managers. If the PCR reports an insolvency that exceeds the reporting threshold, all banks with which the borrower has relations will be able to realize this from the credit report. In this case, banks usually take immediate action, such as closure of lines of credit or debt restructuring.

It is instructive to contrast the information provided by PCRs with that provided by private credit bureaus. Table 2.2 gives an example of an individual credit file for a small company. The file is reproduced with explicit authorization from CRIF, the largest credit bureau in Italy. The credit bureau collects and reports detailed positive and negative information to the bureau's members. The credit report is organized into three different levels so that potential lenders can move from the overall picture to a more detailed account of the company's credit history.

The first-level credit report (panel A in table 2.2) provides aggregate information about the indebtedness of the company. In the example, the company applied for three installment loans, currently has two installment loans, and has paid off one installment loan. The summary report also displays other data, including the number of financial institutions that reported data on the subject (five in the example), the number of financial institutions reporting that the subject has arrears or has defaulted (none in the example), and the presence of other negative events (for instance if the borrower has been classified as nonperforming or has defaulted).

The second-level report (panel B) provides aggregate data on specific types of loans (installment loans in the example). The report contains both positive information, such as the amount of monthly installments, and negative data, such as installment in arrears. The third-level report provides detailed information on individual loans (panel C). For each individual loan, it shows the installments paid, installments due, and the presence of guarantees. The sequence of zeroes in the right part of the report shows the insolvency profile in the twelve months prior to the last update. The number one on the far right indicates that the firm has not paid an installment as of the last update. The sequence of zeroes before the one shows that in the eleven months before the last update there was no insol-

Table 2.2
Example of a credit report issued by a credit bureau

CRIF: Centrale Rischi Finanziaria

Data on a company or on an individual can be requested from CRIF by the members of the credit bureau when the following conditions are met:

1. The company or the individual has applied for credit, or when the company or the individual is currently engaged in a credit relation with the member institution.
2. The company or the individual has regularly authorized his or her file to be transferred to CRIF and approved future data treatment by CRIF.

It follows that a member of the CRIF credit bureau can access CRIF data only:

1. To control and forecast insolvency.
2. After complying with law 675/96 (the Italian privacy law).

CRIF credit reports are organized in three different levels of detail. They allow CRIF members to study the credit history of the individual or the company in successive steps. The first stage provides aggregate information about the debt situation of the subject on which the request for credit report has been filed. The second stage report provides aggregate data on specific types of loans (for instance, installment loans). The third stage report provides disaggregate information on individual loans.

Panel A: First-level information (general summary)

Tax ID	002138975601	VAT ID	002138975601
NAME	ROSSI SNC		
ADDRESS	VIA FASSI, 20		
ZIP CODE	41012		
CITY	CARPI		
PROVINCE	MODENA		
COUNTRY	ITALY		

---------------------------- Operation stage ------------------------------
----

	RC/IS	RF	RN	AC	EA/ES
INSTALLMENTS :	3			2	1
NONINSTALLMENTS :					
CARDS :					
Number of institutions reporting data	: 5				
Of which report nonperforming loans	:				
Of which report defaults	:				
Negative events on the subject	:				

Source: © CRIF. Reproduced with explicit CRIF authorization of May 6, 1999. Further reproduction is prohibited.

Note: The first part of this report gives basic information about the credit applicant: Tax ID, VAT ID, and the legal address. The second part of the report summarizes the credit history of the firm. In particular, one can read the number of loans in the credit bureau file. Each loan is classified by operation stage and type of loan.

The operation stage of the loan are classified as: application (RC), under review (IS), denied (RF), withdrawn (RN), active (AC), extinguished (ES), extinguished before terms (EA). The types of loans recorded by CRIF are classified in three sections:

Table 2.2
(continued)

1. *Installment loans* (for instance, personal loans, mortgage loans, and leasing).
2. *Noninstallment loans* (for instance, lines of credit, and factoring).
3. *Cards* (for instance, revolving credit, and credit cards).

In the example the company has applied for three installment loans, currently has two installment loans, and one installment loan has been paid off. The summary report also contains other information: number of financial institutions that have reported data on the subject (five in the example), number of financial institutions that report that the subject has arrears or has defaulted (none in the example), and the presence of other negative events (such as if the subject has been classified as nonperforming or defaulted). From the summary report the client can access the second information level for the section on which he or she is interested (installment, noninstallments, and cards).

Panel B: Second-level information (section on installment loans)

--------------------- «Summary section on installment loans» ---------------------

«Number of operations considered 2»

Monthly installments	R + C :	3.000	G :
Residual installments	R + C :	60.000	G :
Installments due and not paid	R + C :	1.000	G :

-------------------------- «List of operations» ----------------------------

S	Type of loan	Operation stage	Role	Loan granted
—	LS	AC	R	05/08/1998
—	LA	AC	R	01/06/1998
—	MG	ES	R	01/02/1986
—	List of not completed operations			

Source: © CRIF. Reproduced with explicit CRIF authorization of May 6, 1999. Further reproduction is prohibited.

Note: This example of second-level credit report shows summary information on installment loans. The first part under "summary section on installment loans" reports aggregate values relative to total installment loans granted. The values are:

• *Amount of monthly installments.* This shows the total monthly burden of the debtor for current installment loans, divided between installments in which the firm appears as applicant $(R + C)$ and installments for loans for which the firm is a guarantor (G). In the example the firm has total monthly obligations for installment loans, as direct applicant (R), of 3 million lire.

• *Amount of residual installments.* This shows the residual debt on current installment loans, shown separately for the case in which the firm is the direct applicant $(R + C)$ or the guarantor (G). In the example the firm has a residual debt of 60 million lire as direct applicant (R).

• *Amount of installment in arrears.* This shows the total amount of unpaid installments on all installment loans (either on current installment loans or on extinguished installment loans), shown separately for arrears in which the firm appears as applicant $(R + C)$, and those in which it is a guarantor (G). In the example the firm has total arrears, as direct applicant (R), of 1 million lire.

Table 2.2
(continued)

The second part of the report (under *"list of operations"*) reports the type of loans granted (current loans or extinguished loans) and some information on each of these loans. In the example there is information on three loans:

• Instrumental leasing (*loan type LS*); the loan is not extinguished (*operation stage AC*); the firm has applied for the loan (*role R*); the loan was granted on 05/08/1998.

• Car leasing (*loan type LA*); the loan is not extinguished (*operation stage AC*); the firm has applied for the loan (*role R*); the loan was granted on 01/06/1998.

• Aided loan (*loan type MG*), the loan is extinguished (*operation stage ES*); the firm had applied for the loan (*role R*); the loan was granted on 01/02/1986.

By clicking *S* next to each operation (*LS, LA, LG*), one can access information about each single loan. Clicking *S* next to "list of not concluded operations" one can further access information on current applications, withdrawal from credit by the firm and loan denials by members of the credit bureaus.

Panel C: Third-level information (details on single operations)

-------------------- N. 001   Current Operation out of 003 ---------------------

Role	R	Number of residual installments 11	
Operation stage	AC	Amount of residual installments 11.000	
Type of loan	LS	Last payment 05/02/1999	
Starting on	05/08/1998	N. of installment due and unpaid 1	
Ending on	05/02/2000	Amount due and unpaid 1.000	
Last update 08/04/1999	---		
Payment	AD	Max 1 For 100000000001	
Personal/real guarantees	/	State	
N. of inst. and period	18 M	Role and CRIF links	
1 installment due	1.000	G 300002635	
Monthly installment	1.000		

Source: © CRIF. Reproduced with explicit CRIF authorization of May 6, 1999. Further reproduction is prohibited.

Note: The report contains details on the first loan of the second-level report. In the example:

• *Role*: indicates if the firm has applied for credit or if the firm was a guarantor. In the example it has applied directly (*R*).

• *Operation stage*: indicates the stage of the operation. In the example the loan is active (*AC*).

• *Starting on and ending on*: indicate the day of start and end of the operation.

• *Last update*: indicates the day of the last update of the information contained in the report.

• *Payment*: indicates how the firm will pay the installments to the financial institutions. In this case payment is by order through the checking account (*AD*).

• *Personal/real guarantees*: indicates if the firm has provided real or personal guarantees for the loan. In this case there are none.

• *N° of installment and period*: indicates the total number of installments and when they are due. In the example there are 18 monthly (*M*) installments.

Table 2.2
(continued)

• *One installment due*: indicates the amount of the next due installment as of the last update. In the example the installment is 1 million lire.
• *Monthly installment*: indicates the value of the average monthly installment. In the example it is 1 million lire.
• *Number of residual installments*: indicates the number of installments as of the last update. In the example the number of residual installments is eleven.
• *Amount of residual installments*: indicates the total amount of the residual installments due. In the example it is 11 million lire.
• *Last payment*: indicates the day of the last payment. In the example it was 05/02/1999.
• *Number of installments due and unpaid*: indicates the total number of installments due and unpaid. In the example there is one installment due and unpaid.
• *Amount due and unpaid*: indicates the amount of the installment due and unpaid. In the example it is 1 million lire.
• *Max ... For*: the number next to "max" indicates the maximum number of insolvency that has been notified during the life of the contract. The number next to "for" indicates for how many months the firm was insolvent. In the example the maximum number of insolvency is one, and the number of months is one.
• The twelve numbers that follow max/for show the insolvency profile in the last twelve months. The number on the far right indicates that the firm has not paid one installment as of the last update. The sequence of 0 before the 1 shows that in the eleven months before the last update there was no insolvency.
• *State*: refers to the state of the loan process (under judicial dispute, nonperforming, defaulted). In the example this does not apply.
The last part of the report under *"role and CRIF links"* shows the ID of subjects that have participated in various ways to the loan operation (for instance, guarantors). The example shows that a guarantor (G) is present in the operation. The third-level reports for the other two loan types (non-installment, cards) shown in the second-level report contain similar information.

Panel D: Third-level information (details on operations not concluded)

---------- «Summary of installment section/Operations not concluded» -----------

Type	Stage	Role	Date	Inst.	Prd.	Amount.	Other	Role
MI	RC	R	29/04/1999	120	M	100.000	600003470	G
LI	RF	R	18/04/1999	120	M	150.000	600003470	G
MI	RF	R	01/04/1999	120	M	200.000	600003470	G

Source: © CRIF. Reproduced with explicit CRIF authorization of May 6, 1999. Further reproduction is prohibited.
Note: The third-level report shows details on operations not concluded (under approval, firm withdrawn, or credit denial). It is available separately for installment loans, noninstallment loans, and cards. For each operation the following information is given:
• *Type*: Type of loan.
• *Stage*: indicates the stage of the loan: under approval, withdrawn, denied. In the example the first operation is under approval (RC), and the other two have been denied (RF).

Table 2.2
(continued)

- *Role*: if the subject is involved as applicant or as guarantor. In the example in all three operations the firm has applied for credit directly (*R*).
- *Date*: refers to the date of the loan application. In the example the firm has made three applications in April of 1999.
- *Inst.*: the number of installment loans in the loan application. In the example it is 120 for each loan.
- *Prd*: indicates when the installments are due. In the example they are due each month (*M*).
- *Amount*: indicates the amount of the application. In the example the firm has applied for three loans of 100 million, 150 million, and 200 million.
- *Other*: indicates the presence of other subjects in the operation. In the example the same subject appears in all three operations (the CRIF ID is 600003470).
- *Role*: indicates in what capacity other subjects are involved in the operation. In the example the subject is a guarantor (*G*) in all three operations.

vency. The third-level report also shows detailed information on loan applications not concluded or under review by one or more credit bureau members (panel D). The example shows that in April 1999 the company ought credit from three different sources. Two loan applications were already turned down, and another one was under review. The credit report also contains cross-references to the individual files that the bureau has recorded in the names of the guarantors.

The lesson that can be drawn from comparing the public credit report of table 2.1 and the private credit report of table 2.2 is that they feature a different level of detail. The private credit bureau reports information on individual loans, while the PCR aggregates loans and reports the overall indebtedness of the borrower. On the other hand, the PCR draws on the universe of lenders that are required to report information to the PCR; the credit bureau instead draws on voluntary information and therefore seldom covers the entire banking sector.

2.2.2 Common Features

Table 2.3 sets forth the main characteristics of PCRs in Europe, based on a questionnaire submitted to the central banks and on public national sources. Seven European countries operate a PCR (Austria, Belgium, France, Germany, Italy, Spain, and Portugal). European PCRs share several common features, including compulsory participation, confidentiality, privacy protection, a reporting threshold for loan information, and a computer-intensive technology.

Table 2.3
Characteristics of public credit registries in Europe

Country	Participating institutions	Access by participating institutions	Sanctions and fees
Austria	Financial institutions, insurance, leasing and factoring companies and their foreign subsidiaries	Fixed intervals and upon request. Unrestricted access.	Civil and criminal sanctions. No fees.
Belgium	National credit institutions and their foreign subsidiaries	Fixed intervals and upon request. Access to data about own borrowers and new credit applicants.	Administrative and criminal sanctions. Fees exist.
France	National credit institutions and foreign branches; leasing and factoring companies	Fixed intervals and upon request. Access to data about own borrowers and new credit applicants.	Administrative, civil and criminal sanctions. Fees for statistical consultation via Minitel.
Germany	National credit institutions and their foreign subsidiaries; national insurance companies	Fixed intervals and upon request. Access to data about own borrowers and new credit applicants.	Administrative, civil and criminal sanctions. No fees.
Italy	National credit institutions and their foreign subsidiaries, national branches of foreign banks	Fixed intervals and upon request. Access to data about own borrowers and new credit applicants.	Administrative sanctions. Fees for data requests about new credit applicants.
Portugal	National credit institutions and national branches of foreign banks; leasing, factoring and credit card companies	Fixed intervals and upon request. Access to data about own borrowers and new credit applicants.	Administrative and criminal sanctions. No fees.
Spain	National credit institutions and national branches of foreign banks; leasing and factoring companies	Fixed intervals and upon request. Access to data about own borrowers and new credit applicants.	Administrative sanctions. No fees.

Participation is compulsory for all financial institutions under the supervision of the central bank. In Austria, France, Portugal, and Spain, as shown in table 2.3, participation extends to finance companies, in Portugal to credit card companies and in Germany to insurance companies. The rules governing a PCR are rigidly imposed by regulation, rather than contracted among participants as in credit bureaus. As shown in section 2.2, the compulsory and universal nature of participation is the key difference with private credit bureaus. In contrast, credit bureaus are less complete in their coverage of financial institutions but offer details on individual loans and merge credit data with data from other sources, such as courts, public leasing and property registers, tax authorities, and so forth.

The mandatory nature of PCRs explains why administrative sanctions are invariably threatened to any lender who fails to supply data or provides inaccurate information. The European experience reveals that most lenders supply their information regularly and accurately, and therefore sanctions are seldom inflicted.

PCRs invariably operate under the principles of confidentiality for participating institutions and privacy protection for individual borrowers. Participating institutions are assured that the data they provide will be disseminated only in aggregate form, only to other credit institutions, and only for the purpose of credit granting. Individual borrowers are entitled by privacy protection laws to inspect and correct their files in the PCR.

Table 2.4 reports detailed information on the seven PCRs that operate in Europe, plus Finland, where the PCR is contracted out to a private company. The oldest registers are in Germany (1934), Finland (1961), and Italy (1964). Though universal in their coverage of lending institutions, PCRs do not collect data on all loans. Data are reported only above a specified *threshold value*. Despite its large variation across European countries, in most countries this threshold is sufficiently high so as to cut off most data on household lending and in some countries even those on small business loans. A further reason why PCRs do not convey information about household indebtedness is that finance companies and credit card companies, which are major suppliers of household credit, are generally outside the supervision of the central bank and therefore exempted from reporting duties. In two countries where household credit is also covered (Belgium and France), this is done via a separate, specialized PCR, which reports only negative information.

Table 2.4
Public credit registries in Europe

Country	Starting date	Number of subjects covered	Credit reports issued	Minimum reporting threshold (US$)	Data reported by participating institutions	Return flow to participating institutions
Austria	1986	58,111 (1999)	11,901 (1999)	430,700	L, G	L, G
Belgium	1985	360,000 households (1997), 400,000 firms (1990)	3,550,000 for households (1997)	223 for households, 27,950 for firms	D, A for firms, D, A, L for households	D, A for firms, D, A, L for households
Finland	1961	213,000 (1991)	3,500,000 (1990)	0	D, A	D, A
France	1989 for households, 1984 for firms	370,000 (1990)	5,400,000 (1990)	118,293 (1990)	D, A for households, L, G, undrawn credit facilities for firms	D, A for households, L, G, undrawn credit facilities for firms
Germany	1934	1,200,000 (1998)	1,800,000 (1998)	1,699,800 (1998)	L, G	L, G
Italy	1964	2,200,000 (1994), 6,536,914 (1998)	1,400,000 (1994)	0 for non-performing and insolvent loans, 86,010 for other loans	D, A, L, G	D, A, L, G
Portugal	1977	2,400,000 (1998)	N/A	5 (1998)	D, A, G	D, A, G
Spain	1983	4,600,000 (1991)	758,000 (1997)	6,720 for residents, 336,000 for nonresidents	D, A, L, G, regional, sectoral and currency risk	D, A, L, G, regional, sectoral and currency risk

Note: Figures about public credit registries are based on a questionnaire sent to central banks. The data reported to the registry are defaulted loans (D), arrears (A), total loan exposure (L), and guarantees (G). The exchange rates used to convert the minimum reporting threshold into dollars are those of September 1, 1998.

Currently, European PCRs rely heavily on computer-intensive technology, sophisticated software, and direct electronic connections to manage the two-way flow of information from and to participating institutions. This explains why they require a modest amount of labor, between ten and sixty employees as of 1990 (10 in the Belgian PCR for households, 30 in the Belgian PCR for companies, about 60 in France, and about 10 in Spain).

An accessory, but nevertheless important, function of PCRs is their use for supervisory purposes by the central bank. Their data can always be accessed in full detail for banking surveillance. In European countries, the PCR is the statistical basis to provide supervisory authorities with an up-to-date overview of large borrowers' or banks' exposures. The data of the PCR can be crucial to detect borrowers' imminent insolvency, insofar as it allows the supervisory authorities to assess the overall exposure of banks to a particular borrower. It also allows monitoring individual banks' exposures toward particular borrowers.[4] In some countries that do not feature a PCR, data on bank loans are nevertheless collected for the exclusive use of supervising authorities.[5] The surveillance role of PCRs also explains why in some countries the information to be reported is not limited to credit data. For instance, German banks must report the equity stakes they own in their borrowers' capital when these exceed 25 percent.

2.2.3   Main Differences

Table 2.4 shows that the types of data that lenders must report to the PCR vary considerably across countries. For instance, in Italy lenders are required to report data on defaults, arrears, loan exposure, and guarantees. In Germany, only loan exposure and guarantees are reported. In Belgium, only defaults and arrears are reported.

The main differences among European PCRs concern the reporting threshold, the type of information collected, and the design of the memory system. Even though PCRs invariably specify a reporting threshold, this varies considerably across countries. At one extreme, in Germany and Austria the threshold is so high that these PCRs focus only on large borrowers. This interest in the behavior of large borrowers is confirmed by the fact that the German PCR consolidates loans by company groups not only individual borrowers. This is also an increasing concern in other countries, such as Italy, whose industrial sector is dominated by groups, controlled by a financial holding, even in the sector of small- and medium-size firms. At the other extreme, in Portugal the low reporting threshold implies that the Portuguese PCR also effectively covers loans to many households. This also happens in Belgium and France due to the existence of PCRs specialized in consumer debt.

Clearly, the higher the threshold set by regulators, the fewer the borrowers covered and the credit reports issued, as shown in table 2.4. The threshold also demarcates the market segment where private credit bureaus operate without competition from the PCR; for loans above the threshold, credit bureaus must take into account that lenders can also turn to the public register's reports.

Another important difference is the type of information collected. In several countries PCRs collect both positive and negative information about firms, except Germany and Austria, where only positive information (loan data) is reported, and Portugal, where only negative information is collected (on defaults and arrears). The household credit registries in Belgium and France collect only negative information.

The detailed description of the individual country experiences also brings out distinctive national features in the design of the memory of the system. As explained in appendix 2.A, in Belgium the memory of the household PCR is proportional to borrower misconduct; defaults are kept in the database longer than arrears, witnessing the disciplinary role of the PCR. In all cases the PCR eventually "forgets," offering defaulting debtors a second chance, which may be justified not only on equity grounds but also for economic efficiency. A PCR with infinite memory would eliminate all incentives that defaulted debtors may still have to undertake new projects or even take regular employment, and ex ante would make people extremely wary of taking on any debt for fear of defaulting.

In Italy the design of the memory of the PCR is equally interesting, but for a totally different reason. The system provides each lender with a complete picture of its existing borrowers (irrespective of the dates of their loans), but only one-year information on new credit applicants. This reflects a concern that PCRs may foster excessive competition among lenders by giving access to information about their respective borrowers. The system's memory allows lenders to monitor their own borrowers, but at the same time it discourages them from using the PCR's data as tools to penetrate other banks' market areas.

2.2.4   Toward a European Public Credit Registry?

The growing integration of national credit markets within the EU poses several problems to European PCRs. As of 1999, PCRs are strongly if not exclusively oriented to their respective domestic markets. For instance, Italian banks are required to report to the Italian PCR loans made by their foreign branches. But these loans are not reported to the host-country PCRs. Similarly, Italian companies can borrow abroad without being reported to the Italian PCR. The integration of capital markets thus implies that PCRs are losing the capacity to provide full, accurate, and reliable information on the overall indebtedness of a company.

The efforts made by the EU commission in the past to set up an international credit reporting system have not met with success due to the differences among the national systems already in place and to the unwillingness to set up a national credit reporting system in countries that do not have one. Apart from the problems due to the differences in the information technology they rely upon, the existing registers often feature a totally different design. Some aspects, such as their coverage, reporting thresholds, type of information reported, and privacy protection clauses, are so different as to pose formidable problems to their integration. These substantive problems are compounded by the inertia that is so often typical of bureaucratic organizations, which have a soft budget constraint and lack the competitive pressure under which private organizations operate.

As a first step toward closer cooperation, existing PCRs have managed to agree on a cross-border exchange of information on borrowers' indebtedness in specific cases. To date, however, such information can be used only for prudential purposes. To enable commercial banks to obtain information on their customers' borrowing abroad, PCRs currently plan to extend existing cooperation and in the future provide commercial banks with access to the information stored at other PCRs.

As EU countries have not yet met the legal requirements for this exchange of information, nor solved the relevant technical and organizational problems, it is impossible to say if and when this cooperation will become effective. In the long run, national PCRs may gradually be displaced by the growth of private, transnational private credit bureaus, or by cross-border agreements among national credit bureaus. Since the seven EU countries that have PCRs have so far found it difficult to agree on a common set of rules, this outcome appears likely.[6]

The difficulties so far experienced in linking European PCRs may partly depend on the fact that these national registers are quite old and feature deeply ingrained differences. By the same token, countries that are establishing a PCR for the first time have the opportunity of designing them to ensure compatibility with the systems of their main commercial partners. In this regard, latecomers may be better positioned than their predecessors.

2.3 Role of Public Credit Registries

This section addresses two main issues. First, what are the likely effects of a PCR on interest rates, defaults rates, and lending? Second, is it socially desirable to establish a PCR if it does not emerge spontaneously? The answers to these questions depend on the model of the credit market and of competition among lenders. Jappelli and Pagano (2000) elucidate the various roles that information sharing can have in credit markets, and they point out that exchanging information about borrowers can have four effects.

First, credit bureaus improve banks' knowledge of applicants' characteristics and permit more accurate prediction of repayment probability. This allows lenders to target and price their loans better, easing adverse selection problems.

Second, credit bureaus reduce the "informational rents" that banks could otherwise extract from their customers. When a bank has superior knowledge about a borrower, it can charge interest rates just slightly below those offered by an uninformed competitor and earn a rent from its information. Pooling information with other banks reduces this advantage and the implied rent by forcing each lender to price loans more competitively. Lower interest rates increase borrowers' net return and augment their incentive to perform.

Third, credit bureaus work as a borrower discipline device. Borrowers know that if they default their reputations with all other potential lenders are spoiled, cutting them off from credit or making it more expensive. Like the previous point, this mechanism heightens borrowers' incentive to repay, thus reducing moral hazard.

Finally, a borrower has the incentive to become over-indebted if he or she can draw credit simultaneously from many banks without any of them realizing it. Anticipating this temptation, banks are less willing to lend to credit applicants in the first place. Credit bureaus and PCRs disclose the borrower's overall indebtedness, thereby eliminating this incentive the implied inefficiency in the provision of credit.

One might be tempted to conclude that information sharing always attenuates asymmetric information in credit markets and improves social welfare. Therefore one may wonder why it is not spontaneously produced by market forces in all countries. Both the desirability of information sharing arrangements and the need of public intervention in this area deserve closer scrutiny. There are models in which information sharing is socially beneficial. In the model by Padilla and Pagano (1997), for instance, the regime with information sharing about borrowers' characteristics turns out to be Pareto superior. Lenders gain because they are able to lend more and therefore earn larger profits; borrowers gain because they get access to valuable credit opportunities that would be precluded otherwise.

But this need not always be the case. Padilla and Pagano (2000), for instance, show that information sharing may increase or reduce efficiency, depending on the level of effort to ensure repayment that is elicited by the disciplinary effect. There are situations in which sharing information about defaults may elicit an equilibrium level of effort that exceeds the socially efficient level and others in which it still falls short of it.[7] In some instances, however, the first-best level of effort can be obtained as an equilibrium outcome by a careful design of the information sharing mechanism. This happens when sharing only default information would induce an excessive level of effort, relative to the social optimum. Then, sharing also a certain amount of data about borrowers' characteristics can temper the disciplinary effect of default disclosure. One can thereby fine-tune the system to achieve the efficient outcome. Thus the social efficiency of information exchanged among lenders also depends on the type of information shared and, more generally, on the design of the sharing mechanism.

Another reason why a compulsory information sharing mechanism such as a PCR may be damaging is that it may discourage banks from searching for information on their own and thereby reduce their screening and monitoring activities. On one hand, each bank may find it cheaper to free ride on the information collected by others. On the other, it may not want to spend costly resources searching for information that others may then easily exploit. Compulsory information sharing may therefore kill relationship lending, which by its very nature rests on a high level of screening and monitoring activity by the lender.

However intuitively appealing, this argument should be made with great care. First, it does not apply to spontaneous information sharing such as that occurring via credit bureaus. In that case, banks can refrain from becoming part of the agreement and keep their data for themselves; alternatively, they can choose to share certain data and not others. Second, the free-riding problem could be solved or attenuated by appropriate pricing of the information contributed by banks to the bureau. Banks that are net suppliers of information to the system should be compensated for it, and banks that are net buyers of data should pay for such compensation. If the access fees of the information system can be designed to implement such transfer payments, a PCR may not discourage banks from producing information because they would expect to be compensated for such production. If such a system is not (or cannot be) engineered, however, it should be acknowledged that forced communication among lenders could reduce their information production. This can be socially damaging insofar as it leads to a worse allocation of credit.

Thus information sharing among lenders is not always efficient. It would be a comforting thought, however, if one could conclude that whenever it is, market forces will spontaneously produce an information sharing arrangement designed to maximize efficiency. Unfortunately, one cannot be sure of this either.

In some cases, information sharing might be efficient, but generate winners and losers (i.e., fail the Pareto criterion), and still not be introduced because the relevant initiative can only be taken by the would-be losers. In the adverse selection model by Pagano and Jappelli (1993), for instance, if banks have no other source of monopoly power except superior information about their local clients, they will never want to share information because this would eliminate their profits and transform the market into a perfectly competitive one. This would be socially efficient, and in principle consumers could compensate banks for the profits they lose. It is hard to imagine, however, a private scheme through which this could happen. Alternatively, one could ask why potential borrowers themselves do not set up an arrangement to certify and publicly disclose their credit-relevant information. The answer is that most likely they cannot easily coordinate such a scheme, because they are too dispersed and individually have too feeble an interest to set it up. Therefore, when information sharing depends on private initiative, it may not be implemented despite its social efficiency. It would elicit too much competition for banks.

One can imagine, however, a policy intervention capable of introducing an information sharing mechanism and compensating the banks with adequate transfers. Transfers are not even necessary because those who gain from the more competitive credit market are the same as those who lose as shareholders due to the banks' lower profits. Therefore, the introduction of a PCR could be justified on the same grounds as any antitrust policy. It could be seen as an act designed to stimulate competition and attain the associated efficiency gains.

Another reason why the creation of a PCR may be justified is to enhance the stability of the banking system. Bank managers may take an inefficiently high level of risk, for instance, because of the moral hazard caused by public deposit insurance or by the implicit bailout promise of the government. The existence of a public register may help indirectly by making real-time data on the lending policies of banks available to the central bank for supervision and prudential intervention. In practice, this may have been a decisive reason for the establishment of a PCR in many countries. It is particularly relevant in France, the only European country in which the PCR database is merged with other data (balance sheets, judicial records, etc.) and is used to produce managers' and firms' ratings (turnover, credit, and payment ratings). These ratings are crucial parameters for the conduct of the central bank's policy, because on their basis private claims are eligible for banks' refinancing operations with the central bank.

A PCR could also help directly by reducing banks' mistakes in the evaluation of credit risks and thereby making banks less likely to enter distress. The latter effect, however, may be balanced by the banks' greater tendency to take risks under the pressure of the more aggressive competition brought about by information sharing.

Finally, a PCR register may even help conglomerate banks get a clearer picture of their own overall consolidated liability position. Surprisingly, some Italian conglomerate banks have no internal method to assess routinely their consolidated liabilities; they rely instead on the Italian PCR for this task. The complexity of some bank holding groups makes this less surprising than may appear at first.

2.4 Where Are Public Credit Registries More Likely to Appear?

This section investigates whether or not PCRs are created to remedy the lack of private credit bureaus or the poor protection of creditor rights. If PCRs are created to remedy the lack of private initiative, the preexistence of a credit bureau should be negatively related to the presence of a PCR. In testing for this relationship, one should control for the severity of moral hazard in the credit market. In the presence of moral hazard, information sharing mechanisms can increase borrowers' incentives to repay and lead to a welfare gain.[8] Therefore, if credit bureaus fail to arise spontaneously (say, because of coordination problems), the case for the creation of a PCR by a regulator is particularly strong in countries where debtors' opportunistic behavior plagues credit relations and where institutions afford a weaker protection to creditor rights. These factors can be controlled for via the rule-of-law index and the creditor rights variable reported by La Porta at al. (1997).

To gain sample size, the information on non-European countries reported in Jappelli and Pagano (2001) was also exploited.[9] The first three columns of table 2.5 display descriptive statistics on forty-three countries, of which seventeen operate a PCR. A private credit bureau existed in only 30 percent of the countries where there is a PCR, against 65 percent where there is none. Interestingly, PCRs tend to be established in countries where creditor rights are less protected (1.59 versus 2.50) and there is less respect for the law (the rule-of-law variable is 6.67 against 7.34). They are also more likely to be found in countries whose legal system derives from the French civil code tradition (the French-origin dummy is 0.71 against 0.19).

To test the statistical significance of these relations, probit regressions were estimated where the presence of a PCR is the dependent variable. The results, displayed in columns 4 and 5 of table 2.5 show that the probability of the presence of a PCR is significantly and negatively related to the preexistence of a credit bureau. The coefficient indicates that preexistence of a private credit bureau raises the probability of establishing a PCR by 40 percent. If the legal origin

Table 2.5
Determinants of the presence of public credit registries

Variable	Averages			Probit regressions	
	Total sample (1)	PCR present (2)	PCR absent (3)	(4)	(5)
Creditor rights	2.14	1.59	2.50	−0.16 (−2.37)	−0.07 (−0.81)
Rule of law	7.08	6.67	7.34	−0.01 (−0.11)	−0.01 (−0.09)
Preexistence of a private credit bureau	0.51	0.29	0.65	−0.39 (−2.24)	−0.41 (−2.04)
English origin	0.38	0.12	0.54		
French origin	0.39	0.71	0.19		0.49 (3.35)
German origin	0.14	0.11	0.15		0.57 (1.77)
Scandinavian origin	0.09	0.06	0.12		0.48 (1.16)
Number of observations	43	17	26	43	43

Note: Countries are divided according to the presence of public credit registries. Presence of a PCR is 1 if the registry is operating in 1998, 0 otherwise. Preexistence of a private credit bureau is 1 if at least one private credit bureau was in operation before the establishment of the PCR, 0 otherwise. Other data are taken from La Porta et al. (1997). In the probit regressions, the dependent variable is the presence of a PCR prior to 1998. The probit coefficients indicate the effect of the variable on the probability of establishment of a PCR. T-statistics are reported in parentheses. Countries included in the probit estimation are reported in note 9.

dummies are not introduced in the probit regression, the creditor-rights variable also appears with a negative and significant coefficient. When the origin dummies are added as explanatory variables, the coefficient of creditor rights is still negative but not precisely estimated, whereas the French-origin dummy takes a large, positive and statistically significant coefficient. The reason is that creditor rights has a strong negative correlation with French origin; that is, the countries whose legal system is rooted in the French civil code are also those that afford the weakest legal protection to creditors. Finally, the coefficient of the rule-of-law variable is close to zero.

Overall, the historical experience is consistent with the hypothesis that the establishment of PCRs has been largely motivated by their "substitution" role. First, they have often been created to make up for the lack of private credit bureaus. Where the market alone has not produced information sharing, governments have taken the initiative. Second, PCRs tend to compensate, at least partly, for the weak protection that the state offers to creditors' interests and thus contain the implied moral hazard in lending.

2.5   Conclusions and Policy Issues

In many European countries lenders share data about their customers' creditworthiness or can access databases that help them assess credit applicants. The type, quality, and quantity of data available, however, vary greatly, and so do the information-sharing mechanisms. Often lenders agree to exchange information spontaneously, via information brokers known as credit bureaus. In other cases they are obliged to do so by the authorities via public credit registries.

A systematic description of public information-sharing arrangements in Europe has been provided, documenting their common features and main differences and explaining their economic rationale. The increasing financial and output market integration of the region is gradually reducing the usefulness of national PCRs. A solution would be to consolidate the existing national registries into a pan-European one or else link their databases. This may entail considerable transition costs, which are likely to be compounded by political attrition. The European experience suggests that countries currently setting up a credit information system are well advised to make its design compatible for future integration with the registries of their main commercial and financial partners.

The important policy issue of the desirability of a PCR has also been discussed. Information sharing among lenders is not always efficient. There are instances, however, in which information sharing is not provided spontaneously, and nevertheless it can increase social welfare. Here is a case for the creation of PCRs. Its benefits are greatest where moral hazard in the credit market is more severe. The incentives to repay created by the existence of a PCR can partially substitute for the lack of incentives arising from weak legal protection and enforcement of creditors' rights. Indeed, the historical experience suggests that PCRs have generally been created where private initiative failed to set up credit bureaus and where creditor rights are less protected.

Appendix 2.A   Description of Public Credit Registries in Europe

The institutional characteristics of European PCRs are described here—in particular, the type of information collected, the minimum reporting threshold, and the number of credit reports issued.

Austria

The Austrian PCR, established in 1986 and operated by the central bank, in early 1998 covered more than 55,000 borrowers from about 1,600 lenders. All credit institutions, finance companies, and insurance companies in Austria are required to report to the central bank loans in excess of Austrian shillings 5 million. Defaults are not reported, so the PCR only contains positive information.

As in the other European PCRs, the Austrian PCR aggregates these data and returns them to the participating credit institutions, but in contrast to other PCRs each credit institution is not restricted to receiving data about its own borrowers or credit applicants. They have access to the entire database. In 1997 the number of reports to credit institutions was over 10,000.

Belgium

Belgium has two PCRs, one for firms and one for individuals. The PCR for firms contains positive and negative information, while that for individuals contains only negative information.

The Central Office for Credits to Enterprises has been in operation since 1967.[10] The management of credit-recording activity is given to the National Bank of Belgium. The reporting obligation is imposed on all credit institutions established in Belgium, and it can be extended by royal decree to other financial institutions and to certain categories of insurance companies. In the case of credit granted to nonresidents, there is a simplified reporting procedure whereby only credit granted must be reported.

The Central Office for Credits to Enterprises records for each debtor data about credit above 1 million Belgian francs (BF), listing both the amounts granted and the amount drawn. The credit is described according to the type of credit (granted or drawn), the form of credit, and the currency in which the credit was granted or drawn. The reporting threshold is 100 million BF for credit granted to a nonresident by a branch of a participating credit institution located abroad. There is no requirement to report transactions to the Belgian state, to international institutions, and consumer credit and mortgage loans granted to individuals (the latter being recorded in the Central Office for Credits to Private Individuals).

After sending the information, participants are informed by an acknowledgment of receipt. Participating credit institutions may consult the data collected in two ways: (1) by subscribing to the automatic return, a system periodically supplying credit institutions with a full credit position report about all the debtors of the institutions supplying data to the central office; (2) by inquiring about the credit position of one or more debtors.

The Central Office for Credit to Private Individuals was established in 1985. It records defaults about installment contracts (sale, loan, and personal installment loans). Since 1991 it also records consumer credit and leasing, and since 1992 it records mortgages. The register has four features: it reports only negative information, it has limited "memory," it requires preliminary consultation by consumer credit grantors, and it allows consumers to inspect and correct erroneous data.

Negative information must be reported on amount, number and due date of installments, amount of arrears, date of cancellation and due amount, date and amount of repayments. Arrears are defined as either three unpaid amounts, or payments that for three months have not been effected completely. Lenders must also report all reimbursements to the register. Before granting consumer credit, it is compulsory to consult the register, while for mortgages it is optional. When a request is filed, the report by the central office will contain all the information about the person's identity and the loan contracts registered in that name (without mentioning the lenders' identities).

The PCR "memory" is designed in an interesting fashion: borrowers who redeem their debt disappear more quickly from the register than borrowers for whom a repayment commitment continues to exist. In case of repayment of arrears, the information is automatically removed after one year; in case of repayment of defaults it is removed only after two years. Irrespective of the type and status of the obligation, the database does not keep any registration for more than ten years. So "punishment" is stricter for more serious misconduct (defaults are pushed more than arrears), but eventually there is forgiveness for everyone.

France

Like Belgium, France has two distinct PCRs, one for firms—with both positive and negative information—and another for individuals with negative information only.

Reporting to the French PCR for firms (Central des Risques, part of the Direction des Entreprises of the Banque de France) has been compulsory since 1984 for all financial institutions operating in French territory, including leasing and factoring companies. Data on corporate groups are not reported. In contrast with other European PCRs, the French PCR for firms integrates the information received from credit institutions with other information about firms and their managers, drawn from legal announcement bulletins, courts, and the financial press.

Participating institutions must report monthly credit drawn above French francs (FF) 680,000. The threshold applies to credit extended by a single branch rather than by the bank as a whole. The choice to apply the threshold to the branch rather than to the bank as a whole is warranted by the tendency of French firms to seek credit from only one branch of the same bank. Reported loans are classified according to maturity and guarantees.

The Banque de France also keeps a PCR for individuals, which is a national file of personal loan delinquencies. All credit and financial institutions must report monthly delinquencies on installment purchase credit, leasing, personal loans, credit lines, and overdrafts. Delinquencies are defined as follows. For installment loans, delinquency occurs if the amount overdue exceeds the last installment due by three times. For credit without a regular repayment schedule, delinquency occurs if the debt is overdue for more than ninety days. For all other credit, delinquency occurs when the lender starts a legal action. The item is deleted from the file when repayment is made.

The central bank also keeps a database on firms, managers, judicial incidents, and court ordered bans. This database, known as FIBEN, records and elaborates information on the credit worthiness of the securities held by credit institutions. Currently FIBEN files almost 2.5 million firms and 1.5 million managers.

FIBEN does not limit itself to the collection of data on companies and managers; it also provides ratings for managers and three types of rating for firms (a turnover rating, a credit rating, and a payment rating). The turnover rating is simply an index of the level of turnover, net of taxes. The payment rating (in three categories) signals if payments are made on time or if there are cash flow difficulties. The most important rating is the credit rating, which is based on the analysis of the financial position of the firm, the assessment of managers, holders of capital, and the existence of payment incidents or legal proceedings. The rating goes from 3 (an excellent rating for firms whose ability to repay is guaranteed beyond any possible doubt) to 6 (for firms whose financial situation gives cause for serious concern, for instance, because of negative profitability or cash flow for the previous three years, inability to meet debts, existence of court proceedings, etc.).

The ratings can be used only by the central bank and by credit institutions for their business, and they cannot be published or communicated to third parties. They serve two main purposes. First of all, they are crucial parameters for the conduct of monetary policy, because on the basis of the ratings private claims are eligible for banks' refinancing operations with the central bank. Second, banks can use the ratings to screen and monitor credit applicants and existing borrowers.

Germany
The German PCR was established in 1934. According to section 14 of the Banking Act, all credit institutions in Germany, their branches and subsidiaries abroad, insurance companies, risk capital investment companies, own account dealers and factoring enterprises (after 1988), domestic and foreign credit institutions subordinated to a domestic parent credit institution (after 1995) are required to report data quarterly to the Deutsche Bundesbank. Data must be provided only for borrowers whose indebtedness exceeded Deutsche mark (DM) 3 million (DM 1 million from 1948 to 1993) during the three calendar years before the reporting date. Other financial institutions are required to report only if they are controlled by an institution that is required to report. The report must only indicate the indebtedness (including short-term interbank lending and exposure to public credit institutions) at the end of the quarter. No information on collateral and nonperforming loans must be provided. Banks must also report any holdings of more than 25 percent of their borrowers' equity.

Currently the PCR records 1,200,000 borrowers of which 304,000 are active. In 1997 it issued 1,800,000 notifications to credit institutions. On the basis of the reports submitted on loans above DM 3 million, the PCR computes the total indebtedness of each borrower. Two or more persons or corporations are consolidated to form a single borrower unit if one can exercise a dominant influence on the other(s). This is the case for companies that belong to the same group or of majority owned enterprises. If a borrower has raised loans for DM 3 million or more from several lenders, the PCR is required to notify the lenders with exposure to this borrower. To maintain bank secrecy, the notifications to lenders contain only data on the total indebtedness of the borrower and the number of lenders involved, and not the names of other institutions that have extended credit to the same borrower. The notification is broken down by type of indebtedness (on-balance-sheet and off-balance-sheet transactions, derivatives, guarantees for derivatives, leasing/factoring claims, mortgage loans, publicly guaranteed loans, interbank lending).

Lenders who have reported loans of 3 DM million or more to foreign borrowers receive an additional list showing the number of lenders that have reported exposure to debtors in the country concerned and the total amount of exposure. The aggregation of the indebtedness of all reportable borrowers of a particular country yields the total indebtedness of that country to German lenders and their foreign subsidiaries, making assessment of country risk more transparent.

Since January 1998, participating institutions also have the option of obtaining information on the level of debt of a potential borrower prior to granting the loan via an advance inquiry at the PCR if the envisaged loan amounts to 3 DM million or more and if the customer agrees to the inquiry.

Italy

The Italian PCR (Centrale dei Rischi) was established in 1962 and became operative in 1964.[11] In several respects the Italian PCR is the most complete and accurate service of this kind in Europe. Currently the PCR has almost 7 million records and issues more than 12 million reports per year. Participation is compulsory for commercial banks and other financial institutions under the supervision of the Bank of Italy and for branches of foreign banks operating in Italy.

Currently all loans in the following categories must be reported if: (1) credit granted or effectively used by the borrower in each month exceeds Italian lire (LIT) 150 million; (2) the value of guarantees exceeds LIT 150 million; (3) the loan is nonperforming, regardless of the amount. Information must also be provided on maturities and guarantees.[12] Participating institutions are required to submit information monthly.

The PCR provides two types of return information flows. First, each month the PCR provides each credit institution with information on each reported customer's aggregate position versus the whole banking system, distinguishing performing and nonperforming loans. This information is complete in the sense that all the outstanding loans are reported, regardless of when they were granted. The PCR also reports on a regular basis the indebtedness of persons acting as guarantors of the borrower as well as aggregate statistics about loans by category, geographical location, and sector of activity of the debtors. This flow of information, which is supplied at no cost, allows a bank to monitor clients' indebtedness over time and also to evaluate its own position relative to other banks and to the economy.

The second type of return information consists of data on potential borrowers. For a fee, each bank can request information on a credit applicant who it never extended credit to in the past. Considering the confidentiality of the database, banks can only ask information for an admissible purpose, that is, the granting of credit and evaluation of credit risk. In such cases the information that is released only concerns loans granted in the previous twelve months (i.e., in the data that are made available to banks there are 12 monthly files and each month the oldest file is deleted). Thus, the information that banks can obtain for new borrowers is far less complete than that available for their existing clients. Each inquiry on the part of single banks is recorded in the PCR files.

Banks and other financial intermediaries must provide accurate data. They are required to check the return information flow from the PCR and are required to notify mistakes or inaccuracies. In case of a mistake in reporting data, banks are required to send back information for the previous twelve months; all banks are notified of these corrections. The Bank of Italy does not correct the data but samples regularly its archive to detect anomalous reports; the anomalies are then reported to the banks for further checking.

The PCR also serves an important prudential role in the supervision of banking activity, in the conduct of monetary policy, and in the monitoring of the allocation of credit. To this end, the Bank of

Italy can access all data stored in the PCR beyond the twelve-month limit set to banks.

Portugal

The Portuguese PCR was established in 1977 and is operated by the central bank.[13] In early 1999 it covered 2.4 million borrowers. All credit institutions, finance and leasing companies, and credit card companies in Portugal are required to report monthly to the central bank defaulted loans and arrears in excess of Portuguese escudos 1,000. Information on guarantees on these loans also must be reported. Interbank loans are not reported. Thus, the Portuguese PCR contains mainly negative information.

The PCR aggregates data on defaults and arrears at a monthly frequency and returns to each bank the aggregate position of their respective customers. Banks can also request data on new credit applicants, but in this case the information is limited to the most recent aggregate data on that particular applicant and prior authorization of the borrower is required. No information is made available about the location where loans were extended or on originating lenders. Data cannot be transmitted to third parties. Misreporting is a criminal offence, while other misconduct is sanctioned with exclusion of further access of the PCR.

Spain

The Spanish PCR, established in 1963, is similar to the Italian one and is managed by the Bank of Spain.[14] Under current regulation, all credit institutions, deposit insurance funds, savings banks, cooperative banks, specialized credit institutions, and mutual guarantee companies must report direct and indirect credit exposures to the Bank of Spain (interbank lending is excluded). The direct exposures include risks arising from loans granted by the reporting institution or credit extended to it, from financial leasing and fixed-income securities held by the institution, excluding securities issued by the central government. Indirect exposures include risks incurred by the institution as guarantor of directly granted credit as well as guarantees received as security for guarantee given. At the end of 1998, 425 institutions were required to supply data to the PCR, and 758,000 specific reports were required by the institutions.

Each month, institutions must report information on borrowers about credit drawn, maturity, guarantees, arrears, defaults, identification, sector, economic activity, province, judicial insolvency situations, suspension of payments, bankruptcy, moratorium, or insolvency. For resident borrowers, information must be reported when the loan is above pesetas (PTA) 1 million for activities in Spain (PTA 10 million for activities in other countries). If the borrower is a local authority, a foundation, a semipublic enterprise or company owned or connected to a local authority, all credit must be reported. For nonresident borrowers, information must be reported when the loan is above PTA 50 million or greater for activities in Spain. Risk arising from shares or participation must also be reported when the book value is equal or greater that PTA 1 million.

The PCR supplies three types of information to the reporting institutions. First, each reporting institution receives the aggregated information on its own borrowers with all the data available, except for the origin of the operation. The information is broken down into written-off debts, bad debts, and other debts. Second, all reporting institutions receive monthly aggregate statistics by sector, class of loans, province, and so forth on borrowers of the whole system. Third, upon request, credit institutions can obtain data on their new credit applicants. For this purpose the institution must previously obtain an authorization signed by the beneficiary.

Circulation of the data is restricted to the participating institutions, local banks, and the Inspectorate of the Bank of Spain responsible for supervision. The Inspectorate maintains a computerized archive (the so-called minicentral credit registry) with files of case histories of borrowers with a significant loan exposure.

Notes

1. Definition derived from the report on Banking Supervisory Subcommittee of the former Committee of Governors of the Central Banks of the member states of the EEC "Central Credit Registers in the Community Countries," October 1992.

2. In Finland not only financial institutions but also the general public can access the PCR. In Greece a database on large loans is collected for supervisory reasons by the central bank, but this information is not made available externally.

3. Austria is an exception, since its banks receive data on all borrowers, even if they have not lent to them nor received a credit application from them.

4. European banking directives mandate banks to disclose once a year large exposures exceeding a specified percentage of the lending institution's liable capital. This has been enforced in EU countries by national regulations; for instance, in Germany lenders are required to report exposures above 10 percent (after January 1, 1999, pre-

viously 15%). Given the large liable capital of the major German banks, however, this "large exposure clause" is rarely triggered; German banks file virtually no large exposure reports.

5. In Greece, for instance, where a PCR as defined here does not exist, banks must still report loans, arrears, and defaulted loans in excess of Greek dracmas (GRD) 1 billion (about U.S.$ 3.3 million) to the Bank of Greece for supervisory purposes. All banks established in Greece, including branches of foreign banks, file a report to the Supervision Department every six months. The reports include credit lines used, collateral, and nonperforming loans. The system can aggregate loans per debtor, but the information can be used only as a prudential supervision tool and cannot be transmitted in any way to the banks or any other party.

6. It may already be occurring. In October 1998, the main Italian credit bureau (CRIF) announced a link-up with other European credit bureaus.

7. The situation is complicated further by the multiplicity of equilibria, characterized by different levels of effort and therefore by a different probability of default.

8. Padilla and Pagano (2000) show that, if these mechanisms are appropriately designed, borrowers' effort to perform is closer to the socially optimum level.

9. The countries included in the analysis are Argentina, Australia, Austria, Belgium, Brazil, Canada, Chile, Colombia, Denmark, Egypt, Finland, France, Germany, Greece, Hong Kong, India, Ireland, Israel, Italy, Japan, Kenya, Mexico, the Netherlands, New Zealand, Nigeria, Norway, Peru, Philippines, Portugal, Singapore, South Africa, South Korea, Spain, Sri Lanka, Sweden, Switzerland, Taiwan, Thailand, Turkey, the United Kingdom, Uruguay, the United States, and Zimbabwe. The list of countries that in 1998 operated a PCR includes Argentina, Austria, Belgium, Chile, Colombia, Finland, France, Germany, Israel, Italy, Kenya, Mexico, Peru, Portugal, Spain, Sri Lanka, and Uruguay.

10. Its activities are currently regulated by title VI of the law of 22 March 1993 on the status and supervision of credit institutions. Detailed rules on supplying of information and consultation are set out in the royal decree of 12 December 1994.

11. It is currently regulated by Law 385 of September 1993 and by the directives of the Bank of Italy.

12. The largest commercial banks have also agreed to provide data on the loan rates charged on each individual loan or line of credit. These data cannot be reported to participating institutions under any circumstance.

13. It was created by Decreto-Lei n. 47909 of 7/9/1967, later modified by circular serie A n. 191 of 24/11/1988.

14. Currently the PCR is regulated by circular 3/1995, modifying circular 18/1983.

References

Jappelli, Tullio, and Marco Pagano. 2000. "Information Sharing in Credit Markets: a Survey," CSEF working paper no. 36, University of Salerno.

Jappelli, Tullio, and Marco Pagano. 2001. "Information Sharing, Lending and Defaults: Cross-Country Evidence." *Journal of Banking and Finance* 26, no. 10 (October): 2023–2054.

La Porta, Rafael, Florencio Lopez-de-Silanes, Andrei Shleifer, and Robert W. Vishny. 1997. "Legal Determinants of External Finance." *Journal of Finance* 52, no. 3 (July): 1131–1150.

La Porta, Rafael, Florencio Lopez-de-Silanes, Andrei Shleifer, and Robert W. Vishny. 1998. "Law and Finance." *Journal of Political Economy* 106, no. 6 (December): 1113–1155.

Padilla, A. Jorge, and Marco Pagano. 1997. "Endogenous Communication among Lenders and Entrepreneurial Incentives." *The Review of Financial Studies* 10, no. 1 (Winter): 205–236.

Padilla, A. Jorge, and Marco Pagano. 2000. "Sharing Default Information as a Borrower Discipline Device." *European Economic Review* 44 (10): 1951–1980.

Pagano, Marco, and Tullio Jappelli. 1993. "Information Sharing in Credit Markets." *The Journal of Finance* 43, no. 5 (December): 1693–1718.

3

Credit Reporting Agencies: A Historical Perspective

Rowena Olegario

3.1 Introduction

The credit reporting agency (CRA) was an institutional response to the problem of information asymmetry. (The term "agency" is a historical one that has attained the force of custom. More accurately, these organizations should be thought of as private, for-profit firms.) CRAs originated in the United States during the 1830s. Dun & Bradstreet, the oldest agency still in existence, traces its roots to the Mercantile Agency, established in New York City in 1841. The CRA model has since spread throughout the world; today, there is scarcely a country or region that does not have at least one and often several CRAs. Along with the establishment of PCRs, which access information primarily from banks, the recent appearance of CRAs in nearly every developing and transitional economy promises to provide local and foreign creditors with better information on a growing number of potential trading partners.

The original American CRAs were an attempt to manage the riskiness of mercantile, or trade, credit. This form of credit is the extension of goods to another business—for example, from a wholesaler to a retailer—based on the promise that the receiver of the goods will pay for them at a later date. It is, therefore, a form of unsecured business-to-business lending. During the American colonial era, credit terms stretched to a year or more. They shortened considerably in the intervening years, and today they generally span from thirty to ninety days, depending on the type of goods involved. Interest is generally not charged unless the buyer pays late, and a discount is given for early payment.[1] In the United States, business credit reporting appeared much earlier than did consumer credit reporting, which became a significant industry only in the twentieth century. This progression is generally not the case today in developing and transitional economies, where agencies and bureaus often do not distinguish between the two types of credit.

Trade credit was, and continues to be, an important source of funding for small businesses. It functions as short-term working capital because it allows businesses to have full use of goods before they are paid for, an important benefit when capital is scarce. In the nineteenth-century United States, it was often the only type of credit available to businesses operating in small towns and rural areas. No reliable statistics on the volume of trade credit used during that period exist, but the anecdotal evidence suggests that it was used almost every time goods changed hands. When the United States became a capital-rich economy toward the end of the nineteenth century, trade credit continued to be important. What began as a practical necessity when capital was in short supply became a tool for retaining the loyalty of customers, stimulating sales, and gaining a competitive edge over rivals.

This chapter contributes to recent scholarship that attempts to locate institutions such as CRAs within a system of risk prevention and risk taking, a framework that includes laws and regulations affecting solvency, transparency, and privacy. Yet there are other frameworks that also critically influence how organizations such as CRAs develop. Among the most important of these is the cultural framework; that is, the set of societal norms that restrict, promote, and (in the most successful cases) legitimize institutional development. Like the legal and regulatory framework, the cultural one has a significant impact on whether or not institutions succeed and thrive within particular countries.

The cultural dimension of institutional change and development is difficult to measure, but one way to approach the problem is to take a long historical perspective on the institutions in question. One can ask, for example, when, where, and how credit reporting agencies emerged. Why did they first appear in the early nineteenth-century United States? Why did this particular solution to information asymmetry succeed there while other models did not? What were the cultural consequences of this model? What cultural "baggage" do these institutions carry with them today, and does this baggage restrict the successful transfer of the CRA model to other countries?

This chapter focuses on the important effects that CRAs had on the U.S. business culture, where the new institution played a significant role in transmitting the business values of the large commercial centers to nearly every community. These values included a preference for transparency and reliance on a particular set of character traits as an indication of creditworthiness. Through its branch structures, the agencies helped to standardize the criteria for creditworthiness in a country that was large, regionally varied, and heterogeneous. These criteria tended to focus on an individual's ability and willingness to pay rather than on family, social, or political connections.

Over the course of their long history, CRAs also helped to legitimize business credit and its practices, thereby preparing the way for the professionalization of credit managers that occurred in the United States at the turn of the twentieth century.

Locating the origins of CRAs within a specific time (1830s–1840s) and place (the United States) is useful for several reasons. First, this perspective demonstrates that the business assumptions upon which CRAs were originally founded were not necessarily natural or universal; they merely happened to have been good innovative solutions to the peculiar conditions that existed in the United States during the early to mid-nineteenth century. In the intervening time, these assumptions have become naturalized. But it is worth keeping in mind that in the beginning many Americans found strange and offensive the idea that businesses should be transparent and open to scrutiny by outsiders. A common complaint about the CRAs was that they were "inquisitorial"—hardly a desirable attribute in a society whose citizens were deeply attached to notions of personal "independence" and "liberty." Today, CRAs in many developing and transitional economies face similar problems as they attempt to instill an unfamiliar idea (transparency) into their countries' business cultures.

Second, CRAs have existed in the United States for some 170 years, much longer than in any other country. They evolved alongside other important institutions, including the country's commercial and bankruptcy laws. The agencies had ample time not only to experiment but also to accommodate the demands of the larger culture, which in turn had the opportunity to adjust to the new agencies. A long process of give-and-take occurred among the agencies, the courts, legislatures, the press, and the public before CRAs became deeply embedded in U.S. business culture.

A historical perspective makes clear that efforts to transplant CRAs to developing and transitional economies, whether by governmental bodies or by private entrepreneurs, involve risks. An institution whose underlying assumptions were forged in the frontier United States may not be compatible with the institutions and cultures of countries that have different historical traditions. Transplanted institutions are often not given the time to adjust because both policymakers and entrepreneurs feel pressure to demonstrate their effectiveness as quickly as possible. There is also the danger that these imported institutions may replace ones that are already working fairly well, are more deeply embedded in local culture, and are therefore perceived by locals to be more "legitimate."

These and other cultural issues should be regarded as part of the system in which risk assessment and risk taking occurs.

3.2 History of CRAs

3.2.1 Industry Groups versus Third-Party-Providers

Before turning to the development of credit reporting agencies in the United States, it is worth noting the radical and discontinuous nature of the CRA model.

Prior to the establishment of CRAs, information about individuals' creditworthiness flowed through networks composed of merchants linked by kinship, marriage, religion, and other personal ties. Alternatively, the information was transmitted within merchants' groups, such as roundtables, associations, and mutual protection societies. (For example, Creditreform, a large CRA based in Germany, began as a mutual protection society in 1879.) In all of these instances, information sharing was restricted to members, and there was little or no attempt to profit from the services provided.[2]

Because of the vast geographic scale of the United States and the high mobility of its population, mutual protection societies and other merchants' groups did not evolve as an effective response to business credit risk during the first half of the nineteenth century. In fact, robust and long-lasting organizations of this type did not appear even in places such as New York City, Chicago, and New Orleans, where one might have expected to find them. In the 1820s a group of New York wholesalers formed a society and hired a credit investigator, but the arrangement did not last. In the 1870s national manufacturers' and wholesalers' trade associations began appearing, but their primary goal was to maintain prices rather than to share credit information. One of the first national wholesaler's groups devoted to the sharing of credit information, the Credit Clearing House, was established only in 1888.[3]

In contrast to such groups, the CRA was a third-party provider of information, and it departed from previous information arrangements in a number of ways. The most obvious was that CRAs were profit-seeking ventures; they earned revenues by turning information into a commodity that could be appraised, bought, and sold. Information was transformed from being something that was available only to members of closed networks to a commodity that could be accessed by anyone willing to pay the agencies' subscription price.

The other major difference between the two models involved the CRAs' attempts to gather information on a wide array of businesses, not just those that were of interest to a particular network. Because competition among CRAs was robust in the early years, broad coverage came to be seen as a competitive advantage, and agencies often instructed their local correspondents to report on even the smallest businesses in their locality. In this way, peripheral establishments were brought under the agencies' purview. (One of the unexpected and welcome features of these early credit reports, especially for social historians, is the large variety of businesses they cover, including ones owned by women, ethnic minorities, and African Americans).[4]

Table 3.1 summarizes the most important differences between the two models of information transmission.

As table 3.2 shows, these inherent differences resulted in different motivations and in widely varying ideologies about markets and business behavior. Credit reporting agencies were the products of the dynamic and highly mobile American society of the early nine-

Table 3.1
Traditional networks versus credit reporting agencies

Within networks, information is	While information from CRAs is
An intrinsic part of the transaction	Separated from the transaction and made into a commodity
Not sold for profit	Sold for profit
Circulated only to members	Available to anyone willing to pay for it
Concerned with only those in network or its immediate periphery	Usually highly inclusive because broad coverage is perceived to be a competitive advantage

Table 3.2
Traditional networks versus credit reporting agencies: Motivations and ideologies

Traditional networks	While CRAs
Attempt to stabilize relationships among traders	Arise because markets are volatile and dynamic rather than stable
Limit trade to relatively few participants	Tend to support openness and inclusiveness
Do not share information with outsiders	Seek a large market for their information
Are secretive	Promote transparency as a virtue
Promote rules of behavior only among members	Promote and disseminate rules of behavior that can be widely understood (i.e., certain character traits)

teenth century, where stable and closed networks did not easily develop. Not surprisingly, the early CRAs tended to argue for a business environment that was open, dynamic, and transparent—precisely the kind of environment that benefited them. Moreover, competition drove the agencies to greater inclusiveness, as ambitious agency managers strove to demonstrate that they could provide subscribers with more thorough coverage than their competitors. The agencies' preferences and methods happened to dovetail with the rhetoric of fairness and opportunity that characterized American politics during the 1820s to the 1850s, when modern American ideas about democracy first took shape.[5]

Credit-reporting agencies, in other words, helped to entrench the very conditions that gave rise to them, and which made their work possible. It might be argued that the strong embeddedness of these values in U.S. business culture resulted in part from the CRAs' early appearance and success there. If so, CRAs provide a vivid example of how organizations can transmit, embed, and legitimize particular business values within the larger society.

3.2.2 Early U.S. Agencies

Credit reporting agencies emerged first in the United States because of the comparative absence of entrenched interests, such as a nationally integrated banking system or national merchants' associations. The setting was highly conducive to institutional experimentation. Until the early nineteenth century, the small scale of trade had allowed businesses to rely on letters of recommendation for information on individuals' creditworthiness. Recommenders were usually local or distant suppliers with whom an individual had previously done business or, less frequently, respectable members of his or her community, such as lawyers and bankers. Some large mercantile houses such as Baring Brothers of the U.K. hired local agents to conduct credit investigations of their U.S. customers, but this was a costly arrangement and was confined to the largest firms. By the second decade of the nineteenth century, the expansion of the country and the accompanying increase in the volume of trade rendered letters of recommendation inadequate and (it was generally felt) unreliable. Wholesalers, in particular, needed a better way to assess quickly the creditworthiness of a growing number of potential and existing customers, many of whom operated country stores in distant states and territories.[6]

During the 1830s, enterprising individuals in New York City invented a new type of organization, the credit reporting agency. The new CRAs were better suited to the peculiar needs of American society, where creditors needed to obtain information on individuals whose business experiences frequently were dispersed over a wide territory. The most successful CRAs achieved scale and scope efficiencies by setting up branch structures that linked local offices into an association trading under a common name. (These agencies were, in fact, among the first U.S. businesses to be national in scope.) CRAs were run along the lines of modern-day franchises: the local offices, called "branches," were partly or wholly owned by individuals or partners. Branches contributed a share of their profits to the head office in return for access to the network's growing scale advantages, including its ability to provide information on individuals living in other localities. In the typical arrangement, local correspondents sent their reports to their local branches, which in turn forwarded them to the head office, usually based in New York City. The head office helped to coordinate the interbranch exchanges of information, an arrangement that one scholar has aptly described as a "hub and spoke" system.[7] Although not perfect, the innovative branch structure proved more effective at tracing individuals who moved from state to state than any local network could have done. As Barron and Staten have pointed out (see chapter 8 in this volume), information sharing is most useful in large markets with high borrower mobility and heterogeneity, a situation that perfectly describes the United States during this period.[8] In addition to their primary service of credit reporting, agencies typically offered a range of related services and products, including debt collection and analyses of local economic conditions, both of which exploited the advantages provided by a network structure.

The agencies did not emerge fully formed. Rather, they evolved through experimentation and innovation as entrepreneurs attempted to gain comparative advantages over rival establishments. CRAs responded to four constituencies, all of whom had an impact on the agencies' strategies and structures: (1) their subscribers, who desired accurate and timely information; (2) correspondents, whose interests needed to be aligned with the agencies'; (3) the subjects of the reports, who often resisted the agencies' scrutiny and demanded fair treatment; and (4) the general public, who had to be persuaded of the agencies' usefulness and legitimacy. Like many institutional innovations, CRAs initially prompted suspicion even among groups whose interests they purportedly served.

Most of the early agencies' records have not survived, so some of the details concerning their evolution can only be a matter of conjecture. Fortunately, however, those of the R. G. Dun Co. (established in 1841 as the Mercantile Agency and the forerunner of today's Dun & Bradstreet) have been preserved, and they constitute the single largest source of historical information on this otherwise hidden industry.[9] The Dun records are particularly useful, given the firm's unusual position. After the Civil War this firm, along with its archrival the Bradstreet Co. and perhaps one or two others, came to dominate the field of national and interregional credit reporting. (Local and trade-specific agencies—for example, ones covering the shoe trade—also continued to flourish.)

In 1870, R. G. Dun claimed to have 7,000 subscribers; by the 1880s, it had an estimated 40,000, including the country's largest wholesalers, importers, manufacturers, banks, and insurance companies.[10] As table 3.3 shows, by 1900 Dun was reporting on well over one million establishments.

3.3 How Did the Early Agencies Determine Creditworthiness?

Payment histories—records of how well a business has met its past obligations—are among the most important pieces of information collected by credit reporting agencies today. This kind of information is particularly valuable for small debtors, whose financial state-

Table 3.3
Number of entries in R. G. Dun reference volumes, 1859–1900

Year	Number of entries
1859	20,268
1870	430,573
1880	764,000
1890	1,176,988
1900	1,285,816

Source: Edward Vose, *Seventy-Five Years of the Mercantile Agency: R. G. Dun & Co., 1841–1916.* New York: R. G. Dun & Co., 1916, p. 98.
Note: These are net numbers that do not reflect the significant number of entries dropped between each date. In reality, the agency covered many more businesses than these figures indicate.

ments are often not carefully audited.[11] The early agencies, however, could not systematically collect payment data; at best, they were able to obtain anecdotal information only. To compensate, the agencies used informal but effective mechanisms to predict the likelihood of payment.

3.3.1 Credit Analysis Today versus Credit Analysis in the Nineteenth Century

Before examining how the early agencies determined creditworthiness, it is worth noting how this is done today. In modern times credit scoring models have become available, usually on a proprietary basis, from providers such as Fair, Isaac, and Dun & Bradstreet. These techniques enable credit managers to benchmark companies against their peers to determine whether a particular account is likely to pay on time, late, or not at all. The models are most useful to businesses that receive large numbers of applications because they allow credit managers to identify the higher risk candidates who can then be separately assessed.

D&B's proprietary measure, called the Paydex score, is one widely used analytical tool. It is a composite statistic that allows creditors to compare their borrowers' record with up to two years' worth of aggregated and weighted data on hundreds of other borrowers in the same industry. The data are provided to D&B on a voluntary basis, mostly by major companies who may also share the data with other credit reporting agencies; additional data are also gathered by D&B reporters. The Paydex score ranges from 100 ("anticipate," meaning the payment can be safely anticipated) to 20 (meaning that the borrower has been up to 120 days late in making payments).[12] Credit scoring was made possible by the willingness of business debtors to share their payment records with credit reporting agencies, a relatively recent phenomenon.

Today D&B covers a broad array of businesses that are neither large nor publicly owned.[13] This is an important service because, as of the late 1990s, only some 50,000 to 60,000 of the world's companies were public. In 2000, D&B covered over 62 million businesses worldwide, about 32 percent of them in North America. The vast majority of these were privately owned and comparatively tiny: in 1998, nearly 40 percent of the U.S. companies in D&B's database had only twenty or fewer employees.[14]

D&B's data-gathering resources today are extensive. In 1998, a workforce of 1,400 employees contacted some 15 million U.S. businesses (mostly to verify addresses and phone numbers) and conducted more thorough interviews of management personnel in an additional 3 million companies. A small minority—almost 200,000 in the United States—shared their payment and bank information with D&B, and some 6,000 of those supplied accounts receivable data electronically. D&B accesses items on suits, liens, and judgments from the federal and state bankruptcy courts. Other sources of information include the offices of the states' attorneys general, insurance commissioners, and secretaries of state; over 2,000 daily newspapers, publications, and electronic news services; the U.S. Postal Service; and telephone and other utility companies.

The American creditor of the nineteenth century, in contrast, faced much more serious obstacles to obtaining good financial information on business owners. Not only were payment histories unavailable; financial statements also were difficult to obtain, and creditors were reluctant to request them for fear of offending existing or potential customers.[15] Moreover, even if creditors succeeded in procuring financial statements, these were not necessarily reliable. Statements were almost never audited, ignorance about bookkeeping was widespread, and no generally accepted accounting principles (GAAP) existed. Financial information was typically limited to an individual's total wealth and liabilities, primarily mortgages; little or no information was provided on a business's revenues, profits, expenses, and cash flow. Although credit practices and expectations varied among different lines of business, there was no industry data available to use as benchmarks.[16]

Reporters obtained financial information by interviewing the individuals in question, consulting newspapers and county and state tax and property records, or through local gossip. These sources typically provided very limited financial data. In a sample report from the 1850s presented in figure 3.1, note the scarcity of precise financial information (underlined for emphasis).[17]

The sample in figure 3.1 was found among the papers of one Elijah Morgan, an attorney in Ann Arbor, Michigan, who worked as a correspondent for a number of CRAs. Because the sample represents an idealized report, it serves to illustrate the kinds of information that CRAs during the mid-nineteenth century believed their correspondents could obtain with a reasonable (although presumably not excessive) amount of detective work. What the sample underscores is the limited nature of the available information about a borrower's current liquidity.

According to the report, the senior partner (Jones) was deemed to be worth some $25,000, of which $5,000 consisted of "unincumbered real estate." But of what, exactly, did the remaining $20,000 consist—cash, securities, merchandise, or personal property? And what of the real estate? Was it the owner's home, a property he rented out, or a store? The report indicates that one of the junior partners, Smith, paid in $5,000 in cash when he was admitted into the partnership. But that was a full two years earlier, which means that the financial information, even if it was reported by the correspondent within the previous six months, was at least two years out of date. The $5,000 was "principally a gift from his father, who is well off," but there is no precise measure of the father's wealth nor any indication that he would be willing to contribute more cash to the business.

3.3.2 "Character" as a Substitute

In any event, because credit terms could stretch from six to twelve months, a business owner's current liquidity was not as helpful as past behavior. (There was little to be gained from knowing how much cash a business currently had if payments weren't due for another year.)[18] Ideally, past behavior would have included an individual's payment record from other suppliers; but as already noted,

```
Jones, Smith, & Brown

Alfred Jones, John Smith, Wm. Brown, Gen'l Dealers
```

"J." is about 50 years old, and a merchant at this place for 20 years, during which time he has been doing a good business and has made money, never failed, is of good character, and a shrewd business man. Is now *estimated worth about $25,000, of which $5,000 is in unincumbered real estate.* He does a legitimate business, and never ventures into rash speculations. "S" and "B" are each about 35 years old, and smart businessmen. "S" had been in business and failed, settled honorably, acted as clerk, for "J." for two or three years, and was admitted a partner some two years since, *paying in $5,000 in cash, principally a gift from his father, who is well off.* "B" has been a clerk in the house about four years, and a good and popular one, is just admitted a partner, but does not add any capital. They continue to do a good business, are in good credit, and worthy of it.

Figure 3.1
Sample report, 1850s. Financial information is highlighted

information interchanges of this kind did not exist until the end of the nineteenth century.

As a proxy for past business behavior, reporters conveyed their assessments about the borrower's "character." At first glance, this term carries much scope for imprecision. One of the most significant features of the early credit reports, however, was the clear pattern of specificity and consistency that they exhibited. Not all character traits were considered to be potentially important. Instead, creditors focused primarily on those directly linked to borrowers' willingness and ability to pay, which are summarized in table 3.4.

Table 3.4
Summary of borrower's characteristics

Important signals	Not important
"Honesty," "Honor"	Political or social connections
Punctuality	Religious affiliation (except Jews)
"Extravagance," "Thrift"	Education
Experience	Churchgoing
"Energy"	Marital infidelity, sexual deviance
"Vices" (drinking and gambling only)	or misbehavior
Ethnicity (but not consistent: sometimes explicitly mentioned, at other times implied or ignored)	
Other:	
Marital status	
Age	

These traits were shorthand for a specific set of questions.[19] For example:

"Honesty," "Honor"

· Has the borrower always made a good faith effort to pay?

· Does the borrower keep creditors informed of the risks faced by his or her business?

· Does the borrower pay all suppliers on time? (It was possible to maintain a good record with only one or two suppliers, who were then asked to provide a positive recommendation.)

· If the borrower failed in the past, did he or she deal fairly with all creditors? (One reliable source estimated that some 60 percent of retailers ran into problems in paying their suppliers. Note in the sample report in figure 3.1 that a record of failing did not necessarily result in an unfavorable assessment as long as the borrower made an effort to pay eventually.)

"Extravagance," "Thrift"

· Are the store and its inventory appropriate to the market?

· Are family expenses in line with income? (This was important, as most businesses in the nineteenth century were run as sole proprietorships or partnerships, not as limited-liability corporations.)

Jones, Smith, & Brown

Alfred Jones, John Smith, Wm. Brown, Gen'l Dealers

"J." is about *50 years old*, and a *merchant at this place for 20 years*, during which time he has been doing a good business and has made money, *never failed*, is of *good character*, and a *shrewd* business man. Is now estimated worth about $25,000, of which $5,000 is in unincumbered real estate. He does a *legitimate* business, and *never ventures into rash speculations*. "S" and "B" are each about *35 years old*, and *smart* businessmen. "S" had been in business and *failed, settled honorably*, acted as *clerk, for "J."* for *two or three years*, and was admitted a *partner some two years* since, paying in $5,000 in cash, principally a gift from his father, who is well off. "B" has been *a clerk in the house about four years*, and a *good and popular* one, is just admitted a partner, but does not add any capital. They continue to do a good business, are in good credit, and worthy of it.

Figure 3.2
Sample report, 1850s

"Energy"

· Does the borrower show commitment and willingness to work?
· Is the borrower spreading him/herself too thin on other projects?
· Does the borrower engage in speculation?

Looking again at the sample report from the 1850s, this time the "character" traits are highlighted (figure 3.2). As the sample demonstrates, character functioned as an effective substitute for more precise payment information that for cultural and practical reasons was simply not available.

Note, moreover, that the rules for assessing creditworthiness were relatively simple; there was little need for specialized knowledge or training to understand and apply them. Although the rules appear quaint to modern eyes, it was the sheer folksiness of this method that makes it historically important. Because the method was relatively simple to understand and so congenial to larger American values, it spread quickly. Transmission was aided by the CRAs' network structure, which broadcasted the agencies' assumptions and expectations from their base in the large commercial centers to communities throughout the country. Trade creditors, whether operating in New York, Charleston, St. Louis, or San Francisco, shared an understanding about the precise set of traits that constituted creditworthiness. Surviving credit reports show little deviation among the major commercial centers, despite political and social differences among the regions which, in the most extreme and tragic instance, led to the Civil War.[20]

In 1857 Bradstreet began publishing a bound reference book that contained information, presented in the form of rating keys, on the creditworthiness of some 20,000 businesses scattered throughout the country, primarily in the large cities. The 1857 volume, called *Bradstreet's Improved Commercial Agency Reports*, had 110 pages containing ratings for 17,100 establishments (mostly large concerns) in nine locations.

The traits presented in table 3.5 appeared in Bradstreet's 1860 reference volume. Each trait was assigned a number that was used as a shorthand to describe the individuals listed. Note how both negative and positive traits were included. The key that was used to indicate the reporter's judgment as to the individual's creditworthiness is given in table 3.6. In later volumes, the keys began designating an individual's or firm's estimated capital strength and the amount of credit a borrower could safely be extended.

Bradstreet's innovative ratings system was a much more convenient method for putting information into the hands of subscribers, whose clerks were no longer obliged to spend such onerous amounts of time at the agencies' offices. Moreover, the rating keys replaced the descriptive and highly impressionistic language of the credit reports, so that subscribers could more easily compare potential borrowers. After some hesitation due to concerns about libel suits, R. G. Dun in 1859 issued its own reference book, a 519-page volume containing over 20,000 rated firms in the United States and Canada.

Table 3.5
Borrower's traits

Making money	Does not always pay accounts at
Losing money	maturity
Expenses large	Credits prudently
Economical	Takes large risks in creditoring
Business too much extended	Does not value prompt payments
Business not too much extended	sufficiently
Temperate	Sued
Not temperate	Not sued
Attends closely to business	Pays promptly
Does not attend very closely to business	Rather slow pay
Pays large interest	Honest
Does not pay large interest	Honesty not fully endorsed
Often hard run for money	Good business qualifications
Often pays before maturity	Medium business qualifications
Good moral character	Endorses too much
Not very good private character	Does not endorse
Sometimes suffers notes to be protested	

Source: Bradstreet Commercial Report, v. VII, 2d ed., July 31, 1860, p. 8.

Table 3.6
Key used to indicate the reporter's judgment as to the individual's creditworthiness

Aa	Good for any amount required
A	Best of credit
B	Very good credit
C	Good credit
D	Good for smaller lines
E	Fair for small lines

Source: Bradstreet Commercial Report, v. VII, 2d ed., July 31, 1860, p. 8.

(Only larger firms were included because Dun believed that small traders could be judged only by consulting the full records.) The reference books were issued with a lock and key to emphasize the confidential nature of its information, and the contract specified that outdated volumes had to be returned to the agency. It is important to note, however, that the reference volumes did not replace the more detailed reports. The agencies continued to offer these special reports to subscribers and strongly advised that they be consulted before making a final decision about extending credit.[21]

To summarize, the shared method for assessing creditworthiness that CRAs helped to transmit throughout the United States probably encouraged commercial transactions by providing simple and consistent rules for managing ambiguity. It is fair to say that no other country during this period exhibited such a widespread popular understanding of the demands imposed by a credit economy, circumstances that can partly be explained by the existence of CRAs.

Obviously, the credit reporting agency system worked only if business owners acquiesced to the agencies' scrutiny of past behavior, including personal spending habits. Many Americans were profoundly disturbed and offended by what they saw as the agencies' inquisitorial system. Yet resistance to the CRAs, although vocal, was nevertheless relatively mild, and during the latter decades of the nineteenth century the initial suspicion gave way to an almost bland acceptance. As the practice spread, the business press affirmed the agencies' usefulness, and courts further advanced acceptance by generally ruling in the agencies' favor.

3.3.3   Regulatory and Legal Environment

After the panic of 1873, a number of U.S. state legislatures introduced bills that would have punished the agencies in cases where the information they provided proved to be incorrect and resulted in losses to subscribers. None of these was enacted into law. Instead, the courts emerged as the most active controllers of credit reporting agencies during the first half-century or so of their existence.

The agencies' unprecedented methods of collecting and transmitting sensitive information, some of it erroneous or outdated, made them the targets of numerous lawsuits. One of the earliest occurred in 1851 when two Ohio merchants brought a libel suit (*Beardsley v. Tappan*) against the Mercantile Agency (the R. G. Dun Co.'s predecessor) for inaccurately stating that their firm was about to fail. The technical issue in this case, as in many subsequent others, was that of privileged communication; counsel for the agency argued that the reports fell under this legal heading and therefore did not constitute libel. The judge in *Beardsley* interpreted the question narrowly, however, reasoning that because the information was available to a large number of partners and clerks, and potentially to any subscriber who requested it, credit reports did not enjoy protection as "privileged communication." The agency appealed, but the decision was upheld by the U.S. Circuit Court. The case did not put the agencies out of business; however, it became a nagging worry when the firms began to publish reference books.

In later decades, the courts tended to broaden the definition of privileged communication. Seventeen years after the Beardsley case, *Ormsby v. Douglass* (1868) resulted in an important rethinking of the issue. Once again, a libel suit was brought against the R. G. Dun Co.; this time, however, the court accepted the firm's arguments and stipulated only that the communication must be "made in a proper manner, without evil intent or malicious motive." The decision provided important safeguards for the agencies, who were transmitting larger amounts of information to their rapidly growing subscriber base. Meanwhile, the agencies refined their contracts with their subscribers to include disclaimers about the accuracy of the information they provided. In the 1870s several decisions established that the agencies needed only to be "reasonably diligent." In most cases, the court rejected the argument that the agencies were liable for losses that resulted from reliance on the information they provided. At the same time, the courts punished individuals who knowingly submitted erroneous financial statements.[22]

Lawsuits were a constant source of concern to the agencies, but they functioned as an important check on an otherwise unregulated industry. Courts forced the agencies' managers to curb their worst impulses while at the same time allowing them to continue what increasingly was accepted as a necessary and valuable service. Equally important, the court decisions helped to legitimize the agencies' activities. Throughout the post–Civil War period the resistance to credit reporting agencies slowly gave way to acceptance, as greater convenience and uniformity, increased protection from the courts, and the sheer prevalence of the practice succeeded in embedding CRAs as permanent elements of the country's commercial infrastructure.

3.4   Current U.S. Industry Structure and Characteristics

The early industry pioneers who struggled to establish the agencies' legitimacy in the United States would have marveled at how tightly CRAs are now woven into the fabric of the country's business establishment. In a recent annual report, D&B itself acknowledged that the public perceives it to be "conventional," "old-fashioned," and "rigid," an unfortunate side effect of being one of the world's most trusted and recognized brand names.[23] Today the question is not whether D&B carries sufficient authority, but whether it has an inordinately large effect on the allocation of business credit. The evidence suggests that a number of factors mitigate the power that D&B, or any business credit reporting firm, could potentially wield. These factors include robust competition from a host of industry-specific agencies and Internet start-ups, the reluctance of the agencies themselves to overstate their authority (due to the threat of lawsuits), and recent legislation, which has extended the protection accorded to consumer borrowers to business borrowers.

3.4.1 D&B's Dominance

Dun & Bradstreet's dominance of this industry has historically been extensive. After the Civil War, an industry shakeout resulted in an oligopoly consisting of R. G. Dun, the Bradstreet Company, and one or two others.[24] When the two largest firms merged in 1933, a monopoly on national credit reporting appears to have been achieved. Official statistics do not treat credit reporting agencies as a separate category, so it is difficult to find a total industry figure; there is general consensus, however, that D&B currently accounts for a large majority of the total industry.[25]

D&B's long history and exceptional dominance make the firm a unique case study of how scale efficiencies can work in the credit reporting business. With 2000 revenues of some $1.4 billion, Dun & Bradstreet is one of the world's largest providers of business credit information.[26] Its closest competitor in the United States is Experian, a subsidiary of the United Kingdom's Great Universal Stores (GUS) plc. (GUS's annual report does not indicate how much of Experian's revenues are obtained from credit reporting vs. its other businesses, such as target marketing.) In 2000 D&B operated wholly or majority-owned firms in thirty-three countries and had minority interests in joint ventures in a further six, while Experian had operations in nineteen countries. North America remains D&B's largest market, accounting for $968 million of revenues in 2000, followed by Europe ($382 million), and Asia Pacific/Latin America ($67 million).

The firm's influence extends to other areas. In addition to its role as an information-sharing mechanism, D&B serves as a source of official data. It is a major compiler of statistical information, including failure rates, and its proprietary numbering system for businesses, called the D-U-N-S number, is used as a global standard by the United Nations, the federal government, and over fifty industry and trade associations worldwide. The Dun numbering system was used by the federal government until the 1950s, when standard industrial classification (SIC) codes were introduced.

3.4.2 Limits to the CRAs' Authority

At first glance, the field of business credit reporting appears to be concentrated in a mere handful of powerful entities and in one firm in particular. The situation is not surprising, as scale advantages are extremely important in this industry. D&B's own history shows, however, that its position as the largest of the national agencies was mitigated by competition from smaller local and industry-specific agencies as well as the industry groups that had become well established by the early twentieth century.

Today competition has intensified, particularly from local and regional firms, as well as Internet start-ups. Recent international directories produced by two private firms, Creditworthy.com and Creditsafe (U.K.), confirm that the credit reporting business attracts substantial entrepreneurial interest. Throughout the world, individuals and groups have sought to fill niches that are not adequately served by the large international CRAs. (No comprehensive survey has yet determined how market share is divided up among the large international firms vs. smaller locally owned and managed agencies.)

Another important mitigating factor is the fact that no laws or regulations compel trade creditors to obtain a credit report as a precondition to transacting. This contrasts with the fixed-income securities market where, according to the *Financial Times*, "state laws and legal precedents restrict the investments of trusts and fiduciaries to investment-grade securities" and some "investors can only legally buy bonds that meet certain criteria imposed by Moody's and S&P." As a result of such requirements, these two players account for some 80 percent of the credit ratings market.[27] Moody's and S&P have opened offices in a number of foreign locations; in contrast, foreign rating agencies have not been successful in penetrating the United States because, crucially, they must first be designated by the Securities and Exchange Commission as a nationally recognized statistical ratings organization (NRSRO). The *Financial Times* reports that the "NRSRO designation process is somewhat mysterious and considerably frustrating for non-U.S. ratings agencies. There are no formal criteria for the designation and it is alleged that applications from several non-U.S. rating agencies have been in limbo for several years."[28]

Thanks to such regulatory requirements, Moody's and S&P have acquired what one scholar has called "epistemic" authority, an advantage that inhibits competition from new technologies such as the Internet. The very authority that Moody's and S&P have managed to construct in the course of nearly a century, and which is now upheld by powerful bodies such as international banks, the IMF, other transnational organizations, and governments, has effectively shut out all competition in the credit rating industry. In contrast, the worldwide credit reporting industry is characterized by robust competition and innovation. D&B's dominant position is continually challenged by Experian and a host of new Internet-only entrants, including Creditworthy, CreditFYI, Creditsafe (U.K.), eCredit, and businessCredit.

In addition to the checks imposed by competition, D&B itself has always openly acknowledged the limits of its own authority, a stance that is probably motivated by the threat of lawsuits. Despite the much improved quantitative methods that it makes available today, D&B analysts frequently stress that models must be supplemented by the judgment of the individual creditor, a claim that is accepted by most credit practitioners. (One of these has aptly characterized the granting of trade credit as being similar to the practice of medicine, in that it is an "inexact exact science.")[29] The authority of credit reporting agencies is debated constantly and publicly by those who rely on their services; the inaccuracies and inconsistencies of their information are freely discussed by credit professionals in trade publications such as *Business Credit*. Investigative journalists have questioned the accuracy of reports simply by obtaining several different ones on the same company, comparing the information contained in them, and then reporting their findings.[30] The nature of the credit reporting agencies' authority is, therefore, more limited than that of Moody's or S&P. Unlike these agencies, firms such as D&B do not make authoritative judgments about an account; rather, they provide a range of information so that creditors themselves can make the call. "We can provide plenty of background and qualitative information," states a D&B analyst based in the United Kingdom. But it "is up to the managers in the supplier firm to evaluate the data and make a judgment about how the trading relationship should proceed and whether credit should be given."[31]

Although credit reporting was long dominated by one firm, its authority—and the authority of credit reporting agencies generally —is more contestable than is the case with credit rating agencies, which "see themselves as quasi-regulatory institutions," according to Timothy Sinclair.[32] The authority of CRAs is checked by competition, the relative ease with which competitors' products can be compared to one another, the absence of regulations requiring creditors to use the services, and their own sense of the limited nature of their authority, an attitude that is shared by the entire credit profession.

3.4.3 Current Regulatory Environment

In the United States, recent legislation has further restricted the power and authority of credit reporting firms. Since the 1960s, most new federal laws have been aimed at the consumer sector.[33] Although the line separating business and consumer credit has historically been clearer in the United States than is the case in developing countries today, that line can sometimes blur, particularly for small business borrowers. In 1990, for example, the Equal Credit Opportunity Act (ECOA), originally enacted to regulate consumer creditors, also became mandatory for business creditors. The act stipulated that business creditors must provide notice within thirty days to applicants who are denied credit. The law also requires that an applicant's records be kept for sixty days after notification; if the applicant requests in writing the reasons for the credit decision, the creditor must keep the records for at least twelve months.

In 1997, the U.S. Congress reauthorized the Fair Credit Reporting Act (FCRA), which was followed by the drafting of new regulations by the Federal Trade Commission. Aimed at enhancing the protection of consumer credit borrowers, the new regulations threatened to restrict access to the credit reports of business owners. The National Association of Credit Management objected to the new regulations, arguing that they should not apply to transactions between businesses (as opposed to between businesses and consumers). "It is very common for corporate creditors to receive an application for the extension of open, unsecured business or trade credit to a sole proprietor who may be a consumer," states a recent NACM newsletter. The issue "is whether business creditors have a legitimate business need to obtain consumer credit reports, without obtaining specific written permission."[34]

Thus, credit reporting firms are subject to evolving legislation aimed at protecting the privacy of individuals. As Barron and Staten point out, all credit information-sharing devices necessitate the loss of a certain amount of privacy; it is what potential borrowers give up in return for access to credit.[35] But the extent to which individuals are expected to tolerate this loss is continually contested in the United States, particularly in the field of consumer credit reporting. New restrictions can affect access to information on business borrowers, especially sole proprietors. Currently, laws limit the information contained in consumer credit reports to the following: the consumer's name, address, Social Security number, place of employment, and spouse's name; open credit lines, outstanding credit balances, credit limits, history of timeliness of payments, and amount of last payment; and bankruptcies, liens, and public judgments against the consumer. Reports cannot include information about a person's lifestyle, religion, political affiliation, driving record, or medical history.

The FCRA mandates that only those with a "permissible purpose," such as creditors, insurers, employers, and landlords, may purchase the reports.[36] Although restrictive, the laws are laxer than similar laws in Europe, Australia, and many other countries. In Portugal, for example, credit bureaus need to have a person's consent before they can either collect or sell any credit data, and the permission can be withdrawn at any time.[37] Australian bureaus report only negative information; creditors do not have access to the files of individuals with positive records.[38]

3.5 Credit Reporting Agencies in Developing and Transitional Economies

This section gives a brief overview of CRAs in developing and transitional economies, including their structures and services, the challenges they face, and the effects they may have on their countries' business norms. Before proceeding, it is useful to clarify that the firms referred to in this chapter as CRAs perform in-depth investigations on individual businesses as a key part of the services they provide. Some also collect payment history data or other basic information from courts or corporate registries on a larger number of firms, in the mold of the credit reporting firms and credit bureaus discussed previously by Miller. An important distinction exists, however, between the CRAs discussed here and the firms surveyed by the World Bank and by Jappelli and Pagano. Both of those surveys focused only on firms that collect standardized payment history information, not on CRAs that also do detailed firm analysis of individual businesses. No comprehensive directories of this rapidly growing part of the industry are currently available.[39]

3.5.1   The Spread of CRAs

Existing surveys and directories make clear that credit reporting agencies and other private credit registries and bureaus have appeared in nearly every developing country, many in the past two decades. The World Bank's survey, focused primarily on Latin America, notes that approximately half of the private credit registries in its sample began operating only since 1989.[40] The directory compiled by Creditworthy, a private provider of business credit information, indicates that CRAs have been present in Central and South America for several decades but have become more common in Asia and Eastern Europe only since the mid-1980s.

As was true of the U.S. experience in the nineteenth century, government initiatives have not played a direct role in the establishment of most CRAs in developing and transitional economies. In general, they were set up by entrepreneurs trying to exploit the growing demand for reliable information on local businesses, many of which are privately owned and comparatively small.[41] The World Bank survey found that a growing number of governments have encouraged the establishment of public credit registries to supervise and monitor bank lending activity. From the point of view of trade creditors, however, the information available from these sources is limited. The biggest drawback is simply that, unlike private credit registries, public ones do not collect information on trade credit.[42] As Margaret Miller cautions elsewhere in this volume, public credit registries should not be expected to substitute fully for private ones because their objectives vary too widely for significant overlap to occur.[43]

Several recent developments have stimulated the establishment of foreign CRAs. In some countries, CRAs have stepped in to provide information previously obtainable from banks, which one U.S. credit practitioner claims "have clammed up" in recent years. Another information vacuum occurred when the U.S. Department of Commerce decided to discontinue its Foreign Company Background

Reports.[44] Financial crises have also contributed. After the 1998 crisis in Asia, a number of firms sought to take advantage of the desire of companies in that region to appear more credible to lenders. Chinese business leaders, for example, sought the help of D&B personnel to learn how to manage a credit department. As a result, D&B immediately made plans to double the size of its database on Chinese companies, and the firm expected to implement a similar policy in Singapore and Malaysia.[45] The financial crisis also inspired the appearance of a large number of local start-ups. According to the manager of a Chinese CRA, there are currently some one hundred large and small CRAs operating in China, almost ten times the number of five years before.[46]

Even so, the worldwide credit reporting industry today cannot simply be characterized as one of unfettered competition; instead, it is a mixture of competition and cooperation. This is because increased cross-border trading compels CRAs, whether large or small, international or local, to ally with one another to provide better coverage—circumstances that further complicate attempts to gauge the degree of concentration within this industry. Networks include ALIAC (Latin American Business Credit Reporting Association), TCM Group International (headquartered in Australia), American Business Information Association (based in New York City), and Eurogate, among many others. Along with opening foreign branches, industry giants D&B, Experian, and Equifax have formed alliances with, or buy information from, foreign agencies.[47] (The establishment of foreign branches by large agencies is not a new phenomenon; as early as the 1850s, U.S. agencies began establishing them in countries where American companies conducted sizeable trade, such as Canada, Mexico, and the U.K. By 1901, the R. G. Dun Co. had several offices in Canada as well as in London, Glasgow, Paris, Melbourne, Sydney, Mexico City, Guadalajara, Havana, and Cape Town.) It is not clear how direct a role the parent companies play in monitoring the quality of the information provided by their foreign subsidiaries and partners.

To gain at least an impressionistic picture of the goals and problems faced by CRAs in developing and transitional economies, the author conducted interviews in late 2000 with owners and managers in Argentina, Chile, China, the Dominican Republic, India, Kenya, Lithuania, Mexico, Thailand, and Ukraine. Although the results of this small-scale survey are preliminary and highly tentative, the

respondents' goals, problems, and challenges are probably representative of ones faced by their counterparts elsewhere. Despite their
diversity, these ten countries share common concerns, such as the
difficulty of obtaining reliable information and the need to educate
their native populations about the business norms of the developed
world. It is therefore likely that the survey results would be replicated in a larger sample size.

The survey uncovered disagreements, however, about the desirability of welcoming the international agencies versus encouraging
the growth of locally owned establishments. A respondent in China
regarded the entry of the international agencies in a positive light:
"More and more foreign credit reporting companies, like D&B, are
rapidly developing the market in China. They will bring experience
and knowledge of the industry [which will be] very helpful." In
contrast, an agency owner in Mexico criticized the international
agencies for their lack of regard for local circumstances and culture.
He wrote: "Culture plays a big role since the market is divided
[between locally based agencies and] international companies which
just want to sell reports and do not look at the regional facts. They
produce reports the same way they do in the U.S. or Europe ...
I strongly believe that reports must consider the culture within each
country."

3.5.2 Limits to Information Gathering

Like the early U.S. agencies, foreign CRAs are information-sharing
mechanisms that are, or are becoming, key components of their
countries' business information infrastructure. The author's survey
suggests that CRAs in developing and transitional economies are
established to meet the needs of both outside and local business
creditors.[48] Typical clients include exporters-importers, insurance
companies, banks and other financial institutions, lawyers, manufacturers, construction companies, consulates and trade organizations, collection agencies, chambers of commerce, embassies and
foreign diplomatic missions, other credit reporting agencies, and information resellers.

Although each agency is constrained by the particular economic,
social, and political circumstances of its host country, all share a
number of common features. Subscribers typically are offered services ranging from a simple company profile to a thorough investigation that may include personal interviews of a company's

Table 3.7
Sevices provided by CRAs in developing and transitional economies

Debt collection

Market and consumer research, including feasibility research for joint ventures, local market conditions, product pricing, consumption patterns, public opinion surveys

Search and retrieval of public registry and stock exchange documents, annual reports of local companies

Networking: facilitating contacts among international and local businesses searching for mutual opportunities

Prospecting: helping outsiders search for local business opportunities

Surveying agents for cargo insurance companies, including inspection of damaged cargo and preparation of all documents

Real estate and property investigations and appraisals

Life insurance investigations

Consulting

Personnel training

Publishing, especially reference books on local business topics and conditions

Insurance claims

Direct mailing

representatives. Some produce original reports while others simply wholesale the information prepared by others, but in general the agencies attempt to provide the kind of credit reports that the older U.S. agencies have made standard.[49] In addition to credit reports, CRAs offer other services that take advantage of their local presence and ability to provide first-hand knowledge and information (see table 3.7).[50]

Accessing the types of information that U.S. creditors take for granted, however, is difficult for CRAs in developing and transitional economies.[51] Official data sources do exist, but respondents to the survey noted that these sources frequently are inadequate. Information from China's Administration of Industry and Commerce (AIC) "is not open to the public," the agency manager reported. "At present, we get this kind of information from the AIC through lawyers, which is expensive." The manager in Lithuania spoke of inadequate technology as an obstacle. The "main problem," he wrote, "is that information is insufficient, as most government institutions keep data not in computers or other digital form, but on simple paper blanks." In India, "many a time obtaining this information is extremely difficult as there are no public records available for nonincorporated companies, and on incorporated companies, the extent of the information available at the Registry of Companies is quite often incomplete." Many countries also limit access to particular kinds of data; for example, some Latin American countries, including Costa Rica, Ecuador, and Guatemala, prevent banks from sharing information on their customers' accounts. A number of the survey respondents stated that privacy laws further restricted the type of information they could obtain and report.[52]

Irregular business practices such as tax evasion and the lack of GAAP throw into question the reliability of financial statements. Agency managers in Kenya and China referred specifically to these problems: "No company in Kenya will give you their monthly accounts receivable, plus most companies keep five sets of books, one for the tax man, one for the owners, etc. Which one do you rely on?" In China, "[m]ost accounting offices do not follow the accounting laws [but instead] follow the requirements of companies in audit reports who pay them. Most, especially private companies and small businesses, do not follow the accounting laws. Very often a company has some secret bank accounts to avoid tax." This manager added, however, that "some big companies and foreign-invested companies do well in following accounting practices," and although "the figures in the financial statements are often inaccurate, they are still valuable for credit reporting, as most ... [inaccuracies] cannot be so large as to affect the overall financial condition of the company. If [they are], it is regarded as a serious violation of the law." The World Bank survey of credit registries finds that private registries use a variety of methods to correct for inaccurate information, including requesting a review from the reporting institutions when a data problem arises, suspending access to the data by institutions with recurrent data problems, and providing consumers with a free copy to encourage review of the data.[53] Because these mechanisms have not been systematically studied, their effectiveness remains unknown.

Perhaps the most disturbing obstacles are the security fears of business owners. In Mexico, companies "are not very willing to provide financial information any more. In the past we had 90 percent of reports with financials, but by 1998 we went down to 75 percent. Today we are at 50 percent. This is a response to insecurity in the country ... [where owners fear] the risk of being robbed or the principals being abducted." The manager in Ukraine pointed to a similar problem. She wrote: "people are frightened by the criminals, and that's why they do not like to give truthful information."

Valuable information, however, need not be complex. Sometimes local sources can add tremendous value simply by visiting the facility to see whether the business actually exists. They can also be valuable allies in international debt collection, which is frequently hampered by simple breakdowns in communication, such as when debtors fail to receive invoices because they neglect to inform their creditors of an address change. Cultural misunderstanding also frequently occur, which leads one practitioner to advise: "before turning to the legal system, try to contact the company directly, or through another company or division where there are collection people who have native language speaking capacities and familiarity with local customs. In many cases the problem can be resolved with a few telephone calls." Having access to a reliable local source such as a credit reporting agency can help minimize communication problems for overseas creditors and reduce the need to appeal to the legal system.[54] Foreign CRAs are well aware of their advantage in this area and frequently highlight it in their promotional literature.

3.5.3 Effects on Business Norms

The author's survey indicates that the managers and owners of CRAs in developing and transitional economies have distinct ideas about how their agencies affect their countries' business norms and vice versa. Not surprisingly, respondents stressed the agencies' positive effects, and their statements tend to be prescriptive rather than objectively descriptive. Even so, their responses shed light on these agencies' agendas and the often tacit assumptions that underlie their work.

To a remarkable extent, the ideology expressed by the agency managers mirrors that of the early U.S. agencies. In the same way that CRAs transmitted the values of the large commercial centers across the U.S. continent during the nineteenth century, CRAs are spreading these values to developing and transitional economies during the twenty-first century. Whether wholly or partly owned by a larger international agency or completely local in ownership, these firms are helping to establish standards of transparency. Collectively, CRAs are helping to bring about a globally consistent set of criteria for business credit analysis.

Some of the respondents mentioned the educative function of the agencies, including their role in transmitting the business norms of more developed countries. The respondent in Lithuania believes that native producers there have begun to realize the benefits of obtaining information on potential trading partners. Credit reporting agencies, he wrote, have "changed the attitude toward the cost of information and [its role] in company strategy and marketing decision making. For example, there have been increased [requests for information on] foreign partners." Similarly, the Ukrainian manager wrote that in "the last two years we have seen changes produced in the minds of Ukrainian businessmen. They have become more open and credible during interviews. Most of them now accept the European standards in managing their business." This manager expressed the opinion that credit reporting would not succeed fully until more stringent financial accounting and credit reporting standards are put in place. Native business owners, she wrote, "do not want to spend money for the information because they think the money will be wasted. The only way to overcome these problems is to educate our businessmen about the standards of developed countries."

Other respondents focused on more fundamental changes. The manager in Kenya stated that credit reporting agencies and bureaus can help to stem the corruption endemic in that country, which in turn would increase investment:

We are one of the most corrupt countries in the world. We have the ability to substantially change the way business is conducted in this country. Exposing the abuse of credit can only result in greater liquidity in the market, reduction of the consumer price index which directly translates into increased local and foreign investment. Who wants to invest in a country where no one pays their bills and the legal system is open to debtor manipulation? Basically, our culture has developed into one of gross fiscal irresponsibility. A strong, unencumbered and independent credit bureau is deemed the only sustainable method of changing the way consumers honour their obligations.

This manager cautioned, however, against the wholesale transplanting of the CRA model to sub-Saharan Africa, where he felt a conventional credit agency or bureau would not work. For one thing, "to arrive at a [conventional] credit rating you must have both positive and negative components, and our markets are unwilling to provide positive information [because] the culture dictates that you will steal their customers!"

In the Dominican Republic, a manager emphasized the way credit reporting agencies have equalized access to credit: "One very important and almost always overlooked issue is that the credit reporting system has allowed 'democratized' access to credit, thus to wealth creating mechanisms, heretofore only available to those who were either wealthy to begin with or simply had the 'right connections.'"

In general, the respondents' stated goals and the language they used strongly echo the early U.S. credit reporting pioneers, who also spoke of the positive economic and social benefits that flowed from their services.

3.6   Analysis and Discussion

Credit reporting agencies have come a long way from the 1830s, when they first appeared in New York City to help wholesalers assess the creditworthiness of traders from distant localities, including the country's frontier areas. Yet the original goal of the early CRAs—reducing information asymmetry—remains intact. Recent research has confirmed that CRAs can reduce default rates by improving the ability of creditors to predict outcomes.

At least three areas are worth discussion from a policy perspective: (1) the role that CRAs can play in shaping and transmitting globally consistent business norms, (2) their ability to enhance opportunity, and (3) the proper role of government in establishing CRAs.

3.6.1   Shaping Business Norms

The history of credit reporting agencies provides a vivid example of how institution can shape and standardize business norms. The early U.S. agencies' branch structure became an important mechanism for transmitting and embedding the standards for creditworthiness that were established by New York City merchants. These standards traveled via the CRAs' branch networks to the furthest corners of the continent. Such norms were important because good quantitative information was unavailable, so ideas about which character traits mattered functioned as an effective substitute for information that was either lacking or suspect. Although the methods employed by the pioneer CRAs appear quaint from a modern perspective, it is important to note that the rules about how to operate in a credit-driven economy were simple to understand, and that this fact helped to ensure that they were consistently and widely applied. The agencies thus provided a homogenizing force in a country whose population was constantly supplemented by fresh waves of immigrant entrepreneurs. CRAs also helped to engender a widespread popular understanding about what it takes to succeed in a credit-driven economy.

Today foreign CRAs exhibit a similar pattern, as they strive to emulate the standards and the underlying cultural assumptions of international agencies such as D&B. The managers of these foreign agencies express the desire to educate their native business owners about the standards that prevail in the United States and Europe. This is a significant development because, as the U.S. experience demonstrates, consistent norms can reduce transaction costs by minimizing ambiguity among traders who do not know one another personally. As Douglass North has argued, the existence of clear rules, whether formal or informal, results in enhanced business confidence and a greater willingness to trade.[55]

CRAs also helped to legitimize credit in the public mind. The historical literature demonstrates that credit has often been poorly understood and is prone to being blamed for societal ills, especially during times of economic crisis. Problems with credit have in the past been popularly associated with lax morality and the breakdown of social order, and credit itself has been perceived as a tool of oppression used by the haves against the have-nots.[56] The danger for developing and transitional economies is that business credit could be curtailed by regulators acting out of benign but misinformed motives or to appease a public that traditionally associates credit with social instability, social injustice, or both. In the United States, credit reporting agencies, in association with nonprofit organizations such as the National Association of Credit Men (founded in 1896 and now known as the National Association of Credit Management), have been an important force in legitimizing business credit. They promote the professionalism of credit managers, develop more quantitative methods for assessing risk, monitor legislative, regulatory, and legal developments, and actively promote the interests of business credit grantors.

3.6.2 Enhancing Opportunity

There is evidence that credit reporting agencies tended, sometimes inadvertently, to increase competition and opportunity. The early agencies were third-party providers, meaning that they made information available not just to members of an exclusive industry group (the traditional arrangement) but to any creditor willing to pay the subscription fee. By equalizing the access to information, CRAs may have enlarged the pool of creditors and enhanced competition among them. The appearance of more creditors increased the opportunities available to business owners. Moreover, by making reputations portable, CRAs may have reinforced the dynamism and mobility of American society. As the research on consumer credit by Barron and Staten suggests, the enhanced information made available by credit bureaus in the United States has

[l]owered the prices for other financial products as customers have been freed from their binding relationships with banks and other depository institutions. In the past the customer's own bank was frequently the lowest cost source for a loan because other creditors lacked the information needed to measure risk. Consequently, banks have been forced to become more competitive for customers at all margins. [Bureaus have also made] consumers (and workers) more mobile by reducing the cost of severing established relationships and seeking better opportunities ... the portability of information makes us more open to change. There is less risk associated with severing old relationships and starting new ones, because objective information is available that helps us to establish and build trust more quickly.[57]

It is important to note, too, that the credit reporting industry in the United States was itself characterized by strong competition from an early date. This drove them to cover a large portion of the business population, including the smallest enterprises run by women, African Americans, and members of ethnic and religious minorities. Tens of thousands of these businesses appear in the R. G. Dun ledgers, covering the period 1841–1889. Many small, minority-owned businesses are described, frequently in some detail. There are even reports on black business owners that date from before the Civil War. If inclusion is, in itself, a virtue—because acknowledgment is the first step to legitimacy—then the credit reports can be deemed progressive rather than exclusionary.[58]

The character traits that the early reports emphasized focused on individuals' ability and willingness to pay rather than on their social or political connections. The early credit reports seldom mentioned which political party an individual belonged to, a significant omission during a time when membership in political parties played an important role in the construction of (white) men's social identities.

Nor did the reports tend to note membership in social clubs or churches—again, a noteworthy omission given the crucial position these institutions held, especially in small-town life. By insisting on the primacy of traits such as "honesty" (does the individual make a good faith effort to pay? does the individual pay all suppliers on time?), the agencies helped to embed these values more deeply and thereby opened up opportunities to groups that might otherwise have been excluded from participating fully in market activities because of class, ethnic, or gender barriers.

Clearly, the effectiveness of credit reporting agencies and bureaus in this area can be overstated, and policymakers should note that the system currently has serious shortcomings. Critics have suggested that credit-scoring models commonly used today contain hidden biases against minorities and women. This is because banks that lend to small businesses tend to place a heavy emphasis on the owner's personal credit history, a practice that works against minorities, who tend not to engage in practices—such as taking out home-equity loans—that are more common among whites. Instead, minority business owners are more likely to have accessed loans from community groups, subprime lenders, and local finance companies, which tend not to report their loans to credit bureaus; indeed, some predatory lenders have even withheld good payment records to prevent their customers from seeking refinancing from competitors.

Women are also often subject to bias in the credit markets. For example, many married women do not have credit histories in their own names because their accounts are held in the names of their husbands. Women are also more prone to gaps in employment because of child rearing and other family responsibilities. And because they tend to start their businesses on a less formal basis than men (working from their homes or only part-time), women are more likely to report that their businesses have operated for less than two years, a significant negative in the eyes of lenders.[59] Obviously, problems such as these merit further scrutiny from lenders, credit reporting agencies, and regulators.

3.6.3   Other Institutional Considerations

Before tackling this issue, it is useful to keep in mind that credit reporting agencies already operate in nearly every developing and transitional economy, and that the spread of globalization makes them likely to flourish. In countries such as China that are currently in a state of rapid transition, credit reporting agencies are in a pioneering, highly pliable stage of development. Any policy recommendations must take into account the quickly evolving nature of this industry and its historically high level of responsiveness to changes in the business environment. Nearly all countries today have official bodies that collect information on the largest business establishments; many are also establishing public credit registries to collect data from lending institutions. Yet the information provided by official sources is often inadequate for trade creditors, and this situation provides a substantial opportunity for private organizations.

The American experience suggests that private providers need not be closely monitored by government bodies; however, some effective form of dispute resolution would be desirable as a way to curb abuses. In the United States it was the courts rather than legislatures or official policymaking bodies that functioned as the instruments by which the larger society exerted control over the new agencies. The courts were supplemented by a vigorous press that allowed criticism or support to be aired and debated. In addition, trade organizations such as the National Association of Credit Men (NACM) complemented and supported the work of the agencies through education and lobbying activities. Because the credit profession was not regulated by the states or the federal government, the NACM stepped in to fill the function, and the profession continues to be self-regulating today. These complementary institutions and organizations underlay the work of the agencies; without them, it is doubtful that CRAs could have succeeded to the extent that they did.

Moreover, in the United States, many institutions and infrastructures that were important to commerce worked fairly well even at an early date. These included the post office, the court system, railroads and canals, the market for bonds and commercial paper, banks, and the insurance industry, to name only the most important. American merchants also benefited from a long period of trading with Britain and its other colonies as well as southern Europe and parts of the Far East. The country's trading history began in the seventeenth century and continued when the United States became an independent republic. Today the least developed countries often lack these kinds of robust institutions and infrastructures, and local merchants frequently do not have the experience with overseas trade that American merchants acquired from an early date.

Finally, one must pay attention to the problems that arise when institutions are transplanted from one culture to another. Credit reporting agencies had their origins in the early nineteenth-century United States, whose business environment was characterized by the relative lack of entrenched interests such as an established church, aristocracy, and national military, among others—circumstances that are often not replicated in developing countries today. Credit reporting in the United States evolved along with the country itself and was able to adjust to changing cultural norms and an evolving regulatory and legal environment, which in turn accommodated the innovations introduced by the new institution. Today this kind of extended experimentation is a luxury that is denied to transplanted institutions. Instead, they are forced to prove their effectiveness within a highly compressed time period, during which they must become embedded; that is, locals must view them as endogenous and therefore legitimate, rather than as exogenous entities that have been imposed on them by outsiders.[60]

Appendix 3A.1   Information Provided by CRAs on U.S. Businesses

(The following is an ideal list. Not all of the information is always available.)

• Full company name, address, phone number, SIC classification, addresses of branches (if any), year of incorporation

• Name of chief executive, other officers; their ages, education, and experience

• Sales, net worth, current and fixed assets, current and long-term liabilities, profits; amount of authorized capital, type of capital, and who owns it

• Total employees

• Recent news, such as fires

• Supplier risk score ("predicts likelihood of a firm ceasing business without paying all creditors in full, or reorganizing, or obtaining relief from creditors under state/federal law over the next eighteen months.")

· Incidence of financial stress (compares the company with the national average and with companies in its industry segment)

· Company's payment history (i.e., incidence of slow payments); evidence of open suits, liens, or judgments, along with details

· Quick ratio (current assets minus inventory divided by current liabilities); comparison to others in its industry

· Whether business owns its facilities; description

· Ratio of accounts payable as percentage of sales; comparison to others in its industry

· Return on assets; comparison to others in its industry

· Ratio of total liabilities to net worth; comparison to others in its industry

· Financial appraisal ranking (a calculated average of the supplier's quartile ranking based on the available ratios)

· Number of customer accounts, collection terms, market territory, seasonal or nonseasonal

· Whether candidate for government programs, based on socioeconomic factors (e.g., small business, minority-owned, women-owned)

Source: Based on sample report provided by Dun & Bradstreet online at ⟨www.dnb.com⟩, 2000.

Appendix 3A.2   Information Provided by CRAs in Developing and Transitional Economies

(This is an ideal list. Not all of the information is always available, and some countries restrict access to some types of information, such as bank accounts.)

· Company name, address and phone number, ownership structure, nationality, line of business, principal brands

· Executive officers: their ages, place of birth, marital status, education

· Business history: where and when established, range of products

· Relevant local economic and industry conditions

• Financial information: total capitalization, revenues, profit, fixed and current assets, current liabilities, shareholder equity

• Financial ratios: net margin, profitability, leverage, liquidity, solvency

• Auditors and bankers, insurance coverage

• Terms of payment (i.e., percentage of its supplies bought for cash vs. credit, terms of credit) and sales (i.e., percentage it sells on cash vs. credit, terms of credit)

• Payment history; names of trade references

• Names of closest competitors

• Key customers and sales territory

• Whether seasonal or nonseasonal

• Imports and exports

• Number of plants and warehouses; location and appearance; capacity utilization; whether owned or leased, equipment owned (such as trucks, computers)

• Number of employees

• Legal record

Sources: Based on sample reports provided on-line by Profancresa-PCR (Mexico) and Delos Infocenter (Romania), 2000. The reports can be found on-line at ⟨www.alaic.com/mex⟩ and ⟨www.delos.ro⟩, respectively.

Appendix 3A.3   Responses to Survey Conducted by Author, September–October 2000

Question 1: What types of clients use your service most?

Question 2: In your experience, what is the most reliable source of information for determining the creditworthiness of a business? Is it easy or difficult to get this information?

Table 3A

Country	Customers: Local or foreign?	Typical lines of business?
Argentina	50% local, 50% foreign	Foreign: export credit insurance companies Local: banks and other financial
Chile	65% local	Manufacturers, insurance companies, dealers, etc.
China	Mostly foreign	Credit reporting agencies, companies that are partly or wholly foreign-owned, international trade
Dominican Republic	Mostly local	
India	Foreign	Export credit insurance, credit reporting agencies
Kenya	Mostly local	
Lithuania	Mostly foreign	Credit insurance
Mexico	80% local	
Thailand	80% foreign	Lawyers, commercial companies, and credit reporting agencies
Ukraine	Mostly foreign	Insurance companies, banks, big foreign companies doing business with Ukrainian partners

Country	Types of information sought	Difficult to obtain?
Argentina	Recent financial statement, good description of payment record, clear business history of firm and owners	Can access central bank database for some of this information
Chile	Financial statements, payment records	Not easy to find this information; however, can obtain some information on banks, big companies, insurance companies, from Superintendent of Stock Companies
China	Financial statements considered most important, although these are often unreliable	Very difficult to get directly from company interviews. Some agencies can get statements from local/state Administration of Industry and Commerce (AIC). But this information is not open to the public. At present, we get this from the AIC through lawyers, which is expensive
Dominican Republic	Past payment of obligations is primary, then financials, commercial references, interviews	Very difficult; about 40% of the time not even possible

Table 3A
(continued)

Country	Types of information sought	Difficult to obtain?
India	Financial information, background information, market conditions, etc.	Often extremely difficult since there are no public records available for nonincorporated companies, and on incorporated companies, the extent of the information available at the Registry of Companies is quite often incomplete
Kenya	Bad debt information only	Very difficult. No company will give you their monthly accounts receivable, plus most companies keep five sets of books, one for the tax man, one for the owners, etc.
Lithuania	Financial statements, payment records, interviews with management	Very difficult. Information is insufficient, as most government institutions keep data not in computers or other digital form, but on simple paper blanks.
Mexico	Financial statements, trade references, location description, products, commercial activities, insurance	Obtain information through fieldwork, to make sure company actually exists. Most difficult to obtain is the financial. No place in Mexico where companies have by law to send their statements. Insecurity in the country makes owners unwilling to share their financial information for fear of being robbed or abducted
Thailand	Financial statements taken from the ministry, background checks of directors	Some information not easy to obtain
Ukraine	Registration and financial data	Very difficult. Most reliable source is Ministry of Statistics. Management often strictly refuse to give any information, particularly financial

Source: Survey conducted by author, September–October 2000. The respondents were guaranteed anonymity.

Acknowledgments

The author wishes to thank Alexander Dyck, Roumeen Islam, and Margaret Miller for their comments on earlier drafts of this chapter.

Notes

1. Roy A. Foulke, *The Sinews of American Commerce* (New York: Dun & Bradstreet, 1941).

2. Greig, C. McNeil, *The Growth of Credit Information: A History of UAPT-Infolink plc.* (Oxford, U.K.: Blackwell Publishers, 1992). Today, industry groups flourish as important mechanisms for information sharing. They do not compete with credit reporting agencies so much as provide overlapping and complementary services. Some industry groups are run independently while others operate under the auspices of larger trade groups such as the National Association of Credit Management. Some are affiliated with credit reporting agencies; D&B, for example, sponsors several such forums. In the United States, these "interchange groups" must be monitored by an outside party to ensure that the information complies with antitrust regulations.

3. William H. Becker, "American Wholesale Hardware Trade Associations, 1870–1900," *Business History Review* XLV, no. 2 (summer 1971): 179–200; Peter P. Wahlstad, *Credit and the Credit Man* (New York: Alexander Hamilton Institute, 1917), 125; E. M. Skinner, "Essentials in Credit Management," *Credits, Collections & Finance: Organizing the Work, Correct Policies and Methods; Five Credit and Collection Systems* (Chicago: A. W. Shaw Co., 1914), 16–17; B. H. Blanton, *Credits: Its Principles and Practices* (New York: Ronald Press Co., 1915), 99–100; William A. Prendergast, *Credit and Its Uses* (New York: D. Appleton-Century Co., Inc., 1906), 203.

4. Recent studies of female, African American, and ethnic business owners that have made extensive use of nineteenth-century credit reports include Wendy Gamber, *The Female Economy: The Millinery and Dressmaking Trades, 1860–1930* (Urbana, Ill.: University of Illinois Press, 1997); Juliet E. K. Walker, *The History of Black Business in America: Capitalism, Race, Entrepreneurship* (New York: Macmillan Library Reference USA, 1998); and Elliott Ashkenazi, *The Business of Jews in Louisiana, 1840–1875* (Tuscaloosa: University of Alabama Press, 1988).

5. See Harry L. Watson, *Liberty and Power: The Politics of Jacksonian America* (New York: Hill and Wang, 1990).

6. Ralph W. Hidy, "Credit Rating Before Dun and Bradstreet," *Bulletin of the Business Historical Society* 13 (December 1939): 84–88; Lewis E. Atherton, "The Problem of Credit-Rating in the Antebellum South," *Journal of Southern History* 12 (November 1946): 534–556.

7. Daniel B. Klein, "Credit Information Reporting: Why Free Speech is Vital to Social Accountability and Consumer Opportunity," p. 5. Available at *http://lsb.scu.edu/faculty/creditreporting.html*. (Klein is associate professor of economics at the University of California, Santa Clara, and he is the editor of *Reputation: Studies in the Voluntary Elicitation of Good Conduct*.) Until the 1870s the Mercantile Agency transmitted the information orally; that is, a representative from the subscriber's office would go to the agency in person to obtain the information. This was done because the agency feared

lawsuits. By the mid-1870s, this was no longer felt to be an issue. The invention of the typewriter and use of carbon paper allowed the reports to be produced in multiple copies, resulting in much greater efficiencies.

8. See chapter 8.

9. R. G. Dun Historical Collection, Baker Library, Harvard Business School. On the history of credit reporting, and of R. G. Dun in particular, see James D. Norris, *R. G. Dun & Co. 1841–1900: The Development of Credit-Reporting in the Nineteenth Century* (Westport, Conn.: The Greenwood Press, 1978); James H. Madison, "The Evolution of Commercial Credit Reporting Agencies in Nineteenth Century America," *Business History Review* 48 (summer 1974), 164–186; Bertram Wyatt-Brown, "God and Dun & Bradstreet, 1841–1851," *Business History Review* 40 (winter 1966), 432–450; Owen Sheffield, "The Mercantile Agency . . . A Private History," 3 vols., Dun & Bradstreet, privately printed, 1965.

10. Norris, *R. G. Dun & Co.*, p. 189 n. 68. On the transformation of the American economy, and especially of the role of distributors, see Glenn Porter and Harold Livesay, *Merchants and Manufacturers: Studies in the Changing Structure of Nineteenth-Century Marketing* (Baltimore: Johns Hopkins University Press, 1971).

11. See chapter 5.

12. D&B, Supplier Evaluation Report Sample, obtained from ⟨www.dnb.com⟩, 1999. Obtaining this information is neither easy nor cheap. Not only must D&B expend effort to collect the data; once collected, it must convert numerous diverse reporting formats into a consistent one. Jarl G. Kallberg and Gregory F. Udell, "The Value of Private Sector Credit Information Sharing: The U.S. Case," unpublished paper, June 7, 2000, p. 5n.7.

13. Some industries, such as construction, remain extremely fragmented. Obtaining good financial information on companies in these industries remains difficult, even for the large agencies.

14. Of the 62 million companies in its database in 2000, 45 million were active and 17 million were inactive (D&B provided only historical information on these companies). D&B delivers its reports in a variety of formats, depending on the need (and budget) of its clients. These products and services continue to evolve in response to the changing business climate.

15. Judging individuals, particularly men, primarily on the basis of their character rather than on financial statements was a powerful cultural idea that changed very slowly, and it persevered even into the early twentieth century. See Judy Hilkey, *Character Is Capital: Success Manuals and Manhood in Gilded Age America* (Chapel Hill: The North Carolina Press, 1997).

16. Firms reporting to D&B provide income statement data much less often than balance sheet data. Kallberg and Udell, "The Value of Private Sector Credit Information Sharing," pp. 19, 23.

17. Elijah W. Morgan, correspondence with American Collecting Agency. Morgan Family Papers, ca. 1830–1900, Box 1, Michigan Historical Collections, Bentley Historical Library, Ann Arbor.

18. See chapter 1.

19. These were compiled from a number of contemporary books and articles. See especially Samuel H. Terry, *The Retailer's Manual* (Newark, N.J.: Jennings Bros., 1869).

20. In some cases, the credit reporting agencies' norms were forcibly imposed. This was the case with immigrant Jews, the only group that managed to form business networks that resisted the agencies' demands for transparency. See Rowena Olegario, "'That Mysterious People'": Jewish Merchants, Transparency, and Community in Mid-Nineteenth Century America," *Business History Review* 73 (spring 1999): 161–190.

21. Norris, *R. G. Dun & Co.*, chapter 4. Norris overstates the extent to which the reference books replaced the descriptive reports. The reports continued to be important sources of information. See Madison, "The Evolution of Commercial Credit Reporting Agencies in Nineteenth Century America," p. 174, and B. H. Blanton, *Credits: Its Principles and Practices* (New York: Ronald Press Co., 1915), p. 82.

22. Madison, "The Evolution of Commercial Credit Reporting Agencies in Nineteenth Century America," pp. 177–182; Norris, *R. G. Dun & Co.*, pp. 54, 132–133; *Beardsley v. Tappan*, 5 Blatchf. 498 (1867); *Ormsby v. Douglass*, 37 N.Y. 484 (1868).

23. Dun & Bradstreet company Web site ⟨www.dnb.com⟩, 1999; company annual report, 1998, frontispiece.

24. Due to a paucity of historical data, the exact market shares of the leading players are unknown.

25. See chapter 5.

26. On September 30, 2000, D&B spun off its Moody's credit rating subsidiary into a separate publicly traded company. Its 2000 annual report restated the revenues of previous years to make them compatible.

27. Roy C. Smith and Ingro Walter, "Rating Agencies: Is There an Agency Issue?" Paper presented at The Role of Credit Reporting Systems in the International Economy, a conference sponsored by the World Bank, New York University, and the University of Maryland, Washington, D.C., March 1–2, 2001, p. 3.

28. "Evaluating the Bond-Rating Agencies," *Financial Times*, May 27, 1997, p. 2.

29. Joyce R. Ochs and Kenneth L. Parkinson, "Using Credit Screening to Manage Credit Risk," *Business Credit*, March 1998, pp. 22, 24–27; Jeff Brill, "The Importance of Credit Scoring Models in Improving Cash Flow and Collections," *Business Credit*, January 1998, pp. 16–17; Michael G. Ash, "Analyzing Credit Information: What You See Isn't Always What You Get," *Business Credit*, March 1996, pp. 7–8.

30. "Online Credit-Rating Reports Are Not Always Credible," *Los Angeles Times*, August 19, 1998, part D, p. 6.

31. "Survey—FT Exporter," *Financial Times*, June 1, 2000, p. 4.

32. Timothy J. Sinclair, "Reinventing Global Authority: Embedded Knowledge Networks and the New Global Finance," *Environment and Planning C: Government and Policy 2000* 18: 487–502, p. 496.

33. U.S. Department of Commerce, *Credit and Financial Issues: Responsive Business Approaches to Consumer Needs*, May 1995.

34. National Association of Credit Management, newsletter, n.d., at ⟨www.nacm.org⟩, 2000.

35. See chapter 8.

36. Daniel B. Klein, "Credit Information Reporting," pp. 2–3.

37. "Tagging Deadbeats is Big Business," *Crain's Chicago Business*, November 18, 1996, p. 15.

38. See chapter 8.

39. Creditworthy, a private firm, has compiled one of the most complete publicly available global directories of CRAs. Yet a comparison with the directory compiled by the U.K. firm Creditsafe showed little duplication, indicating that neither list is exhaustive.

40. See chapter 1.

41. There are exceptions. For example, China ProDiligence (based in Vancouver, Canada) describes itself as having been "established with the support of the Chinese authorities." Its shareholders include the China Industrial and Commercial Enterprises Consultants (under the State Administration for Industry and Commerce), the China International Tax Consultancy Corporation (under the State Administration of Taxation), the China International Commercial Information Centre (under the State Bureau of Internal Trade), and the China Financial Information and Consultancy (under the People's Bank of China). See the company's Web site, ⟨www.prodiligence.com⟩. Keppel Communications, one of Southeast Asia's leading telecommunications and logistics providers, is 33 percent owned by the Singapore government. In early 2000, Keppel agreed to form a 50–50 joint venture with New Zealand's BayCorp to build on-line credit information bureaus throughout Asia. Keppel also has an interest in a Thai internet company, Anew, which has an online business venture with D&B.

42. See chapter 1. The manager of a Mexican-based credit reporting agency, however, states that public and private bureaus in that country "do not carry any information regarding commercial transactions" and "will not provide any other verified topics [such as] present locations, present board of directors, trade references, etc." These observations were in response to a survey conducted by the author, September–October 2000.

43. See chapter 1.

44. "Savvy Exporters Do Credit Checks," *Journal of Commerce*, May 3, 2000, p. 10.

45. "Asian Firms Seek Stamp of Approval from D&B," *Journal of Commerce*, December 17, 1998, p. 2A.

46. Response to survey conducted by author, September–October 2000.

47. See chapter 1.

48. See appendix 3A.3, survey question 1.

49. "Savvy Exporters Do Credit Checks," p. 10.

50. Based on information on the web sites of international credit reporting agencies linked to Creditworthy.com.

51. See appendix 3A.3, survey question 2.

52. The Web sites of Latin American credit reporting agencies, accessible through Creditworthy.com, warn about the restrictions on bank data.

53. See chapter 1.

54. Lynnette Warman, "An Overview of Legal Issues Impacting Collections in Mexico and Latin America," *Business Credit*, November–December 1999, pp. 36–39; Les Kirschbaum, "Managing Risks by Selling Internationally on Open Account," *Business Credit*, January 1996, pp. 13–15.

55. Douglass C. North, *Institutions, Institutional Change and Economic Performance* (New York: Cambridge University Press, 1990).

56. In the United States, the issue of credit was most politicized during the "bank wars" of the 1830s. The technical issue involved was whether banks should be liberal or conservative in issuing bank notes, which at the time constituted the country's currency. There is a large literature on this topic. See especially Watson, *Liberty and Power*, and Bray Hammond, *Banks and Politics in America From the Revolution to the Civil War* (Princeton: Princeton University Press, 1957). Other works that discuss how credit became closely tied to political, social, or religious issues include Rosa-Maria Gelpi and Francois Julien-Labruyere, *The History of Consumer Credit: Doctrines and Practices*, trans. Mn Liam Gavin (Basingstoke, U.K.: Macmillan Press Ltd., 2000); Lendol Calder, *Financing the American Dream: A Cultural History of Consumer Credit* (Princeton: Princeton University Press, 1999), and Julian Hoppit, "Attitudes to Credit in Britain, 1680–1790," *Historical Journal* 33 (June 1990): 305–322.

57. See chapter 8.

58. This is not to suggest that the reports were free of bigotry; on the contrary, they are filled with descriptions of Jews, African Americans, and other "peripheral" business owners that are deeply offensive to modern sensibilities. But in the context of nineteenth century society, the reports can be seen as progressive. They are mostly respectful of and frequently complimentary about female business owners, for example; that is, they legitimized women's participation in business during a time when most women were barred from engagement in the political sphere.

59. "No Credit Where Credit is Due," *Business Week*, May 22, 2000, p. F50.

60. Sinclair, "Reinventing Global Authority," p. 489.

II

The Role of Credit Reporting Data in Financial Systems

4

Credit Information and Market Performance: The Case of Chile

Kevin Cowan and José De Gregorio

4.1 Introduction

A common assumption of theoretical studies on lending is that consumers (or entrepreneurs) applying for a loan are better informed than the lenders about their capacity to repay their loans (or the quality of the projects they are borrowing for). This information asymmetry leads to the issues of moral hazard and adverse selection. Informational asymmetry, however, is not exogenous and lenders can develop mechanisms to improve their knowledge about borrower characteristics or actions. In this context, a growing literature has focused on the theory and empirical evidence of the role of credit bureaus, and more generally, information sharing in credit markets. The literature discusses both the effects of information sharing on the credit market and the incentives that exist for lenders to share information on a voluntary basis. It also addressees the role of the public sector in information sharing. Should the government promote or enforce information sharing? What role does the government have in protecting consumer privacy? How does information sharing relate to the governments' role as a regulator of the banking system?

Although there is a growing literature on information sharing, very little work has been done on this issue in the Chilean case.[1] Fuentes and Maquieria (1998) analyze the wider issue of determinants of loan repayment in Chile. They discuss the evolution of the Chilean banking sector and different aspects that affect loan repayment, mainly: (1) limitations on access to credit, (2) the degree of macroeconomic stability, (3) type of loan collection technology, (4) the bankruptcy code, (5) the existence of information sharing agreements, (6) characteristics of the judicial system, and (7) the effect of major changes in financial market regulation. A time series study of the Chilean banking sector since the 1960s concludes that information sharing is one of the variables that has had a significant (positive) effect on the level of banking sector loans.[2] Additional time series regressions show a positive impact of information sharing on defaults.

This chapter attempts to address the following issues.

First, what are the effects of information sharing on Chilean banking loans? This question seeks to answer how existing cross-country results carry through in a time series setting for a country that has experienced an important development of its banking system in the last twenty years. For this purpose, time series behavior of consumer loans is analyzed.

Second, what are the roles of the public credit registry (PCR) in Chile? Specifically, interest here is in determining to what degree information collected for regulation purposes is also distributed and used by lenders. To put this question in context, the evolution of the banking sector and banking supervision over the past two to three decades is briefly described.

Third, what information needs to be shared between lenders? Is the existing combination of negative or positive information necessary?[3] Could recent changes in the laws governing information disclosure hurt the banking system? Answers to these questions will also shed light on the incentives that exist for department stores to participate in providing positive information. These issues are examined here by evaluating a cross-section of consumer information currently available in the banking system.

Fourth, in Chile a growing amount of credit is being intermediated outside the banking system, mainly by department stores. The stores do not share information through the PCR, and although this sector is not subject to banking supervision (for the obvious reason that they lend their "own" money), there is the issue of whether they should share information, which may allow a more accurate evaluation of bank's customers. This issue has been particularly debated in Chile. Unfortunately, there is not enough data to rigorously address these issues here, but it is an important area where data could help to evaluate different proposals.

The chapter proceeds as follows. Section 4.2 briefly reviews the theoretical and empirical literature that underlies our investigation. Section 4.3 describes the institutional setting of information sharing in Chile. Section 4.4 provides an overview of the Chilean banking system over the past years, focusing on aggregate behavior and the regulatory framework. Section 4.5 estimates the effects of information sharing on the volume of consumer credit in Chile in the 1980s and 1990s. Section 4.6 is a cross-section study on a database of 3,000 consumers which evaluates and discusses the capacity that different subsets of information have for predicting default among consumers. Finally, section 4.7 concludes.

4.2   Information Sharing and the Credit Market

A credit bureau (CB) is characterized by the voluntary exchange of information among lenders.[4] The bureau collects the information provided by its members and combines it with other sources to produce an applicant's credit report. CBs are based on the principle of reciprocity; only those lenders who comply and provide adequate and timely information on their debtors are granted access to the credit reports. Public credit registries (PCRs), on the other hand, are set up by the economic authorities and participation is compulsory. Lenders are required by law to provide information to the PCR, and in turn they are allowed access to consolidated credit information.

The information shared among lenders can be of two main types: negative information refers to past defaults or arrears, while positive information includes detailed reports of the applicants' current assets and liabilities, income and employment, and guarantees in which the applicant is involved.

What are the implications of existing models of credit information sharing on the loan market?[5] First, by favorably altering borrowers incentives, information sharing will induce greater levels of effort by debtors and reduce nonpayment. Second, the effect of CBs on the volumes of loans is ambiguous (and thus an interesting empirical question), and depends on the degree of competition among creditors. Third, increased information sharing will translate into a greater variance on interest rates within loan categories as banks and finance houses adjust the price of credit to suit their more exact estimates of debtor characteristics. Theoretical research also generates predictions about the creation of CBs and the structure of information sharing: (1) Private credit information sharing should develop in countries with large credit markets, high mobility of households, and lower levels of competition among credit providers. (2) Participation in CBs should increase as the costs of information sharing decrease and as information accumulates in the bureau. (3) CBs will usually be few in number, possibly only one due to economies of scale. This chapter concentrates on the effects of information sharing on the loan market.

Empirical studies on credit information sharing fall into two categories: (1) macroeconomic cross-section or time series studies that evaluate the impact of information sharing on aggregate dimensions of the credit market; and (2) microeconomic studies that discuss the effects of different measures of information sharing on the capacity of lenders to correctly predict creditor default.

Jappelli and Pagano (1998), based on data from an international survey of CBs and PCRs, test various implications discussed earlier. They find that breadth of credit markets is positively associated with information sharing. In particular they find that the consumer credit market is broader in countries where CBs exist, the positive effect on loan volume of CBs and PCRs increases with the number of years the credit bureau has been in place, and provision of both negative and positive information contributes to higher loan volumes. They also find weaker evidence that public and private credit information sharing reduces defaults. On the rise of private credit information sharing, Jappelli and Pagano find that CBs are more likely to rise if borrowers are mobile, protection of credit rights is weak, and banking competition is lower. This last variable indicates that incentives for information sharing are higher when additional nonfinancial costs are higher.[6]

4.3   Credit Information in Chile

Credit information in Chile is provided by a mixture of private and public institutions that collect and process information on both a voluntary and obligatory basis. Both positive and negative credit information is available. Most information is collected by public institutions that then make it available either to the general public or in the case of reserved information; to financial institutions. Private companies have evolved that collect this information from the different public sources, process it, and complement it with privately collected data. These companies are not CBs—they do not collect data directly from lenders or financial institutions—but they have been an important aspect of the loan market in Chile during recent years. An interesting feature of Chilean legislation, the existence of a unique tax identification number (RUT) assigned to all individuals and companies, allows information from different sources to be merged easily and accurately by these companies or the financial institutions themselves. A summary of institutions and their role in providing information is shown in table 4.1.

The bank regulators, the Superintendence of Banks and Finance Houses (SBIF) keeps a permanent record of all persons and companies that hold debts within the financial system.[7] Financial institutions are obliged to provide individual debt information on a monthly basis, which is then checked for internal consistency, aggregated by the SBIF, and returned to the banks and finance houses. Financial institutions accessing what is effectively a PCR know the total amount of debt each borrower (or potential client) holds, but not the creditor institutions involved. This last issue is important when it comes to determining costs and benefits of the information sharing system; under the existing framework, information about a bank's client base is not revealed to competitors. The PCR provides information on total and unpaid debt so that both positive and negative information on individuals and companies is available. For privacy purposes this information can only be accessed by the same financial institutions that surrender the information and by individuals who wish to know their personal credit record. Retail stores providing credit to customers cannot access the SBIF database.[8]

In addition to the information in the PCR maintained by the SBIF, there are a series of other sources of information. A commonly used source of negative information is the *Boletin de Informes Comerciales* published on a weekly basis by the Chamber of Commerce. It contains comprehensive current and historic information on bad checks and overdue bills of exchange with the financial system and with nonfinancial companies and individuals. Information is provided by banks and public notaries and consolidated by the Chamber of Commerce. This information is publicly available.

Not all credit granted in Chile is registered in the SBIF database. Retail stores grant close to 20 percent of consumption credit. Information on current outstanding debt and credit lines granted by the stores is not available. The *Boletin de Morosos del Comercio*, however, set-up in the 1990s by seven of the largest department stores, contains information on individuals who have arrears in any of these stores.

Table 4.1
Sources of credit information in Chile

Institution	Information provided	Who provides information

SBIF	Total debt of individuals and companies in the financial system classified:
	  By type: consumption, commercial, and mortgage
	  By status: up to date, overdue, and defaults
	  Direct and indirect: whether the debt is as a guarantor to third-party debt
	Information on people who are prohibited from opening a current account
		Banks and financial companies

Central Bank	Information on people who have not paid fines or who have been prosecuted due to violations in international trade law	Central bank
Official paper	Record of new companies, legal amendments to charters, lists of partners in firms	Affected parties

National Chamber of Commerce	Current bad checks and overdue bills of exchange
	  By type of document: check, bill of exchange, etc.
	  By face value of document
	Historic bad checks and overdue bills of exchange
	  By type: cleared, rectified[a], or not payed after five years
	Information on companies that have violated labor laws
		Notaries and banks

	Morosos del Comercio Arrears with the seven largest department stores	Department stores

a. Refers to a mistake that has been cleared by the corresponding institution.

The main private company operating in the credit information sector (DICOM) was set up in 1979 by the National Chamber of Commerce and private entrepreneurs. Initially DICOM provided clients with four categories of information: information in the *Boletin de Informes Comerciales* (Chamber of Commerce), address verification, job verification (self-generated), and information on arrears in department stores from SICOM (consolidated system of defaulted credit from department stores). The debt information provided was negative. Then, in the early 1980s DICOM was awarded a public bid to provide information services to the SBIF.[9] Finally, in 1989 DICOM established individual contracts with banks and finance houses to process the reserved information distributed by the SBIF to the banks. Currently DICOM offers on-line information to banks and finance houses from the following eight databases:

1. Tax identification number (RUT). Provides information about an applicants name, RUT, and whether the RUT belongs to a person or a company or organization. All information queries through DICOM are made with the RUT.

2. Residence registry and verification. Generated by DICOM, it provides information on the applicant's address, verification of the address, type of construction, area, time of residence, and basic information on the residents.

3. Report registry. Keeps track of the number of times information has been requested for a particular applicant in the preceding three months.

4. Prohibited from opening current accounts. Informs on people who are prohibited (for legal reasons) from opening a current account.

5. Current bad checks and overdue bills of exchange. From *Boletin de Informes Comerciales*.

6. Consolidated debt in the banking system. The information obtained from the PCR.

7. Historical registry of bad checks and overdue bills of exchange. From the *Boletin de Informes Comerciales*.

8. Credit score. DICOM also provides a credit score.

DICOM receives an average of 600,000 information requests each month. The total number of companies and individuals in the global database system is close to 2.5 million.

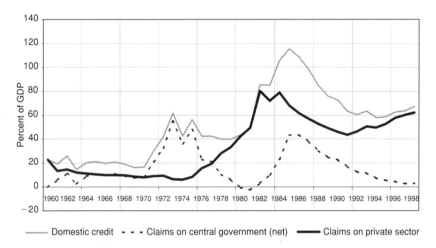

Figure 4.1
Evolution of the Chilean banking sector, 1960–1998
Source: IMF International Financial Statistics and Central Bank.

4.4   The Chilean Banking Sector[10]

4.4.1   The Past Twenty Years

Chile began a process of financial deregulation in 1974.[11] Before the reforms, interest rates where fixed and credit was directed, entry was restricted and reserve requirements were high and uneven. Virtually all financial institutions had been nationalized between 1970 and 1973. The result was an extremely narrow financial market.

Figure 4.1 shows the evolution of two aggregate measures of banking sector development—total domestic credit and claims of banks on the private sector. As shown in the figure, although domestic credit expanded in the early 1970s, most of the loans where directed at the government with claims on the private sector falling to below 10 percent of GDP in 1974.

In the first stage of reform barriers to entry were relaxed, and finance houses (*financieras*) were allowed to operate without the interest rate restrictions placed on banks. In the next stage, the ceiling on bank interest rates was lifted, banks were privatized and foreign banks were allowed to open branches in Chile.

The privatization of state banks started in 1975 and by 1978 only one bank, the *Banco del Estado*, remained under state control. Entry barriers were relaxed in two stages. During 1974 foreign banks were allowed to begin operations in Chile. In that same year *financieras* were allowed to operate. In 1977, foreign investment in domestic banks was allowed. Interest rates were partially deregulated in 1974 and by December 1975 were freed completely. Reserve requirements were gradually relaxed, leveling out at 10 percent and 4 percent for sight and time deposits respectively. Financing sources were also subject to reform. 1977 marks the beginning of a period where restrictions on international financing of banks was gradually reduced. By April 1980 most restrictions were abolished.

Financial intermediation grew rapidly in the period following the reforms. By 1982 claims on the private sector had grown to over 70 percent of GDP. In the same period the number of banks and finance houses increased from twenty-one to forty-nine.[12]

The process of reform, however, failed to provide adequate regulation and supervision in the context of implicit guarantees, so that the economic crisis of the early 1980s lead to serious difficulties in the financial system.[13] Weak collateral, excessive concentration of lending (particularly to related companies or conglomerates called *grupos*), and most importantly deficient information on the (low) quality of bank assets are some of the elements cited behind the crisis. Particularly relevant here is the fact that the SBIF did not introduce a method to classify loans according to risk, and therefore correctly measure the value of the loans, until 1980. Thus, neither the public nor the regulators had accurate measures of the quality of bank portfolios with which to judge profitability or solvency of the banks. It is estimated that up to 30 percent of all banks' credits in 1982 were not able to be paid back. As a result of this crisis, bank claims on the private sector fell to 40 percent of GDP by 1986 only to approach precrisis levels in the mid-1990s.

Reactions to the crisis involved a series of temporary measures aimed at supporting the ailing financial system and the development of a new regulatory framework for the banking sector, including a new banking law, which was enacted in 1986.[14] One objective of the law was to minimize government intervention by encouraging self-regulation; transparent and timely information is a key aspect if depositors are to self-select financial institutions based on their financial soundness. In addition to self-regulation, the SBIF initiated close supervision to minimize the risk of insolvency. The reforms also looked to eliminate many of the practices that had led to problems in the past, such as concentration of lending and lending to related groups.

All of these policies required timely and detailed information on loans. Thus, a large part of information currently available to lenders is the result of regulatory changes that took place in response to a severe banking crisis. As discussed above, this information was available to the banking sector since 1986; however, it was not until 1989 that DICOM started systematically processing and distributing this information.

4.4.2 The Current Situation

Table 4.2 provides an overview of bank and financial company credit during the period 1986–1998 in which total loans grew by 165 percent. The highest growing segment of banking system loans was consumption credit, which grew tenfold, followed by housing loans, which tripled during the period. Due to the high rate of growth, consumption credits expanded from close to 2 percent of total loans in 1986 to approximately 10 percent in 1998. Housing loans in 1998 made up 15 percent of total loans compared to 10 percent in 1986.

An interesting characteristic of the Chilean credit market, and in particular of consumption loans, is the importance of nonbanking sector loans.[15] Unfortunately data on these loans is scarce and limited to the last five years. Table 4.3 summarizes available information on nonbanking loans for this period. Department store loans accounted for 21.2 percent of total consumption loans in 1998, up from 11.1 percent in 1993.

By international standards, nonperforming loans in the Chilean banking system are extremely low. According to available data, they are among the lowest in the world.[16] Figure 4.2 shows the decline in arrears during the 1986–1998 period. Loan losses fell from 11.6 percent to 2 percent and loans past due drop from 5.7 percent to 1.9 percent despite large fluctuations in economic activity.

Currently, Chile is one of the developing countries with the largest banking sector (measured in terms of banks loans to the private sector over GDP). La Porta et al. (1997) estimate the effect of legal rules and law enforcement on capital and debt markets. Based on the cross-country regressions carried out in their paper (which include levels and rates of growth of GDP), the fitted value of debt over GDP corresponding to Chile is estimated in table 4.4. The result—53 percent—is lower than the observed value of 63 percent.

Table 4.2
Composition of bank and financial corporation credit, 1986–1998

	Real loans (1986 = 100)[a]				Annual percent change				Percent of total loans		
	Con-sumption	Com-mercial	Housing	Total	Con-sumption	Com-mercial	Housing	Total	Con-sumption	Com-mercial	Housing
1986	100.0	100.0	100.0	100.0					2.2	74.6	10.3
1987	116.4	101.0	101.1	101.3	16.4	1.0	1.1	1.3	2.6	74.4	10.3
1988	146.5	108.6	105.5	109.7	25.8	7.6	4.4	8.3	3.0	73.9	9.9
1989	187.2	117.1	127.8	120.2	27.8	7.8	21.0	9.6	3.5	72.6	11.0
1990	192.9	113.5	166.5	120.1	3.0	-3.1	30.3	-0.1	3.6	70.5	14.3
1991	211.3	107.8	176.5	117.8	9.6	-5.0	6.0	-1.9	4.0	68.3	15.5
1992	308.8	124.2	189.2	135.3	46.1	15.2	7.2	14.8	5.1	68.5	14.4
1993	467.4	146.3	204.3	158.4	51.4	17.7	8.0	17.1	6.5	68.9	13.3
1994	572.4	155.1	226.8	171.8	22.5	6.0	11.0	8.5	7.4	67.3	13.6
1995	715.9	167.4	258.7	191.0	25.1	7.9	14.1	11.2	8.3	65.4	14.0
1996	945.7	188.5	309.8	220.3	32.1	12.6	19.7	15.3	9.5	63.8	14.5
1997	1195.8	202.7	363.9	246.4	26.5	7.5	17.5	11.9	10.8	61.3	15.2
1998	1258.3	226.3	413.7	273.9	5.2	11.7	13.7	11.1	10.2	61.6	15.6
Average 1986–1990					23.5	7.0	12.6	8.8	3.0	73.2	11.2
Average 1991–1998					17.8	3.2	13.6	4.7	7.7	65.6	14.5
Average 1986–1998					26.4	9.0	12.1	10.9	5.9	68.5	13.2

Source: Authors calculations based on SBIF information.
a. Deflated by CPI.
Consumption credit: short- and long-term credit, and reprogrammed consumer credits.
Housing: *creditos hipotecarios vivienda, hipotecarios endosables vivienda, letras credito vivienda, dividendos hipotecarios reprogramados.*
Commercial: short- and long-term comercial loans, short- and long-term foreign trade loans, reprogramed productive loans, general use mortgage loans, and *efectos comercio.*

Table 4.3
Nonfinancial loans in Chile, 1993–1998

	Consumption loans				Total loans[a]	
	Stock of loans in mm $ December 1997					
	Department stores	Banks and financial corporations	Total	Department stores/Total	Department stores/Total	Consumption loans/Total
	1	2	3	1/3 (%)	(%)	(%)
April 1993	98,462.1	791,587.3	890,049.4	11.1	0.8	7.0
April 1994	198,283.0	1,016,759.6	1,215,042.6	16.3	1.4	8.6
April 1995	308,003.8	1,226,922.0	1,534,925.8	20.1	2.1	10.0
April 1996	400,839.7	1,617,229.7	2,018,069.4	19.9	2.3	11.4
April 1997	530,982.6	2,108,357.3	2,639,340.0	20.1	2.7	13.1
April 1998	629,078.3	2,339,315.6	2,968,393.9	21.2	2.8	13.0

Sources: Chamber of Commerce and SBIF.
a. Net lending among financial corporations and banks.

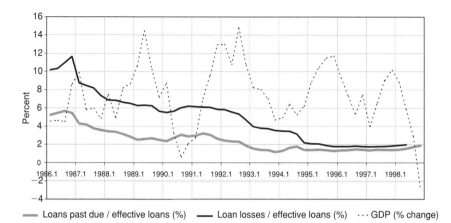

— Loans past due / effective loans (%)   — Loan losses / effective loans (%)   ··· GDP (% change)

Figure 4.2
Nonpayment in the Chilean banking system, 1986.1–1998.4
Source: Fuentes and Maquieria (1998).

Table 4.4
Debt/GNP fitted and actual values

Variable[a]	Estimated coefficients (a)	Variable values (b)	(c) = (a) ∗ (b)	Average value complete sample[b]
GDP growth	0.0310	3.35	10.4	3.79
Log GNP	0.0667	10.69	71.3	11.72
Rule of law	0.0615	7.02	43.2	6.85
Creditor rights	0.0518	2.00	10.4	2.30
Intercept	−0.8261	1.00	−82.6	
Fitted Debt/GNP (1994)			52.6	
Actual Debt/GNP (1994)			63.0	

Source: La Porta et al. (1997).
a. All variables significant at 10 percent.
b. Sample includes forty-nine countries.

Asset quality evaluation is a central part of current banking regulation in Chile. The objective of this mechanism is to provide regulators, depositors, and investors with a correct estimate of a bank or finance house's assets, based on estimates of potential cash flows from the creditors or the collateral and not on accounting information alone.[17] Banks are required to rate all of their loans according to a preestablished risk scale. According to the type of loan (commercial, consumption, or housing) the bank must then make a provision (reduce the value of the asset) that varies by risk category. The SBIF then evaluates (using a sample of loans) the banks classification procedure and can possibly reevaluate the risk category of a particular loan. These corrected measured of banks assets are then incorporated in traditional solvency measures.[18] Risk categories for loans to companies (commercial loans) are determined on a case-to-case basis on information such as past payment behavior, current payment capacity, and value of collateral. Note that risk is determined based on total debt of the company in the financial system so that an integrated database is required. For consumer loans, risk categories are determined solely on the basis of current delay in payments.

Initial asset evaluation by the bank and later supervision by the SBIF both require a centralized register of creditors that contains information on past and current debts, arrears, and the classification given to the individual debts. This information comes from the database maintained by the SBIF.

Summing up, there is a significant overlap between information distributed to lenders and the information used (and collected) by regulators of the Chilean banking system. Past experiences with banking crisis and efforts to avoid them in the future have been behind the development of adequate regulation and the provision of accurate and comprehensive information. The SBIF database was developed initially as a monitoring tool and only later became a central ingredient in information sharing among lenders. Information is crucial for good regulation and increased efficiency in intermediation.

4.5 Evaluating Credit Information Sharing in Chile

The objective here is to evaluate the role of credit information sharing on loans given by the banking sector. Existing theory predicts an unambiguous improvement in loan repayment, but it is not unequivocal on the effects on the volume of loans. This section looks at the latter effect, concentrating on consumption loans. As mentioned above, Fuentes and Maquieira (1998) estimate volume of banking sector loans as a function of GDP, and a set of dummies that capture the changes in the banking system described in the previous section and the existence of DICOM. Their sample includes annual data from 1960 to 1997. Estimates here build upon their work by including additional variables and allowing the importance of credit information sharing to evolve over time. Consumption loans are the focus here because it is likely that the existence of credit information sharing will impact consumer loans to a greater extent, as it allows for a low cost method for evaluating small consumption credits. A bank evaluating a credit to a company is likely to devote more resources to estimating repayment capacity due to the amounts involved, and at the same time can access additional information contained in the companies accounting records.

4.5.1 Estimating the Consumption Credit Demand Function

The following reduced form expression is estimated for quarterly data from 1986 to 1998. This is a period with no significant changes in the regulatory framework of banks and finance houses.[19] The equation to estimate is:

$$\Delta(l_c) = \alpha_1 + \alpha_2 \Omega + \alpha_3 r_{-1} + \alpha_4 \Delta(ys) + \alpha_5 \Delta(m) + d_i$$

Behind this expression is a model of loan demand in which individual demand for loans increases with growth of income and decreases in r—and the number of "credit-worthy" consumers is a function of information sharing where:

l_c: log of total consumption loans of the banking system (banks and finance houses) measured in real terms (deflated by CPI). Data on total consumer loans (banking system and retail stores) are only available since 1993. *Source:* SBIF.

r_{-1}: average interest rate on 90–365 day loans in the banking system lagged one quarter. The interest rate on consumption loans alone is not available. Annual rates in UF.[20] *Source:* Central bank.

Ω: a measure of information sharing. The last quarter of 1989, the date at which DICOM started distributing information from the PCR to banks, is taken as the start of information sharing in Chile. This follows Fuentes and Maquieira (1998).[21]

Table 4.5
Estimation results

	Equation 1		Equation 2		Equation 3		Equation 4	
	Coefficient	t-stat	Coefficient	t-stat	Coefficient	t-stat	Coefficient	t-stat
Least squares estimation: Dependent variable is log (consumption loans)								
intercept	0.127[a]	5.147	0.129[a]	5.419	0.093[a]	3.946	0.101[a]	3.739
$d(L_{-1})$					0.486[a]	3.875	0.602[a]	4.798
t	0.005[a]	5.177	0.005[a]	5.234	0.003[a]	3.071		
t^2	0.000[a]	−5.243	0.000[a]	−5.299	0.000[a]	−3.325		
duminfo							0.016[c]	1.706
r_{-1}	−0.011[a]	−5.448	−0.011[a]	−5.649	−0.007[a]	−3.478	−0.009[a]	−3.293
ys	0.241[b]	2.022	0.237[b]	2.022	0.051	0.446	0.002	0.017
d(m)	0.023	0.322			0.086	1.338	0.095	1.369
d1	0.010	0.932	0.012	1.245	−0.004	−0.377	−0.006	−0.535
d2	−0.028[a]	−2.894	−0.028[a]	−3.008	−0.043[a]	−4.493	−0.045[a]	−4.431
d3	−0.021[b]	−2.035	−0.023[b]	−2.451	−0.014[c]	−1.548	−0.012	−1.203
Test results on OLS estimation								
R^2	0.740		0.740		0.810		0.770	
D. Watson	1.220		1.210		2.120		2.000	
LM Test								
Stat	8.170		8.340		1.770		5.270	
p-value	0.080		0.080		0.780		0.260	
White								
Stat	2.510		2.070		16.870		21.030	
p-value	0.990		0.990		0.260		0.050	
Hausman								
p-value	0.059		0.060		0.060		0.020	

Least square estimation: Newey/West standard errors

intercept	0.127[a]	5.249	0.129[a]	4.955	0.093[a]	6.284	0.159[a]	6.468
$d(l_{-1})$					0.486[a]	3.333		
t	0.005[a]	3.748	0.005[a]	3.784	0.003[a]	2.806		
t^2	0.000[a]	-4.052	0.000[a]	-4.096	0.000[a]	-3.139		
duminfo							0.032[c]	2.611
r_{-1}	-0.011[a]	-7.228	-0.011[a]	-6.951	-0.007[a]	-5.092	-0.016[a]	-7.659
ys	0.241[b]	2.199	0.237[b]	2.118	0.051	0.550	0.231	2.320
$d(m)$	0.023	0.526			0.086	2.042	0.016	0.300
d1	0.010	1.052	0.012	1.513	-0.004	-0.307	0.012	1.149
d2	-0.028[a]	-2.792	-0.028[a]	-2.758	-0.043[a]	-3.733	-0.025[a]	-2.428
d3	-0.021[b]	-2.482	-0.023[b]	-2.921	-0.014[c]	-1.786	-0.020	-2.068
R^2	0.740		0.740		0.810		0.770	

Note: Variables are defined in text. LM test is a Lagrange multiplier test for serial correlation. The null hypothesis is that there is no serial correlation up to 4 lags. The statistic presented is the #obs*R^2, the p-value is from a χ^2 with 4 degrees of freedom. White test for heteroskedasticity. The statistic presented is the #obs*R^2. The p-value is from a χ^2 with degrees of freedom equal to number of coefficients-1.

a. Significant at 1%.
b. Significant at 5%.
c. Significant at 10%.

1. Trend from when DICOM started distributing SBIF data. The effects of information sharing are expected to increase with the number of years that information sharing has taken place. A squared trend to capture diminishing effects was also used.

2. Alternatively, dummy indicating when DICOM began distributing SBIF data among banks and finance houses.

ys: Annual growth rate in GDP measured in 1986 pesos smoothed with a Holt Winters filter. This variable is used as a proxy of changes in permanent income. Income and disposable income series are only available on an annual basis. *Source:* Authors' calculations based on central bank data.

m: log of the monetary base in 1986 pesos, deflated by CPI. *Source:* Central bank.

d_i: seasonal dummies.

4.5.2 Results

Table 4.5 summarizes the results from quarterly data for 1986 to 1998.

The first rows of the table show the results from an OLS estimation, followed by results of specification tests. For equations 1 and 2 a Lagrange multiplier test rejects the null of no serial correlation; for equation 4 a White test rejects the null hypothesis of homoscedasticity. For this reason we concentrate on the results of equation 3, which includes a lagged term of the dependent variable, and on the lower section of the table—estimations using Newey/West standard errors. A Hausman test was also carried out to confirm the hypothesis that by using the interest rate lagged with one lag eliminates potential endogeneity problems. The Hausman test rejects inconsistency of the estimated coefficients.

In all four equations the measures of information sharing are significant at 10 percent and have the expected signs. Both the trend and the square of trend variables are statistically significant. The interest rate is also significant in all four specifications; a rise in the rate of interest on loans (as expected) reduces the volume of loans. The measure of income growth is significant and positive in all equations in which the lagged variable is not included, but when the lagged variables are introduced it looses significance because of the correlation of growth with past growth of loans. Equation 1 was also estimated with GDP growth without smoothing, and the coefficient

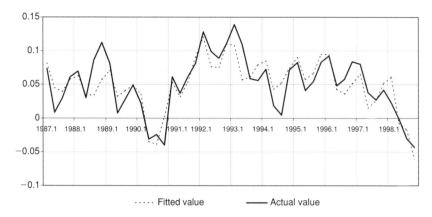

Figure 4.3
Consumption loans, 1987–1998
Actual and Fited Values—d(log(loans))
Source: SBIF and author calculations.

also had the expected sign but was less significant and the overall fit declined. The results would therefore indicate that information did contribute to the growth of consumption credit in Chile in the 1986–1998 period. High-powered money is not significant in any equation. The fitted and actual values are presented in figure 4.3.

Two questions remain to be answered. Are the trends and dummy variables used to capture the effects of information sharing actually capturing the effect of omitted variables or structural changes that took place within the sample period instead of information sharing? And second, what is the magnitude of the effect that information sharing has on the Chilean consumer loans evolution?

The answer to the first question is both quantitative and qualitative. First, this was a period of relative stability in Chilean economic history both in macroeconomic terms and, more importantly, in terms of rules and legislation affecting banks and finance houses. Thus, it can be argued that there were no other significant structural changes in this period. Second, figure 4.4 shows the outcome of $cusum^2$ tests of structural change for the four equations. In all cases the hypothesis of structural change other than that captured by the information sharing variables is rejected. Finally, figure 4.5 shows the result of an ad hoc exercise carried out to determine the validity of measures of information sharing. A series of OLS regressions were carried out with equation 1, changing the starting period of the in-

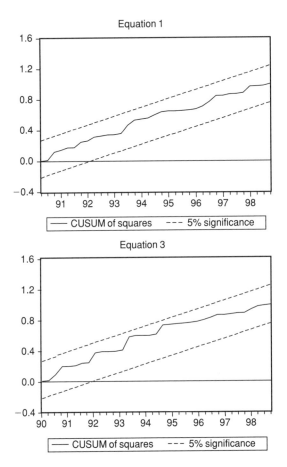

Figure 4.4
Tests of structural change

formation sharing dummy or trend. The graph shows the t-statistics obtained. Similar exercises for the other equations show that starting the dummy and trends at the end of 1989 gives one of the highest significance levels,[22] indicating that the best fit is obtained using the period in which information sharing started.

It is important to note that our estimate does not capture the effect the *existence* of a PCR or other databases have on loans in Chile, but the effects of setting up and adequate system to *distribute* this information.

The answer to the second question is shown in figure 4.6. The graphs show the fitted values of the equations with and without

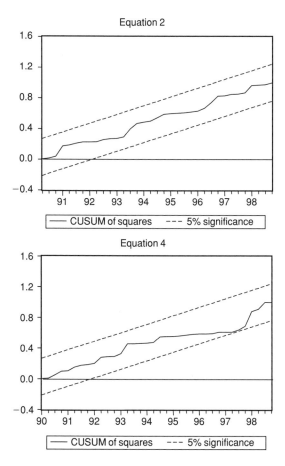

Figure 4.4
(continued)

the information sharing measures. As can be seen the effect is large. Table 4.6 shows the same results for the period 1990–1998. As can be seen from the table, the effect of information sharing is large. Consumer loans would be 40 percent lower without it. Furthermore, this effect is not excessive considering the explosive growth in consumer credit during this period.

Summing up the conclusions from results shown here:

First, results point in the same direction as previous studies on information sharing in Chile. There is a significant increase in loans that coincides with the start of information sharing. The results also

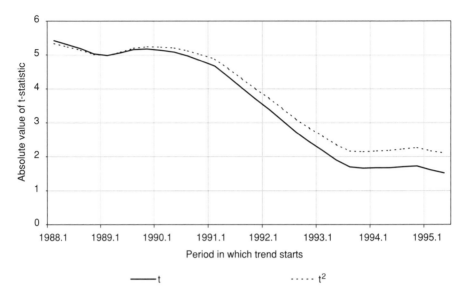

Figure 4.5
Significance of trends

point in the same direction as cross-section international evidence: information sharing increases the volume of loans.

Second, the effect of information sharing measured here depends on the time the providers of information have been in existence and potentially (although it can not be tested directly) on the volume of information in the PCR and other databases. This result is also in line with international evidence on credit bureaus.

One of the main caveats to the results presented above relates to the information that is publicly available on consumption credit in Chile. Banks and finance houses are not the only providers of credit—all credit granted by retail stores has been left out. Furthermore (and this is the most serious criticism of these findings), information sharing can undoubtedly be quantified with more precision if measures of the level of activity of DICOM and other companies were available. For lack of better information, the trend variable was used here. The authors recognize, however, that omitted variables may be driving part of these results.

Section 4.4 argued that the credit market in Chile was more developed than what could be expected, controlling for GDP per capita, growth rates, and legal environment. No attempt is made here to argue that information sharing is the sole cause for this difference—undoubtedly there are many other causes—but it does appear to be at least one potential cause. The reader is referred to Fuentes and Maquieria for a discussion of a larger range of determinants.

4.6 The Effects of Information Sharing on Credit Risk

This section evaluates the capacity that existing sources of information (public and private) have of predicting individual's default on loans. In doing so we seek to address the third issue discussed in the introduction: what information needs to be shared by lenders? Two questions and answers are proposed:

1. Does existing information contribute to predictions on loan default? Although this question can be easily answered, since banks and finance houses use this information while deciding on credit, it is a necessary step toward answering question 2.

2. Which information is important for correctly predicting default? There are at least three important sources of consumer credit information in Chile:

a. PCR: maintained by the SBIF, the PCR contains information on current debt in the financial system classified by type of debt and by payment status.

b. BIC: the *Boletin de Informes Comerciales* contains current information on bad checks and overdue bills of exchange within the financial system and with nonfinancial companies and individuals. A historic record of the information contained is also available.

c. API: this contains an applicant's personal information that can be requested by the bank or finance house granting the credit. Examples are the applicant's age, income, marital status, collateral, profession, and number of dependents.

The significance of each of these three sources of information was tested for predicting default. The significance of positive and negative credit information was also tested.

The sample consists of 3,000 individuals randomly drawn from the SINACOFI database who have been in the SBIF database for the last thirteen years and had outstanding debt with the financial system in 1999.[23] A probit model was estimated on a set of variables coming

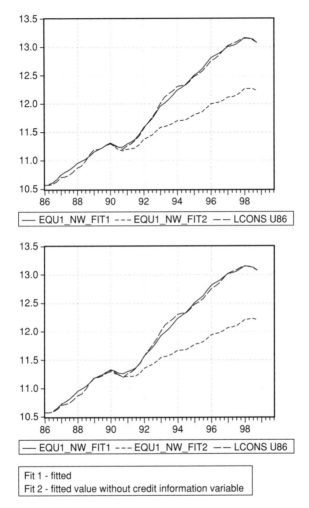

Fit 1 - fitted
Fit 2 - fitted value without credit information variable

Figure 4.6
Impact of information sharing on consumption loans

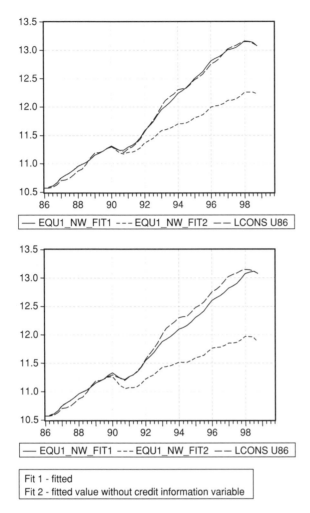

Fit 1 - fitted
Fit 2 - fitted value without credit information variable

Figure 4.6
(continued)

Table 4.6
Quarterly averages consumption loans, 1990–1998

	Consumption loans $86 (mm)					
	Fitted values without information sharing from equation				Average	Actual value
	1	2	3	4		
Mean	123313	123255	119979	101196	116936	211386
Median	122038	122176	117639	100373	115557	224632
Maximum	211496	211240	203414	158147	196074	513836
Minimum	71049	71140	73311	63177	69669	72963
Observations	36.00	36.00	36.00	36.00	36.00	36.00
Ratio of fitted to actual variables						
Mean	0.58	0.58	0.57	0.48	0.55	1.00
Median	0.54	0.54	0.52	0.45	0.51	1.00
Maximum	0.41	0.41	0.40	0.31	0.38	1.00
Minimum	0.97	0.98	1.00	0.87	0.95	1.00

Source: Author calculations as described in text.

from these different sources of information:

$$Prob(default) = f(PCR, BIC, API)$$

The variables used in the estimation group by source are described below. The sign at the end of each variable description indicates the expected sign of the estimated coefficient. Choice of variable and samples were conditioned by data availability.

A. Public Credit Registry Data from the SBIF. For SBIF data, two periods were considered for variable averages: September–November 1999 or May–November 1999.

1. Default: a binary variable taking on a value of 1 if the consumer defaults in the respective period. Default is defined as having arrears for a period of thirty to ninety days.[24] Two periods were considered for defining default: September–November 1999 or May–November 1999. These periods are labeled 1999 and 99II, respectively.

2. Debt: total debt with the financial system. It includes direct debt held by an individual, and indirect debt held by others but for which the individual is also responsible in case of primary default (thousands of $). Period average. (+)

3. dir_debt: direct debt with financial system (thousands of $). Period average. (+)

4. Used: the SBIF database also contains information on total credit lines granted to the individual. The variable "used" is the fraction of the total debt approved (granted loans + credit lines) that has been disbursed. Period average. (+)

5. dir_used: Fraction of total direct debt approved that has been disbursed. Period average. (+)

6. Punished: punished debt at the beginning of the period (i.e., May or September) (thousands of $). (+)

7. Institutions: number of institutions with which the person has consumption credits. Period average.

B. *Boletin de Informes Comerciales from the Chamber of Commerce.*

B1. Current Data

1. bad_amounts: total amount in pesos of bad checks and overdue bills of exchange that the debtor currently has. The information remains in this database for five years. This information is available for May 1999. (+)

2. bad_number: number of bad checks and overdue bills of exchange that the debtor currently has. The information remains in this database for five years. This information is available for May 1999. (+)

B2. Historic Data

After the five-year period mentioned above, bad checks or overdue bills are switched to another database which is also maintained by the Chamber of Commerce. This database also contains information on checks or overdue bills that have been paid or where a mistake was corrected. Information remains in this database indefinitely.

1. h_bad_amounts_cle: total amount in pesos of bad checks and overdue bills of exchange that have been cleared. (?)

2. h_bad_number_cle: total number in pesos of bad checks and overdue bills of exchange that have been cleared. (?)

3. h_bad_number_ncle: total number of bad checks and overdue bills of exchange that have not been cleared. (+)

4. h_bad_amount_ncle: total amount in pesos of bad checks and overdue bills of exchange that have not been cleared. (+)

Table 4.7
Estimation results

Dependent variable: / Error distribution:	1. Default 1999 Probit		2. Direct Default 1999 Probit		3. Direct Default 1999II Probit		6. Direct Default 1999 Logit	
	Coefficient	t-stat	Coefficient	t-stat	Coefficient	t-stat	Coefficient	t-stat
Intercept	-3.167[a]	-5.318	-2.990[a]	-4.986	-2.746[a]	-4.546	-5.689[a]	-4.831
ypc	-0.001[a]	-3.726	-0.002[a]	-4.369	-0.002[a]	-3.854	-0.003[a]	-4.134
sex	-0.007	-0.090	0.008	0.102	0.016	0.186	-0.012	-0.084
prof	-0.205[b]	-2.170	-0.256[a]	-2.620	-0.357[a]	-3.374	-0.406[b]	-2.274
age	0.016	1.179	0.014	0.996	0.017	1.100	0.026	1.026
debt	0.000	1.323						
dir_debt used			0.000[b]	2.100	0.000[b]	1.938	0.000[b]	2.089
dir_used	1.431[a]	3.932	1.399[a]	3.908	0.905[a]	3.413	2.940[a]	3.706
punished	0.000[c]	1.937	0.000[b]	2.233	0.000[b]	2.139	0.000[c]	1.720
institutions	0.272[a]	7.324	0.245[a]	6.371	0.263[a]	6.493	0.427[a]	6.322
bad_amounts	0.000[a]	-4.774	0.000[a]	-4.779	0.000[b]	-2.556	0.000[b]	-5.160
bad_number	0.112[a]	13.083	0.110[a]	13.028	0.064[a]	10.902	0.221[a]	11.079
h_bad_amounts_cle	0.000	-0.122	0.000	0.133	0.000	0.731	0.000	0.078
h_bad_number_cle	0.045[a]	4.682	0.036[a]	3.780	0.023[a]	2.285	0.066[a]	3.833
h_bad_amounts_ncle	0.000	-0.564	0.000	-0.613	-0.001[c]	-1.626	0.000	-0.602
h_bad_number_ncle	-0.030	-1.458	-0.021	-1.033	0.040	1.313	-0.046	-1.147
Log likelihood	-769.5		-733.6		-643.9		-728.9	
Restricted log likelihood	-1063.1		-1013.4		-827.6		-1013.4	
LR statistic	587.3		559.7		367.3		569.2	
p-value LR Statistic	0.000		0.000		0.000		0.000	
Obs with dep = 0	1526		1454		1466		1454	
Obs with dep = 1	452		431		313		431	
Total	1978		1885		1779		1885	

Dependent Variable: Error distribution:	4. Direct Default 1999 Probit		5. Direct Default 1999II Probit	
	Coefficient	t-stat	Coefficient	t-stat
Intercept	-2.901^a	-8.331	-2.407^a	-9.669
sex	-0.018	-0.230	-0.032	-0.392
prof	-0.250^a	-2.635	-0.337^a	-3.309
dir_capacity/ypc	0.000	1.255	0.000	0.864
dir_used	1.617^a	4.481	1.073^a	4.145
dir_punished/ypc	0.039^a	2.664	0.024^b	2.292
institutions	0.251^a	6.543	0.221^a	5.542
bad_amounts/ypc	-0.005^a	-5.310	-0.003^a	-3.018
bad_number	0.109^a	12.958	0.065^a	11.158
h_bad_amounts_cle/ypc	0.007	1.425	0.005	1.558
h_bad_number_cle	0.026^a	2.903	0.017^a	1.880
h_bad_amounts_ncle/ypc	-0.012	-0.635	-0.149^b	-1.722
h_bad_number_ncle	-0.016	-0.805	0.044	1.362
Log likelihood	-741.2		-659.2	
Restricted log likelihood	-1013.4		-827.6	
LR statistic	544.5		336.7	
p-value LR Statistic	0.000		0.000	
Obs with dep = 0	1454		1466	
Obs with dep = 1	431		313	
Total	1885		1779	

Note: Restricted log likelihood: maximized log likelihood when all slope coefficients are restricted to zero. LR statistic: tests the null hypothesis that all slope coefficients are zero. p-value: is obtained for the LR statistic from a χ^2 distribution with $n - 1$ degrees of freedom.

a. Significant at 1%.
b. Significant at 5%.
c. Significant at 10%.

C. Additional Personal Information

Banks or finance houses have access to a wealth of data that cannot be directly obtained from the above databases. We did not have access to this data but built variables from a publicly available database kept by the National Elections Registry.

1. sex: male or female. (?)

2. dum_prof: dummy that takes on the value of 1 if the debtor states to have a profession requiring post secondary education. (?)

3. age: age in years. (?)

4. ypc: per capita income. This variable was constructed with the CASEN, a national socioeconomic survey carried out every two years. Each individual is registered to vote in the commune in which he or she lives. Incomes were assigned to each individual based on communal per capita income in 1994. (−)

4.6.1 Estimation Results

Table 4.7 shows the results of regressions of the dependent variable default against the independent variables described above. The equations were estimated by maximum likelihood.[25] Estimations were carried out assuming normally distributed error terms (no. 1 to 5) and logistic distribution of error terms (no. 6). The similarity between the results of equation 2 and 6 in coefficient sign and significance, and the derivatives presented in table 4.8, indicated that the results do not hinge on a specific assumption for the distribution of the error terms.

Equation 1 shows the results when default on total debt (including indirect commitments) is considered; all other equations consider default on direct debt only. Given that direct debt reflects to a larger extent variables and decision over which the individual debtor has control (or information), we concentrate on estimates of direct debt. Equations 4 and 5 adjust all monetary variables for per capita income. Comparing equations 2 and 3 indicates if results are dependent on the period we chose to determine default. All coefficients that are significantly different from zero at 5 percent are also similar in magnitude and identical in sign across both equations. Therefore, the sample period does not make a significant difference.

Table 4.8
Derivatives

Variable	Equation 2	Equation 3	Equation 6
Intercept	**−2.545524**	**−2.4575776**	**−2.9400**
ypc	**−0.0013453**	**−0.0013579**	**−0.0015214**
sex	0.0069	0.0139364	−0.0062
prof	**−0.2177004**	**−0.3196987**	**−0.2099012**
age	0.0119141	0.0151	0.0134581
dir_debt	0.0000	0.0000	0.0000
dir_used	**1.1908657**	**0.8097274**	**1.5217717**
punished	**0.0002228**	**0.0001857**	**0.0001853**
institutions	**0.2088216**	**0.2349444**	**0.2211951**
bad_amounts	0.0000	0.0000	0.0000
bad_number	**0.0940443**	**0.0571042**	**0.114276**
h_bad_amounts_cle	0.0000	0.0000	0.0000
h_bad_number_cle	**0.0310619**	**0.0205013**	**0.0339129**
h_bad_amounts_ncle	−0.0001042	−0.001188	−0.0001154
h_bad_number_ncle	−0.0176722	0.0358431	−0.0237794

Note: Coefficients that are significant at 5 percent are in bold type. The derivatives were calculated taking the sample average of the derivatives, not the derivative evaluated at the sample average.

Table 4.8 shows that the derivatives for both specifications are very similar. Because of these results, the discussion concentrates on equation 2.

Table 4.9 provides information on the variables used in the model grouped according to the value of the dependent variable. Individuals who defaulted on debts have lower income, are more likely not to be professionals, have higher levels of debt at the time of default, and have a larger fraction of their debt "capacity" used. They also have a higher level of punished debt and owe money to a larger number of banks or finance houses. On average, individuals who default also have a poorer past performance in checks and bills of exchange.

An LM test was carried out for heteroskedasticty using the artificial regression method. The null was tested against the alternative of heteroskedasticty of the form $var(e_i\}) = exp(2z_i d)$, where d is an unknown parameter and z is one of the independent variables. For all variables in equation 2, the test fails to reject the null hypothesis.[26]

Table 4.9
Descriptive statistics for explanatory variables

Variable	Mean		
	Dep $= 0$	Dep $= 1$	All
ypc	169	124	159
sex	0.39	0.31	0.37
prof	0.25	0.19	0.23
age	35.69	36.20	35.80
dir_debt	34624	37543	35292
dir_used	0.88	0.97	0.90
punished	21.34	284.19	81.44
institutions	1.16	1.33	1.20
bad_amounts	211	1297	459
bad_number	0.63	9.53	2.66
h_bad_amounts_cle	121	538	216
h_bad_number_cle	0.91	3.10	1.41
h_bad_amounts_ncle	18.38	48.31	25.22
h_bad_number_ncle	0.26	1.10	0.45
number of observations	1454	431	1885

How well do these models allow to predict default? First, as can be seen in the lower rows of each estimation, a LR test rejects the null hypothesis that coefficients except the intercept are zero in all equations. The likelihood ratio (LRI) is also shown in the lower section of table 4.7, and although forward interpretation is not possible, it does shed some light on the goodness of fit of the model. In this case the LRI is different from zero for all equations.

Another option is to compare default predictions that would be made from equation 2 with predictions that result from a model that only contains the intercept. Forecasts for equation 2 are obtained by making $y = 1$ whenever P, the predicted probability value is above a critical value c. In this case c was set at 0.2, the approximate proportion of $y = 0$ observations in the sample. With this "decision rule," approximately 75 percent of observations are correctly predicted. This was compared to the results obtained by giving all the observations a value of 0 or 1. The gain from improved forecasts is an indicator of the predictive ability of the model. In this case correct predictions increase 54 percent in absolute terms and 70 percent in terms of the incorrect classifications in the constant probability

Table 4.10
Significance of data sets on credit information

		Equation 1	Equation 2	Equation 3	Equation 6
SBIF	Statistic	21.630	27.880	28.310	24.430
	p-value	0.000	0.000	0.000	0.000
Current bad checks	Statistic	76.060	70.730	67.410	64.670
and bills	p-value	0.000	0.000	0.000	0.000
Historic bad checks	Statistic	171.380	169.730	118.970	127.000
and bills	p-value	0.000	0.000	0.000	0.000
Personal characteristics	Statistic	36.470	25.270	15.050	26.240
	p-value	0.000	0.000	0.000	0.000

Note: p-value is determined with the Wald statistic for a χ^2 distribution with degrees of freedom equal to the number of coefficients restricted to zero.

model. Therefore, one can conclude that the model presented above does contribute significantly to the prediction of default.

Which sets of variables are significant in the model? Wald tests in table 4.10 show that at 1 percent significance all datasets are significant. Thus it appears that all three sets of data are important for determining default.

Summing up, the results indicate:

First, information in existing databases that is intermediated by DICOM and other private companies does significantly contribute to explaining default and reduces information asymmetry.

Second, all three sources of information are significant. Furthermore, both positive and negative information are important.

The first implication of these results applies to retail stores that grant consumer credit. At present they cannot access the data contained in the SBIF database. This has a cost both for the stores and the soundness of the financial system. For the stores the cost stems from not having access to significant information on a consumer's credit record and current situation in the financial system. From a global perspective it implies lending to a customer who may have a high default probability, which will not only affect the department store but banks and finance houses as well. The fact that department stores are not interested in sharing their information with the SBIF, however, implies that they face some other costs to prevent them from sharing information that may increase their ability to predict default. A closer look at the payoffs for department stores from entering a information sharing system is undoubtedly an important research topic, and it may also shed light on the costs and benefits faced by banks and finance houses for which entering the credit bureau is not an option.

The second implication is about current and future changes to legislation on information disclosure. In estimations discussed here, all sources of information are significant in explaining defaults, hence, reducing this information inevitably involves increasing information asymmetry. This does not mean, however, that these changes should not take place, but it does imply that the costs of doing so, in terms of information loss, must be considered and weighed against the benefits of these proposals.

Two main caveats must be considered regarding these results. The first relates to the information available for estimation here and the nature of the default variable defined. Ideally, default should be estimated by following the evolution of individual loans from beginning to end. This information is only available to the financial institutions granting the credit. Furthermore, it is likely that the database used here fails to capture all the information relevant for explaining default. These are data limitations that cannot be solved at this stage. The method used above, however, does shed light on the questions we set out to answer with this model.

The second caveat refers to the changes in behavior produced by the existence of different information sharing arrangements. The most important case is the one discussed by Vercammen (1995), who argues for an optimal length in the credit record beyond which the creditor has an almost complete "picture" of the creditor and therefore the later has reduced incentives to not default. Estimations made here do not capture this type of behavior change. A more complete database is required to address this point.

4.7 Conclusions

After deregulation and a profound crisis in the early 1980s, Chile has experienced a sustained increase in loans over the last twenty years. Furthermore, arrears are low and have remained so for most of the period despite large fluctuations in economic activity. The existence of credit information sharing, and more specifically the existence of private companies that process and distribute this information, are possible determinants of the high level of growth of consumption loans in Chile. Supporting this result, we find that the information distributed as of 1989 by DICOM, and later by other private companies, is significant for explaining default probabilities on consumption loans.

These results (subject to the caveats mentioned in the text) are in line with cross-country studies that find higher loan volumes in counties in which either a CB or a PCR exists. Also in line with cross-country evidence is the fact that until recently the credit information market was dominated by one company, hinting at potential economies of scale in providing information. The low level of arrears in Chile may also be attributable to information sharing; however, this hypothesis is not tested in this chapter.

More generally, we find that both positive and negative information is relevant for predicting default. All of the positive information is obtained from a database maintained by the bank regulators. Thus, we find that there is an important overlap between information deemed important by regulators for an adequate supervision of the banking sector and information useful for lenders who wish to reduce information asymmetry. This result should no be surprising—ultimately both the regulators and the banks wish to adequately forecast the expected value of an asset.

Finally, we touch on the issue of department store credit. Department stores in Chile do not provide detailed credit information to the bank superintendence, so there is no record of positive information about this type of consumer loans. This creates two questions. How important is it for regulators to obtain this information, as high consumer borrowing in department stores may ultimately result in default on consumer loans? This question is particularly relevant, given the importance of this type of credit in total consumer credit. The second question relates to the costs and benefits for stores of belonging to a credit bureau, and more importantly, what they can show of the costs and benefits to banks and finance houses that are not free to choose.

Acknowledgments

We thank Margaret Miller and an anonymous reviewer for helpful comments. We also thank SINACOFI, especially Ingrid Baraona, and Rodrigo Fuentes for providing data.

Notes

For a description of credit information sharing in Chile from the perspective of the bank regulator see SBIF (1999).

1. Specifically they find that a dummy variable for the period (1989–1997) is significant in a repression that also controls for banking sector reforms, per capital GDP and the new bank law enacted in 1986.

2. It may be possible that black information is a better predictor of default behavior as argued by Chandler and Parker (1989). This is discussed in more detail in Padilla and Pagano (1997) and Vercammen (1995).

3. A detailed description of information-sharing institutions and the types of information available in different countries is given in Japelli and Pagano (1998).

4. A review of existing literature is included in appendix 4A.

5. These results corroborate previous findings from Jappelli and Pagano (1993).

6. Finance corporations in Chile are those that together with banks intermediate funds. They are subject to many of the same laws as banks and regulated by the same institution, but they are prohibited from issuing current accounts. This chapter includes financial corporations in the definition of the banking sector.

7. In addition to credit information, the SBIF also publishes listings on all those individuals or companies that are legally prohibited from opening a bank account. The central bank maintains a record of individuals and companies that have defaulted on payment of fines or have been prosecuted due to violations of international trade and exchange laws.

8. Currently the international company Equifax owns DICOM.

9. Throughout the chapter, "banking system" refers both to banks and finance houses.

10. For a detailed description of Chilean banking law, see Ramirez and Rosende (1992). Edwards (1995, pp. 200–250), provides an overview of financial reform in Latin America and Chile.

11. Financial liberalization is not the only factor behind the dramatic increase in credit and intermediation. Optimistic expectations (Barandiarian 1983), increased demand for liberalized imports of consumer goods and overstocking due to expectations of a real devaluation and, lending to grupos (financial and productive conglomerates) seeking to purchase assets are among the demand factors behind the boom. Held (1997) also argues that rolling over bad debt also contributed significantly to the expansion of bank credit.

12. As stated by Velasco (1991): "Obviously severe shocks can disequilibrate even the soundest of markets. But whereas a sound market tends to cushion the effects of perturbations, an unsound one tends to magnify them. Unfortunately the Chilean market seems to belong in this latter category. Regardless of the role played by other factors, it is difficult to escape the conclusion that the Chilean financial problem had perverse microdynamics of its own, which in turn was made possible only by the peculiar pattern of ownership and regulation...."

13. For a discussion of the solutions to the financial crisis see Sanhueza (1999) and Velasco (1991). Rojas-Suarez and Weisbrod (1996) compare the Chilean solutions to those carried out in Argentina in the same period.

14. For a detailed discussion on consumption credit in Chile, see Butelman and Landeretche (1998).

15. See Japelli and Pagano (1998). This is also one of the issues that motivated Fuentes and Maquiera to study the determinants of loan repayment in Chile.

16. A detailed description of the system implemented in Chile to evaluate and classify bank assets can be found in Ramirez (1997).

17. A detailed description of Chilean prudential regulation can be found in Held (1997).

18. A combination of government guarantees, international capital opening, capital inflows to Latin America, and lack of prudential regulation were part of the scenario in Chile up to 1982. The subsequent crisis and intervention marked the next few years as did a sweeping reform of bank regulation in 1986.

19. The U.F., or Unidad de Fomento, is a constant purchasing power unit of account used extensively in the Chilean economy. It is updated daily according to the previous month's inflation.

20. Ideally one would also want to work with data on the amount of information shared, for example the number of information requests to DICOM; however, this information is not publicly available.

21. The probability above the t-distribution corresponding to the t-statistics on information sharing measures.

22. The selection criteria follows from the fact that initially the authors intended to take into consideration SBIF information for every month since the database started in the mid-1980s. Resource constraints and regulatory issues prevented the authors from doing so, but it leaves open issues for useful future research.

23. If delays in payments are shorter than thirty days in the Chilean system, the debt is considered outstanding; delays of more than ninety days force banks to consider the debt as punished and remove it from their assets. Punished debt, however, remains in the SBIF database until it is canceled providing a useful source of historical information.

24. Parameter estimates were estimated using quadratic hill climbing. Likelihood maximization using Newton-Rhaphson and Berndt-Hall methods for equation 2 led to nearly identical results.

25. Ideally the authors would also wish to test for omitted variables since the presence of either heteroskedasticity or omitted variables leads to inconsistency of the coefficient estimates in a binary choice model. The authors, however, did not have access to a complete set of personal characteristics of the debtors.

26. It is possible that a "naive" model like the one presented here predicts better according to this criterion than a behavioral model. This follows from the fact that the estimation method seeks to maximize a likelihood function and not the fit of the equation, for example, as is the case in OLS.

References

Barandiarian, E. 1983. "La Crisis Financiera Chilena." *Documento de Trabajo*, Centro de Estudios Públicos, no. 6.

Butelman, A., and O. Landerretche. 1998. "Evolución e Importancia Del Crédito de Consumo en Chile." *Economía Chilena* (Banco Central de Chile) 1 (2): 5–18.

Chandler, G., and L. Parker. 1989. "Predictive Value of Credit Bureau Reports." *Journal of Retail Banking* 11 (4): 47–54.

Edwards, S. 1995. *Crisis and Reform in Latin America: From Despair to Hope*. World Bank, Oxford University Press.

Fuentes, R., and C. Maquieria. 1998. "Determinants of Loan Repayment in Chile." Mimeo., Departamento de Economía Universidad de Chile.

Held, G. 1997. "Bank Regulation, Liberalization and Financial Instability in Chile." In G. Held and Y. Akyuz, eds., *Finance and the Real Economy: Issues and Case Studies in Developing Countries*, 245–291. United Nations University/World Institute for Development, ECLA, United Nations Conference on Trade and Development.

Jappelli, T., and M. Pagano. 1993. "Information Sharing in Credit Markets." *Journal of Finance* 48 (5): 1694–1718.

Jappelli, T., and M. Pagano. 1998. "Information Sharing in Credit Markets: International Evidence." Paper prepared for the Conference on Willingness to Repay in Financial Markets, organized by the IADB, Inter-American Development Bank Buenos Aires.

La Porta, R., F. Lopez-De-Silanes, A. Shleifer, and R. Vishny. 1997. "Legal Determinants of External Finance." *The Journal of Finance* 52 (3): 1131–1150.

Padilla, J., and M, Pagano. 1997. "Endogenous Communication Among Lenders and Entrepreneurial Incentives." *The Review of Financial Studies* 10 (1): 205–236.

Ramirez, G., and F. Rosende. 1992. "Responding to Collapse: Chilean Banking Legislation after 1983." In P. L. Brock, ed., *If Texas Were Chile. A Primer on Banking Reform*, 193–226. Sequoia Seminar Publications, ICS Press.

Ramirez, G. 1997. "Evaluación y Clasificación de Activos: La Experiencia Chilena." In G. Held and R. Szcalachman, eds., *Regulación y Supervisipon de la Banca: Experiencia de América Latina y el Caribe*, 115–143. ECLA, UNDP.

Rojas-Suarez, L., and S. Weisbrod. 1996. "Manejo de Crisis Bancarias: Lo que Debe Hacerse y lo que no Dede Hacerse." In L. Rojas-Suarez and S. Weisbrod, eds., 3–26.

Sanhueza, G. 1999. "La Crisis Financiera de los Años 80 en Chile: Análisis de Sus Soluciones y sus Costos." *Economía Chilena* (Banco Central de Chile) 2 (1): 43–68.

Staten, M. E. 1997. "Regulating the Collection and Storage of Personal Credit Information: The U.S Experience." Paper prepared for the workshop on the Role of Timely and Reliable Credit Information in the Development of Stable Financial Markets organized by the Argentine Central Bank and the World Bank, Buenos Aires.

SBIF, Superintendencia de Bancos e Instituciones Financieras. 1999. *Desarrollo de los Credit Bureau en el Sistema Financiero Chileno.*

Velasco, A. 1991. "Liberalization, Crisis, Intervention: The Chilean Financial System." In T. Baliño and V. Sundararajan, eds. *Banking Crises: Cases and Issues*, 113–174. IMF.

Vercammen, J. 1995. "Credit Bureau Policy and Sustainable Reputation Effects in Credit Markets." *Economica*, no. 62: 461–478.

5 Private Business Information Exchange in the United States

Jarl G. Kallberg and Gregory F. Udell

5.1 Introduction

A crucial aspect of credit extension is the quality of information that lenders possess on prospective borrowers. While of great practical importance, the quality of, and access to, credit information is also a significant issue from the perspective of financial system architecture, since better credit information can lead to increased lending and other forms of investment in a country's economy. Thus, an important public policy issue is the degree to which governments should become involved in establishing credit gathering mechanisms or whether private information gatherers can be as, or more, effective. A closely related issue is which types of information make sense to gather.

The overall objective of this chapter is to analyze the value of the institutionalized exchange of business credit information. The emphasis is on private information exchanges, using the United States as a reference point. The mechanism of private information exchange is examined, and an overview of the institutional setting in the United States is provided. The theoretical motivation for information exchange is also explored. This examination includes a discussion of the extant theoretical literature in this area and our own extension of this literature. Specifically, this chapter offers a new theoretical model that clarifies the sources of economies of scale in private information exchange associated with mercantile trade information—that is, information about how companies pay their trade credit. Most of the theoretical literature in this area has focused on single lender models and thus ignored the advantages of collecting information from multiple credit sources. The principal contribution here to the theoretical literature is to emphasize the economies of scale that derive from the positive association between the number of credit payment observations and the quality of the credit signal generated by the information exchange. The model used here also explores the relative value of information payment experience information (i.e., information accumulated by a formal information exchange) versus information that can be culled from a borrower's financial statements.

The empirical literature on the value of information exchanges is also examined. The limited literature in this area has addressed the value added from formal information exchanges at the macro level and the micro level. Macrolevel analysis focuses on the connection between the presence of formal information exchange in a financial system and aggregate economic performance at the country level. Micro-level analysis focuses on the information content of credit data produced by formal information exchange and its value in assessing borrower quality. Because the focus here is on the mechanics of information exchange in the United States, particular emphasis will be placed on micro-level analyses. This includes a discussion of recent empirical research that assesses the incremental value of the various types of business credit information used in the United States, that is, the value of trade credit information relative to other types of information that do not require formal information exchange.

Emphasis here is placed on commercial credit and the associated business-to-business exchange of credit information. Similar information collection mechanisms exist in the consumer credit market. Thus, many of the conclusions in this chapter should hold in the consumer arena as well. The United States is a particularly interesting case because of the dominance of one large private information broker: Dun and Bradstreet (D&B). Analyzing business credit information exchange in the United States affords the opportunity to examine the mechanics of information collection in what may be its most scale efficient form. D&B's database contains information on over 59.4 million businesses in over 200 countries.[1] D&B collects many different types of information about a company's business activities, including its size, history, public filings (liens, lawsuits, judgments, bankruptcy), and in some cases financial statements. The most valuable information for credit granting, however, is trade payment history. As emphasized in the theoretical model presented here, the principal source of scale economies stems from the collection of this type of data.

The organization of the chapter is as follows. Section 5.2 describes the institutional structure of private information sharing in the United States, emphasizing the type of data collected by D&B. Section 5.3 examines the theoretical literature related to formal information exchange. This section also presents a new model of formal information exchange. Section 5.4 examines the extant empirical evidence on the value of the business credit information, and section 5.5 offers some conclusions.

5.2   The Institutional Structure of Private Formal Information Exchange in the United States

The quality of credit information and the mechanisms for gathering it vary enormously by country. At one extreme is the United States, where extensive credit information is inexpensively available on almost every individual and business entity of significant size. At the other extreme are developing countries, where credit information is virtually nonexistent and few mechanisms are in place for its efficient collection. A recent example of the value of credit information is Indonesia, where ethnic Chinese for generations have supplied credit to local farmers using their specialized local knowledge to gauge a given farmer's creditworthiness. During the latest period of political unrest and "ethnic-cleansing" in 1998, many of these Chinese left Indonesia. The result was a drastic shortage of credit to this agrarian sector and a subsequent collapse of the rural economy.[2]

5.2.1   Information Exchange in the United States

The focus here is on the United States and its dominant formal information exchange, Dun & Bradstreet Corporation (D&B), which was formed as a result of the 1933 merger between R. G. Dun & Co. (founded in 1841 in New York) and the Bradstreet Company (founded in 1849 in Cincinnati).[3] It has approximately 90 percent of the U.S. market for business credit information and is also a major player globally. D&B's only major U.S. competitor is Experian. In addition to these private information exchanges, several industry groups pool credit information for their members. The types of business credit decisions for which these types of data are most useful are relatively small dollar transactions. The typical user would be a leasing company, a factor or a supplier extending credit in the $3,000 to $100,000 range. For transactions of this type, credit grantors are unwilling to undertake a more expensive investigation. Often, the timeliness of the decision is also important, making automated credit granting techniques much more viable. This time line is increasingly important as the Internet becomes a larger channel for business-to-business and business-to-consumer transactions.

The most important data accumulated by D&B are the payment experiences of individual companies. Essentially, D&B collects information from vendors (i.e., suppliers) and other creditors on how individual firms are paying their bills. Participation in public credit registries (PCRs) is typically compulsory. This is decidedly not the case, however, with private information exchanges like D&B. Almost all firms enter D&B's database as a result of a credit inquiry by one of D&B's customers (i.e., a company that wants credit-related information on a company to which it is contemplating extending credit).[4] Specifically, when a customer request cannot be matched to existing data, the customer is asked if he or she would like D&B to initiate a report on the firm. If D&B does this, the customer receives a report without incurring any extra costs. D&B thus absorbs a loss to build its database. In general, credit suppliers will only share information with a private information exchange to the extent that it is in their financial interest to do so. For D&B, this remains a rather murky area. D&B claims not to pay suppliers of credit information; however, it is plausible that during price negotiations the fact that the customer supplies D&B data gives the customer a valuable bargaining chip.

The process of data collection for a private business information exchange is illustrated in figure 5.1. Vendors (such as hypothetically Sears, Staples, and Dell) who sell on credit to their customers and lenders (such as hypothetically Bank One) supply payment history information on their customers/borrowers (such as ABC Co., DEF, Co., and GHI Co.) to the information exchange (such as D&B). The information exchange then aggregates the information in the form of credit reports on these individual firms (i.e., ABC Co., DEF, Co., and GHI Co.) which often includes summary statistics that capture their payment quality. These summary statistics can be in the form of a credit rating or a summary statistic that captures payment timeliness. The information exchange then sells these credit reports to cli-

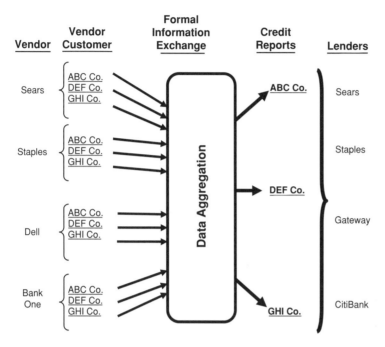

Figure 5.1
Formal information exchange mechanism

ents (i.e., lenders) who are composed in part of the same vendors and lenders who supplied the information originally. These clients then use the information in these reports as input data in their credit analysis.

D&B's credit report traditionally has been delivered in the form of its business information report (BIR). This document contains a wide variety of text and numerical data in addition to the payment information data described in figure 5.1. For many decades this report has been an essential part of commercial credit granting in the United States. It is typically delivered to the lender by the Internet, fax, mainframe, PC, or dedicated terminal. The advent of automated commercial credit granting procedures caused D&B to develop a mechanism for delivering the data element-by-element, rather than only processed into reports like the BIR.

Prior to about 1988, the basic report delivered to the vast majority of D&B clients was the BIR, described above. As several of D&B's major customers began to develop automated processes for credit decisions, however, this text-based report was inadequate. Customers wanted individual data elements as input to their decision-making software. At that point, D&B began to sell its data "by the pound." Customers, through a service called DunsLink, could request specific data elements, including, for example, Paydex (a summary statistic that captures payment timeliness), D&B's credit rating, SIC code, years in business, and so forth. D&B's customers would pay only for the items that D&B could deliver. In contrast, BIR customers paid a flat fee, independent of the amount (or quality) of the data it contained. In many cases, particularly for small and young firms, the BIR had little usable data; often there were no trade experiences, filing or financing data given, which rendered the report of little use for making credit decisions. The lack of information on a BIR, however, is taken as a negative signal of the firm's creditworthiness. Similarly, individuals without an established credit record are often turned down for consumer credit.

It is quite likely that the ability of D&B to deliver specific data elements (rather than just structured credit reports), which began in 1989, significantly enhanced the efficiency of the commercial credit granting process, at least for relatively small transactions. This part of D&B experienced considerable growth in the 1990s, but it was hampered by the conflicts between D&B wanting to sell as much data as possible versus finding the best model. Currently a number of independent consulting firms build credit and fraud detection models using D&B, consumer, and other sources of data.

5.2.2   Information and Data Provided by D&B

D&B collects a variety of information about businesses. The most important information provided by D&B is information about trade experiences which reflect a firm's credit status with a supplier, other corporation, or bank. As reflected in figure 5.1, the sources of these data are the vendors and lenders that report to D&B the current payment history of their business customer base. These data are augmented by a smaller number of additional trade experiences that are manually gathered by D&B, usually by their field reporters.

D&B reports the total number of trade experiences over the past thirteen months as well as the total dollar amount; the highest credit amount and the percentage of the trade payments that fall into each "aging bucket." Aging buckets refer to invoice payment status by timeliness: current, overdue less than 30, overdue between 31 and 60

Table 5.1
D&B payment index: Paydex

Paydex	Payment
100	Anticipate
90	Discount
80	Prompt
70	Slow to 15 days
50	Slow to 30 days
40	Slow to 60 days
30	Slow to 90 days
20	Slow to 120 days

Note: This table gives an interpretation of the Paydex measure of aggregrate payment behavior. Paydex requires at least four trade experiences within the last thirteen months from different credit grantors.

days, overdue between 61 and 90 days and overdue past 91 days. It should be noted that these data are not typically voluntarily released by the firms, so for most creditors this information is only available from an information exchange.

D&B generates a summary statistic on trade experience called Paydex. In its computation of Paydex D&B makes an effort to use representative trade experiences. In essence Paydex gives a composite evaluation of the most recent thirteen months of reported payment history. It can be converted into dollar-weighted average days past due. (It should be noted, however, that the specific transformation calculation involves more than just this measurement.) As shown in table 5.1, for example, a Paydex of 80 corresponds to prompt payment; a Paydex of 70 would correspond to average payments slow fifteen days; a Paydex of 40 would correspond to payments late sixty days. Arguably Paydex is the most important single product (i.e., output) provided by D&B. As shown in section 5.4, recent empirical evidence suggests that the power of Paydex to predicate firm failure may substantially exceed other sources of public and quasi-public information.

D&B also sells a bond-type rating, its D&B rating, that incorporates an estimate of net worth together with payment experiences. This D&B rating is described in table 5.2. The first term in the rating (ranging from a high of 5A to a low of HH) is an estimate of net worth. The second component (ranging from a high of 1 to a low of 4) is a measure of payment history. Often used by D&B customers

Table 5.2
D&B rating

Estimated financial strength		Composite credit appraisal			
		High	Good	Fair	Limited
5A	$50,000,000 and over		1	2	3	4
4A	$10,000,000 to 49,999,999		1	2	3	4
3A	1,000,000 to 9,999,999		1	2	3	4
2A	750,000 to 999,999	1	2	3	4
1A	500,000 to 749,999	1	2	3	4
BA	300,000 to 499,999	1	2	3	4
BB	200,000 to 299,999	1	2	3	4
CB	125,000 to 199,999	1	2	3	4
CC	75,000 to 124,999	1	2	3	4
DC	50,000 to 74,999	1	2	3	4
DD	35,000 to 49,999	1	2	3	4
EE	20,000 to 34,999	1	2	3	4
FF	10,000 to 19,999	1	2	3	4
GG	5,000 to 9,999	1	2	3	4
HH	up to 4,999	1	2	3	4

Note: The table gives a breakdown of the two segments of the D&B rating. It plays the role of a bond-type rating for small firms. A rating of — is commonly assigned when D&B does not have sufficient data to establish a rating. Ratings of NQ (not quoted) or INV (under investigation) are usually interpreted negatively.

for small dollar credit decisions, this rating is widely distributed on CD-ROM.

D&B also collects information beyond trade experience. This encompasses information on public filings, including data on lawsuits, liens, tax liens, and judgments filed against the firm. It should be noted that these data are available publicly, but probably at a much higher cost for most creditors than the cost at which they are available from D&B. A variety of firm-specific information is also collected by D&B, including most importantly SIC code, years in business, and firm organization (corporation, sole proprietorship, or partnership). This may include firm financial statements, but only if they are publicly available (i.e., the firm has issued registered securities which would not be the case for small firms), or if the firm voluntarily provides them to D&B (which many small firms will not). It often also includes qualitative information about the principals of the firm, characteristics of the place of business, and so forth. Some

Table 5.3
U.S. information sources for D&B credit data

Source	Number (in thousands)
Management interviews	3,908
Direct mail requests	1,004
Businesses sharing trade data	93.7
Banks sharing banking experiences	1.7
Daily newspapers	8.0
Filing locations for suits, etc.	2.6
Others	

Source: ⟨www.dnb.com⟩.
Note: The table gives the primary U.S. sources for D&B's business credit data. The data are as of June 2001. The "Others" category includes the fifty secretaries of state, the U.S. Postal Service, utilities and telephone companies.

of this information is collected by D&B fieldworkers who may visit the firm's place of business.

Table 5.3 summarizes the major information sources of the D&B database. Figure 5.2 shows the frequency with which they are updated. Nearly one million trade experiences, for example, are added to the database each month.

5.2.3   D&B Customers

Virtually any extender of business credit might purchase credit information from D&B. The incremental value of this information, however, crucially depends on the type of lender. Five different types of commercial lenders or lending technologies can be identified: (1) financial statement lending, (2) asset-based lending, (3) relationship lending, (4) credit scoring, and (5) trade credit.[5] A brief description of each technology will be illuminating.

Financial statement lenders emphasize the strength of a company's financial statements in their lending decisions. The stronger a firm's balance sheet and income statements, the more likely it will be able to obtain credit from a financial statement lender. Because this type of lending requires a relatively high level of transparency, it is reserved for larger firms or particularly strong small firms with informative financial statements. This type of lending is typically delivered by commercial banks in their traditional commercial lending operations.

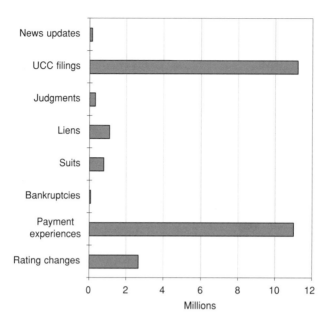

Figure 5.2
D&B information updates
Source: ⟨www.dnb.com⟩
Note: This figure shows the numbers of annual updates to various types of business credit data. The data are as of June 2001.

The credit decision in an asset-based loan is based primarily on the quality of the borrowing company's assets, particularly its accounts receivable and inventory. The condition of the company as reflected in traditional financial ratios is far less important than the value of collateral based on ratios such as accounts receivable and inventory turnover, invoice payment timeliness, and return items as a fraction of sales. The bulk of asset-based lending is extruded through secured lines of credit, although about 25 percent is in the form of factoring which involves the outright purchase of accounts receivable. Asset-based lenders will often lend in debtor-in-possession (DIP) situations or pre-DIP situations. Asset-based lending is provided by commercial finance companies and the asset-based lending divisions of large and mid-sized commercial banks. Asset-based borrowers are typically middle market companies.

Relationship lending typically emphasizes soft qualitative information acquired by the bank over time and across multiple services about the credit quality of the company and the skills and trustworthiness of the entrepreneur. This type of lending is particularly important for small, informationally opaque firms. For organizational reasons, this lending technology is most likely to be employed by smaller community banks. That is, it is likely that the transmission of soft information within large banking organizations makes it more difficult for them to extend this type of credit where the primary determinant of availability and pricing is the degree of mutual trust between the loan officer and the entrepreneur.

Credit scoring is the application of statistical techniques (such as logistic regression or discriminate analysis) to credit evaluation. It has been the principal technique used in consumer lending for well over three decades. Only in the last half-dozen years has it been extensively applied to business lending as a primary lending technology.[6] Credit scoring used in this fashion has been limited to "microbusiness lending," which is typically defined as credits less than $250,000. Credit scoring has now been rather widely adopted by large banks. It has not yet been widely adopted by smaller banks, however, but the recent availability of generic credit scoring models (such as those available for consumer credit scoring) will likely lead to their adoption of credit scoring in the next decade.

Trade credit can also be considered a separate lending technology. Arguably trade creditors have certain information advantages over other lenders in understanding their borrowers' (i.e., their customers') product markets. Because many trade creditors extend credit in small amounts, they may see credit deterioration early. The combination of these factors could give them a strategic advantage over other creditors as companies become financially distressed.[7]

The information provided by D&B is of value to all five types of lenders and is widely used by all of them. Its relative importance, however, differs significantly. It is one of the most important inputs in trade credit and credit scoring, but it is a much less important input in financial statement lending and asset-based lending. These latter two technologies generate a considerable amount of information about borrower quality (apart from any information generated by D&B)—information generated from expensive audited financial statements in the case of financial statement lending and from expensive collateral monitoring in the case of asset-based lending. The high fixed cost associated with each of these two technologies, however, is amortized over a relatively high loan dollar amount. The incremental information content of a D&B report in the context of these two technologies is relatively small. Nevertheless, it is generally still justified because of its small cost per loan dollar.

For trade creditors and credit scorers (and, to a lesser extent, relationship lenders), on the other hand, the incremental value of D&B data is quite high. Because the transaction size associated with these types of loans is so small, the low cost of D&B data makes it a cost-effective source of information about borrower quality.

5.3   The Theory of Formal Information Exchange

In addition to producing information about their own borrowers, lenders can share information about their borrowers with other creditors through a variety of sharing arrangements. Sharing can be conducted on a bilateral basis or through an exchange. Usually bilateral sharing occurs on an informal basis when one lender agrees to share information with another. Alternatively, information sharing can be extruded through a formal information exchange either through PCRs or private information exchanges.

Information sharing is useful both at the origination stage and after credit has been extended. At the origination stage, information sharing can augment the due-diligence process in mitigating problems of adverse selection. Much of the limited theoretical literature in this area has focused on bilateral, single lender information sharing. The setting here typically involves two periods where a first period lender may exchange information with a potential second period lender. Pagano and Jappelli (1993) use a pure adverse selection model to find that information sharing improves the borrower pool, reduces loan interest rates, and decreases loan defaults in a model of bilateral sharing. Moral hazard problems can also be addressed through information sharing. Padilla and Pagano (1997) show that information sharing can have an incentive effect on borrower behavior. In their model, lenders have private information about borrower quality that gives them a degree of market power over their borrowers. By precommitting to exchange information about borrower quality, however, lenders reduce their ability to extract future informational rents. By reducing the holdup problem, information sharing has positive incentive effects, encouraging borrowers to expend more effort. Padilla and Pagano (1999) show that, even in the absence of holdup problems, information sharing can have a disciplinary effect when lenders exchange information about past defaults.

Formal information sharing among lenders to small business, particularly trade suppliers, may be the most valuable (and possibly the only) mechanism available for reducing coordination costs in the small business credit market. It may afford trade creditors, in addition to any bank lenders,[8] an opportunity to observe in real time the performance of their borrowers on contracts with other creditors. One could speculate that formal information sharing among multiple trade creditors and lenders would mitigate adverse selection and moral hazard problems in a manner similar to the single lender models discussed above.[9]

Formal information sharing mechanisms may encourage a more competitive loan market in addition to mitigating potential adverse selection and moral hazard problems. This occurs, for instance, in the Padilla and Pagano (1997) model because information sharing reduces the extraction of informational rents. In their model, a holdup problem is created because lenders are endowed with an informational advantage stemming from private information about their borrowers. As noted earlier, the incentive effects derived in their model are a result of competition, which discourages predatory pricing in the second period.

Another issue is the quality of the information exchanged through formal information sharing mechanisms. For these mechanisms to deliver the benefits noted above, not only must the information they provide be of a type that is useful to lenders, it must also be reliable. Presumably, in the case of PCRs, the credibility of the institution itself (i.e., the credit registry) is less of an issue. With only one exception (Finland), Jappelli and Pagano (1999) report that PCRs are managed either by central banks or banking supervisory authorities.[10] In addition, as agents of the government, PCRs may have an advantage in ensuring that lenders supply accurate information. The relative reliability of public versus private information likely depends on the extent to which PCRs can solve the agency and organization problems associated with running a government bureaucracy, and the extent to which reputation effects can solve the incentive problems associated with private information gathering.

There is one model, Klein (1992), that examines the economies of scale associated with a formal information exchange. Klein uses a repeated game setting with a modified prisoner's dilemma problem at each stage. Firms can join a formal information exchange, which allows them to obtain the credit history of any potential borrower. Belonging to the exchange commits the firm to truthfully supply all of its own credit experiences. From this framework one quickly sees the economies of scale: the larger the exchange, the more costly it is for borrowers to default.

5.3.1 A New Model of Formal Information Exchange

Much of the extant theoretical literature on information exchange focuses on single-lender bilateral information exchange rather than formal information exchanges. Klein's model (1992) is an exception. It captures the economies of scale associated with an information exchange that derive from increasing the likelihood that borrowers will be included in the data base. It does not, however, capture the essence of private information exchanges like D&B which collects information from multiple sources on each borrower. Rather than modifying the approach used in Klein, some of the framework developed in Leshchinski (2000) is adopted instead. His model describes a setting where traders may choose to give valuable private information to generate a more favorable price movement. This approach is used here to address the absence in the theoretical literature of a model that captures the economies of scale associated with formal information exchanges that collect information from multiple sources on each individual borrower.

The model used here also addresses the absence in the theoretical literature of a model that identifies the conditions under which information exchange-generated information will dominate alternative sources of information, such as the financial statements used by financial statement lenders and the collateral valuation information used by asset-based lenders. Here, a theoretical model is offered that clarifies the economies of scale in information exchange that derive from multiple payment observations and the conditions under which formal information exchange dominates an alternative information source.

A simple, one-period model is developed that captures the differing nature of payment experience data versus single source data such as the firm's financial statement information. Specifically, the focus is on the difference between obtaining a one-time signal of firm quality, for example, a set of financial statements, versus a series of signals. The latter information structure can be thought of as a sequence of signals generated by payment experiences of a single borrower with multiple lenders. The above distinctions are purely for interpretation; the model structure is quite general.

Thus, we assume that during the period borrower i $(i = 1, \ldots, I)$ generates a series of J_i firm-specific signals

$$s_{ij} = q_i + \varepsilon_{ij}$$

Here q_i represents the realizable value of the debt claim. The error term, ε_{ij}, $j = 1, \ldots, J_i$ is a function of firm, country, and industry characteristics. It is assumed to be normally distributed with mean zero and standard deviation ε_p. We can interpret these signals as payment experiences; each is a noisy, dynamic signal of the firm's (or the debt claim's) true quality. A supplier observes its individual s_{ij} as a result of granting credit to the firm. The role of a formal information exchange is to aggregate these experiences and offer, at price C_B, a composite payment experience signal. The basic tension here is between the cost of aggregating the individual signals versus the value of the increased signal precision.

In addition, each firm generates a single signal, τ_i, from a static information technology (e.g., firm financial statements), which is obtainable at price C_F

$$\tau_i = q_i + \delta_i$$

where the error term, δ_i, is normally distributed with zero mean and standard deviation σ_F. This information technology can be thought of as financial statement data.

Now consider the first pair of choices the credit grantor has in determining the information on which to base its credit granting decision:

• *Case (1):* Use only on s_{ij} and incur no extra credit investigation costs. Here we have assumed that the lender obtains a signal at no cost through some initial credit granting decision.

• *Case (2):* Use both s_{ij} and τ_i; expend the cost C_F to gain further information from the other signal of quality.

Below we discuss the problem with a formal information exchange present, denoted case (3). In the first case the signal has precision (reciprocal of the standard deviation) of $\dfrac{1}{\sigma_P}$. In the latter case the lender observes a signal with precision[11]

$$\frac{2}{\sqrt{\sigma_P^2 + \sigma_F^2 + 2\,\mathrm{cov}(\varepsilon_{ij}, \delta_i)}} \equiv \frac{1}{\sigma_{PF}}$$

Assume that the credit grantor has constant absolute risk aversion (CARA) utility with absolute risk aversion of $\beta > 0$.[12] It maximizes the end-of-period expected utility of granting credit under the two possible information structures.

The following derivations make repeated use of the following integration[13] for x normally distributed with mean μ and standard deviation σ. Here f_x denotes the corresponding density function.

$$\int \exp(ax) f_x \, dx = \exp\left[\mu a + \frac{(a\sigma)^2}{2}\right]$$

In case (1) we have the following objective value:

$$EU_1 \equiv -\int \exp[-\beta(q_j + \varepsilon_{ij})]\,d\varepsilon_{ij}$$

$$= -\exp(-\beta q_j)\int \exp[-\beta \varepsilon_{ij}]\,d\varepsilon_{ij}$$

$$= -\exp\left[-\beta\left(q_j - \frac{\beta\sigma_P^2}{2}\right)\right]$$

In case (2) the objective function is similarly

$$EU_2 \equiv -\int \exp[-\beta(q_j - C_F + \mu_{ij})]\,d\mu_{ij}$$

$$= -\exp\left[-\beta\left(q_j - C_F - \frac{\beta\sigma_{PF}^2}{2}\right)\right]$$

Therefore, the lender will expend C_F if

$$q_j - C_F - \frac{\beta\sigma_{PF}^2}{2} > q_j - \frac{\beta\sigma_P^2}{2}$$

Equivalently

$$C_F + \frac{\beta}{4}[\sigma_P^2 + \sigma_F^2 + \mathrm{cov}(\varepsilon_{ij}, \delta_i)] < \frac{\beta\sigma_P^2}{2}$$

$$C_F < \frac{\beta}{8}[3\sigma_P^2 - \sigma_F^2 - 2\,\mathrm{cov}(\varepsilon_{ij}, \delta_i)]$$

This formulation admits a number of comparative statics results: The lender is more likely to expend C_F if:

- The lender is more risk averse (i.e., β is higher)
- The precision of the static signal is higher (i.e., $\dfrac{1}{\sigma_F}$ is higher)
- The precision of the payment signal is lower (i.e., σ_P is higher)
- The covariance between the two signals is lower

Of these observations, perhaps the most interesting is the last; the extent to which the payment experience and financial statement signals are uncorrelated is crucial to the value of obtaining further information.

Now consider the case of a formal information exchange, which aggregates the individual J_i payment signals and offers, at price C_B, a composite signal u_i,

$$u_i = q_i + \gamma_i$$

Now the standard deviation[14] of the error term γ_i is σ_C, given by

$$\sigma_C^2 = \mathrm{var}\left[\frac{1}{J_i}\left(\varepsilon_{i1} + \cdots + \varepsilon_{iJ_i}\right)\right]^2 = \frac{\sigma_P^2}{J_i}$$

Proceeding as earlier, we now determine conditions under which the lender will expend C_B to acquire this composite signal. In the first case, assume that the lender has not acquired the static signal. The variance of the combined signal is

$$\frac{1}{4}\left[\frac{\sigma_P^2}{J_i} + \sigma_P^2 + \frac{2\sigma_P^2}{J_i}\right] = \frac{\sigma_P^2(3 + J_i)}{4J_i} \equiv \sigma_{PB}$$

Now the expected utility is

$$EU_3 \equiv -\int \exp[-\beta(q_j - C_F + v_{ij})]\,dv_{ij}$$

$$= -\exp\left[-\beta\left(q_j - C_F - \frac{\beta\sigma_{PB}^2}{2}\right)\right]$$

The lender will expend C_B if

$$q_j - C_B - \frac{\beta\sigma_{PB}^2}{2} > q_j - \frac{\beta\sigma_P^2}{2}$$

Equivalently, if

$$C_B < \frac{\beta}{2}\left[\sigma_P^2 - \frac{\sigma_P^2(3+J_i)}{4J_i}\right] = \frac{\beta\sigma_P^2}{2}\left[\frac{3J_i-3}{4J_i}\right]$$

Now the comparative statics show that the lender will be more likely to expend C_B if:

- The lender is more risk averse (i.e., β is higher)
- The precision of the payment signal is lower (i.e., σ_P is higher)
- J_i increases

The first two points parallel the previous case. The third observation shows the effects of scale. As more payment experiences are accumulated, the precision of the composite signal increases, making it more valuable. This captures the key source of economies of scale associated with information exchanges that collect information from multiple creditors of the same firm. This model could apply to both private information exchanges and PCRs. It would not, however, apply to those public credit registries that only collect information from single lenders. Thus, for example, it would not apply to a credit registry that collects only specific payment information on a firm's bank lender and not its trade creditors.[15]

The final case is when a borrower that has already accumulated the static signal, will also expend C_B to acquire the composite payment signal. Without supplying the details[16] here, it is clear that the same intuition outlined in the previous two comparative statics analysis will also carry forward in this notationally more complex case.

5.4   Empirical Evidence on Formal Information Exchange

The theoretical motivation for information sharing in general, and formal information exchanges in particular, have been analyzed, including offering our own contribution to this literature. The model here specifically clarifies that the economies of scale from formal information exchange principally derive from aggregating information from multiple lenders to produce a less noisy signal of borrower quality. What is the evidence that formal information exchange works? Does it add value in the real world? This issue is addressed next.

There have been a number of empirical studies that shed light on the value added from formal information exchange. First, note that information exchange mechanisms are widespread. Based on questionnaires sent to forty-nine countries, Jappelli and Pagano (1999) found that nineteen countries had PCRs and twenty-nine countries had voluntary information exchanges.

Some of the empirical research on formal information exchanges suggests that the presence of formal information sharing has a significant impact on aggregate economic performance. To the extent that information sharing represents an efficient vehicle for reducing contracting costs associated with asymmetric information, then one would expect more credit availability and a lower cost of capital in countries that had either public credit bureaus or private information brokers. Jappelli and Pagano (1999) find that countries with more developed formal information sharing, either via credit registries or voluntary information exchanges, exhibit greater bank lending as scaled by GNP. They also find that credit risk is negatively related to measures of formal information sharing. One policy implication of this finding is that countries without any exchange mechanisms may find it advantageous to establish a PCR. Jappelli and Pagano (1999) explore this policy issue further by finding empirical evidence that suggests that PCRs can be effective substitutes for voluntary information exchanges. They find that countries with voluntary credit information exchanges were less likely to start a PCR. In their empirical tests of lending and substitutability, however, no distinction is made between business credit information sharing and consumer information sharing.

Only limited empirical work has been done at the microlevel on the value added from information sharing. Petersen and Rajan (2001) provide some indirect evidence on the benefits of information sharing in an empirical study of the effect of improved information availability. They study the changing relationship between small U.S. firms and their lenders using data from the 1988 and 1993 National Survey of Small Business Finance. They find that the average distance between small firms and their lenders has increased significantly over time. They attribute this, at least partially, to improvements in bank productivity due to increased availability of borrower credit records. More generally, it could be viewed as consistent with an overall increase in the availability of information about borrowers and a decrease in the cost of this information. It is possible that information sharing among lenders and through formal information exchange could be included as part of this overall increase in information availability. Given data limitations in Petersen and Rajan's (2001) study, however, specific sources of improved information availability were not identifiable.

One recent study specifically focuses on the value added from formal information exchanges at the microlevel. Kallberg and Udell (2002) analyze the incremental value of information generated by a formal private information exchange in assessing borrower quality. Specifically, they examine the U.S. case by analyzing the value of information accumulated by D&B, including most importantly D&Bs mercantile credit information (including trade experiences). In particular, they empirically test the power of D&B's key payment behavior index in models of firm failure prediction using D&B data on 2,723 firms, 241 of which failed during the sample period. They also test whether information accumulated and sold by D&B adds value above and beyond information that is otherwise publicly available and/or accessible to private lenders such as ratios from financial statements. D&B's key measure of payment behavior is Paydex, which gives a composite evaluation of the most recent thirteen months of reported payment history. As noted, this statistic can be converted to average days past due (dollar-weighted), although the actual calculation involves more than just this measurement. The close relationship between Paydex and firm failure is shown in figure 5.3 which shows the normalized failure rate. For example, a value of one indicates that the failure rate is the same as the overall population failure rate. This figure shows how dramatically the failure rates increase as Paydex declines. At a Paydex of 50 (which roughly corresponds to payments averaging 30 days slow), the failure rate is more than five times the average. At a Paydex of 30 (slow 90 days), the failure rate is over nine times the average.

Kallberg and Udell estimate logistic regression models to discriminate between bankrupt and nonbankrupt firms. They test three models: a model based on information in the D&B database (including Paydex and firm characteristics); a model based on just financial statement data (mostly financial ratios); and a model including both types. They found that Paydex is the most significant variable in the first and third models. This finding implies that credit information produced by a formal information exchange—particularly information aggregated from multiple trade experiences—adds information

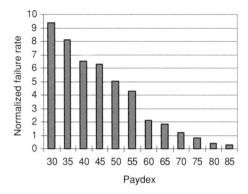

Figure 5.3
Paydex and firm failure rate
Note: The horizontal axis shows the Paydex level and the vertical axis shows the normalized firm failure rate associated with that Paydex level in the KU sample. A normalized failure rate of one indicates that the failure rate is the same as the overall population failure rate. A normalized failure rate of 6 indicates that the failure rate is over six times the population average.

above and beyond the information that is otherwise available to lenders. They also found that the first model significantly out performs the second model. The performance of these models is displayed in figure 5.4 which shows the error rates for the three models in sample. This result suggests that payment performance information is even more powerful than financial statement information in evaluating borrower creditworthiness.

Figure 5.4 also shows the performance of the Kallberg and Udell models out-of-sample for quartiles based on total assets, quartile one is the smallest. While it appears reasonable that model 2, which uses only financial statement data, should improve as firms size increases, this is not apparent in the data. The error rate (percentage misclassified) in the largest and smallest quartiles are approximately the same. Comparing the out-of-sample error rates for models 1 (using just D&B data) and 3 (using all available data) shows that the incremental impact of adding financial statement variables to model 1 is small; the error rates are almost identical in each quartile. In the total out-of-sample group, the error rate for model 1 is 12.8 percent while it is 11.7 percent for model 3. It is also interesting to observe that the error rates for models 1 and 3 decline by almost 50 percent as firm size increases. This suggests that as the number of trade experiences increases (because of greater firm size), the models that use

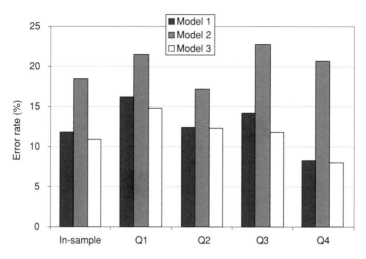

Figure 5.4
Model error rates
Note: This figure shows the error rates for each of the three models in-sample and out-of-sample. The last four sets of columns correspond to KU's out-of-sample groups divided into asset size quartiles from smallest to largest. Model 1 refers to model using only mercantile credit data; Model 2 uses only financial statement data and Model 3 uses both types.

D&B data perform better. The Kallberg and Udell study provides rather powerful evidence that the information contained in information exchange-aggregated trade performance (and modeled here in section 5.3) is a powerful tool for lenders in assessing borrower quality.

5.5 Conclusions

The quality and availability of information is an important determinant of the efficiency of the credit markets that provide external funding to business. From the perspective of financial system design, this is a particularly challenging issue for small businesses, which tend to be acutely informationally opaque. Moreover, because their credit transactions tend to be small, the high fixed costs generally associated with information production can make credit origination proportionately more expensive for small businesses than large businesses. Information sharing mechanisms could play a major role here. These mechanisms can either take the form of a public institution or private one. This chapter analyzed one of the world's largest private information exchanges, Dun and Bradstreet.

We have noted in the analysis that theoretical models of information sharing have demonstrated that the exchange of credit information can be useful in addressing adverse selection problems at the origination stage and in addressing moral hazard problems after funding. We extensively discussed the types information produced by D&B and used by its customers in their credit decision making, with particular emphasis on the D&B trade credit database. We also offer here a new model that clarifies the value added by a formal information exchange. The model isolates the key source of economies of scale in information exchange: the reduction in the statistical noise when multiple trade experience data are aggregated by an information exchange in generating a signal about borrower quality. The model also examines the conditions under which lenders will incur the costs associated with purchasing such a signal from a formal information exchange.

Finally, we noted that there is a paucity of empirical evidence on the value of business credit information exchange mechanisms. Two studies that directly examine this issue empirically were discussed, one addressed the issue at the macrolevel and one at the microlevel. The former study analyzed the relationship between the existence of information exchange and macroeconomic performance at the country level. It found that countries with formal information exchanges exhibit greater bank lending and lower credit risk. The latter study examined the value of the information provided by an information exchange, in this case D&B, in the credit decision-making process. It found that the information produced by an information exchange, particularly aggregated trade experience data, added significantly to a lender's ability to assess borrower quality as measured in failure prediction models. They also found that information from D&B was significantly more important in predicting firm failure then financial information.

Our analysis of the theoretical and empirical work in this area indicates that the information produced by formal information exchanges, particularly information about trade credit behavior, adds significant value. This is reflected both at the microlevel in improved lender underwriting and at the macrolevel in improved macroeconomic performance. More generally, our analysis leads to the conclusion that formal information exchange mechanisms improve the efficiency of credit markets. Our analysis also suggests that private information exchanges are a viable alternative to public information exchanges (i.e., PCRs). One argument in favor of PCRs is that they may be a superior mechanism in solving the agency and organizational problems that affect the reliability of the information they produce. Thus, to some extent, it is an empirical issue as to whether reputation effects and other mechanisms are sufficiently powerful to ensure the viability of private information exchanges. The longevity of D&B by itself strongly suggests that these problems can be overcome. The empirical finding that D&B's trade payment information is significant in predicting firm failure, and that it is more powerful than financial statement information, provides further evidence that a private information exchange can overcome these credibility problems and generate data that improve lender underwriting ability.

Acknowledgments

The authors would like to thank Margaret Miller and an anonymous referee for very helpful comments. We are grateful for the comments of our discussants—John Barry of Heller Financial, Dan Corcoran of Equifax and Thomas Holloway of Freddie Mac—at the World Bank International Conference on Credit Reporting Systems, Miami Florida, June 23–24, 2000. We would like to acknowledge the assistance of the members of D&B's Technical Services Group. All errors remain the responsibility of the authors.

Notes

1. See ⟨www.dnb.com⟩ for these and related figures.

2. See "Wages of Hatred," *BusinessWeek*, October 9, 2000, pp. 71–74.

3. See Newman (1997) for a historical perspective.

4. While strictly speaking, a firm may not yet be in the database in the sense that a credit report has not been generated on the firm. It is often the case that D&B has trade experiences on this firm already available, but these remain unmatched to the firm until a credit inquiry is created.

5. See Berger and Udell (2001) for a more detailed discussion of these technologies and related theoretical and empirical work.

6. Credit scoring has been used in loan monitoring for some time. Its application here, however, was limited to large credits because the credit-scoring models were calibrated using data on large publicly traded firms.

7. Trade creditors will often use credit-scoring models themselves. This would represent a melding of these two technologies.

8. Berger and Udell (1995) report that most small firms that obtain working capital financing borrow only from a single bank.

9. The simultaneous observation of performance across multiple loan contracts (via formal information sharing), coupled with the continuous recontracting nature of trade credit, may be analogous to the enforcement of cross-default covenants found in multiple-lender financing for large firms.

10. This is not to say that these government organizations are devoid of agency problems, only that these problems are probably of second-order importance relative to the credibility problems associated with private information brokers. Specifically, it appears reasonable to assume that the objective function of central banks is more likely to be aligned with maximizing social welfare.

11. The variance of the combined error is $\frac{1}{4}[\sigma_P^2 + \sigma_F^2 + 2\,\mathrm{cov}(\varepsilon_{ij}, \delta_i)]$. Note that the authors are not attempting to determine the optimal weights on the two signals here or in the subsequent derivations. This would be easy to do but would complicate the notation without changing any of the comparative statics, which are the focus in this section.

12. In this context one can assume without loss of generality that the initial wealth is zero.

13. It can be most easily derived from properties of the moment generating function for the normal distribution.

14. Here the authors have assumed that the series of signals generate serially uncorrelated estimates of "true" quality.

15. There also may be economies of scale associated with the vendors who generate the data used by the information exchange. If these vendors are large and extend trade credit to many customers, then the costs associated with collecting, storing, and transmitting that information to the information exchange may be lower. Economies of scale from this indirect source are not modeled here.

16. These are available from the authors upon request.

References

Berger, A. N., and G. F. Udell. 1995. "Relationship Lending and Lines of Credit in Small Firm Finance." *The Journal of Business* 68 (3): 351–382.

Berger, A. N., and G. F. Udell. 2001. "Small Business and Debt Finance." In *Handbook of Entrepreneurship*, ed. Z. J. Acs and D. B. Audretsch. Dordrecht: Kluwer Academic Publishing.

Cox, R., and J. Shulman. 1985. "An Integrative Approach to Working Capital Management." *Journal of Cash Management* 5 (6) (November–December): 64–67.

Jappelli, T., and M. Pagano. 1999. "The European Experience with Credit Information Sharing." Universitia di Salerno: mimeo.

Kallberg, J., and G. Udell. 2002. "The Value of Private Sector Business Credit Information Sharing: The U.S. Case." Stern School of Business, NYU, Working paper, December.

Klein, Daniel B. 1992. "Promise Making in the Great Society: A Model of Credit Information Sharing." *Journal of Economics and Politics* 4: 117–136.

Leshchinski, Dima. 2000. "Does It Pay to Voluntarily Disclose Private Information?" Working paper, INSEAD.

Newman, J. Wilson. 1997. "Dun and Bradstreet: For the Promotion and Protection of Trade." In *Reputation: Studies in the Voluntary Solicitation of Good Conduct*, ed. Daniel B. Klein. Ann Arbor: University of Michigan Press.

Padilla, A. J., and M. Pagano. 1997. "Endogenous Communication Among Lenders and Entrepreneurial Incentives." *The Review of Financial Studies* 10 (1): 205–236.

Padilla, A. J., and M. Pagano. 1999. "Sharing Default Information as a Borrower Discipline Device." University of Salerno: CSEF working paper no. 21.

Pagano, M., and T. Jappelli. 1993. "Information Sharing in Credit Markets." *The Journal of Finance* 43: 1693–1718.

Petersen, M. A., and R. G. Rajan. 2001. "Does Distance Still Matter? The Information Revolution in Small Business Lending." *Journal of Finance*.

6

**The Use of Public Credit
Registry Information in
the Estimation of
Appropriate Capital and
Provisioning
Requirements**

Michael Falkenheim and
Andrew Powell

6.1 Introduction

In common with the majority of the credit registries created by central banks and analyzed in this book, the original motivation for the creation of the credit registry in the Central Bank of Argentina in 1991 was also prudential in nature. In particular, the primary concern was to collect information on the larger debtors of the financial system and to understand how those debtors provoked risks for the financial system and for individual banks. For this reason, the credit registry began life as a database including only information on large debtors.

Over time, however, the power of this tool for other objectives was realized. First, the importance of sharing information among financial institutions was realized, and at an early stage the database was given to virtually all the financial institutions at low cost. Second, the power of this information to address "willingness to pay" issues prompted both an extension of the database and its wider distribution. Today, the database covers virtually all loans in the financial system, numbering over six million entries, is updated monthly and is freely available to anyone for consultation through the Internet.[1]

As the database grew, it became clear that there were yet further potentially interesting uses of these data. In chapter 7, Berger et al. use the data to study the relations between lenders and borrowers (especially small and medium sized enterprises). A further exciting use of this database, however, is to analyze appropriate capital and provisioning strategies for banks and, in particular, to assess whether current capital and provisioning regulations match up to actual risks. That is the focus of this chapter.

In particular, simple techniques are developed to estimate the expected loss and the variance of potential losses of a portfolio of Argentine loans. The authors advocate that provisions should cover expected losses and that capital requirements should cover potential losses over and above expected losses subject to some statistical level of tolerance. They then assess how actual capital and provisioning requirements match up to estimated requirements given by the theoretical model and calibrated using a particular sample of recent data.

The chapter is organized as follows. Section 6.2 gives a brief account of the history of the credit registry. Section 6.3 describes a potential differentiation between provisioning and capital requirements with reference to the probability distribution of loss of a portfolio of loans. Sections 6.4 and 6.5 describe briefly the recent debate about the definition of provisioning and capital requirements and suggest that capital requirements may need to reflect portfolio considerations. Section 6.6 presents the methodology and estimates for implied provisioning requirements, given a simple model to derive expected losses, and compares these estimates to actual provisioning requirements. Section 6.7 presents a simple portfolio model to evaluate credit risk over and above expected losses, and section 6.8 presents results comparing implied to actual capital requirements. Section 6.9 offers some conclusions.

6.2 The History of the *Central de Deudores del Sistema Financiero* Database

The source of data for studying credit risk here is the *Central de Deudores del Sistema Financiero* (CDSF) database, a public credit registry (PCR) which currently carries information on virtually every loan in the Argentine financial system. The CDSF originated in January 1991 when the Central Bank of Argentina began to collect and disclose information about the largest debtors (with debts over $200,000) of the financial system. Financial institutions provided the information, and after validation it was then redistributed to all contributors. The information on debtors originally included only the classification assigned to each debtor by each financial firm.[2] Later the Central Bank required banks to report more detailed information, including the principal activity of the debtor, its links, if any, to the lending institution, the business group to which it belonged, debts by currency denomination, collateral, provisions, and net worth. In September 1994, the Central Bank decided to make the information available to the public by charging a modest fee, through an agency named the Risk Center (Diaz 1998; Roisenzvit 1997).

In 1995 the Central Bank decided to extend the range of debtors through the creation of the Credit Information Center (CIC). This new register included information on debtors from the nonfinancial sector with debts greater than $50, thus covering practically the entire range of borrowers. The CIC began to operate in January 1996 together with the Risk Center. For each debtor, the CIC provided the following information to the public: principal activity, total debt, collateral, and the financial institution's classification of the debtor. In October 1996 the Central Bank decided to disclose the information contained in the CIC for an annual fee.

By March 1997 the amount of information processed per month by the Risk Center was approximately 45,000 records, corresponding to 25,000 debtors, while the CIC processed around 4.5 million records per month. In July 1997 both risk centers were unified in the *Central de Deudores del Sistema Financiero* CDSF. This central bank agency now allows access to the public via the Internet. This history is summarized in table 6.1.

Employing the CDSF to study credit risk entails a number of practical problems. For example, the database does not contain information on individual debts, but instead groups all of the debts of each individual at a financial institution together. Many credit risk models developed recently, such as J. P. Morgan's CreditMetrics™

Table 6.1
History of the *Central de Deudores del Sistema Financiero* database

January 1991	A database is established with information on debtors with credits of more than $200,000
September 1994	The information is made available to the public through the "risk center" agency
January 1996	The credit information center (CIC) begins to operate, reporting information on debts larger than $50.
October 1996	The Argentine Central Bank begins to disclose the CIC information for a monthly fee.
July 1997	The "risk central" and CIC are unified in the *Central de Deudores del Sistema Financiero* (CDSF) database

(see Gupton, Finger, and Bhatia 1997), require information on the interest rate and structure of payments of debts.[3] The CDSF does not provide information about the structure of debts, and only recently it has begun to provide information on loan duration and the interest rate of debts. Moreover, until recently, it was difficult to track individual debtors over time. Recently the Argentine Central Bank has begun a project to store historical data in a more accessible form and also to improve the information on the interest rate and duration of debts. These improvements will be invaluable for this type of research going forward. For these practical considerations, it was decided here to use data from January 1998 giving us some fifteen months of information.

6.3 Provisions, Capital Requirements, and Credit Risk

Provisioning and capital requirements both attempt to control credit risk by creating a buffer against credit losses (Basle Committee on Banking Supervision 1999a,b). On a practical level it is sometimes difficult to differentiate between provisions and capital. For example, in the Basle 1988 Accord, it was agreed that a general provisioning requirement might be recorded as capital against requirements. In theory, however, provisions and capital serve two quite distinct purposes. Provisions should protect banks against ordinary levels of credit loss, while capital requirements should protect banks against unforeseen losses. In statistical terms, while provisions should reflect the expected value of credit losses, capital requirements should protect against unexpected losses subject to some level of statistical tolerance. This means that in theory both provisioning and capital requirements may be specified from the same distribution (the distribution of potential credit losses), but they reflect different statistics of that distribution.

Figure 6.1 illustrates the implied level of provisions and capital requirements by means of an example. The graph plots a distribution of potential credit losses (for a single loan or a loan portfolio). Marked on the graph is the expected loss, $12,500 in the example, and this is then the appropriate level of provisions. Capital requirements on the other hand should reflect unexpected losses, which are usually defined as the difference between a given percentile level and the expected loss. In this example, appropriate capital requirements were calculated as equal to the difference between the 99.9

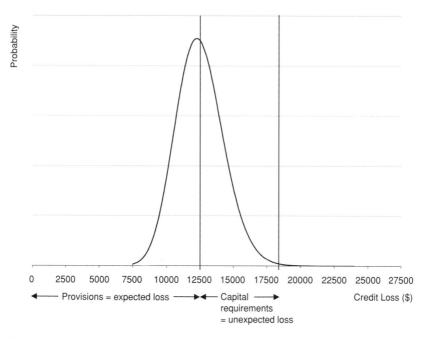

Figure 6.1
The credit loss distribution

percentile of credit losses and the expected value. The 99.9 percentile defines a line that places just 0.1 percent of the distribution to the right and in the example is at \$18,000. Thus appropriate capital requirements here are \$18,000 − \$12,500 = \$5,500. Note that credit losses should exceed the 99.9 percentile in only one out of 1,000 possible economic scenarios (just over once every eighty-three years, considering monthly drawings from this distribution).

If a financial institution charges interest over and above expected losses, this could also protect it against credit losses. Interest rates might be higher than what is required to cover expected losses for a number of reasons. First, if the financial institution has market power, it may be able to set interest rates above the level that would prevail in a competitive market. Second, the competitive market's interest rates might reflect a risk premium associated with systematic risk. Escudé (1999), for example, presents a Capital Asset Pricing Model (CAPM) approach where expected loan returns in excess of the risk-free rate depend on the loan's risk contribution to a common optimally diversified market portfolio. He argues that capital requirements should be proportional to this excess component of interest rates, automatically accomplishing the goal of requiring capital in proportion to portfolio risk. Addressing the role of excess interest rates could then potentially give a more complete picture of risk. It was decided that at this point, however, it was not worthwhile to attempt to estimate the effect of such excess interest on portfolio risk. The authors of this chapter do not have adequate information on interest rates to study how they relate to default risk. Also, their studies have indicated that financial institutions vary substantially in their level of diversification. Some diversify their portfolio in a way that is consistent with established finance theory and others do not. Many institutions have large concentrations in individual debtors and industries, and probably they are not compensated for this with higher interest rates. Thus, the relationship between risk and interest rates is not uniform across financial institutions, and measuring it on an institution by institution basis would be highly complicated. It is not necessarily desirable to lower the capital requirements for institutions with interest rates in excess of the expected value of credit losses. It is not good regulatory policy to reward banks that exercise market power and charge higher interest rates, even if this protects them against credit losses. Doing so would reinforce their monopoly power. As the central bank gathers more information on interest rates in the future, research will be better able to identify the elements that comprise them, and the authors will incorporate this information into our future analysis.

6.4 Provisioning Requirements: A Discussion

In Argentina, as elsewhere, the central bank requires a minimum level of provisions for each individual loan, which depends on the economic classification of the debtor. For commercial loans, financial institutions are required to "rate" the debtor on a scale of 1 to 5, depending on the economic condition of the obligor through an analysis of their expected cash flow. For consumer and housing loans, financial institutions must base the classification of debtors on their current payment status. Commercial loans of less than $200,000, according to current regulations, may be treated as consumer loans based on these requirements. One of the central purposes of this study is to evaluate the current system of provisioning requirements. In particular, credit registry data was used to assess whether the level of provisions for each classification is adequate given observed loss probabilities.

In evaluating the current levels of provisions, the authors first develop a financial model of loan value, which takes into account expected credit losses. Then this model was estimated with the available credit registry data to estimate the level of provisions needed to cover those expected losses.

6.5 Capital Requirements: A Discussion

The recent literature stresses the need for capital requirements to maintain a healthy financial system by limiting the risk of bank failures. While in the past the level of requirements reflected "rules of thumb," or arguably were the outcome of complex political negotiations, more recently there have been greater attempts to quantify appropriate levels of regulatory capital. The methodology normally applied is to consider what stock of capital would cover potential losses in all but a small percentage of scenarios that could prevail in the relevant horizon. The relevant horizon is normally seen to be the time needed to take risk-mitigating actions such as the sale of risky loans or the replenishment of capital.

The Basle 1988 Capital Accord formally establishes the current form of capital requirements for "internationally active" banks in G-10 countries. Over 100 countries, however, including Argentina, have explicitly adopted the Basle Accord either in their own banking regulations or in some cases in law. In many countries, however, the rules are applied not only to internationally active banks but also to domestic banks. Moreover, in some countries while the general Basle methodology has been adopted, the actual requirements adopted have been stricter than the minimum 8 percent of assets at risk recommended by the Basle document. Countries have then adopted their own limits within the general methodology depending on the perceived level of credit risk.

In Argentina, the central bank sets capital requirements for the banking system and has established (since the end of 1994), a minimum ratio of 11.5 percent for capital to risk-weighted assets for counterparty risk. The Basle Accord defined risk-weights for different assets in an attempt to capture the different levels of risk in their returns. In Argentina these weights are used, but they are complemented with a risk indicator that is based on the interest rate charged on each loan. This additional risk indicator is a factor that multiplies the base capital requirement. Under this system, loans with higher interest rates have higher capital requirements because they are presumed to have a higher level of risk. Argentine capital requirements also include a factor that depends on the CAMELS[4] rating assigned by the superintendency to each financial institution. On top of counterparty risk capital requirements, the central bank has also imposed capital requirements for market risk and for interest rate risk. The current Argentine capital requirements may then be specified by the following formula:

overall capital requirement

$$= 11.5^*IR^*W^*K + \text{market risk} + \text{interest rate risk}[5]$$

Where IR is the interest rate factor, W is the average Basle risk weight for assets and K is the CAMELS factor assigned by the superintendency.

One shortcoming of Basle-style capital requirements is that they do not take into account how individual exposures are combined in the loan portfolio. One large loan to a single company for $100 million has the same capital requirement as 1,000 loans of $100,000 each to 1,000 different companies if these loans are in the same risk category. Maintaining a diversified portfolio, however, will in general reduce the total credit risk of an institution. Moreover, requirements do not differ according to the level of correlation of asset returns in a portfolio. A portfolio of loans exclusively to companies in the textile sector would have the same capital requirement as a portfolio of loans spread across various industries, assuming they were all in the same risk category. If the standard rules do not reflect well the actual risks of financial institutions' credit portfolios, then this may result in either too little or too much capital and distort capital allocation decisions.

A recent proposal to remedy this situation is the use of internal models to assess capital adequacy. Under this system, financial institutions would apply to use their own measures of credit risk to determine the capital requirement. Regulatory authorities would need to decide which models deserve authorization based on their technical merit and historical performance. Recent analyses of such models, however, still place this possibility at an early stage of development. Indeed, a recent proposal to modify the Basle 1988

Accord, while including many ideas to improve credit risk assessment of individual debtors, shies away from methods to analyze portfolio risk including internal models.

In using a credit risk model, it is important to evaluate provision and capital requirements to recognize the current limitations of this approach. The Basle committee and other institutions studying credit risk models all concluded that they were not yet sufficiently well developed to use in a capital requirement system. According to the Basle Committee on Banking Supervision (1999a,b) and many scholars (see Jackson, Nickell, and Perraudin 1999), important issues, such as the correct shape of the loss distribution, have not been resolved and the short span of historical data makes it impossible to properly validate credit risk models. Furthermore, other risk factors such as operational risk have not been adequately studied. The basic ratio established in the Basel Capital Accord might also provide a needed hedge against operational and other risks.

The problems with the implementation of internal models for credit risk regulatory capital is mirrored in an emerging country context. Moreover, it is likely that some of the problems are magnified. For example, model assumptions both about structure and parameters are likely to be more unstable and technical, and human resources are likely to be more constrained. Faced with this reality, the objectives in the exercise below are more modest. Namely, the authors consider that such models might be employed as a check to see whether current regulations match, in broad terms, implied theoretical levels. Here the concern is with the total amount of provisions and capital available to an institution or to the financial system as a whole. The authors do not consider, for example, how this capital is distributed across the loan portfolio. In this way, the exercise does not address questions of efficiency but rather questions of overall prudential standards.

Another possible use of credit risk models is in supervision. Capital requirements in Argentina depend on the CAMELS rating that the Superintendency of Financial Institutions assigns to each institution. Supervisors in Argentina rate institutions between 1 and 5 based among other things on the level of risk of their assets. This rating translates into a lower or higher capital requirement, since each rating leads a different multiplier to be applied to the global capital requirement. A reasonable objective is then that credit risk models may help supervisors quantify the credit risk of institutions and perhaps become an explicit part of their (CAMELS) ratings decisions.

In developing a credit risk model, it is necessary to measure to what degree diversification reduces insolvency risk. Diversification cannot completely reduce portfolio risk when credit outcomes are positively correlated. Credit registry information can reveal the economy-wide correlation between the default risk of loans based on their characteristics, thereby discovering the relationship between diversification and risk, and also inform one about the nature of credit risk in moments of crisis. Credit registry information can play an important role in measuring (1) the risk of different types of loans and (2) the risk of each bank's portfolio to determine the proper level of provisioning and capital requirement.

The first step in the following investigation will be the development of a methodology that estimates the variance of the return on banking portfolios using the CDSF information. This information is used to study loan outcomes based on debtor variables, calculate the variance of loan returns, and calculate the covariance between loans with different characteristics. These are then used to parameterize a function that estimates the variance of the returns of banking portfolios in the Argentine system.

6.6 Calculating Provisions as a Function of Loan Classification

To measure the economic cost of credit deterioration, let us assume that the value of a loan depends on its classification. The provisions should reflect the difference between its balance sheet value and its economic value so that the loan's net balance is equal to its economic value. This difference should reflect, among other things, the expected loss due to credit risk. The classification (or "state") is a number between 1 and N. Assume that a loan with a balance of B and classification s has an economic value of V_sB dollars where $0 \leq V_s \leq 1$. Then also add the state 0 for the case in which the loan is paid in full before the end of the next period, and $N+1$ is the state in which the loan becomes irrecoverable in the next period. $V_0 = 1$, since a loan that is paid in full will yield its entire balance. Then assume that when a loan becomes irrecoverable that its value is zero.[6] Thus

$$V_{N+1} = 0$$

The loan's value in any given period must be equal to its present expected value in the following period when there is some probability that the loan will either become irrecoverable or that it will be completely paid. There is also some probability that it will retain the same classification or that it will change to any one of the other classifications. Let us assume that these probabilities depend on the current classification of the loan. These probabilities can then be used to derive a value of the loan for each classification in the form developed by Cyert, Davidson, and Thompson (1962). Define $q(r,s)$ as the probability that a loan in classification r will change to classification s.

In the next period the loan will accrue interest so that its balance or payment will be R times its current value $(R > 1)$ provided that the loan is in classification 1 or 2. In Argentina, if a loan is in classification 3 or worse, it generally does not accrue interest. If it does, the bank must set aside the entire amount of accrued interest as provisions as recommended by international standards (Basle Committee on Banking Supervision 1999c). It is necessary to discount future cash flows to reflect their present value. The discount factor is defined here as β and assume that $0 < \beta < 1$. If one knew with certainty that a loan with a current balance of B_i pesos would be in classification s in the next period, then its present value would be $\beta R V_s B_i$ if it begins the period in classification 1 or 2, and $\beta V_s B$ if it begins the period in classification 3–5. If a loan is paid in the next period, it will yield RB_i pesos representing a present value of $\beta R B_i$ pesos. If the loan becomes irrecoverable in the next period, then assume that its value is zero as stated above. The restriction that a loan's current value is equal to the present expected value in the next period gives the following expressions:

$$V_r = \beta R \sum_{s=0}^{6} q(r,s)V_s \quad \text{for } r = 1, 2 \tag{1}$$

and

$$V_r = \beta \left[\left(\sum_{s=1}^{5} q(r,s)V_s \right) + Rq(r,0) \right] \quad \text{for } r = 3, 45 \tag{2}$$

If one knows β and R, and estimate the matrix of elements $q(r,s)$, then it is possible solve this set of five equations for the five unknown elements: $V_r, r = 1, \ldots, 5$.

Table 6.2
Monthly transition probabilities for loans by classification, February 1998–April 1999

Classification at the beginning of the month	Classification at the end of the month (percentage)						
	0 (paid)	1	2	3	4	5	6 (irrecoverable)
1	5.4	91.7	2.6	0.1	0.1	0.2	0.0
2	6.0	24.3	51.8	16.8	0.3	0.8	0.0
3	5.0	7.4	4.1	64.0	19.1	0.4	0.0
4	2.9	2.7	0.6	1.3	83.3	9.2	0.0
5	0.0	2.1	0.2	0.1	0.3	94.2	3.1

Table 6.3
Estimated values for loan classifications (percentage)

Classification	Definition	Value	Implied provision	Current minimum provision
1	Normal	99	1	1
2	Potential Risk	91	9	5
3	Substandard	77	23	25
4	Doubtful	63	37	50
5	Loss	40	60	100
Total for the financial system (Argentine pesos)			4.6 billion	6.2 billion

Averaging over the fifteen-month period, the authors obtained transition matrix presented in table 6.2.

To perform the calculation indicated in equation (2), assume R to be equal to 1.01, which is approximately one plus the average monthly interest rate in Argentina over the relevant period. Assume β to be equal to $\frac{1}{1.005}$ since the average monthly deposit rate in Argentina is approximately 0.5 percent. With these assumptions, the authors acquired an estimate of the vector V, of loan values in each of the five classifications. Provisions for loans with classification s should be equal to $1 - V_s$ of the balance as shown in table 6.3.

It can be seen that the levels of provision for classifications 1–3 are close to those implied by the model. The figures suggest, however, that provisioning requirements for category 2 could be tightened, whereas they are too strict for categories 4 and 5. Loans rated as 5 seem to have some value, even though the category is defined as a "loss." This is because a small proportion of these loans eventually repay.

The total minimum level of actual provisions for the entire financial system is above the level that is implied by the model. This suggests that on a global basis the provisions of the Argentine financial system are sufficient. Note, however, that the results imply that current provisioning levels may be too low for category 2 and too high for categories 4 and 5. Thus, the model suggests that it might be appropriate to alter the distribution of provisioning requirements somewhat across the different categories, but at the same time it suggests that current provisioning requirements in aggregate represent a conservative approach to covering expected credit losses. At the same time, one must remember the limitations of the model discussed above in drawing strong policy conclusions from these results.

6.7   Estimating the Variance of Portfolio Returns Using the CDSF

The same model of loan value used to calculate the adequate level of provisions can be used to estimate the variance of portfolio returns. The variance of a portfolio return can indicate a notion of the value at risk. Two important building blocks in these calculations of portfolio return variance are the variance of individual loan returns and the covariance of returns between different loans.

The balance of loan A is defined here as B_A for $A = 1, \ldots, N$ the variance of the return as a percent of its value of loan A as σ_A^2 and the covariance of the return of loan A with the return of loan B as σ_{AB}. With this notation, observe that the variance of the return of the loan portfolio, σ_P, is:

$$\sigma_P = \sum_{A=1}^{N} B_A^2 \sigma_A^2 + 2 \sum_{\{A,B:A \neq B\}} B_A B_B \sigma_{AB} \tag{3}$$

To estimate σ_P, it is first necessary to estimate σ_A^2 and σ_{AB} for all loans A and all pairs of loans A and B.

To do this, divide loans into groups and assume that their statistical properties are homogeneous within each group. Then assume that loans of the same sector and classification form a group. For example, all of the loans in classification 3 in the agricultural sector form a group. In each period, the probabilities of changing to each possible classification are identical for all loans within each group. The assumption here will allow us to express σ_A^2 and σ_{AB} as functions of their sector and classification, and estimate them using economy-wide data.

First note that if loan A in classification r_A and sector j_A has the probability $q_A(r_A, s)$ of ending in each of the seven possible classifications s, then the mean and variance of its return are the following:

$$\mu_A = \sum_{s=1}^{S} q^{j_A}(r_A, s) \left(\frac{R}{V_r} V_s \right)$$

(4)

$$\sigma_A^2 = \sum_{s=1}^{S} q^{j_A}(r_A, s) \left(\frac{R}{V_r} V_s - \mu_A \right)^2$$

This gives an expression for the variance of a loan in any group that depends on its probabilities of transition, $q^j(r, s)$ and the values of loans in each classification V_s. To apply it, use the values V_s developed in the previous section and estimate $q^j(r, s)$ for all sectors j and all classifications r and s, using data from the entire sample period.[7]

To estimate the covariance of loan returns, the authors model individual loan returns as the sum of two random components: a group component and an individual component. The return of loan A, x_A^t, in period t is:

$$x_A^t = x^{j_A, t}(r_A) + z_A^t$$

(5)

where $x^{j_A, t}(r_A)$ is the group component in period t and z_A^t is a zero-mean component that is independently distributed for each individual. Under the assumption that individual components are independent, the covariance between the returns of loans A and B in any period t is the following:

$$\sigma_{AB} = Cov(x^{j_A, t}(r_A), x^{j_B, t}(r_B))$$

(6)

In other words, the covariance between loan returns is equal to the covariance of the group component of each loan's return. In the case where

$$j_A = j_B \quad \text{and} \quad r_A = r_B:$$

$$\sigma_{AB} = Var(x^{j_A, t}(r_A))$$

(7)

To estimate the covariance between the group components, calculate the average return for each group in each time period, and define the group average for loans in sector j, classification r, and period t as $\overline{x^{j,t}(r)}$. For the group comprising loans in sector j and classification r, the group average at time t is equal to the following:

$$\overline{x^{j,t}(r)} = \frac{R}{V_r} \sum_{s=1}^{S} q^{j,t}(r,s) V_s \tag{8}$$

With the elements $\overline{x^{j,t}(r)}$ one can estimate the variance and covariance of group components over time.[8] In appendix 6A, the authors obtain the following estimate for σ_{AB} using data from periods $t = 1, \ldots, T$, where loans A and B are in different groups, that is, $j_A \neq j_B$ and/or $r_A \neq r_B$:

$$\hat{\sigma}_{AB} = \frac{1}{T-1} \sum_{t=1}^{T} \left[\left(\overline{x^{j_A,t}(r_A)} - \frac{1}{T} \sum_{t=1}^{T} \overline{x^{j_A,t}(r_A)} \right) \left(\overline{x^{j_B,t}(r_B)} - \frac{1}{T} \sum_{t=1}^{T} \overline{x^{j_B,t}(r_B)} \right) \right] \tag{9}$$

In appendix 6B the authors derive the following equation for the covariance of two loans (i and k) in the same group (where $j_A = j_B$ and $r_A = r_B$) where n_A is the number of loans in the group:[9]

$$\hat{\sigma}_{AB} = \frac{1}{T-1} \sum_{t=1}^{T} \left[\left(\overline{x^{j_A,t}(r_A)} - \frac{1}{T} \sum_{t=1}^{T} \overline{x^{j_A,t}(r_A)} \right)^2 \right] - \frac{1}{n_A} \hat{\sigma}_A \tag{10}$$

Having derived an estimate for the variances of the returns of all loans and the covariance of all possible pairs of loans, it is possible to calculate the variance of any loan portfolio.

6.7.1 Data

The data used here come from the *Central de Deudores* database. All loans from the entire financial system in the fifteen months between February 1998 and April 1999 were used. There were approximately 4.5 million loans in each month of this period, and the transition matrices using the data from successive periods were calculated.

The following information for each debtor at each financial institution was used here:

1. The amount of the debt
2. The principal activity of the debtor

Table 6.4
Volatility of industry average returns for loans with "normal" classification

Industry	Standard deviation of monthly return (percentage)
Agriculture and fishing	0.85
Mining	0.09
Manufacturing and utilities	0.23
Construction	0.22
Commercial	0.17
Services	0.43
Personal loans	0.14

3. The classification of the debtor

4. The collateral of the debtor

6.7.2 Parameters

As noted in the earlier analysis, the variances of average returns of different groups and the covariance between the returns of different groups are important parameters in estimating loan portfolio variance. Table 6.4 presents some of the estimated parameters. They show which industry groups had more volatile returns during the period from which data were taken and also the correlation between industry average returns.

Table 6.4 shows that some industries have more volatile loan returns than others. By far the largest level of average return volatility corresponds to the agriculture and fishing industry whose average loan returns had a monthly volatility equal to 0.85 percent. At the other extreme, mining has a very low volatility of returns. This accords with substantial anecdotal evidence from the banking sector. Agriculture is generally considered one of the most risky sectors, given the combination of small, often family-led businesses, climatic risks, and volatile agricultural prices. Although the mining sector has also suffered from extreme price volatility, it is characterized by large companies, many of which have foreign capital.

Table 6.5 shows the correlation of industry average returns. Fifteen of the twenty-one numbers in the table are positive, suggesting that there may be factors that affect the performance of all loans in the economy. Indeed, it is clear that most sectors are cyclical with personal loans, with manufacturing and utilities, commercial loans,

Table 6.5
Correlation between industry average returns for loans with "normal" classification (percentage)

Industry	Agriculture and fishing	Mining	Manufacturing and utilities	Construction	Commercial	Services	Personal loans
Agriculture and fishing	—	30.3	98.7	4.0	89.6	6.7	90.7
Mining		—	31.6	−15.6	40.9	−9.0	16.8
Manufacturing and utilities			—	−5.9	86.0	2.5	89.7
Construction				—	31.9	−20.8	13.7
Commercial					—	−8.2	87.6
Services						—	−8.6
Personal loans							—

agriculture, and fishing all showing high positive correlations. Construction and loans in the service sector appear to be the exception, exhibiting negative correlations with the other group. The significant positive correlations suggest that banks will be limited in the extent to which they can shelter themselves from negative economic conditions with diversification across industries, although this will depend on particular banks' portfolios.

As mentioned before, the variances and covariance ideally would have been estimated using a much longer series of data. Since the data used here span only fourteen months, it is natural to be concerned about the stability of the parameters. In particular, it might be that the high correlations found between the average returns of agriculture and fishing loans and manufacturing and utility loans are a result of particular shocks over the sample period and not a long-run structural phenomenon. The authors will only be able to correct this problem in a few years when they have a longer sample period.

6.8   Implicit Capital Requirements

As discussed in the introduction, there are some serious restrictions in using portfolio credit risk models to establish capital requirement regulations both in theory and in the calibration of any model with available data. Nevertheless, the authors considered it an interesting exercise to estimate what capital requirements would be implied by the variance and covariance estimates. In the above, they have avoided making assumptions about the shape of the loss distribution, so strictly speaking it is not possible to convert the variance estimated in the previous section into a percentile of the loss distribution. Nevertheless, for the sake of comparing these results and the existing system of capital requirements, the authors will assume an implied capital requirement equal to three times the estimated volatility and warn that it is necessary to interpret these results with caution. Naturally, if credit loss distributions are normal, then this will agree with the 99.9 percentile of the distribution. Table 6.6 presents average implicit capital requirements for different types of financial institutions when employing this criterion.

Table 6.6 compares implied capital requirements using the model developed in this chapter versus an estimated Basle capital requirement and the actual Argentine capital requirement. The results are

Table 6.6
Implied capital requirements for different types of financial institutions (percentage)

Type of financial institution	Implied capital requirement	Basle requirement[a]	Argentine average capital requirement[b]	Average capital level
Medium sized Retail banks	6.8	6.6	13.5	19.0
Large retail banks	6.9	5.6	10.2	11.9
Small retail banks	7.8	6.9	16.1	24.7
Privatized banks	7.9	5.0	10.0	15.5
National public banks	8.0	5.5	8.3	13.7
Large wholesale and investment banks	8.1	4.7	7.5	14.4
Small and medium wholesale and investment banks	9.8	7.0	13.7	49.4
Other financial institutions	10.6	7.6	23.4	40.4
Provincial and municipal public banks	12.1	5.8	11.9	11.6

a. The Basle requirement was calculated using the 8 percent capital to assets ratio and the Basle Capital Accord's risk weights.
b. The Argentine capital requirement is derived from the formula 11.5%*K*W*IR. K represents the factor derived from the supervisor's CAMELS rating of the financial institution, W represent the average (Basle-style) risk weight of the assets, and IR is the risk indicator derived from the interest rate of loans in the institution's portfolio.

suggestive. First, the Basle capital requirements are without exception lower than the implied requirements underlining the need for stricter limits than the recommended international minimum. Second, the Basle requirements do not vary much over the different categories of banks (a minimum of 4.7% for large wholesale to 6.9% for small retail), whereas the implied requirements range from a minimum of 6.8 percent for medium retail to 12.1 percent for provincial and municipal banks.

Third, the Argentine capital requirements are in general higher than those of the implied levels (the exception being large wholesale banks). In some cases the actual Argentine requirements are substantially higher than the implied levels, including retail banks and other financial institutions (nonbanks). In the case of retail banks, this gives some support for the benefit of diversification of loan portfolios. On the other hand, large wholesale banks have lower actual requirements probably because in general they have a combination of good CAMELS ratings and low loan interest rates. The implied capital requirement is slightly higher than the actual requirement probably because these banks lend in general to low volatility sectors and there is no benefit for this in current regulations. These results suggest that further work is justified in attempting to see how refinements to current regulations might result in a finer correspondence between actual requirements and credit risk of different types of financial institutions.

It is also worth noting, however, that the actual capital of the banks is significantly higher than both the implied level of capital given by the model and the Argentine regulations. It appears then that banks are, on average, more conservative about capital levels than both the theoretical capital requirements and the Argentine regulations would suggest.[10]

6.9 Conclusions

The objective of this chapter was to use the extensive credit registry data of the central bank to evaluate provisions and capital requirements in the Argentine financial system. Although there are some limitations on the use of this information for credit risk models—the database was not originally intended for this—the authors were able to develop a simple model of loan valuation and portfolio return variance and use the credit registry data to calibrate that model. They have argued that in theory provisioning requirements and capital requirements can be defined with a single distribution (the distribution of potential credit losses), but while provisions should reflect expected losses, capital requirements should reflect unexpected losses relative to some tolerance value.

Using this approach and the credit registry data, actual provisioning requirements were found to be close (but to exceed) implied levels, but that there was an argument to refine the requirements across different categories. The authors also found that implied capital levels generally exceed the Basle minimum recommendation of 8 percent of assets at risk suggesting that Basle requirements need to be stricter in the context of an emerging economy such as Argentina. Implied capital requirements, however, were in general lower than actual requirements depending on the type of financial institution.

This chapter is a first attempt to use a simple portfolio model of credit risk and credit registry data to consider regulatory capital requirements. There are many restrictions and "health warnings" which should accompany this type of analysis. The theoretical assumptions are strong and the data used are limited in their time span and so forth. The results reflect these limitations and should be read as suggestive rather than authoritative. Nevertheless, the authors consider this to be an extremely important potential use of the extensive Argentina credit registry and an additional factor supporting the policy of the central bank to develop this extremely valuable resource.

Appendix 6A   The Covariance of Individual Loan Returns

This section demonstrates that the equation given in (9) is an unbiased estimator of the covariance σ_{AB}. Equation (9) stated the following

$$\hat{\sigma}_{AB} = \frac{1}{T-1} \sum_{t=1}^{T} \left[\left(x^{j_A,t}(r_A) - \frac{1}{T} \sum_{t=1}^{T} x^{j_A,t}(r_A) \right) \left(x^{j_B,t}(r_B) - \frac{1}{T} \sum_{t=1}^{T} x^{j_B,t}(r_B) \right) \right]$$

Define $\mu^{j_A}(r_A) \equiv E[x^{j_A,t}(r_A)]$ and $\overline{x^{j_A}(r_A)} \equiv \frac{1}{T} \sum_{t=1}^{T} x^{j_A,t}(r_A)$

Then

$$E\left[\left(\overline{x^{j_A,t}(r_A)} - \frac{1}{T} \sum_{t=1}^{T} x^{j_A,t}(r_A) \right) \left(\overline{x^{j_B,t}(r_B)} - \frac{1}{T} \sum_{t=1}^{T} x^{j_B,t}(r_B) \right) \right]$$

$$= E \left[\begin{array}{c} \left(\left(\overline{x^{j_A,t}(r_A)} - x^{j_A,t}(r_A) \right) + \left(x^{j_A,t}(r_A) - \mu^{j_A,t} \right) \right. \\[1em] \left. + \left(\mu^{j_A,t} - \frac{1}{T} \sum_{t=1}^{T} x^{j_A,t}(r_A) \right) + \left(\frac{1}{T} \sum_{t=1}^{T} x^{j_A,t}(r_A) - \frac{1}{T} \sum_{t=1}^{T} \overline{x^{j_A,t}(r_A)} \right) \right) \\[1.5em] \left(\left(\overline{x^{j_B,t}(r_B)} - x^{j_B,t}(r_B) \right) + \left(x^{j_B,t}(r_B) - \mu^{j_B,t} \right) \right. \\[1em] \left. + \left(\mu^{j_B,t} - \frac{1}{T} \sum_{t=1}^{T} x^{j_B,t}(r_B) \right) + \left(\frac{1}{T} \sum_{t=1}^{T} x^{j_B,t}(r_B) - \frac{1}{T} \sum_{t=1}^{T} \overline{x^{j_B,t}(r_B)} \right) \right) \end{array} \right]$$

This is equal to

$$
= E \left[
\begin{array}{l}
\left(\left(x^{j_A,t}(r_A) - \mu^{j_A,t} \right)\left(x^{j_B,t}(r_B) - \mu^{j_B,t} \right) \right. \\[2ex]
\left. + \left(\mu^{j_A,t} - \frac{1}{T}\sum_{t=1}^{T} x^{j_A,t}(r_A) \right)\left(x^{j_B,t}(r_B) - \mu^{j_B,t} \right) \right) \\[3ex]
\left(\left(x^{j_A,t}(r_A) - \mu^{j_A,t} \right)\left(\mu^{j_B,t} - \frac{1}{T}\sum_{t=1}^{T} x^{j_B,t}(r_B) \right) \right. \\[3ex]
\left. + \left(\mu^{j_A,t} - \frac{1}{T}\sum_{t=1}^{T} x^{j_A,t}(r_A) \right)\left(\mu^{j_B,t} - \frac{1}{T}\sum_{t=1}^{T} x^{j_B,t}(r_B) \right) \right)
\end{array}
\right]
$$

since the expected values of the other cross-products are equal to zero.

$$
= E\left[\sigma_{AB} - \frac{1}{T}\sigma_{AB} - \frac{1}{T}\sigma_{AB} + \frac{1}{T}\sigma_{AB} \right]
$$

$$
E\left[\sigma_{AB} - \frac{1}{T}\sigma_{AB} \right]
$$

This means that

$$
\hat{\sigma}_{AB} = \frac{1}{T-1}\sum_{t=1}^{T}\left[\left(\overline{x^{j_A,t}(r_A)} - \frac{1}{T}\sum_{t=1}^{T}\overline{x^{j_A,t}(r_A)} \right)\left(\overline{x^{j_B,t}(r_B)} - \frac{1}{T}\sum_{t=1}^{T}\overline{x^{j_B,t}(r_B)} \right) \right]
$$

$$
= \frac{1}{T-1}\sum_{t=1}^{T}\left[\sigma_{AB} - \frac{1}{T}\sigma_{AB} \right]
$$

$$
= \frac{T}{T-1}\left[\sigma_{AB}\frac{T-1}{T} \right]
$$

$$
= \sigma_{AB}
$$

Appendix 6B The Covariance of the Returns of Loans in the Same Group

Equation (10) stated the estimate of the covariance between the returns of loans in the same group to be

$$\hat{\sigma}_{AB} = \frac{1}{T-1} \sum_{t=1}^{T} \left[\left(x^{j_A,t}(r_A) - \frac{1}{T} \sum_{t=1}^{T} x^{j_A,t}(r_A) \right)^2 \right] - \frac{1}{n_A} \hat{\sigma}_A^2$$

where n_A is the number of loans in group A. This is an unbiased estimator of σ_{AB}. Define $\mu^{j_A}(r_A) \equiv E[x^{j_A,t}(r_A)]$ and $\overline{x^{j_A}(r_A)} \equiv \frac{1}{T} \sum_{t=1}^{T} \overline{x^{j_A,t}(r_A)}$ and note that $j_A = j_B$ and $r_A = r_B$ given that the loans are in the same group. Then

$$E\{\hat{\sigma}_{AB}\} = E\left\{ \frac{1}{T-1} \sum_{t=1}^{T} [(\overline{x^{j_A,t}(r_A)} - \overline{x^{j_A}(r_A)})^2] - \frac{1}{n_A} \hat{\sigma}_A^2 \right\}$$

It is possible to write

$$E(\overline{x^{j_A,t}(r_A)} - \overline{x^{j_A}(r_A)})^2$$

$$= E \left(\begin{array}{c} [\overline{x^{j_A,t}(r_A)} - x^{j_A,t}(r_A)] + [x^{j_A,t}(r_A) - \mu^{j_A}(r_A)] \\ + \left[\mu^{j_A}(r_A) - \frac{1}{T} x^{j_A,t}(r_A) \right] + \left[\frac{1}{T} \left(\sum_{t=1}^{T} x^{j_A,t}(r_A) - \overline{x^{j_A}(r_A)} \right) \right] \end{array} \right)^2$$

$$= \frac{\sigma_A^2}{n_A} + \sigma_{AB} + \frac{1}{T} \sigma_{AB} + \frac{1}{T} \frac{\sigma_A^2}{n_A} - \frac{2}{T} \frac{\sigma_{AB}}{n_A} - \frac{2}{T} \frac{\sigma_A^2}{n_A}$$

$$= \frac{T-1}{T} \sigma_{AB} + \frac{T-1}{T} \frac{\sigma_A^2}{n_A}$$

Thus

$$E\left\{ \frac{1}{T-1} \sum_{t=1}^{T} [(\overline{x^{j_A,t}(r_A)} - \overline{x^{j_A}(r_A)})^2] - \frac{1}{n_A} \hat{\sigma}_A^2 \right\}$$

$$= \frac{1}{T-1} \sum_{t=1}^{T} \left[\frac{T-1}{T} \sigma_{AB} + \frac{T-1}{T} \frac{\sigma_A^2}{n_A} \right] - \frac{1}{n_A} \hat{\sigma}_A^2$$

$$= E\left\{ \frac{T}{T-1} \left[\frac{T-1}{T} \sigma_{AB} + \frac{T-1}{T} \frac{\sigma_A^2}{n_A} \right] - \frac{1}{n_A} \hat{\sigma}_A^2 \right\}$$

$$= E\left\{ \sigma_{AB} + \frac{\sigma_A^2}{n_A} - \frac{\hat{\sigma}_A^2}{n_A} \right\}$$

$$= E[\sigma_{AB}]$$

Acknowledgments

The authors would like to thank Verónica Balzarotti, Guillermo Escudé and George McAndless, conference participants, and an anonymous reviewer for invaluable comments. All remaining errors are the responsibility of the authors. The opinions expressed in this chapter are entirely those of the authors and do not necessarily reflect those of the Central Bank of Argentina.

Notes

1. See the website of the Central Bank, ⟨www.bcra.gov.ar⟩.

2. In Argentina a basic system of five categories ("classifications") is used to classify loans where 1 is "normal" and 5 corresponds to "loss."

3. One model that does not require much information is CreditRisk+ (Credit Suisse Financial Products 1997). In a parallel study, we have applied that model to the same information.

4. The acronym CAMELS stands for Capital, Assets, Management, Earnings, Liquidity, and Sensitivity, which are the six sets of variables that supervisors examine when determining their classification.

5. Argentina, as recommended by Basel, also has capital charges for off-balance sheet activities.

6. This assumption is not as restrictive as it appears. The following analysis can be applied to any loan provided that it is first decomposed into two parts: a part that is recovered in the case of liquidation and a part that is not. The part that is recovered will retain its full value no matter what the classification of the loan.

7. In the future, the authors will allow these values to vary by sector so that the value of a loan depends on both its sector and its classification. They will then recalculate the parameters with the values, V_s^j.

8. The process of deriving the covariance (or correlation) between loan returns using the variance and covariance of group average returns is known in the credit risk literature as reverse-engineering and is quite widely used.

9. The second term on the right-hand side corrects for the fact that in a finite sample, we would expect the group average return to vary even when there is no covariance between loan returns (see appendix 6B).

10. Obviously such levels of capital proved inadequate to confront recent events in Argentina—the default of the public sector and a forced revaluation of loans and deposits at different exchange rates. These events impacted severely on bank solvency and are not contemplated in the modeling exercise.

References

Basle Committee on Banking Supervision. 1999a. "Consultative Paper on a New Capital Adequacy Framework." Mimeo.

Basle Committee on Banking Supervision. 1999b. "Credit Risk Modeling Current Practices and Applications." Mimeo.

Basle Committee on Banking Supervision. 1999c. "Sound Practices for Loan Accounting, Credit Risk Disclosure and Related Matters." Mimeo.

Credit Suisse Financial Products. 1997. "CreditRisk+, A Credit Risk Management Framework." Mimeo.

Cyert, R. M., H. J. Davidson, and J. L. Thomson. 1962. "Estimation of the Allowance for Doubtful Accounts by Markov Chains." In *Management Science*, 287–303.

Diaz, Julio. 1998. "Credit Information: Conceptual Issues and a Description of the Argentine Case." Mimeo.

Escudé, Guillermo. 1999. "El Indicador de Riesgo Crediticio de Argentina dentro de un enfoque de teoría de carteras de la exigencia de capital por riesgo crediticio." Working paper no. 8, Central Bank of Argentina.

Gupton, Greg M., Christopher C. Finger, and M. Bhatia. 1997. "Credit Metrics—Technical Document." Morgan Guaranty Trust Co. New York.

Jackson, Patricia, Pamela Nickell, and William Perraudin. 1999. "Credit Risk Modelling." *Financial Stability Review* (June): 94–102.

Roisenzvit, Alfredo. 1997. "Los institutos de Información Crediticia en Argentina." Internal memo, BCRA.

7 Relationship Lending in the Argentine Small Business Credit Market

Allen N. Berger, Leora F. Klapper, Margaret J. Miller, and Gregory F. Udell

7.1 Introduction

This chapter discusses public credit registries (PCRs), their purposes and the special case of the Argentine PCR which is atypical in the access it provides to information on borrowers in the financial system. The chapter also reviews changes in the Argentine financial system during the 1990s, a period of tremendous change that included financial crises, fundamental changes in banking regulation and supervision, and massive entry of foreign capital into the sector. The expansion of the Argentine PCR was in large part designed to deal with these changes in the financial system.

The chapter also reviews the literature on small business lending which suggests that large banks, foreign-owned banks, and distressed banks may face particularly steep barriers to providing relationship lending services to informationally opaque small businesses. Given the growth in size of Argentine banks, the huge market shares acquired by foreign-owned institutions, and the amount of distress that banks in Argentina appear to experience, significant concerns may be raised about the adequate supply of credit to these informationally opaque small businesses.

Finally, the chapter reviews some specific econometric research by Berger, Klapper, and Udell (2001) that uses data from the Argentine PCR to address these concerns by matching the borrowing firms to their banks and testing three hypotheses about the effects of bank size, foreign ownership, and financial distress on credits granted to informationally opaque small businesses. This chapter also provides some additional cross-tabulations of the data that support these hypothesis tests.

Increasing numbers of central banks have established PCRs, which collect data from supervised financial institutions about the payment histories of borrowers. These registries typically have two principle objectives: (1) to provide information on borrowers to the financial system for credit risk analysis; and (2) to be an input to supervision of financial intermediaries, enabling supervisors to better understand the credit risks facing institutions and more easily identify inappropriate lending practices.

A third use of the data from PCRs is for economic analysis. The availability of disaggregated credit data at an economy-wide level, as found in a PCR, is unique and enables researchers to ask questions that would otherwise be impossible. The detailed loan data in the PCR makes it possible to look at the behavior of different segments of the credit market, such as small businesses, and different types of financial institutions. Data on bank assets are seldom available in adequate detail to answer this type of question.

The rest of the chapter is organized as follows. Section 7.2 provides a literature review related to the three hypotheses to be tested. Section 7.3 briefly describes the Argentine financial system in the 1990s, including changes relevant to the hypotheses tested here. Section 7.4 describes the public credit registry policy of the Argentine Central Bank and the data used. Section 7.5 presents the empirical results, and conclusions are discussed in section 7.6.

7.2   Literature Review

There is ample empirical evidence that small banks devote larger proportions of their assets to small firms than do large financial institutions, including contributions by Berger, Kashyap, and Scalise (1995), Keeton (1995), Berger and Udell (1996), Strahan and Weston (1996) and Peek and Rosengren (1998). When large banks enter the small business credit market, research suggests they look for strategies that reduce their reliance on relationship lending, for example, by standardizing credit policies (examples include Berger and Udell 1998, Scott and Dunkelberg 1999, and Machauer and Weber 2000) and placing reliance on financial ratios (Cole, Goldberg, and White 1999). Large banks, which often have access to lower cost capital than small institutions, may also use their price advantage to attract the highest quality small enterprise borrowers, including those who have been in business longer, are more financially secure, and are seeking transaction-based credit (Haynes, Ou, and Berney 1999).

Another factor that may affect the ability of large banks to service relationship borrowers has to do with the physical distance that often exists between the small firm requesting credit and the credit grantor, who may be in a centralized office at great distance. If an important part of the banking relationship is the ability to frequently monitor the borrower, either directly or through third-parties, then large banks with centralized decision systems may be at a significant disadvantage when compared to small, local institutions. Hauswald and Marquez (2000) find this is the case as does Miller (1995). Recent empirical evidence by Petersen and Rajan (2002), however, suggests that the importance of distance in the small business lending market may be decreasing due, in part, to the increasing availability of reliable credit reports.

Several papers discuss the operations of foreign-owned banks, and they find that such banks adopt strategies favoring larger borrowers. These contributions include DeYoung and Nolle (1996) who find foreign-owned institutions tend to have a wholesale orientation, or Goldberg and Saunders (1981) and Grosse and Goldberg (1991) who find they service large corporate affiliates of customers from their country of origin. Most studies on bank efficiency have also found that foreign-owned institutions are less efficient than their domestically owned counterparts in the host nation, which is consistent with the notion that they are informationally disadvantaged (see Berger et al. 2000 for a review).[1]

The behavior of foreign-owned banks in the Argentine small business lending market has been analyzed in several previous papers with conflicting results. Bleger and Rozenwurcel (2000) find that, between 1996 and 1998, foreign bank participation in Argentina is associated with a reduction in credit going to the small business sector from 20 percent to 16 percent. Escudé et al. (2001), in a comprehensive review of small business lending in Argentina using data from the PCR, find that small business loans represent a smaller fraction of the portfolios of foreign-owned banks compared to domestically owned institutions, but that total foreign bank lending to the sector has increased over the period 1998–2000. Foreign-owned institutions provided 42.7 percent of credit for micro, small, and medium enterprises in June 2000, up from 38.1 percent in June

1998. Private domestically owned banks reduced their share over the same period from 31 percent to 27.5 percent. With these results, Escudé and his coauthors conclude that foreign entry to the banking sector has not been detrimental to small business access to credit.[2] Clarke, Cull, Martinez-Peria, and Sánchez (2001) also analyze the impact that foreign ownership has on bank lending to small business borrowers in a cross-country study using data from Argentina, Chile, Colombia, and Peru. They find that foreign bank ownership is associated with both a smaller share of small business lending in the bank's credit portfolio and with slower growth of lending to this sector. Although in general Clarke et al. find support for the proposition that small business lending is negatively related to bank size, they find that, among foreign-owned institutions in Argentina, larger banks are more rapidly increasing their small business lending.

Argentina may be somewhat unique in the attention paid to the issue of foreign ownership of banks and small business lending. The rapid increase in the share of assets held by foreign-owned banks in the 1990s, discussed in greater detail in the next section, together with concern for the health of the troubled small business sector, made this an important topic which could be explored given the availability of data from the PCR.

The literature on bank distress and lending to small business is limited. Hancock and Wilcox (1998) provide one of the few contributions in this area. They find that lending was reduced more at small banks, per $1 decline in capital, than at large institutions, which would indicate a greater contraction in lending to small versus large businesses, since small firms receive a higher proportion of their credit from small institutions. Much of the literature on bank distress and lending relates to the "credit crunch" experienced in the U.S. economy during the major economic downturn in the early 1990s, but these papers focus on total lending, not loans specifically for small businesses.[3]

7.3   Changes in the Argentine Financial System in the 1990s

The Argentine financial system experienced profound changes during the 1990s. Many banks were closed or merged with other institutions, the average asset size of institutions increased, and foreign participation in the sector expanded to the extent that only one of the top five banks in 2001 was majority Argentine-owned capital. Some of these changes were the result of policy shifts, while others resulted from the 1995 financial crisis.

The Mexican banking crisis in 1994–1995 (the Tequila crisis) had substantial contagion effects throughout much of Latin America. The Argentine stock and bond markets suffered large losses and the financial sector came close to the point of collapse. Consequently, the Argentine banking sector experienced substantial consolidation and increased foreign entry. Mergers, acquisitions, and closures also accounted for a drop in the number of private domestically owned banks—between December 1991 and December 1998, the number decreased from 182 to 112—with most of these changes occurring after 1994. During this period, the percentage of total assets at private domestically owned banks decreased from 66 percent to 30 percent and total loans fell from 65 percent to 32 percent (Raffin 1999).

At the same time, the number of foreign-owned banks was increasing, with purchases of some of Argentina's largest banks by major foreign institutions—Banco Santander purchased Banco Rio, HSBC purchased Banco Roberts and Banco Bilbao Vizcaya (BBV) purchased Banco Frances. Between 1996 and 1998, foreign direct investment in Argentina's domestic banking sector was estimated at over $4 billion in a total investment in Latin America of over $10 billion (Raffin 1999). Between December 1991 and December 1998, the percentage of total assets held by foreign-owned banks increased from 14 percent to 53 percent, total loans grew from 12 percent to 46 percent, and deposits rose from 17 percent to 44 percent (Raffin 1999). The foreign-owned bank growth reflected not only acquisition of large domestically owned banks, but also a flight to quality. Banking market shares held by foreign-owned institutions represented over 40 percent of the market in 2001; more typical levels internationally are less than 10 percent (Levine 1996).

Aggregate data on the banking sector also suggest that foreign-owned banks behave differently than domestic ones. For example, in 1997, foreign-owned banks made loans almost exclusively to borrowers in Buenos Aires, where 95 percent of their portfolios were concentrated, compared with 57 percent in the case of private domestic banks. Foreign-owned banks also appear to favor economic sectors with large borrowers, such as manufacturing and utilities, while domestically owned banks lend to sectors with many small borrowers, including retail, food products, wood and metal industries, and primary production.

The average asset size of banks in Argentina also increased significantly during the 1990s. In 1994 the average asset size of Argentine banks was 420 million pesos and the median size was 130 million pesos. By 1998 these figures had grown to an average of 1.15 billion and median of 244 million pesos.[4]

State-owned banks are another segment of the Argentine financial system. Two of the largest institutions in the country, Banco de la Nacion and Banco de la Provincia de Buenos Aires, continue to be state-owned, but many others have been closed or privatized, especially those owned by provinces or municipalities. Many of these privatizations took place in the aftermath of the 1995 financial crisis, when fifteen institutions were closed in the span of one year (Calomiris and Powell 2000). In 1997, eighteen state-owned banks held 31 percent of Argentine total bank assets and 35 percent of total deposits. State-owned institutions have been plagued by inefficiencies and in some cases have mandates to lend to certain sectors regardless of creditworthiness. As a result, state-owned banks have a high percentage of nonperforming loans. Since these institutions differ significantly in their behavior from private banks and do not necessarily obey market signals, the authors have treated them as a special case in the empirical work.

7.4   Data from the Public Credit Registry

Following the Tequila Crisis, the Argentine Central Bank extended its collection of bank data. The central bank had been collecting information on major debtors, defined as those with total debt in the financial system above 200,000 pesos, in the *Central de Riesgo* (Risk Central) for several years. Following the crisis, this was expanded to include virtually all bank loans in the system. All supervised financial institutions are now required by Argentine Central Bank regulations to report on a monthly basis the status of all bank loans outstanding in excess of 50 pesos. Key information supplied by banks includes the name of the borrower, their taxpayer identification number (QUID), the amount of loans outstanding, the quality category of the loans on a 1 to 5 scale (measured by number of days past due), and details of any guarantees. Borrowers with more than

200,000 pesos in debt are required to provide additional information, including income and property holdings (for individuals) and balance sheet and employment information (for firms). This database, now known as the *Central de Deudores del Sistema Financiero* (CDSF), is the main source of the data used in this chapter.

The data in the Argentine CDSF is similar to that found in many other public registries, but the policy that has been followed on access to this information is unique. Many PCRs aggregate data so that only total exposure in the system is available, and many of them also conceal the names of the reporting financial institutions in deference to bank requests to limit access to the data. Financial institutions in Argentina, in contrast, can consult data from the CDSF to see the exposure of clients with other banks in the system, including both the names of the other institutions, total debt in each, and loan classification on the 1 to 5 scale. Private credit reporting firms operating in Argentina, including the dominant one in the market—Veraz, an Equifax subsidiary—have access to the PCR data on a similar basis as the banks. Veraz and other private credit reporting firms include these data in their products, resulting in unusually widespread availability of positive credit history data in the Argentine financial market. The quality of data in the PCR has continued to improve over recent years, as banks often experience initial difficulties in providing exhaustive loan information on their entire portfolios, especially if they were not previously distributing such information to private reporting firms. There may be reasons to believe, therefore, that the importance of data from the PCR and private reports has increased in recent years, which may have reduced the relative importance of relationship lending.

The database obtained from the Argentine PCR included information on 61,295 nonfinancial firms with loans from banks in Argentina as of the end of 1998. Information identifying the borrower, including both name and tax ID number, was omitted, with a new number assigned to borrowers so that they could be tracked. In most cases, monthly bank reports as of December 1998 were used, but in a few cases in which these monthly reports were unavailable, the November or October reports were used. Since state-owned banks behave differently from private institutions, data were excluded on 19,472 nonfinancial firms that have a state-owned bank as their primary bank. Loans from state-owned banks were included, however, if the borrower had a private bank as the primary source of credit. In all, loans from ninety-eight privately owned banks and seventeen state-owned banks were included in the database.

Data on 1,607 firms with bank loans totaling less than 2,000 pesos were also omitted. Since very small loan amounts are likely to be checking account overdrafts, and more linked to deposit and payments services, they were viewed as less relevant to determining the factors that influence relationship lending.

7.5   Discussion of Empirical Results

Small businesses are one of the most informationally opaque segments of the credit market and these information asymmetries are particularly acute in emerging economies. Small firms in Argentina often mingle the business's finances with those of the owner, may have irregularities about fiscal obligations, and seldom have audited financial statements. Relationship lending may reduce these information asymmetries, as lenders develop knowledge on their small business clients through continuous interaction and observation. Not all financial institutions, however, may be prepared to provide the same level of relationship lending services.

The hypotheses discussed in this chapter are from Berger, Klapper, and Udell (2001). In their paper, data from the Argentine PCR is used to empirically test three hypotheses about the barriers large banks, foreign-owned banks, and distressed banks may face in lending to informationally opaque small businesses. The authors use regressions that control for other factors, including industrial sector of the firm. Their results indicate that both large banks and foreign-owned banks have difficulty extending credit to small firms, but bank distress has no greater impact on small borrowers than on large borrowers. Some additional cross-tabulations of the data are provided here that support these hypothesis tests.

The first hypothesis tested by Berger, Klapper, and Udell is that small banks are more likely to provide relationship lending services to small borrowers than are large financial institutions. Through relationship lending, loan officers learn about the character of borrowers, but this information may not be easily transmitted through the formal communication channels that exist in large organizations. Large institutions may also be headquartered at a significant distance from small business borrowers, again adding to the difficulty of communicating "soft" information about the character and capability of potential clients (Stein 2002). It may also be difficult for one institution to provide transaction lending services and other wholesale capital market services for large corporate clients as well as relationship lending services to small business customers due to Williamson-type organizational diseconomies.

For similar reasons, it may be more difficult for foreign-owned banks to provide relationship lending services than for domestic banks. As was the case with size of bank, foreign-owned banks are more likely to be located at a distance from small business borrowers, either because they are headquartered in the capital city or even have decision makers in other countries. Foreign-owned institutions may also be at a disadvantage with small borrowers due to cultural or language barriers, or if they generally operate in a significantly different type of market or regulatory environment.

Banks in financial distress may also find it difficult to lend to informationally opaque small businesses, especially if these loans are viewed as overly risky or difficult to properly evaluate by auditors, bank supervisors, or others who may be closely watching the bank's operations. On the other hand, banks may try to maintain their relationship lending services, due to the "information rents" they receive from inside knowledge of the borrowers and the cost and difficulty of reestablishing these relationships once they are cut.[5]

Table 7.1, from Berger, Klapper, and Udell (2001), provides the definitions of variables used in the empirical research. Table 7.2 displays bivariate cross-tabulations that look at whether the main hypotheses are generally consistent or inconsistent with the data. The rows represent the dependent variables and the columns represent the key measure of firm opacity—firm size, as proxied by the firm's total loans from banks. Going across the columns, firm size is divided by quartiles, with the smallest 25 percent of firms having loans below 10,000 pesos, the median is 33,600 pesos, and the largest firms are those with more than 126,100 pesos. The data allow examination of bank barriers on firms that are much smaller than is commonly the case in studies of small business lending in the United States, which typically specify small business lending as loans to borrowers with bank credit of $1 million or less.

Each of the main entries in table 7.2 shows the percentage of firms in the size group that have at least one loan from a bank facing one of the potential barriers. For example, the data show that 39.37

Table 7.1
Definitions and summary statistics for variables used to test the main hypotheses

Variable name	Definition	Mean	Standard deviation
Bank barrier variables (dependent variables)			
BNKASSET10% =	1 if a firm borrows from at least one bank that is in the largest 10 percent of banks ranked by asset size (excluding state-owned banks)	65.08%	47.67%
FOREIGN =	1 if a firm borrows from at least one bank that is foreign	52.89%	49.92%
BNKNPL10% =	1 if a firm borrows from at least one bank whose nonperforming loan (NPL) ratio, measured as total bank NPLs to total loans, is in the top 10 percent (excluding state-owned banks)	2.48%	15.55%
BNKLEV10% =	1 if a firm borrows from at least one bank whose leverage, measured as total assets to total debt, is in the top 10 percent (excluding state-owned banks)	19.62%	39.71%
BNKROE10% =	1 if a firm borrows from at least one bank whose ROE, measured as the ratio of profits to liquid assets, is in the smallest 10 percent (excluding state-owned banks)	2.10%	14.35%
SIZE =	The sum of the firm's total loans from all banks	662,148 pesos	6,376,926 pesos

Source: Berger, Klapper, and Udell (2001).
Note: Summary statistics are for the sample of firms used to test the large-bank, foreign-owned bank and distressed-bank barriers hypotheses. The total number of observations is 61,295, which excludes all firms whose primary bank is state-owned and firms with total bank loans less than 2,000 pesos.

percent of firms in the smallest 25 percent in bank loans have at least one loan from a foreign-owned bank. Under the null hypotheses that large banks, foreign-owned banks, and distressed banks face no special barriers in lending to informationally opaque small businesses, the numbers across each row should be the same. For example, if the size of the financial institution is not important in explaining lending to small business borrowers, then firms in the smallest 25 percent should be just as likely to have a loan from a large bank as firms in the largest 25 percent. Alternatively, if the

Table 7.2
Cross-tabulations: The large-bank, foreign-owned bank, and distressed-bank barriers hypotheses

	Firm size (as proxied by total loans from banks)			
	Smallest 25 percent ($\leq$10,000 pesos)	Second 25 percent (10,000 pesos to 33,600 pesos)	Third 25 percent (33,600 pesos to 126,100 pesos)	Top 25 percent ($>$126,100 pesos)
BNKASSET10%	54.55%	59.51%	65.62%	80.66%
FOREIGN	39.37%	46.54%	53.84%	71.85%
BNKNPL10%	1.40%	1.64%	2.27%	4.61%
BNKLEV10%	18.00%	17.40%	20.16%	22.93%
BNKROE10%	0.47%	0.50%	1.00%	6.45%

Note: Variables are defined in table 7.1. Each of the main entries shows the percentage of firms in the size group that have at least one loan from a bank facing one of the potential barriers. For example, the 39.37 percent in the foreign row and smallest 25 percent column indicates that 39.37 percent of firms with less than 10,000 pesos in total bank loans have at least one loan from a foreign-owned institution.

bank size does matter, then one would expect to see the percentages rising from left to right in the table—as firms increase in size, a higher percentage would receive loans from large banks.

The data shown in the tables are consistent with two of the three hypotheses, that size of financial institutions matters as well as whether they are foreign or domestically owned. Smaller firms are less likely than larger firms to have a loan from a large bank or from a foreign-owned bank. This is not to say that large and foreign banks are not important sources of finance for small firms. In the sample, nearly 55 percent of credits going to the smallest firms were from large institutions and almost 40 percent were from foreign-owned banks. The data in these cross-tabulations do not support the hypothesis that distressed banks are less likely to lend to small businesses.

The data can be divided more finely, so that the smallest and largest 10 percent of firms, defined by their total credit exposure, can be studied. The results are even more dramatic and corroborate the findings of table 7.2, with both size and foreign ownership negatively associated with small business lending. For example, only 46 percent of the smallest 10 percent of firms worked with a large bank compared to 58 percent for firms in the next size category (total loan sizes between the 10 and 25 percentile). More than 86 percent of the largest 10 percent of firms, in contrast, had loans from a large bank.

The results on foreign ownership were also emphasized by the more detailed analysis. Although the percentages of small borrowers with loans from foreign-owned institutions did not vary, the percentage did rise substantially among larger borrowers. Approximately 81 percent of the top 10 percent of borrowers by loan size had loans with foreign-owned banks, while in table 7.2, only 72 percent of the top 25 percent by loan size had received loans from these institutions.

7.6 Conclusions

This chapter has presented empirical evidence about the supply of relationship credit in the Argentine small business lending market. The hypotheses tested in this chapter are from Berger, Klapper, and Udell (2001) which provided econometric results that are corroborated here. Using data from Argentina's public credit registry, the authors show that small firms are more likely to receive loans from small banks or from domestically owned banks than from large institutions or foreign-owned institutions. No evidence was found to support a third hypothesis: that distressed banks are less likely to lend to small firms.

These results do not imply, however, that either large or foreign-owned banks cannot or do not work with small firms in Argentina. In fact, both large banks and foreign-owned banks have significant penetration in the small business credit market and since 1998—the year of data used here—evidence has been provided by others, including Escudé et al. (2001) and Clarke et al. (2001), that the share of small business lending by foreign banks is increasing. These papers also confirm that small banks tend to dedicate a higher share of their lending to small firms, although Clarke et al. also finds a wrinkle in this relationship, as large foreign-owned institutions are increasing their small business portfolio at a significantly faster rate than small foreign-owned banks.[6]

The results from this chapter, in the context of other work on this subject, may show that relationship lending takes time to establish, and thus the share of small business lending by foreign-owned institutions may increase for some time after they come to a new market. Improvements in the information available to banks to evaluate risk, including data from the PCR, may be another factor that could explain changes over time in favor of either large or foreign-owned institutions, since they may more readily have resources and technologies, such as credit scoring, to exploit credit data.

Acknowledgments

The opinions expressed here do not necessarily reflect those of the Federal Reserve Board, the World Bank, or their staffs. We would like to thank Jalal Akhavein, Emilia Bonaccorsi, George Clarke, Robert Cull, Laura D'Amato, Chris James, Bob Jennings, Maria Soledad Martinez-Peria, Rick Mishkin, George Pennacchi, Andrew Powell, Rich Rosen, Tony Saunders, Ian Sharpe, Giorgio Szego, and Andy Winton for their helpful comments. This research also benefited from discussions with the participants of the Australasian Conference in Finance and Banking and the Federal Reserve Bank of Chicago Bank Structure and Competition Conference and from comments from seminar participants at the University of Illinois, World Bank, New York Federal Reserve Bank, Banca D'Italia, and European Central Bank. We especially thank Guillermo Escudé and the staff at the Central Bank of Argentina for providing and preparing the data.

Notes

1. Claessens, Demirgüc-Kunt, and Huizinga (2001) is an exception in that they find that foreign-owned banks outperform domestically owned banks in emerging market host nations.

2. Another interesting finding from the Escudé et al. paper is that the share of lending to the micro, small, and medium enterprise sector by public banks fell slightly during this same period, from 28.1 percent to 27.9 percent, with the share of public provincial and municipal banks falling by nearly 40 percent, from 7.7 percent to 4.8 percent of total lending to the sector.

3. Papers on this topic include Berger and Udell (1994), Peek and Rosengren (1995), and Wagster (1999).

4. Data from the Argentine Central Bank. There was little inflation over this period (in 1998 the rate was 1 percent) so most of this growth is in real terms. The nation's convertibility plan pegged the peso to the dollar in 1990 and was still in effect in 2001. By 2000, average asset size in Argentine banks was almost 1.5 billion pesos, with a median of 223 million.

5. It is important to note that relationship lending is of much greater importance in the commercial loan market than in the consumer loan market. Large financial institutions are successfully penetrating even the low-end consumer market relying exclusively upon credit scoring. The use of credit scoring is much more limited in the commercial credit market, however, due to both the typical limitations in business credit data and the greater average loan sizes. In the commercial loan market, the models most often used are "behavioral scores" that model the relationship between the firm and lender over time and grow more reliable the longer the relationship. This points out the difficulty of eliminating relationship lending in the commercial lending sector.

6. The results obtained by Clarke et al. may also be explained by their definition of small firms, which is much larger than that employed in this paper. They used the definition of small and medium enterprise lending used by the Argentine Central Bank: any loan less than $1 million is considered a loan to the small or medium enterprise sector.

References

Berger, A. N., R. DeYoung, H. Genay, and G. F. Udell. 2000. "Globalization of Financial Institutions: Evidence from Cross-Border Banking Performance." *Brookings-Wharton Papers on Financial Services* 3: 23–158.

Berger, A. N., A. K. Kashyap, and J. M. Scalise. 1995. "The Transformation of the U.S. Banking Industry: What a Long, Strange Trip It's Been." *Brookings Papers on Economic Activity* 2: 55–218.

Berger, Allen N., Leora F. Klapper, and Gregory F. Udell. 2001. "The Ability of Banks to Lend to Informationally Opaque Small Businesses." *Journal of Banking and Finance* 25 (12): 2127–2167.

Berger, A. N., and G. F. Udell. 1994. "Did Risk-Based Capital Allocate Bank Credit and Cause a 'Credit Crunch' in the United States?" *Journal of Money, Credit, and Banking* 26 (August): 585–628.

Berger, A. N., and G. F. Udell. 1996. "Universal Banking and the Future of Small Business Lending." In *Financial System Design: The Case for Universal Banking*, ed. A. Saunders and I. Walter, 559–627. Burr Ridge, IL: Irwin Publishing.

Berger, A. N., and G. F. Udell. 1998. "The Economics of Small Business Finance: The Roles of Private Equity and Debt Markets in the Financial Growth Cycle." *Journal of Banking and Finance* 22: 613–674.

Bleger, Leonardo, and Guillermo Rozenwurcel. 2000. "Financiamiento a las Pymes y Cambio Estructural en la Argentina, Un Estudio de Caso sobre las Falles de Mercado y Problemas de Información." *Desarrollo Económico: Revista de Ciencias Sociales* 40 (157): 45–71.

Calomiris, C., and A. Powell. 2000. "Can Emerging Market Bank Regulators Establish Credible Discipline? The Case of Argentina, 1992–1999." Working paper.

Claessens, Stijn, Asli Demirgüç-Kunt, and Harry Huizinga. 2000. "How Does Foreign Entry Affect the Domestic Banking Market?" *Journal of Banking and Finance*, vol. 25: 891–911.

Clarke, George R. G., Robert Cull, Maria Soledad Martinez-Peria, and Susana Sánchez. 2001. "Bank Lending to Small Businesses in Latin America: Does Bank Origin Matter?" Mimeo., World Bank, Washington, D.C.

Cole, R. A., L. G. Goldberg, and L. J. White. 1999. "Cookie-Cutter Versus Character: The Micro Structure of Small Business Lending by Large and Small Banks." In *Business Access to Capital and Credit*, edited by Jackson L. Blanton, Alicia Williams, and Sherrie L. W. Rhine, A Federal Reserve System Research Conference, 362–389.

DeYoung, Robert, and Daniel E. Nolle. 1996. "Foreign-Owned Banks in the U.S.: Earning Market Share or Buying It?" *Journal of Money, Credit, and Banking* 28 (4): 622–636.

Escudé, Guillermo J., Tamara Burdisso, Marcelo Catena, Laura D'Amato, George McCandless, and Tómas E. Murphy. 2001. "Las MIPyMES y el Mercado de Crédito en la Argentina." Argentine Central Bank, working paper no. 15, July.

Goldberg, Lawrence G., and Anthony Saunders. 1981. "The Determinants of Foreign Banking Activity in the United States." *Journal of Banking and Finance* 5: 17–32.

Grosse, Robert, and Lawrence G. Goldberg. 1991. "Foreign Bank Activity in the United States: An Analysis by Country of Origin." *Journal of Banking and Finance* 15: 1093–1112.

Hancock, D., and J. A. Wilcox. 1998. "The 'Credit Crunch' and the Availability of Credit to Small Business." *Journal of Banking and Finance* 22: 983–1014.

Hauswald, Robert, and Robert Marquez. 2000. "Relationship Banking, Loan Specialization and Competition." Indiana University working paper.

Haynes, G. W., C. Ou, and R. Berney. 1999. "Small Business Borrowing from Large and Small Banks." In *Business Access to Capital and Credit*, ed. Jackson L. Blanton, Alicia Williams, and Sherrie L. W. Rhine, 287–327. A Federal Reserve System Research Conference. Federal Reserve System. Available on-line at ⟨www.federalreserve.gov/community.htm⟩.

Keeton, W. R. 1995. "Multi-Office Bank Lending to Small Businesses: Some New Evidence." *Federal Reserve Bank of Kansas City Economic Review* 80 (2): 45–57.

Levine, Ross. 1996. "Foreign Banks, Financial Development, and Economic Growth." In *International Financial Markets: Harmonization Versus Competition*, edited by Claude E. Barfield. Washington D.C.: The AEI Press.

Machauer, A., and M. Weber. 2000. "Number of Bank Relationships: An Indicator of Competition, Borrower Quality, or Just Size?" University of Mannheim working paper.

Miller, Margaret J. 1995. "The Role of Social Relationships in Financial Intermediation: Empirical Evidence from the United States Small Business Credit Market." Ph.D. diss., Department of Economics, University of California at Berkeley.

Peek, J., and E. S. Rosengren. 1995. "Bank Regulation and the Credit Crunch." *Journal of Banking and Finance* 19: 679–692.

Peek, J., and E. S. Rosengren. 1998. "Bank Consolidation and Small Business Lending: It's Not Just Bank Size that Matters." *Journal of Banking and Finance* 22: 799–819.

Petersen, M. A., and R. G. Rajan. 2002. "Does Distance Still Matter? The Information Revolution in Small Business Lending." *Journal of Finance*, forthcoming.

Raffin, Marcelo. 1999. "A Note on the Profitability of the Foreign-Owned Banks in Argentina." *Banco Central de la Republica Argentina*, Technical note No. 6.

Scott, J. A., and W. C. Dunkelberg. 1999. "Bank Consolidation and Small Business Lending: A Small Firm Perspective." In *Business Access to Capital and Credit*, ed. Jackson L. Blanton, Alicia Williams, and Sherrie L. W. Rhine, 328–361. A Federal Reserve System Research Conference. Federal Reserve System. Available on-line at ⟨www.federalreserve.gov/community.htm⟩.

Stein, Jeremy C. 2002. "Information Production and Capital Allocation: Decentralized vs. Hierarchical Firms." *Journal of Finance*, forthcoming.

Strahan, P. E., and J. P. Weston. 1996. "Small Business Lending and Bank Consolidation: Is there Cause for Concern?" *Economics and Finance* 2: 1–6, Federal Reserve Bank of New York.

Wagster, John D. 1999. "The Basle Accord of 1988 and the International Credit Crunch of 1989–1992." *Journal of Financial Services Research* 15: 123–143.

III

The Impact of Public Policies on Credit Reporting

8

The Value of Comprehensive Credit Reports: Lessons from the U.S. Experience

John M. Barron and Michael Staten

8.1 Introduction

Credit bureau data on consumer borrowing and payment behavior has become the cornerstone of the underwriting decision for consumer loans in the United States. Armed with the most comprehensive consumer payment histories on the planet, creditors apply statistical scoring models to estimate an individual's repayment risk with remarkable accuracy. Reliance on risk scoring has fundamentally improved the efficiency of U.S. credit markets and has brought consumers lower prices and more equitable treatment. Perhaps most significantly, credit bureau data have made a wide range of credit products available to millions of households that would have been turned down as too risky just a generation ago.

The full benefits of comprehensive credit reporting have yet to be realized in most other countries. The credit reporting environment varies widely around the globe. Limits on consumer payment histories may be government imposed (perhaps as a result of concerns about consumer privacy, but often due to lobbying for such restrictions by incumbent lenders wishing to limit competition), or they may simply occur as a result of underdevelopment of the legal and technological infrastructure necessary to sustain a comprehensive credit reporting market.

In many countries, consumer credit histories are fragmented by the type of lender originating the loan. This has often occurred when the evolution of the credit data repository was driven by industry affiliation. For example, in some Latin American countries (Argentina, Mexico, and Brazil) banks historically participated in the exchange of information about their consumer loan experience. This exchange led to the construction of comprehensive credit histories on consumers but only on loans held by commercial banks. Nonbank creditors are often barred from using the data built on bank experience and have found it useful to collaborate with each other to build their own credit profiles of customers. In each of these restricted-information scenarios, the data limitations create higher transaction costs for creditors who wish to enter the market, raise the costs of delivering credit, and ultimately restrict the number of consumers who will receive loans and the amounts they borrow.

This chapter discusses what is known about the impact of credit reporting on the availability of credit to households, and it will describe a series of simulations that demonstrate how credit availability is hindered when credit histories are restricted. Section 8.2 reviews both the theoretical and empirical literature on the linkage between credit reporting and information sharing, and the subsequent development of consumer loan markets and economic growth. Because credit reporting environments differ substantially around the globe, much can be learned via cross-border comparisons. The United States has the most complete credit files on the largest percentage of its adult population of any country. Consequently, the U.S. market provides a useful benchmark to compare lending markets in countries with more restrictive reporting environments. Section 8.3 describes the dimensions of U.S. consumer credit markets and briefly summarizes the privacy laws that govern the construction and distribution of credit histories upon which lending activity is based. An example from the U.S. credit card industry highlights how the availability of detailed credit histories has spurred entry and dramatic price competition in that market.

Section 8.4 considers a common restricted-information scenario in which creditors report only borrower delinquency or default. Historically, credit reporting in most countries began with the sharing of negative information (delinquencies, chargeoffs, bankruptcies, etc.) on borrowers. Only gradually and recently has information about the successful handling of accounts (prior and current) been contributed to the data repository. For example, most Latin American countries are moving in the direction of sharing more positive data about consumers (i.e., accounts currently open and active, balances, credit limits). In these countries (e.g., Brazil, Argentina, and Chile), consumer credit files contain some positive information, although the majority of information in credit files is still negative. At the other end of the spectrum of countries that have credit reporting,

Australia provides a stark example of a negative-only reporting environment. Since its passage in 1988, Australia's Commonwealth Privacy Act has allowed only the reporting of negative information about borrowers, plus inquiries from potential creditors.

Section 8.4 also examines the impact that the absence of positive credit information has on a lender's ability to measure borrower risk. Because the Australian statute clearly specifies what information is allowed in credit files, the Australian environment is simulated using large samples of U.S. consumer credit files. The efficiency of scoring models built with U.S. data under U.S. reporting rules provides the benchmark. The simulation drops out the blocks of data banned under Australian law and determines the impact on risk measurement for the same group of consumers. Measurement efficiency is defined as errors of commission (giving loans to consumers who will not repay) and omission (denying loans to good customers who would have repaid). The results of the simulation have implications for the performance of markets for financial services and consumer goods, small business credit, and overall macroeconomic growth and stability. Although the results are derived from a simulation of the Australian environment, they generally apply to any region, including Latin America, in which positive credit data is missing from many consumer files.

Section 8.5 applies the same methodology to consider other restricted-information scenarios that are common in Latin America. In particular, the authors simulate the impact on risk assessment of having past credit performance available only for retail accounts and, in a separate simulation, only for bank card accounts. Section 8.6 offers some concluding discussion and implications.

8.2 The Conceptual and Empirical Case for Comprehensive Reporting

8.2.1 The Problem of Adverse Selection
Lending markets almost always display some degree of information asymmetry between borrowers and lenders. Borrowers typically have more accurate information than lenders about their willingness and ability to repay a loan. Since the expected gains from the loan contract are a function of both the pricing and the probability of repayment, lenders invest resources to try and determine a borrower's likelihood of repayment. For the same reason, borrowers

may also have incentive to signal their true riskiness (if it is low) or disguise it (if it is high). The actions of borrowers and lenders as they try to reduce the information asymmetry has significant consequences for the operation of credit markets, and they give rise to a variety of institutions intended to minimize the associated costs.

A large theoretical and empirical literature about the consequences of such information asymmetry has developed over the past twenty-five years. For purposes of this chapter, Stiglitz and Weiss (1981) provide the conceptual launching point for explaining the evolution of credit bureaus. This seminal paper focuses on lending markets without information sharing, and it theoretically describes the adverse selection problem which reduces the gains to both borrowers and lenders. Simply put, when lenders can not distinguish good borrowers from bad borrowers, all borrowers are charged an average interest rate that reflects their pooled experience. This rate is higher than good borrowers warrant, however, and causes some good borrowers to drop out of the market, thereby shrinking the customer base and further raising the average rate charged to remaining borrowers.

The adverse selection argument embodies the intuition about why better information makes lending markets work more efficiently. Better information allows lenders to more accurately measure borrower risk and set loan terms accordingly. Low-risk borrowers are offered more attractive prices, which stimulates the quantity of loans demanded, and fewer high-risk borrowers are rationed out of the market because lenders can offer them an appropriate price to accommodate them rather than turn them away.

8.2.2   Why Would Lenders Share Information?

The next step in explaining the evolution of credit bureaus was provided by Pagano and Japelli (1993). Their theoretical development explains the factors encouraging voluntary information sharing among lenders as well as those conditions that deter voluntary information sharing. Where Stiglitz and Weiss showed how adverse selection can impair markets, Pagano and Japelli show how information sharing can reduce the problem and increase the volume of lending. Their theoretical model generates the following implications. Incentives for lenders to share information about borrowers (about payment experience, current obligations, and exposure) are positively related to the mobility and heterogeneity of borrowers, to the size of the credit market, and to advances in information technology. Working in the opposite direction (discouraging the sharing of information about borrowers) is the fear of competition from additional entrants.

The intuition is straightforward. Mobility and heterogeneity of borrowers reduce the feasibility of a lender relying solely on its own experience to guide its portfolio management. Thus, these factors increase the demand for information about a borrower's experience with other lenders. The need for information to supplement a lender's own experience grows with the size of the market. In addition, any declines in the cost of sharing information (perhaps through technological improvements) boost the net gains from sharing.

Once the case for information sharing among lenders was established, the next conceptual step was to rationalize the existence of a credit bureau. Padilla and Pagano (1997) develop a theoretical rationale for credit bureaus as an integral third-party participant in credit markets. The authors explain the conditions under which lenders agree to share information about borrowers via a third party that can penalize those institutions who do not report accurately. The paper is directly relevant to credit relationships between firms and their lenders, but it also has implications for the sharing of information in consumer lending markets. As noted in Pagano and Japelli (1993), information sharing has direct benefits to lenders by reducing the impact of adverse selection (average rates tend to ration out low-risk borrowers leaving only the high-risk borrowers remaining), and moral hazard (borrower has incentive to default unless there are consequences in future applications for credit). Information sharing, however, stimulates competition for good borrowers over time, which erodes the informational rents enjoyed by incumbent lenders (who have already identified and service the good customers, the very ones that competitors would like to identify and recruit).

Padilla and Pagano (1997) discuss an additional problem that can arise out of the informational asymmetry between borrowers and lenders. As a lender establishes relationships with customers, it becomes able to distinguish good borrowers from bad borrowers. At that point, the lender has an incentive to either hold back information about the good borrowers or purposely spread false information about them to discourage competitors from making overtures. Borrowers know this and have less incentive to perform well under the loan contract, because such efforts will not be rewarded with lower interest rates in the future (and may be exploited with higher rates and/or spread of misinformation). This tendency to underperform is reversed if borrowers perceive some gain to signaling they are good borrowers. Consequently, a lender's commitment to share accurate information with other lenders, coupled with an enforcement mechanism that ensures that accuracy, can benefit all parties. The third-party credit bureau fills the role of both clearinghouse and enforcer. As a consequence, Padilla and Pagano show that if they share information, interest rates and default rates are lower, on average, and interest rates decrease over the course of the relationship with each client and his or her bank. In addition, the volume of lending may increase as information sharing expands the customer base.

8.2.3 Limits on Information Sharing

Is more information sharing always better? Interestingly, the theoretical models show that this may not be the case. For example, Vercammen (1995) sets forth a conceptual case for limiting the length of time that negative information could remain on an individual's credit history. In part it is the "clean slate" argument: truly high-risk borrowers over time reveal themselves consistently as such. The presence of their deep history convinces lenders they are high risk. Consequently, as their negative credit history dogs them, such borrowers have little incentive to perform better on loans. The possibility of establishing a clean slate would raise the cost to the borrower of handling the new line poorly. The flip side of this argument is the "one free bite" argument: truly low-risk borrowers over time reveal themselves as such. The presence of their deep and good payment history convinces lenders they are good and so reduces the incentive of such borrowers to pay as agreed on the next loan. Limiting the length of the credit history (forced obsolescence), or perhaps eliminating other pieces of information that allow low-risk borrowers to distinguish themselves, would keep both types of borrowers honest by raising the reputational stakes associated with their performance on their next loan.[1]

Padilla and Pagano (2000) provide yet another twist to the case for less-than-perfect information sharing. Building on the ideas in Vercammen (1995), the authors develop a model that shows information sharing among lenders can boost borrower incentives to perform well on loans, but only if the information shared is less than perfect. When lenders share information about past defaults, borrowers do not wish to damage their credit rating because a default will signal future lenders that the borrower is high risk. Thus, information sharing has a positive disciplinary effect on borrower behavior. Suppose, however, that an incumbent lender shared so much additional information about a borrower's characteristics that future lenders knew with certainty that a borrower was indeed low-risk. In the model, future lenders would compete for such borrowers and offer them better loan terms. Consequently, such borrowers would have no more incentive to perform well on the current loan than if no information was shared. Thus, the authors conclude that less sharing could be better, and that lenders will seek to fine-tune the amount of information disclosed to some level below "perfect" so as to maximize the disciplinary effect.

When applying these theoretical concepts to actual lending markets, keep in mind the distinction between perfect and less-than-perfect information signals about a borrower's true risk. As shown in what follows, the presence of both positive and negative credit information about a borrower can improve a lender's assessment of repayment probability, but hardly constitutes a perfect picture of the borrower's true risk. In reality, positive information still does not equate to perfect information. There is plenty of empirical evidence to suggest that borrowers with no negative payment history still vary widely on default probability and experience. While Vercammen, Padilla, and Pagano raise an interesting theoretical point, this is hardly a case for barring positive credit histories from credit reports.

8.2.4 Evidence on the Evolution of Credit Bureaus

How well do the implications of these theoretical models explain the evolution of credit bureaus and the lending markets they support? Japelli and Pagano (1999) provide one of the few attempts to test the predictions of the theoretical models about the impact of information sharing on lending activity. The authors compiled a unique dataset describing the nature and extent of information sharing arrangements in forty-three countries. Consistent with the theoretical models, the authors found that the breadth and depth of credit markets were significantly related to information sharing. Specifically, total bank lending to the private sector is larger in countries that have a greater degree of information sharing, even after controlling for country size, growth rates, and variables capturing the legal environment and protection of creditor rights. The authors also found that greater information sharing reduced defaults, though the relationship was somewhat weaker than the link to additional lending.

8.2.5   Predictive Power of Bureau-Based Risk Models

The conceptual case that information sharing leads to more efficient lending markets hinges on the assertion that data about past payment behavior are useful for predicting future performance. The entire credit scoring industry stands as testimony to this premise. Among the few published attempts, however, to document the gains from utilizing increasingly detailed credit history data are two papers by Chandler and Parker (1989) and Chandler and Johnson (1992). In the earlier paper, the authors document the ability of U.S. credit bureau data to outperform application data in predicting risk. Their analysis was based on comparing credit bureau versus application data in scoring three categories of credit card applications: bank card, retail store card, and nonrevolving charge card.

In their study, application information included variables such as the applicant's age, time at current/previous residence, time at current/previous job, housing status, occupation group, income, number of dependents, presence of telephone at residence, banking relationship, debt ratio, and credit references. Variable values were coded straight from the credit card application without independent verification.

Credit bureau variables were grouped into thee categories so that the authors could examine the impact of simple versus detailed amounts of credit file data. The first category included only the number of inquiries from other creditors in the last six months (under U.S. law, these result from an application for credit), and the worst credit rating on the borrower's file. The next category in the progression from less to more detail included the number of inquiries in the last six months plus additional variables such as the number of new trade lines opened in the last six months, number of satisfactory credit ratings, number of 30-, 60-, and 90-day ratings, the number of public record items, and the age of the oldest trade. The current Australian reporting environment falls somewhere between these first and second categories. Finally, the authors created a third category, including all variables in the previous two categories, plus more detail on the number of accounts by category of lender (bank revolving, bank nonrevolving, consumer finance company, and captive auto finance company) and a variable capturing the percent of all revolving lines currently utilized.

Using models built to score bank card applicants, the authors found that the application data without the credit bureau data yielded the lowest predictive power, and it did not fare well when compared with predictions based on any level of credit bureau data. The predictive power increased substantially at higher levels of credit bureau detail, with the most detailed model exhibiting predictive power 52 percent greater than the simple credit bureau treatment. In fact, a model incorporating the detailed credit bureau data plus application data performed worse than a model based on the detailed credit bureau data alone. Perhaps this is not surprising, given that most application data on bank card products is not verified because of the cost and consequent delay in the accept/reject decision. The bottom line is that the more information available about a borrower's current and past credit profile, the greater was the ability of the scoring model to separate good risk from bad.[2]

In models built to score the retail card applications, the combination of application plus detailed credit bureau information outperformed a model built just on application data as well as a model built just on detailed bureau data. Similar results were found for models built to score nonrevolving charge card accounts. The authors concluded that predictive power rises for every card product as the level of credit bureau detail increased. They also noted that if the credit bureau file was utilized by scoring only the two items in the first category, the real predictive power of the bureau data could easily be overlooked.

Significantly for the simulations conducted below, the first category of bureau variables contains information allowed in Australian credit bureau files, but the second and third categories incorporate "positive data" variables not allowed under current Australian law and often absent in other countries even when they are legally permitted. Because the detailed credit bureau history found in the U.S. files provided the greatest lift in the predictive power of the scoring models, this result suggests that lenders and consumers in restricted reporting environments are missing significant benefits from their credit reporting system.

8.3   Characteristics of a Full Reporting Environment: The U.S. Experience

8.3.1   Dimensions of the U.S. Market for Consumer Credit

By most any measure, the U.S. market for consumer and mortgage credit is vast. At the end of 1998, mortgage credit owed by consumers totaled about $4.1 trillion, including both first and second mortgages and the increasingly popular home equity lines of credit. Nonmortgage consumer credit (including credit cards, auto loans, and other personal installment loans) totaled an additional $1.33 trillion.

Whether or not these sums are large given the size of the population, perhaps the more impressive numbers relate to the growth in the proportion of the population using credit. For the past thirty-five years, federal policy has encouraged the credit industry to make credit and other financial services available to a broader segment of the U.S. population. The result of these public policies has been a dramatic increase in credit availability to all segments of the U.S. population, particularly to those toward the bottom of the socioeconomic spectrum who need it the most. In 1956 about 55 percent of U.S. households had some type of mortgage or consumer installment (nonmortgage) debt. In contrast, by 1998 over 74 percent of all U.S. households held some type of debt. Put another way, 29.7 million households used consumer or mortgage credit in 1956 compared to 75 million households in 1998.[3]

By loan category, the increased availability and use of consumer credit is equally impressive. In 1956 about 20 percent of households (11 million) had an automobile loan. By 1998 this proportion had increased to 31 percent (32 million). A similar pattern is evident for mortgage credit. In 1956 24 percent of U.S. households (13 million) had mortgage debt. By 1998 43 percent of households (44 million) had home mortgage loans. In the case of both products, credit markets enable consumers to purchase and finance durable goods that provide a valuable stream of services to their owners over time. Over the past two generations, millions of Americans have gained access to credit to enable them to make such investments and raise their standard of living.

The same story has unfolded for credit card products, but even more dramatically given the shorter time frame. Figure 8.1 displays

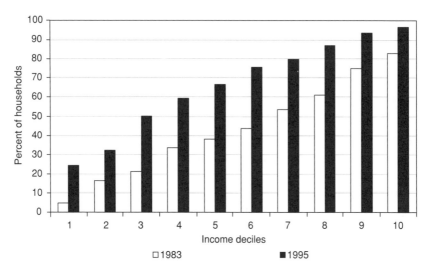

Figure 8.1
Bank card ownership by household income
Sources: Federal Reserve Board.
Note: Percent of households with at least one bank card.

the percent of U.S. households that had at least one general purpose credit card (e.g., Visa, MasterCard, Discover) at two points in time, 1983 and 1995. It reveals that every income grouping of households enjoyed substantially improved access to the versatile "bank card" product even within the relatively short span of a dozen years. By 1995 over 25 million more households had access to bank credit cards than was the case in the early 1980s.

8.3.2   Credit Bureau Information as a Catalyst for Growth
At the heart of the lending decision is information about an applicant's creditworthiness. In this regard, perhaps no industry has been more dramatically affected by the enhanced power of the computer than the consumer credit industry. In the United States, computerized credit files have made it possible to store and instantaneously retrieve many years of payment history for over two hundred million adult residents. Over two million credit reports are sold by the three major national credit bureaus every day. Ready access to such personal credit data, which can be used to evaluate creditworthiness, has fueled the explosion in consumer credit products since the mid-1970s.

Broader access to credit products is widely recognized as the consequence of four simultaneous and interdependent factors:

• Legal rules that permit the collection and distribution of personal credit data to those with an authorized purpose for requesting the information

• Dramatic reductions in data processing costs and equally dramatic improvements in the speed of data retrieval

• The development of statistical scoring techniques for predicting borrower risk

• The repeal of legislated interest rate ceilings that had limited the ability of creditors to price their loan products according to risk

The bank credit card market provides a useful illustration of how and why these combined forces worked to broaden access to credit card products. When bank cards (Visa, MasterCard, and their forerunners) were launched in the 1960s, they typically were priced at only one margin, a finance charge, that was imposed on balances that revolved from month to month. By the late 1970s, card issuers recognized that many customers never revolved a balance. These nonrevolving cardholders were utilizing a package of valuable (and costly) services without being charge for them. Revolvers who paid finance charges subsidized nonrevolvers. The advent of annual fees by the early 1980s gave issuers a method of collecting revenue from the convenience users and reduced the pressure on finance charges to cover all the costs of the card operation. Annual fees were a somewhat clumsy tool for boosting revenues, since they were applied across the board to all customers. Still, they helped issuers to hold down the interest rate on the card and remain competitive in attracting and keeping cardholders who typically revolved. Through the 1980s, other fees (late payment, cash advance, and overlimit) were added to cardholder agreements, each fee aimed at a class of customer who imposed extra costs on the issuer by utilizing specific features of the card. In each case the purpose of adding an extra fee was to reduce the subsidization of one group of users by other cardholders, which occurs whenever extra costs associated with unpriced services are packed into a higher interest rate.

During 1985 to 1991, a wave of new entrants into the bank card market put greater downward pressure on card interest rates and annual fees. Credit bureau data were critical to this explosion in competition both as a way to identify potential customers and to offer them attractive but profitable pricing. New entrants used credit bureau data to identify and target low-risk borrowers for their low-rate cards. Existing issuers saw customer attrition escalate, particularly in the lowest risk categories. Competition forced incumbent issuers to make a choice: either leave the interest rate unchanged and risk defection of their best customers to the new, low-rate entrants, or cut interest rates and fees as a defensive measure.

In late 1991, American Express became the first major issuer to unveil a tiered pricing structure to slow customer defections. For cardholders with at least $1,000 in charge volume during the previous twelve months and no delinquency, the interest rate was lowered to 12.5 percent on revolving balances. Cardholders with smaller charge volume and no delinquency paid 14.5 percent. All other cardholders paid a higher rate. The new rate structure was intended to prevent defection of low-risk, active cardholders to competitors without compromising the higher finance charges imposed on slow payers. A short time later Citibank announced a similar pricing structure for its cardholders who had been paying a 19.8 percent interest rate. Citibank officials estimated that by the end of 1992, nearly ten million Citibank cardholders had benefited from the new tiered rate structure.[4]

The highly publicized tiered rate programs for these two major issuers ignited an unprecedented wave of price competition for the bank card product that continues today. Figure 8.2 illustrates the rapid decline in bank card rates between 1990 and 1992. The proportion of revolving balances being charged an interest rate greater than 18.0 percent plummeted from 70 percent to 44 percent in just twelve months.

Today, issuer portfolios are commonly divided into multiple categories, with different rates and features according to the payment history of the customer. Risk-based pricing, spurred by aggressive entry of new competitors, has eliminated the industry practice of packing the costs of handling delinquent accounts for a small number of customers into higher interest rates for all customers. Consequently, tiered pricing reduces the amount by which low-risk customers subsidize the costs of serving high-risk customers. For the card issuer, the economic success of this strategy hinges on two key factors: (1) the low-cost availability of a comprehensive credit history for cardholders, and (2) the legal ability to charge interest rates

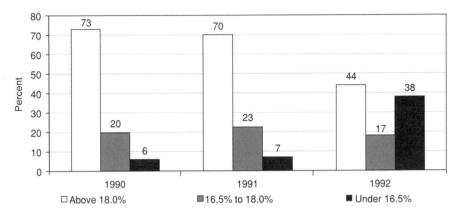

Figure 8.2
Percentage distribution of bank card rates
Source: CardTrak, RAM Research.
Note: Percentage distribution of bank card rates measured as a proportion of outstanding bank card balances. Data derived from survey of 100 top issuers representing 93 percent of U.S. bank card receivables.

commensurate with borrower risk. The occurrence of both in the United States triggered the dramatic improvement in access to bank credit cards displayed in figure 8.1.

In the United States the combination of technological advances and flexible public policy toward data collection have fostered an explosion in consumer credit availability. It is no coincidence that the expansion of credit during the past two decades corresponded to the advent of credit scoring and its eventual widespread use by credit card issuers (late 1980s), automobile lenders in launching risk-based pricing (led by companies such as GMAC in 1989–1990), and mortgage lenders in the early to mid-1990s. By 1998, credit scoring models were being developed and applied to guide small business lending. Personal loans, credit cards, and debit card products are available to the vast majority of the adult population. Moreover, the time between application for credit and the decision to make the loan has fallen precipitously: approval for many auto loans is available in less than thirty minutes. Some retailers advertise "instant credit" available at the point of sale, and can deliver approval for a new account in less than two minutes.

At the same time, across all categories of loans, the dramatic increases in the proportion of the population using credit have come without equally dramatic increases in defaults. The percent of accounts that are delinquent at any point in time varies between 2 and 5 percent nationwide, depending upon the product.[5] Looking at the market from the standpoint of the borrower reveals a similar story: the percent of borrowers nationwide who were delinquent thirty days or more on any account as of September 1999 was 2.8 percent for mortgage holders, 6.9 percent for installment borrowers, and 4.9 percent of credit card borrowers.[6] The U.S. credit reporting environment is the foundation for this remarkable combination of widespread availability and low default rates.

8.3.3 The Balance Between Privacy Rights and Creditors' Need for Payment History

Although quite sensitive to the threat of invasion of privacy, U.S. policy toward the collection of personal information also recognizes that consumers necessarily must reveal some information about past behavior to obtain credit. When a consumer applies for credit, he or she voluntarily trades away some privacy in exchange for goods or services. Loss of some privacy is the price of participating and enjoying the benefits of an information-intensive economy.

In the context of a single loan transaction, a consumer faces a straightforward task of weighing the gains versus the costs of revealing some personal information. Presumably, for some types of transactions, the potential benefits are not worth revealing personal financial information and the customer refuses to continue. For other transactions, such as applying for a loan, the customer gives up much information but places even greater value on obtaining the loan, and so willingly sacrifices some privacy. Since personal information about consumers can be stored and subsequently transferred, however, the consumer loses some control over its use subsequent to the transaction. Thus, a key element of U.S. regulatory policy on the use of credit bureau data is to preserve the consumer's right to authorize release of the information.

To balance the consumer's value of privacy against business need for information and its inevitable storage for reuse, the U.S. Fair Credit Reporting Act (FCRA) stipulates the following:

1. Consumer reporting agencies (credit bureaus) may assemble credit reports but must limit their content to factual information pertaining to past credit experience (no subjective, investigative reports) Under the FCRA, credit bureaus in the United States maintain four categories of personal data in credit files.

• Personal identification information (e.g., name, address, social security number).
• Open trade lines (credit card accounts, auto loans and leases, first and second mortgage accounts, personal loans, etc.) with data such as outstanding balance, credit limit, date account opened, date of last activity, and payment history
• Public record items related to the use of credit, including bankruptcies, accounts referred to collection agencies, legal collection judgments, and liens
• Inquiries on the credit file, including date and identity of inquirer, for at least the previous two years

2. Consumer reporting agencies may release credit files only for permissible purposes. Permissible purposes for release of credit files were defined in the act to be those in conjunction with a variety of voluntary, consumer initiated transactions. These include credit transactions, insurance, and employment applications. Since the consumer must initiate the transaction, no one is in a position to learn the consumer's detailed credit profile unless it is relevant to a transaction the consumer is trying to arrange.

To assist the enforcement of the permissible purposes clause, the FCRA requires credit bureaus to keep a log of all requests for a consumer's credit report (inquiries) for at least two years and to disclose the names and addresses of recipients of reports upon request from the consumer. Disclosure to the consumer also aids in ensuring that the information included in the file is correct. Derogatory information (e.g., delinquencies and charge-offs) can be kept on the file a maximum of seven years, with the exception of personal bankruptcy records which can stay on the file up to ten years. With these provisions, the FCRA allows but limits the centralized storage and use of data about an individual's creditworthiness. Limiting the release of stored data ensures that personal data will only be revealed to those with whom the consumer intends to make a transaction, so that the consumer's sacrifice of some privacy reflects conscious consent to the trade-off.

Recall that section 8.2 reviewed the theoretical arguments and empirical evidence that, by reducing the adverse selection problem, information sharing via credit bureaus promotes the growth of consumer lending and lowers the cost of providing credit. Section 8.3 has focused on the linkage between the availability of comprehensive credit files and dramatic growth in access to consumer credit products in the United States. Next, consider the question of how access to consumer credit products would be impaired if some information about a consumer's past payment history was unavailable. The following section simulates risk scoring under Australian versus U.S. reporting rules to demonstrate that more information is better for a scoring model's ability to distinguish good risk from bad and consequently accept more loans for any target default rate. Specifically, the analysis compares the performance of a risk-scoring model built under the negative only Australian credit reporting rules with the performance of a model built using the greater detail available in U.S. credit reports. The simulation will highlight the cost of artificial restrictions on credit bureau information collection.

8.4   The Impact of Restricting Credit Files to Include Only Negative Information: The U.S. versus Australian Environments

Borrowers in Australia have a credit file only if they have sought credit in the last five years. Information older than five years must be deleted. Credit files contain data on the borrower's name, address (current and previous), date of birth, drivers license number, employer, applications for credit during the past five years showing date the credit was sought, type of credit sought, credit provider to whom application was made, an indication of whether it was a joint or individual application, and whether any account was past due. Creditors can not report date of account openings, highest balance, current balance, credit limit, or similar pieces of positive information. The law allows creditors to report the existence of an account with a given borrower, but Australian industry officials indicate that this option is seldom used because the law also requires creditors to remove such a listing within 45 days of the account being repaid or closed. In any case, no information about account activity can be reported, except for delinquency status.

As indicated in section 8.2, the U.S. and Australian reporting environments differ sharply in that U.S. credit files contain balance and payment status information on all of a borrower's accounts, not just those that have fallen delinquent. This section describes simulations that compare the two reporting environments to determine how a credit scoring model may be impaired by having access to only negative (derogatory) information, but not positive information about the successful handling of accounts. Certainly, a negative only environment gives creditors a profile of applicants that is less complete than if a complete inventory of account and balance information were available. Whether or not this makes a difference in predicting future payment behavior is an empirical question which the simulations are designed to resolve.

8.4.1 Methodology

The simulations in the remainder of this chapter examine the effectiveness of generic bureau scoring models for assessing borrower risk under various assumptions about how much information is available in credit bureau files. The scoring models are generic because they are not specific to a particular creditor's portfolio (and customer characteristics). Instead, they are built on the consumer's experience across all creditors who report to the bureau. The models are bureau-based in the sense that they utilize only the information available in consumer credit reports (no application information or customer demographics).

Generic scoring models have been utilized commercially by U.S. creditors since 1987 to predict bankruptcies, charge-offs, and serious delinquencies. Their application has assisted thousands of creditors in virtually every dimension of the credit granting decision, including new-applicant evaluation, target product solicitations, the setting of credit limits, purchase authorization, credit card reissue and renewals, and appropriate collections activity.

Each of the following simulations builds a risk scoring model utilizing the full complement of both positive and negative information present in U.S. credit files. Then, variables that were available for the construction of the full model, but would not be present in the simulated environments, were dropped from the set of potential variables and the model was rebuilt on the remaining variables. This method allowed for the construction of the best possible model from among the available variables in each environment.

The risk scoring models were built using U.S. credit report data provided by Experian, one of the three major U.S. credit bureaus and a large multinational provider of credit report data and analytical services for risk management. All credit files are anonymous, that is, they have been stripped of unique personal identifying information. The simulations were conducted with samples drawn from a database containing a random sample of ten million individual credit files. For the positive-plus-negative versus negative-only simulation described here, the performance of consumers who opened new accounts from any source in May 1997 was observed over the next two years. Specifically, the models were built to estimate the probability that a new account opened in May 1997 would become ninety or more days delinquent within twenty-four months, that is, by the end of April 1999.

8.4.2 Data and Variable Construction

The precise composition of commercially available scorecards is proprietary and consequently not available for use in an academic simulation. Given access to all variables contained in the credit file and sufficient time and resources for modeling, academic researchers could eventually construct a scoring model that would closely approximate the performance of commercial models. Since the resource requirements to replicate commercial models are typically beyond the scope of academic projects, however, the authors accept that their simulation models will not be as powerful as commercial models and adopt the following approach.

According to the website of a large U.S.-based provider of commercial credit scoring models (Fair Isaac, Co., based in San Rafael, California), the key determinants of a credit bureau delinquency model can be divided into the following four general categories. Simulation models used here include credit bureau variables in each of these categories. For the simulations the full set of bureau variables (500+) were available that were being marketed commercially by Experian in 1999. The models were built using subsets of variables, but include variables from each of the following categories. Inclusion of variables in model building was guided to some degree by the Fair Isaac website that hints at key variables used in commercial models and the direction of their influence on risk scores.

1. *Outstanding Debt and Types of Credit in Use:* Fair Isaac advises consumers who seek to improve their credit score to keep balances low, including credit card balances. People who are heavily extended tend to be higher risks than those who use credit conservatively. They also advise individuals to apply for and open new credit accounts only as needed, as the amount of unused credit is an important factor in calculating credit scores. Table 8.1 lists the variables that have been introduced in the simulations to capture the

Table 8.1
Variables used in the different credit-scoring models

Type of variable: Outstanding debt and types of credit	Variable used in full model	Variable used in negative-only model	Variable exists for bank card-only model	Variable exists for retail-only model
Total number of open, paid, or closed trades	√		√	√
No open, paid, or closed trades	√		√	√
Number of trades open with a balance greater than or equal to zero	√		√	√
No trades open with a balance greater than or equal to zero	√		√	√
Number of trades opened in last six months	√		√	√
No trades opened in last six months	√		√	√
Number of trades opened in last twelve months	√		√	√
No trades opened in last twelve months	√		√	√
Proportion of open trades that is revolving	√			√
Proportion of open trades that is finance installment	√			
Proportion of open trades that is real estate/property	√			
Zero balance on open trades	√		√	√
Average balance across all open trades	√		√	√
Average balance across open revolving trades	√			√
Proportion of debt that is revolving	√			√
Proportion of debt that is finance installment	√			
Proportion of debt that is real estate/property	√			
Bank card balance/limit ratio on all open trades reported in last six months	√		√	
Bank card balance/limit ratio on all open trades opened in last twelve months	√		√	

Table 8.1
(continued)

Type of variable: Length of credit history	Variable used in full model	Variable used in negative-only model	Variable exists for bank card-only model	Variable exists for retail-only model
Age, in months, oldest trade	√		√	√
Age, in months, of most recently opened trade	√		√	√
Age, in months, of most recently opened trade = 9999	√		√	√
Average age, in months, of all trades	√		√	
Ratio of number of open trades reported, last twelve months to age of oldest trade	√			

Type of variable: New applications for credit (Inquiries)	Variable used in full model	Variable used in negative-only model	Variable exists for bank card-only model	Variable exists for retail-only model
Total number of inquiries made for credit purposes	√	√		√
No inquires made for credit purposes	√	√		√
Total number of bank card inquiries made for credit purposes	√	√	√	
No bank card inquires made for credit purposes	√	√	√	
Months since most recent inquiry for credit purposes was made	√	√		
Months since most recent bank card inquiry for credit purposes was made	√	√	√	
Total number of inquiries for credit purposes made, last six months	√	√	√	√
Proportion of inquires to open trades, last six months	√		√	√
Total number of inquiries for credit purposes made, last twelve months	√	√	√	√
Proportion of inquires to open trades, last twelve months	√		√	√

Table 8.1
(continued)

Type of variable: Late payments, delinquencies, and bankruptcies	Variable used in full model	Variable used in negative-only model	Variable exists for bank card-only model	Variable exists for retail-only model
Proportion of all trades never delinquent/derogatory	√		√	√
Proportion of all trades that have never been delinquent, last twelve months	√			
Positive number of trades ever 60+ days delinquent or derogatory	√	√	√	√
Number of trades ever 60+ days delinquent or derogatory	√	√	√	√
Proportion of trades ever 60+ days delinquent or derogatory	√		√	√
Positive number of trades ever derogatory, including collection, charge-off, etc.	√	√	√	√
Number of trades ever derogatory	√	√	√	√
Proportion of trades ever derogatory	√		√	√
Positive number of bankruptcy tradelines ever	√	√	√	√
Total number of bankruptcy tradelines ever (only available for all)	√	√		
Proportion of trades ever bankruptcy tradelines	√			
Months since most recent tradeline bankruptcy	√	√	√	√
Worst status ever (including current) on a trade	√	√		√
Worst status ever on trades reported, last twelve months	√	√		√
Worst present status on an open trade	√	√		√
Worst status ever (including current) on a bank card trade	√	√	√	
Worst status ever on bank card trades reported, last twelve months	√	√	√	

Table 8.1
(continued)

Type of variable: Late payments, delinquencies, and bankruptcies	Variable used in full model	Variable used in negative-only model	Variable exists for bank card-only model	Variable exists for retail-only model
Worst present status on an open bank card trade	√	√	√	
Months since most recent 30–180 day delinquency on any trade	√	√		
Not ever delinquent or derogatory on any trade	√	√		
Months since most recent 90+ delinquency or derogatory, any trade	√	√		
Not ever 90+ days delinquency or derogatory item on any trade	√	√		

extent and type of outstanding debt, with particular focus on revolving and bankcard debt as a proportion of total debt and relative to credit limits.

2. *Length of Credit History:* Fair Isaac advises that the longer someone has had credit established, the better his or her credit score. For example, a borrower who has had credit for less than two years represents a relatively higher risk than someone who has had credit for five years or more. Table 8.1 lists the variables that have been introduced to capture the extent of experience in the credit markets.

3. *New Applications for Credit (Inquiries):* Fair Isaac advises individuals to apply for new credit sparingly if they seek a better credit score. In particular, they suggest that one minimize the number of times creditors are given permission to check one's credit record. Such credit checks are called "inquiries." Table 8.1 lists the variables have been introduced to capture the extent of inquiries.

4. *Late Payments, Delinquencies, and Bankruptcies:* Fair Isaac advises individuals who seek to improve their credit score to always pay their accounts before the due date. Simply put, the fewer late payments, the better the score. Further, Fair Isaac indicates that if there are late payments, those that are most recent are more indicative of future default than those that occurred in the past. Naturally, having no late payments is best. Table 8.1 lists the variables that have been

introduced to capture the extent and timing of detrimental events in an individual's payment history.

8.4.3 The Value of Positive Information

In Australia, only derogatory information and inquiry information can be used in determining a credit score. No variables are permitted on the number of open lines, age of lines, balances, or credit limits.[7] This definition of negative-only is used to simulate the effect of adopting such a system. The full model uses all the variables listed in table 8.1. The negative-only model uses only those variables in table 8.1 that are indicated in the negative-only column. The dependent variable is constructed as equal to one if a new account becomes ninety or more days delinquent within two years, and equal to zero otherwise. In each case a probit model was used to estimate the probability of delinquency for a random sample of 312,484 new accounts opened at the start of the observation period.

There are a variety of ways to evaluate the effect of using only negative information and to present the results once individual credit scores have been calculated for the full model and for the restricted model. For each model, individuals were first ranked according to their credit score. Then a specific approval rate, say 60 percent, was picked and the default rates for the full model were compared to that of the restricted model. For purposes of these simulations, the term "default" refers to the borrower becoming ninety days or more past due on the new account. Alternatively, for a given target default rate one can determine the reduction in the number of individuals who would be offered credit if only the restricted model was available. Tables 8.2 and 8.3 present the results of such comparisons for both the random sample that was used to estimate the credit-scoring models and for a holdout sample of equal size.

At a targeted approval rate of 60 percent, the negative-only model produces a 3.35 percent default rate among accepted applicants compared to a 1.9 percent default rate for the full model. Put another way, table 8.2 reveals that at the given 60 percent approval rate, the default rate using the negative-only model is 76.3 percent higher than if the full model were used. Next, consider the implications of the two models for extending credit to deserving borrowers. Suppose the economics of a lender's operation dictate an optimal default rate of 4 percent. Table 8.3 reveals that the full model approves 83.2 percent of consumers for a loan, while the negative-only model

Table 8.2
Effects on default rates of adopting negative-only credit-scoring model for various approval rates (percentage)

	Default rates estimating sample			Default rate holdout sample		
Target approval rate	Full model	Negative-only model	Percent increase in default rate on loan with negative-only model	Full model	Negative-only model	Percent increase in default rate on loan with negative-only model
40%	1.08	2.92	170.4	1.15	2.91	153.0
60%	1.90	3.35	76.3	1.95	3.36	72.3
75%	3.04	4.07	33.9	3.09	4.10	32.7
100%	9.31	9.31	0.0	9.38	9.38	0.0

approves only 73.7 percent of consumers, a 11.4 percent reduction in loans made. In other words, at a default rate of 4 percent, for every 100,000 applicants, use of the negative-only model would result in 11,000 fewer consumer loans.

The results reported in tables 8.2 and 8.3 suggest that an environment restricting lenders to using the negative-only model produces nontrivial changes in either the likelihood a loan is repaid (and thus, the cost of a loan) or the availability of credit. These results highlight the distinct trade-off between (1) limiting the collection and use of personal credit histories and (2) making credit available to consumers at reasonable prices.

Table 8.4 displays yet another method for assessing the effectiveness of the two models. Suppose one defines a type 1 error as rejecting a borrower who would actually repay. Alternatively, define a type 2 error as accepting a borrower who will become seriously delinquent. Table 8.4 displays the percentage increase in type 1 and type 2 errors for both the full and restricted models, assuming various target loan approval rates. Both types of errors increase in the restricted, negative-only environment.[8,9]

8.5   Bureau Data Restricted by Type of Lender

Credit reporting in Latin American countries has historically been driven by commercial banking consortiums. Positive data are more likely to appear for accounts reported and shared within the bank

Table 8.3
Effects on credit availability of adopting a negative-only credit-scoring model for various default rates (percentage)

Target default rate	Percent of consumers who obtain a loan estimating sample			Percent of consumers who obtain a loan holdout sample		
	Full model	Negative-only model	Percent decrease in consumers who obtain a loan with negative-only model	Full model	Negative-only model	Percent decrease in consumers who obtain a loan with negative-only model
3%	74.8	39.8	46.8	74.3	39.0	47.5
4%	83.2	73.7	11.4	82.9	73.7	11.1
5%	88.9	84.6	4.8	88.9	84.2	5.3
6%	93.1	90.8	2.5	92.8	90.6	2.4
7%	95.5	95.0	0.5	95.6	94.6	1.0
Mean	100.0	100.0	0.0	100.0	100.0	0.0

Table 8.4
Effects on type I and type II errors of adopting negative-only credit-scoring model for various approval rates (percentage)

Type I errors	Percent of good credit risks who do not receive a loan estimating sample			Percent of good credit risks who do not receive a loan holdout sample		
Target approval rate	Full model	Negative-only model	Percent increase in type I error on loan with negative-only model	Full model	Negative-only model	Percent increase in type I error on loan with negative-only model
40%	56.1	57.0	1.6	56.1	56.9	1.4
60%	34.8	35.8	2.9	34.7	35.8	3.2
75%	19.5	20.5	5.1	19.5	20.4	4.6
100%	0.0	0.0	0.0	0.0	0.0	0.0

Type II errors	Percent of bad risks who receive a loan estimating sample			Percent of bad risks who receive a loan holdout sample		
Target approval rate	Full model	Negative-only model	Percent increase in type II error on loan with negative-only model	Full model	Negative-only model	Percent increase in type II error on loan with negative-only model
40%	4.7	12.6	168.1	4.9	12.5	155.1
60%	12.3	21.7	76.4	12.5	21.6	72.8
75%	24.6	32.9	33.7	24.8	32.9	32.7
100%	100.0	100.0	0.0	100.0	100.0	0.0

consortium, but typically are not available to institutions outside the consortium. Information on loans not held by consortium members has tended to be negative when it appears at all. In some countries (e.g., Mexico), retailers and finance companies have attempted to form their own reporting consortiums to improve the quality and scope of data available on consumers to whom they would like to lend. As the consumer finance industry grows, an increasing portion of consumer credit oustandings will likely be held outside the domestic commercial banking system. For example, in the United States at the end of December 1999, approximately 40 to 45 percent of nonmortgage credit outstanding ($560–$640 billion) was originated by nonbanking financial institutions, including finance companies, credit unions, and retailers. A reporting system that provides a credit profile on a consumer's credit experience with either the bank or the nonbank sector, but not both, leaves a substantial gap in the overall profile for a given borrower.

In the absence of efforts to expand the scope of credit reporting, the size of the lender's blind spot in Latin America appears poised to increase as foreign financial institutions recognize the lucrative business opportunities in lending to Latin American consumers. Growth in retail lending is well underway. Until recently, bank credit cards were held by a relatively small portion of well-to-do Latin American consumers, but Latin American charge card volume reported by Visa and MasterCard reached $106.2 billion in 1997, an 81 percent jump. U.S. companies, especially FleetBoston, Citigroup, and Wells Fargo, are moving aggressively to expand their consumer finance operations in Brazil, Chile, and Argentina. U.S. finance companies, including Associates First Capital, GE Capital, GMAC, and Ford Motor Credit, have also been actively courting consumers. Analysts have attribute much of the foreign interest in lending to Latin American consumers to advances in the credit reporting systems in these countries which has, in turn, supported the application of credit scoring.[10] Mexico is also experiencing a rapid influx of U.S. capital since its economy has grown in excess of 3 percent annually from 1996 through 1999, while the domestic banking sector has scaled back lending to the private sector since 1995.[11]

Note that, unlike Australia, there is some positive information reported about Latin American consumers. It tends to be sector-specific, however, relating to bank loan experience or retail loan experience. The following simulations examine the impact on risk-scoring models of having information about a consumer's credit history available only on certain types of loans.

The first restricted-sector simulation approaches the issue from a retail creditor's viewpoint as though the retailer could access credit histories only from a retailer consortium. Thus, in making a loan decision, a retailer would be able to draw on its own experience with a customer (if any) as well as the experience of other retailers in the consortium with the same customer. Relative to the full-information model described in section 8.4, the following simulation examines how well a scoring model built only on retail loan experience performs. That is, the situation is simulated in which a retailer has access to both positive and negative information about a consumer, but only on existing and prior retail loans.

Specifically, the simulation used a probit model to estimate the probability of serious delinquency (ninety-plus days) within two years among a random sample of 67,130 new retail accounts opened in May 1997.

The full-information model employed all the variables in the "full model" column of table 8.1. The restricted, retail-information-only model used only those variables indicated in the retail-only column of table 8.1. Note that all of the variables contained in the retail model were recalculated to apply only to the retail experience. For example, "total number of open trades" would indicate only the number of open retail trades. Some variables are lost altogether in the restricted model because they involve calculations of the proportion of overall debt or delinquency represented by a given type of account. Such a variable would not be available if a retailer could draw only on retail experience but not the experience of other financial institutions.

Tables 8.5 and 8.6 display the results of the retail-only simulations. As in the previous discussion of the negative-only simulation, suppose one uses the estimated models (full and restricted) to estimate credit scores for each individual in the sample and rank them according to their scores. Table 8.5 reveals that at a target approval rate of 60 percent the default rate in the full model would be 1.18 percent, while the default rate using the restricted model would jump to 1.9 percent, a 61 percent increase. Alternatively, for a given target default rate of 3 percent, table 8.6 reveals that the full model approves 83.4 percent of customers, while the restricted model approves only 75.4 percent of customers, a decline of 9.6 percent. Put

Table 8.5
Effects on retail loan default rates of a retail-only credit-scoring model for various retail loan approval rates (percentage)

Target approval rate	Default rates estimating sample			Default rate holdout sample		
	Full model	Retail-only model	Percent increase in default rate on loan with retail-only model	Full model	Retail-only model	Percent increase in default rate on loan with retail-only model
40%	0.53	1.10	107.5	0.55	1.10	100.0
60%	1.18	1.90	61.0	1.10	1.66	50.9
75%	2.13	2.97	39.4	2.01	2.72	35.3
100%	6.03	6.03	0.0	5.87	5.87	0.0

another way, among the pool of borrowers that could be served within the creditor's target default rate, for every 100,000 applicants, 9,600 deserving borrowers would not receive loans if only the restricted, retail-only model were available. Tables 8.5 and 8.6 show these results are validated with a holdout sample of equal size.

Another restricted-sector simulation was conducted assuming only bank credit card experience was available to a bank card issuer. Specifically, the simulation used a probit model to estimate the probability of serious delinquency (90+ days) within two years among a random sample of 110,633 new bank credit card accounts opened in May 1997. The full-information model employed all the variables in the "full model" column of table 8.1. The restricted, bank card-only model used only those variables indicated in the "bank card only" column of table 8.1. Note that all of the variables contained in the restricted bank card model were recalculated to reflect only bank card experience. For example, "total number of open trades" would indicate only the number of open bank card trades.

Tables 8.7 and 8.8 display the simulation results. The most notable difference from the previous simulations is that the degredation in model performance is smaller when a bank card issuer is constrained to use only bank card data. This is an interesting result that suggests, among other things, that much of the predictive power in the full model derives from how customers acquire and handle their bank credit cards. Given the deep penetration of the bank card product in

Table 8.6
Effects on credit availability of a retail-only credit-scoring model for various retail loan default rates (percentage)

Target default rate	Percent of consumers who obtain a loan estimating sample			Percent of consumers who obtain a loan holdout sample		
	Full model	Retail-only model	Percent decrease in consumers who obtain a loan with retail-only model	Full model	Retail-only model	Percent decrease in consumers who obtain a loan with retail-only model
3%	83.4	75.4	9.6	84.6	78.1	7.7
4%	90.6	80.6	11.0	92.1	90.7	1.5
5%	96.3	94.1	2.3	97.3	95.8	1.5
Mean	100.0	100.0	0.0	100.0	100.0	0.0

Table 8.7
Effects on bankcard loan default rates of a bank card-only credit-scoring model for
various bankcard approval rates (percentage)

	Default rates estimating sample			Default rates holdout sample		
Target approval rate	Full model	Bank card–only model	Percent increase in default rate on loan with bank card–only model	Full model	Bank card–only model	Percent increase in default rate on loan with bank card–only model
40%	0.61	0.82	34.4	0.61	0.74	21.3
60%	1.07	1.27	18.7	1.11	1.24	11.7
75%	1.69	1.95	15.4	1.81	2.01	11.0
100%	5.34	5.34	0.0	5.48	5.48	0.0

the U.S. market, relative to the rest of the world, this result may be unique to the United States.

8.6   Discussion and Implications

Based on the results of a burgeoning literature on the impact of information sharing, and also on the results of simulations here that compared the efficiency of scoring models built under comprehensive versus restricted reporting environments, the following implications emerge:

1. Given the prevailing laws governing the reporting of personal credit histories, consumer credit will be less available in countries (e.g., Australia) where credit reporting is confined primarily to negative (delinquent) information relative to the United States. It will also be less available in countries dominated by sector-specific reporting bureaus that exclude consumer borrowing experience with certain types of institutions and/or prohibit access of other institutions to the full bureau files. The effect will be especially noticeable for those consumers who are financially more vulnerable (higher risk categories) such as consumers who are young, have shorter time on the job or at their residence, and lower incomes.

2. As the amount of credit made available per capita increases in countries that lack comprehensive credit reporting, the pricing gra-

Table 8.8
Effects on credit availability of a bank card-only credit-scoring model for various bankcard loan default rates (percentage)

Target default rate	Percent of consumers who obtain a loan estimating sample			Percent of consumers who obtain a loan holdout sample		
	Full model	Bank card–only model	Percent decrease in consumers who obtain a loan with bank card–only model	Full model	Bank card–only model	Percent decrease in consumers who obtain a loan with bank card–only model
2%	79.6	75.6	5.0	77.8	74.6	4.1
3%	89.3	85.6	4.1	88.3	85.3	3.4
4%	95.8	93.4	2.5	95.0	93.4	1.7
Mean	100.0	100.0	0.0	100.0	100.0	0.0

dient will be steeper when compared to the United States. Consumer credit in restricted-reporting countries will likely be more costly in finance charges as well as other features of the loan offer function, including downpayment, convenience of access, credit limits, and fees.

3. Less accessible consumer credit will likely impair the growth of consumer spending and growth in consumer durable industries in countries that lack comprehensive reporting.

4. Restrictions on the storage of past credit history will increase the value to developing other, alternative measures of the likelihood of repayment. Countries that have balked at more comprehensive credit reporting because of concerns over personal privacy should bear in mind that some of these alternative measures may be more invasive and less objective than the payment history itself.

5. The effects of more restrictive rules for reporting credit histories may be moderated by regulatory regimes that provide for harsher collection remedies or limits on access to personal bankruptcy, thus minimizing the reduction in credit availability that would otherwise take place. These, too, may be less desirable from a social standpoint than facilitating the reporting of more complete credit histories.

A quarter century of experience within a comprehensive reporting environment in the United States has produced an impressive list of benefits. Detailed information about a borrower's past payment history, including accounts handled responsibly, as well as a current profile of the borrower's obligations and available credit lines have proved to be an important tool for assessing risk. The resulting benefits include:

• Dramatic penetration of lending into lower socioeconomic groups, making a variety of consumer loans available across the income spectrum.

• Reduction in loan losses that would have accompanied such market penetration in the past

• Ongoing account monitoring and use of behavioral scoring by creditors to adjust credit lines and take early preventive action if a consumer is showing signals of overextension. Preventive measures include contacting customers to offer budgetary counseling or concessions on terms to prevent bankruptcy or charge-off.

• Encourages entry of new competitors, including nonbank financial institutions, which has stimulated vigorous price competition and more convenient products.

• Made feasible the securitization of consumer loan receivables (e.g., mortgages, auto loans, credit cards) which has lowered the cost of providing credit and brought hundreds of billions of additional dollars into consumer lending markets.

• Lowered the prices for other financial products as customers have been freed from their binding relationships with banks and other depository institutions. In the past the customer's own bank was frequently the lowest cost source for a loan because other creditors lacked the information needed to measure risk. Consequently, banks have been forced to become more competitive for customers at all margins.

• Made consumers (and workers) more mobile by reducing the cost of severing established relationships and seeking better opportunities.

This last point may well be the most significant in the long run. Much has been made of the "new economy" in the United States, the remarkable growth in U.S. productivity that's brought the unlikely coincidence of the tightest labor market in thirty years, strong growth in personal incomes (5 percent at the end of 1999, after eight and one-half years of expansion), and extraordinarily low inflation. Economists are increasingly conceding that data sharing (especially about consumers) and free-flowing information has been a key to U.S. economic flexibility and consequent resiliency. It contributes to mobility within a society, so that structural shifts within the economy cause temporary disruptions without crippling long-term effects. As suggested in a speech by New York Federal Reserve Bank President William McDonough, the portability of information makes people more open to change (see McDonough 2000). There is less risk associated with severing old relationships and starting new ones, because objective information is available that helps to establish and build trust more quickly. At the same time, access to personal credit information is protected under U.S. disclosure rules so that the consumer retains some control over the release. It is this commitment to making personal credit information available but only with the consumer's permission that has been the engine behind the stunning growth in U.S. financial services markets in recent years.

Acknowledgments

We are grateful for the technical advice and support of Experian Information Solutions, Inc., which provided the data for the simulations in this project. Special thanks go to Experian analysts Charles Chung, Luz Torres, Gabriel Orozco, Chen-Wei Wang, and Sandra Delrahim for their assistance and guidance throughout. We would also like to recognize and thank Steve Edwards of the Australian Finance Conference, and Melissa Stratton and Andrew Wood of Credit Reference Limited in Australia, for their assistance in acquainting us with Australian credit reports and the implications of the Commonwealth Privacy Act of 1988.

Notes

1. Empirical work conducted in the United States by Fair Isaac on behalf of the Associated Credit Bureaus (industry trade association) has demonstrated that "the presence of derogatory information continues to distinguish levels of credit risk in the studied populations even as the information ages. The implication of this finding is that information predictive of credit risk would be sacrificed by the accelerated deletion of aged references" (Fair Isaac 1990, p. 3).

2. Other authors have noted that when variables that might be available to scoring models are artificially prohibited, the resulting models deliver relatively fuzzy risk predictions. Commenting on the consequence of the U.S. Equal Credit Opportunity Act (which prohibits lenders from using race, sex, religion, ethnic background, and certain other personal characteristics in scoring models) Boyes, Hoffman, and Low (1986) note that the resulting degredation in the lender's ability to separate good risk from bad can prompt them to reallocate loanable funds away from consumer lending and toward other classes of products (for example, commercial loans).

3. These statistics derive from Federal Reserve Board Surveys of Consumer Finances, various years, 1956 through 1998. For an overview of the most recent (1998) survey see Kennickell, Starr-McCluer, and Surette (2000).

4. For discussion of rate cuts by these and other major issuers, see Sullivan, *Credit Card Management*, October 1990; Hilder and Pae, *The Wall Street Journal*, May 3, 1991; Spiro, *Business Week*, December 16, 1991; Pae, *The Wall Street Journal*, February 4, 1992; "Citibank Leads an Exodus from Higher Rates," *Credit Card News*, May 1, 1992.

5. Source: American Bankers Association, *Consumer Credit Delinquency Bulletin*, third quarter, 1999.

6. Source: *Monthly Statements*, a monthly newsletter on consumer borrowing and payment trends, edited by Gregory Elliehausen, Credit Research Center, Georgetown University, and published by Trans Union, LLC, December 1999.

7. Note that this does not imply that Australian creditors do not utilize such information. They can always request this information from the borrower on the credit application, but they must incur the costs and delays associated with verifying the information. Thus, while the information available to the underwriting decision could, in principle, be as detailed as in the U.S. model, in practice the costs of ferreting out the complete borrower profile independently of the credit bureau are likely prohibitive.

8. These results were confirmed in separate simulations conducted by an Experian analytical team using methods typical of commercial scorecard development. There are two primary differences between the methods the authors employed and those underlying commercially available generic bureau scorecards. For a variety of reasons, commercial scorecards are typically constrained to the fifteen to twenty most predictive variables, rather than the longer list employed here in developing a full-information model. Also, generic bureau scorecards marketed to date have generally been customer-based rather than loan-based models. That is, the observation unit for the generic bureau scorecard is a customer, not a loan, and the dependent variable describes whether a customer who opens one or more new accounts at the beginning of the observation period becomes seriously delinquent (90+ days) by the end of the period in at least one of the new accounts. Despite the differences in procedures, the Experian estimates were quite close to those reported here.

9. Note here that the choice of "bad" definition for the model, though widely used in the credit industry, nevertheless limits the model's capacity to make even finer distinctions about borrower risk. For example, a borrower who opens a new account, goes to ninety days delinquent after one year, and then brings the account current for the successive months in the observation period is defined as "bad." Yet, from a profitability standpoint, this borrower may be a more valuable customer than one who is seriously delinquent at the end of the observation period. The argument that two borrowers who experience serious delinquency could differ on profitability is essentially the same argument that supports the addition of positive information to a scorecard that formerly contained only negative payment history. Two borrowers who lack blemishes on the credit histories are not necessarily equally desirable customers from a creditor's viewpoint. Admittedly, these are fine distinctions when applied to borrowers with serious delinquencies on their files. Scorecard builders seeking to fine tune their models and orient them more toward profitability, however, have begun utilizing more complex definitions of the dependent variable.

10. "FleetBoston, Citi Plan Push in Latin Consumer Banking," *American Banker*, March 20, 2000, p. 4.

11. "Credit Programs from GM, Others Help Fuel Growth in Mexican Economy," *The Wall Street Journal*, December 13, 1999.

References

Boyes, W. J., Dennis Hoffman, and Stuart Low. 1986. "Lender Reactions to Information Restrictions: The Case of Banks and the ECOA." *Journal of Money, Credit, and Banking* 18, no. 2 (May): 211–219.

Chandler, Gary G., and Robert W. Johnson. 1992. "The Benefit to Consumers From Generic Scoring Models Based on Credit Reports." *IMA Journal of Mathematics Applied in Business and Industry* 4: 61–72. Oxford University Press.

Chandler, Gary G., and Lee E. Parker. 1989. "Predictive Value of Credit Bureau Reports." *Journal of Retail Banking* 11, no. 4 (Winter): 47–54.

Fair, Isaac Companies. 1990. "The Associated Credit Bureaus, Inc., Study on Adverse Information Obsolescence, Phase 1." September.

Japelli, Tullio, and Marco Pagano. 1999. "Information Sharing, Lending and Defaults: Cross-Country Evidence." Working paper no. 22, Centre for Studies in Economics and Finance, University of Salerno, May.

Kennickell, Arthur B., Martha Starr-McCluer, and Brian J. Surette. 2000. "Recent Changes in U.S. Family Finances: Results from the 1998 Survey of Consumer Finances." *Federal Reserve Bulletin* (January): 1–29.

McDonough, William J. 2000. "Central Banking and Crises Management." Speech delivered in the Capital Markets Research Center's Executive Policy Series, Georgetown University, February 2.

Padilla, Jorge, and Marco Pagano. 1997. "Endogenous Communication Among Lenders and Entrepreneurial Incentives." *The Review of Financial Studies* 10, no. 1 (spring): 205–236.

Padilla, Jorge, and Marco Pagano. 2000. "Sharing Default Information as a Borrower Discipline Device." *European Economic Review* 44, no. 10 (December): 1951–1980.

Pagano, Marco, and Tullio Japelli. 1993. "Information Sharing in Credit Markets." *Journal of Finance* (December): 1693–1718.

Stiglitz, Joseph, and Andrew Weiss. 1981. "Credit Rationing in Markets with Imperfect Information." *American Economic Review* 71: 393–410.

Vercammen, James A. 1995. "Credit Bureau Policy and Sustainable Reputation Effects in Credit Markets." *Economica* 62: 461–478.

9   Privacy Restrictions and the Use of Data at Credit Registries

Raphael W. Bostic and Paul S. Calem

9.1 Introduction

The use of technology to process and analyze information kept by credit repositories increased dramatically in the 1990s. In the United States, for example, the use of automated underwriting tools to analyze credit registry data and quantify the default risk posed by applicants for credit expanded well beyond the consumer credit markets that have used them extensively since the 1960s. Often referred to as "credit-scoring models," these automated underwriting tools have become relatively commonplace in home mortgage markets and are being used increasingly in small business credit markets.

The increase in the use of credit-scoring models places particular importance on the data the models are able to consider. Ideally, models should include all variables that have power in predicting the likelihood of default. In the United States, however, restrictions have been placed on the data that can be collected by credit repositories and how these data can be used in conjunction with credit scoring models. These restrictions objectify society's views about the body of information that should not be considered in assessing an applicant's credit quality. Any such excluded information, regardless of its predictive power, is considered to be private information that lenders and others should not have access to in making lending and other decisions.

In this sense, the restrictions placed on credit registry data are essentially privacy measures establishing privacy boundaries that the market cannot cross in conducting its business. Such privacy measures can have potentially important implications for automated underwriting tools, as models created using data lacking important predictive variables will clearly be less powerful than those created using more complete data sets. For this reason and more generally, privacy restrictions may affect the efficiency of markets that rely on the use of credit registry data.

This chapter examines the potential impact of privacy restrictions on efficiency by examining how one such restriction in the United States—a prohibition on the use of gender information—appears to affect the efficiency of credit-scoring models in the context of a particular lending program. The results highlight the ongoing tension between privacy concerns and the desire for efficiency in market interactions.

9.2 Background on Credit-Scoring Models

Credit-scoring models use statistics to derive measures of the credit risk associated with an application for consumer, mortgage, or small business credit. These measures, known as credit scores, rank order applicants according to their relative credit quality and quantify the likelihood that a given applicant will default (become delinquent) on a loan. Lending institutions use two types of scores: (1) those based exclusively on the credit history of individuals as reflected in credit bureau records and (2) those based on other factors in addition to credit history. The former are commonly called "bureau scores" or "credit history scores" while the latter are often referred to as "application scores" or "origination scores." Because of its focus on the use of data kept by credit repositories, this chapter focuses on credit history scores. The issues highlighted here, however, pertain more generally to both types of scores.

Once developed, scoring models can be used to assess the credit risk of loan applicants. Lenders can input applicant information stored at credit repositories into a model and quickly obtain a credit score for the applicant, which can be used in conjunction with any other information the lender deems necessary to make a judgment of the attractiveness of the application. Because they are automated, scoring models increase the speed, consistency, and objectivity of underwriting decisions and produce judgments about credit risk at far less cost than required if individual loan officers make these decisions. Moreover, evidence from many sources shows that scoring models are quite effective in rank ordering applicants according to their underlying credit risk (for examples, see Avery et al. 1996;

Freddie Mac 1996; Pierzchalski 1996). In these ways, scoring models have been an important element driving increased efficiency in U.S. credit markets.

9.3   Privacy Restrictions in Federal Law

Data restrictions for creditors and credit repositories in the United States using scoring models can be grouped into a few broad categories:

1. Limitations on the information that can be collected or used

2. Time limitations on the storage of adverse information about borrowers

3. Limitations arising from the user's concerns about the public relations ramifications of the use of certain information

The first two categories are established by U.S. statutes and, as such, reflect the set of legal privacy restrictions. The third category is qualitatively different in that it includes restrictions that do not have a legal foundation. Rather, these restrictions are often imposed at the discretion of developers and users of scoring models, and they involve, for example, decisions to limit the use of information related to the potential borrower's geographic location. As the possible efficiency effects of discretionary restrictions of the third category have received some attention in previous work (see below), this chapter will focus primarily on the legal privacy restrictions established in the first two categories.

9.3.1   Limitations on Use of Information

The most significant statute that limits the information that can be used in making decisions to extend credit is the Equal Credit Opportunity Act (ECOA). Part of a group of statutes passed in the mid-1960s and 1970s to address longstanding inequities in access to employment, housing, credit and other markets, ECOA was passed by the U.S. Congress in 1974 in response to concerns that creditors were using gender in assessing applications for credit, with the result that some creditworthy female applicants were unfairly being rejected. In the testimony leading up to the act's passage, two separate problems were highlighted. First, many women were unable to obtain credit, regardless of their underlying credit quality. Second, women as sole signatories were typically not extended credit; only women who had a cosigner, usually the woman's husband, were extended credit.

A key feature of the ECOA is its establishment of a set of characteristics, known as "prohibited bases," that generally may not be used by creditors to evaluate the creditworthiness of applicants. The prohibited bases were originally limited to sex and marital status. In 1976 the act was amended to also include race, color, religion, national origin, and age as prohibited bases as a result of concerns raised at later congressional hearings suggesting that these other noncredit-related characteristics were being used as negative factors in making credit decisions (see the act's section 701, 15 U.S.C. 1691; Regulation B, 12 CFR 202, section 202.2(z)).

Despite the general prohibition against the use of prohibited bases in evaluating an applicant's credit, the ECOA provides some exceptions. In a credit scoring system, for example, a creditor may use age as a predictive factor in evaluating creditworthiness, provided that the age of an elderly applicant is used by the lender to favor (or not adversely affect) the elderly applicant in extending credit (Regulation B, 12 CFR 202, section 202.6(b)(2)).

The ECOA can be violated in three ways: overt discrimination, disparate treatment, and disparate impact. Overt discrimination occurs when credit decisions are explicitly made on a prohibited basis. Disparate treatment occurs when a creditor, while not explicitly using a prohibited basis to assess credit quality, treats applicants with similar credit quality differently based on a prohibited factor. Because of the objective manner in which scoring models are developed and used, neither overt discrimination nor disparate treatment are likely to be associated with the use of scoring models. Credit-scoring models generally do not include prohibited factors among their predictors, and guidelines for the use of scoring models generally promote the same treatment for all applicants who are similarly situated.

The potential for the third type of ECOA violation—disparate impact—remains. Disparate impact occurs when a facially neutral practice negatively impacts members of a protected group and no sufficient business necessity exists for the practice or an equally effective but nondiscriminatory or less discriminatory practice exists.[1] Scoring models may include predictive credit history factors that may be correlated with prohibited bases, which will shift the relative scores of individuals in these protected groups. Thus, despite treating all individuals exactly the same, credit-scoring models that include these predictive factors may result in a disparate impact on members with the particular characteristic. If disparate impact is established, either statistically or otherwise, such practices may be defended if it can be shown they are justified by business necessity. Even if justified, a practice may still be deemed discriminatory if it can be shown that an alternative practice would achieve the same business ends with less discriminatory impact.[2]

9.3.2 Time Limitations on Storage of Adverse Information

The Fair Credit Reporting Act (FCRA) of 1971 is the primary statute that establishes the regulatory structure of the consumer reporting industry. The FCRA regulates the activities of consumer reporting agencies (credit repositories), places disclosure obligations on users of consumer reports, and ensures the fair, timely, and accurate reporting of credit information to credit repositories by creditors.

In the current context, the most important provisions of the FCRA are those in section 605 of the act, which specify information that credit reporting agencies are forbidden from providing to users of consumer credit reports. This information includes any title 11 bankruptcies that occurred more than ten years ago or any civil suits, civil judgments, records of arrest, paid tax liens, accounts placed for collection or charge-off, or other adverse items other than convictions of crimes that occurred more than seven years ago (see 15 U.S.C. §1681c).[3] Thus, credit repositories are prohibited from providing any information on credit applicants other than that pertaining to recent credit experiences of the applicant.

The motivation behind these prohibitions is the belief that, after a certain period of time, adverse information should no longer be held against an individual. The foundation for this belief is the notion that people should have an opportunity to recover from past mishaps and rebuild their reputation and social standing.

Violations of this provision of the FCRA can result in administrative enforcement actions by the Federal Trade Commission. These actions can involve civil penalties, including fines, and injunctions prohibiting the activities that caused the violation. Individual states can also bring actions for violations of the FCRA. Consumers also have recourse, although the remedies are relatively limited.

9.3.3 Limitations Due to Public Relations Concerns

Aside from legally imposed restrictions on the use of data, individual users of the data stored by credit repositories might use their own discretion and decide to restrict their use of certain data items. For example, nearly all credit scoring models lack regional economic forecasts or other geographic factors that might be indicators of an applicant's quality. Research suggests, however, that credit scores may be systematically affected by local economic and broader regional circumstances.[4] The findings of this research imply that such geographic factors can be useful for assessing credit quality and that their inclusion in credit-scoring models could improve model performance and, ultimately, the efficiency of credit allocation.

Despite their potential predictive power, many credit-scoring model developers have decided to omit geographic factors from their models. Indeed, no major bureau credit-scoring model commonly used by lenders includes geographic factors as predictive variables in their algorithms. In most cases, this is likely due to a concern that the inclusion of such factors could lead to serious public relations problems. To gain an appreciation for this, consider the following example.

Assume that the data used to develop a scoring model showed a positive relationship between an individual's past performance with credit and the strength of a regional economy. In addition, assume that over the past five years the local economy in California was considerably stronger than in Mississippi. Now consider applicants that are identical in every way except that one lived in California and the other in Mississippi. In such an instance, a credit-scoring model that incorporated geographic information would rate the Mississippi applicant as a stronger applicant, because this applicant was able to maintain the same payment history as the California applicant while living in a weaker economic environment.

While rational and statistically justified, a decision to grant a loan to the applicant from Mississippi and deny one to the California applicant, even though both applicants had the same credit score save geographic considerations out of each applicant's control, could be difficult to justify to a skeptical public. Virtually all institutions have decided that this possibility is not worth the potential pitfalls. This practice exists even though there is no legal restriction on the use of such geographic factors in making credit decisions.

9.4   The Potential Effects of Privacy on Efficiency—An Example

On the one hand, the various privacy restrictions discussed in the previous section objectify societal decisions pertaining to privacy, fairness, or related important social concerns. On the other hand, these restrictions could impact the efficiency of credit-scoring models, and hence credit markets, although the magnitude of their effects are likely to vary. For example, one might expect time limitations on the storage of adverse information to be relatively innocuous, as more recent behavioral patterns are likely to be better predictors of an individual's future behavior than behavioral patterns almost a decade earlier. Thus, replacing more distant experiences with more recent ones in scoring models should improve, or at least not degrade, model performance. One should point out, however, that empirical evidence demonstrating this point is lacking.

Other statutory and politically motivated limitations may be more costly from an efficiency standpoint. This is because, in both cases, variables are omitted from scoring models and equally or more predictive alternatives are not substituted in their place. Indeed, for factors omitted by statute, it is possible that reasonable alternatives could be found. If true, then a model that incorporates the prohibited or omitted factor could be more predictive than the statute- or policy-compliant model that omits the factor. Use of the former (noncompliant) model could increase allocative efficiency by leading to the extension of more credit, lower-risk credit.

To see this, consider the following gender-based example. Assume that a credit-scoring model is effective at rank ordering applicants by their credit risk in two populations that are identical in every respect except for their gender. Further more, assume that the model does not quantify delinquency rates with the same precision for the two groups. Panel (1) of figure 9.1 shows a case where, at each credit score, the subsequent delinquency rate for females is less than that for males, although the delinquency rate gap varies over the range of credit scores.

Suppose a lender that uses this scoring model has a loan origination policy to approve all applicants with credit scores for which the expected delinquency rate is lower than a given percentage (see panel (2)). If a score of a represents the relevant threshold score, all applicants with credit scores higher than score a (to the right of the

Panel 1

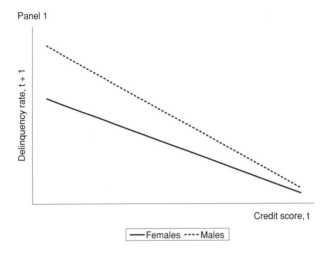

Panel 2

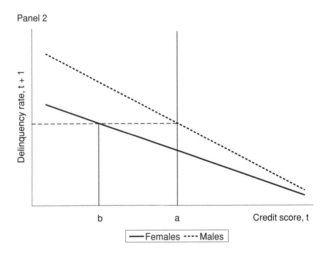

Figure 9.1
Sample credit score/delinquency rate distributions

vertical line) are approved and all applicants with credit scores lower than a (to the left of the line) are denied. Panel (2) shows that this policy results in the denial of applications by females who would have lower expected delinquency rates than approved males (females with credit scores between scores a and b).[5]

This is an inefficient outcome, as the lender could extend additional credit to all females with credit scores between scores a and b and still comply with the origination policy. Similarly, if the lender had a fixed amount of credit that it could extend and was unable to make additional loans, the lender could increase efficiency by shifting credit from males with credit scores slightly greater than a to females with scores slightly less than a. In this case, efficiency would be increased because the average credit quality of the pool of credit recipients would be higher after the credit shift.

9.5   Evidence on the Efficiency Effects of Privacy Considerations

While this example makes it clear that privacy restrictions can theoretically affect the efficiency of scoring models and the allocation of credit, it remains an open question as to whether these effects are observed in any credit market. This section examines this empirical question in the context of privacy restrictions prohibiting the use of gender information in making credit decisions. The analysis relies on repayment performance data from a sample of home purchase loans obtained from a major depository institution in Philadelphia (referred to as Bank). All of these loans were underwritten under a flexible mortgage-lending program known as the Delaware Valley Mortgage Plan (DVMP).[6] The authors augment the DVMP data with credit scores obtained from a national credit bureau and attempt to determine whether the use of credit scoring for borrowers in the sample would have predicted different repayment frequencies by gender.[7]

Using a database of close to 1,200 seasoned and new loans, the relationship between serious loan delinquency and, with controls, credit scores are analyzed. It is important to state that Bank did not obtain or use credit scores in evaluating DVMP applicants. The credit score variable is stratified into a number of ranges and then gender-based dummy variables are used to trace out the expected delinquency-credit score relationship (represented in figure 9.1) for male and female mortgage holders. Significant differences in these distributions, with females having a higher repayment rate than males in given score ranges, would suggest that privacy restrictions on the use of gender information have constrained the efficiency of this lending market, particularly regarding potential uses of credit scoring.

9.5.1 Loan Performance

Data on loan performance were drawn from Bank's servicing files as of November 15, 1994. These files contained records on all (2,390) outstanding loans that had been originated under the DVMP prior to August 1, 1994, and for which first payments were due on or after June 1, 1988. All were fixed-rate, conventional loans for the purchase of single-family, owner-occupied properties. The information obtained includes due date of the first payment, date of the last payment received as of November 15, 1994, and number of months delinquent (if delinquent) as of November 15, 1994. The records also provide the loan amount, contract interest rate, term to maturity, required monthly payment (principal, interest, and escrow amount), and whether the loan was backed by private mortgage insurance. Because the loan servicing records did not include the gender of the borrower and did not provide a credit score, data from other sources were merged to obtain this information.

9.5.2 Borrower Gender

Data collected by federal regulatory agencies under the Home Mortgage Disclosure Act (HMDA) were used to identify the gender of the borrower. HMDA records were merged with DVMP files by matching loan amounts and census tract locations and by requiring that the date of the first payment for a DVMP loan be close to the origination date recorded in the HMDA record. The authors were unable to accomplish this in cases where the loans appeared to be missing from the HMDA data and in cases where multiple matches were obtained. These cases were not included in the final sample.

The race, income, and gender of the borrower and whether a coborrower was present were identified via the HMDA data for 1,222 loans, which comprise the final sample for the analysis here. Delinquency rates and other characteristics of the subsample with HMDA data were similar to those of the full sample.[8] The income data provided in the HMDA records allowed for the calculation of the borrower's housing expense-to-income ratio (front-end ratio), which is used as a control variable in this analysis. Because the census tract location of each loan was provided by BANK, the analysis also was able to control for neighborhood characteristics.

The purchase price of the property being financed was determined from data obtained from the Philadelphia Board of Realtors for nearly all of the loans in the sample obtained from Bank, and it is used to construct additional control variables. The loan-to-price ratio is used in this analysis as a proxy for the loan-to-value ratio. The ratio of the price to the census tract median house value is also used here.

The distribution of the sample by year of origination, gender of the borrower, presence of a coborrower, and repayment status is shown in table 9.1. Female borrowers make up 39 percent of the sample. Approximately 9 percent of the loans were delinquent 60 days or more as of November 15, 1994, and another 8 percent were 30 to 59 days past due. During the period covered by this study, very few loans were foreclosed. Given the relatively small loan amounts,

Table 9.1
Sample characteristics

Characteristic	Number	Percent
Year of origination		
1990	164	13.4
1991	244	20.0
1992	411	33.6
1993	331	27.1
1994	72	5.9
Number of applicants		
Single	956	78.2
With coapplicant	266	21.8
Gender		
Male	745	61.0
Female	477	39.0
Delinquency		
Current	1008	82.5
30–59 days delinquent	102	8.3
60–89 days delinquent	37	3.0
90–180 days delinquent	37	3.0
180 or more days delinquent	39	3.2
Number of observations	1222	

forbearance was viewed as generally less costly than foreclosure. Bank's policy was to proceed with foreclosure only when it became clear that a borrower had little prospect of resuming payments.[9] Because of this policy, the data include a substantial number of loans that were delinquent six months or more.

9.5.3 Borrower Credit Scores

For 682 of the loans in the sample, a score of the borrower's credit history was obtained as of the date of loan origination. Specifically, "The Mortgage Score" (TMS), a credit score developed by Equifax Mortgage Services, was utilized.[10] TMS scores are statistically derived measures of the credit risk associated with a given credit history. This scoring system, which was developed by Equifax on the basis of the credit records of a large general population of mortgagors and the payment performance on their mortgage accounts, weighs such factors as the number and severity of recorded episodes of delinquency, records of bankruptcy, number of credit lines, and age of the oldest credit line. While such credit history information was considered by BANK in evaluating applications for DVMP loans, credit scores were not used.

For the remaining 540 loans in the sample, a credit history score was imputed.[11] For the subsample with scores, the credit score was regressed on characteristics of the loan and borrower including income, race, and sex of the borrower, presence of a coborrower, several race and sex interaction terms, and dummy variables controlling for year of origination and the loan category. The estimated regression equation was then used to impute missing scores.[12]

The use of imputed data may produce biased estimates if the error term of the regression model used to impute credit scores is correlated with the error term of the statistical model of loan delinquency. Another limitation of the imputation procedure is that the imputed scores are fully determined by the variables included in the imputation equation—there is no random variability. As a result, the use of imputed credit score data may bias statistical tests of the relationship between credit scores and loan performance. These issues are addressed below.

9.5.4 Empirical Model

BANK's servicing data, together with borrower characteristics from HMDA, purchase prices, tract-level census data, and TMS scores (known or imputed) form the data for the multivariate logit analysis of loan performance. Specifically, loan performance was regressed on a series of variables expected to influence repayment. Two measures of loan performance were used as the dependent variable: whether a loan is 60 days or more delinquent and whether a loan is 90 days or more delinquent.

The independent variables included in the specification to represent the factors influencing repayment are only briefly described. These variables and their expected relationships to loan performance are more fully described in Calem and Wachter (1999). It should be emphasized that data limitations constrained the selection of control variables.

The potential effects that trends in property values may have had on likelihood of delinquency, as well as any potential effects of loan seasoning, are considered by including dummy variables for when the loan was originated. Since the sample contains observations from only part of 1994, the second half of 1993 to 1994 was appended; otherwise, half-year periods are employed to control for date-of-origination. The equations are estimated with the second half of 1992 as the omitted year dummy variable.

Additional dummy variables are included to control for the relationship between loan performance and the loan-to-value ratio at time of origination. Specifically, those loans originated with a loan-to-value ratio of 80 percent or less and those originated with a loan-to-value ratio of 91 to 95 percent at the time of origination were identified. (Loans originated with a loan-to-value ratio between 80 and 90 percent are the omitted group.) Another dummy variable indicates whether the purchase price of the property exceeded the 1990 tract median value by 33 percent or more (RELPRICE). The authors also include a dummy variable identifying the small subsample of loans backed by private mortgage insurance, one identifying households with a front-end ratio exceeding 28, and, to control for the presence of a coborrower, one identifying individual (as opposed to joint) borrowers.

Three neighborhood factors—census tract housing market activity, squared activity, and the proportion of residents age fifty-five or older—are included as additional control variables. Housing market activity is measured as the number of HMDA-reported home purchase loans in a census tract from 1990 to 1993 per ten owner-occupied units in the tract, and it is included in the model because theory suggests that neighborhood housing market activity may affect credit risk.[13] The proportion of residents aged fifty-five or older is included because previous research suggests that in the early 1990s, Philadelphia neighborhoods with larger proportions of older residents had more stable populations, contributing to overall neighborhood stability (Calem 1996).[14]

Because lenders typically implement credit scoring models by establishing rules based on score thresholds, categorical credit score dummy variables were included rather than a single continuous credit score variable. The cutoffs used to establish the TMS categories—600, 660, and 720—correspond to widely cited thresholds for generic credit history scores used to represent different general levels of risk.[15] A credit score below 600 is generally associated with low credit quality, and scores above 660 are generally associated with high credit quality. A "greater than 720" category was included to examine whether the repayment performance of borrowers with high credit quality differs from those of others. In this specification, the "greater than 720" category is the omitted group. To ensure that results are not sensitive to the selection of particular cutoffs, additional regressions were run using a number of alternative category combinations.

To determine whether the relationship between loan performance and credit scores varies by gender, interaction terms between credit score and gender were included in the specification. Significant differences in these coefficients across borrowers of different genders would indicate that repayment performance varied significantly by gender.

Several borrower characteristics that prior studies have found to be related to loan performance were omitted from the estimated equations due to lack of data. These include nonmortgage debt payments as a proportion of income, cash reserves, and measures of income stability such as employment tenure. These omitted factors may be correlated with the borrower's credit score and gender, in which case the regression results may need to be reinterpreted. For instance, it is possible that female borrowers with higher TMS scores have a lower likelihood of delinquency than male borrowers with comparable scores in part because female borrowers have more stable income. In evaluating the results, the possibility that estimated relationships between credit score, gender, and the likelihood of delinquency may in part reflect omitted variables should be borne in mind.

9.5.5   Results

Table 9.2 shows the results of estimates with 60- and 90-day delinquency, respectively, as the definitions of nonrepayment.[16] The authors restrict attention to the coefficient estimates for variables of interest—the interactions of the credit score categorical variables with gender. The coefficient estimates for the control variables conform to the findings in Calem and Wachter (1999).

The estimates reveal significant differences by gender in the relationship between credit scores and subsequent repayment performance. Looking first at male borrowers and sixty-day delinquency, the estimates indicate that declines in credit scores are associated with declines in the frequency at which borrowers were current on their payments. Compared with males with credit scores above 720, males with credit scores between 600 and 720 were significantly less likely to pay as agreed. Those with credit scores between 660 and 720 were slightly more likely to be delinquent than males with credit scores between 600 and 660, but these rates are not statistically different from each other ($t = 0.05$, $p = 0.76$). Males with credit scores below 600 were even less likely than the 600 to 720 credit score group to make payments on their mortgages in a timely fashion. These borrowers were delinquent a statistically significant eight times more often than borrowers with scores greater than 720 ($t = 2.10$, $p < 0.05$).

Among female borrowers, only those with credit scores below 600 performed significantly differently than male borrowers with scores above 720. These female borrowers were delinquent on their loans as frequently as male borrowers with comparable scores ($t = 0.38$, $p = 0.38$). The repayment behavior of female borrowers with scores above 600, however, was not statistically significantly different from that of male borrowers with scores above 720. This is in stark contrast to the distribution of repayment among male borrowers, in which all male borrowers with scores below 720 had significantly lower repayment frequencies. Thus, at each point over the credit score distribution, female borrowers had a delinquency rate that was less than or equal to that of male borrowers. This result is also observed in the case where the dependent variable was ninety-day delinquency.

Given the regression results, the predicted repayment performance-credit score relationship for males and females can be traced out. To do this, the predicted sixty-day delinquency rate of male and

Table 9.2
Regression coefficients for estimates of loan repayment performance (Dependent variable: Days of delinquency)

	60-day		90-day	
	Coefficient	Standard error	Coefficient	Standard error
Intercept	−3.38	1.04[b]	−4.02	1.35[b]
Insured	−1.16	0.75	−0.77	0.77
Activity in tract	19.19	11.75[a]	10.53	13.58
(Activity in tract)^2	−138.70	64.49[b]	−109.80	77.04
Front-end ratio	0.94	0.33[b]	0.63	0.41
Tract population over 55 years	−0.02	0.01[a]	−0.03	0.01[b]
Single	0.41	0.27	0.79	0.35[b]
(TMS ≤ 600) * female	1.76	0.86[b]	2.01	1.16[a]
(600 < TMS ≤ 660) * female	0.57	0.79	0.91	1.08
(660 < TMS ≤ 720) * female	0.24	0.85	0.42	1.15
(TMS > 720) * female	−0.67	1.25	−0.03	1.45
(TMS ≤ 600) * male	2.25	0.79[b]	2.48	1.09[b]
(600 < TMS ≤ 660) * male	1.42	0.75[a]	1.71	1.04[a]
(660 < TMS ≤ 720) * male	1.51	0.75[b]	1.71	1.05
Relative Price	0.56	0.23[b]	0.72	0.27[b]
Loan-to-Value Ratio ≤ .80	−0.74	0.55	−0.55	0.63
Loan-to-Value Ratio > .90	1.00	0.80	0.99	1.26
N	1172		1172	
Number of delinquencies	112		75	

a. Significant at 10%.
b. Significant at 5%.
Note: Omitted category is male applicant with a coapplicant, a loan with a loan-to-value ratio between 0.80 and 0.90, and a TMS score of greater than 720. Regressions include separate dummy indicator variables for the first six months of 1990, 1991, 1992, and 1993, for the second six months of 1990 and 1991, and for the period of July 1993, through September 1994 (seven in total). The second six months of 1992 is the omitted category.

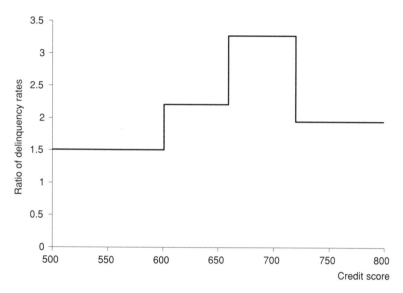

Figure 9.2
Male delinquency rate in relation to female delinquency rate

female borrowers was compared with credit scores in the same score range and with identical tract and loan characteristics. The borrowers were assumed to be single. Tract variables were set equal to their sample means. The hypothetical loan was originated in the second half 1992, had a loan-to-value ratio in the 81 to 90 percent range, was not backed by private mortgage insurance, had a front-end ratio less than 28 percent, and was to purchase a property whose price was not relatively high (RELPRICE = 0). Figure 9.2 shows the results of this simulation.

Figure 9.2 shows that, for single borrowers with the selected tract and loan characteristics, sixty-day delinquency rates for males are between 1.5 and 3 times higher than those for females across the four credit score ranges. The figure also shows that the male-female performance gap varies across the credit score ranges, with the widest gap occurring in the 660 to 720 credit score range. These differences illustrate that the same credit score is associated with substantially different repayment frequencies across gender categories. Moreover, the size of the gender-based performance gap does not consistently increase or decrease with the credit score, which suggests that the gap is not an artifact of omitted credit characteristics but is indicative of fundamental differences in the relationship between repayment performance and credit scores for borrowers of different genders. There is little reason to believe, for example, that gender-based differences in employment history would be greatest for borrowers in the middle score range.

9.5.6 Robustness

This result was remarkably robust in the data. Because of concerns that the presence of coapplicants might influence lender origination decisions, thereby reducing the information value of the applicant's credit score alone, the regressions were run on a sample that only included single applicants. These results are shown in table 9.3. Female borrowers again were observed to repay at significantly higher frequencies than male borrowers over some credit score ranges and at least as frequently in the remaining credit score ranges. Similarly, to ensure that the result was not simply an artifact of the cutoffs chosen for the credit score ranges, all regressions were rerun using several different cutoff combinations. In these cases, the repayment behavior of female borrowers was also equal to or exceeded the repayment behavior of male borrowers.

The results also are robust to adding any of the following variables to the estimated equation: borrower income; dummy variables identifying black borrowers and Hispanic borrowers; a dummy variable identifying observations with imputed credit scores, and various census tract characteristics (unemployment rate; median income; median house value; proportion of residents of age 45–54; proportion of housing units that are rental properties; percent of households earning under $15,000 per year; and dummy variables identifying predominantly minority areas and blighted areas.) When these variables were added to the empirical model, none of associated coefficients was found to be statistically significant.

As noted, there is no random variability in the imputed credit history scores. Consequently, the estimation results reported above may be biased. Moreover, the use of imputed data can yield biased estimates if the error term of the imputation regression equation is correlated with the error term of the loan performance equation. The robustness of the estimated relationships was checked in two ways. First, variability to the imputed scores was added by employing a randomized imputation procedure. To the imputed scores, the authors added simulated "noise" generated from a normal distribution with mean zero and variance equal to the mean square error of

Table 9.3
Regression coefficients for estimates of loan repayment performance, single applicants only (Dependent variable: Days of delinquency)

	60-day		90-day	
	Coefficient	Standard error	Coefficient	Standard error
Intercept	−2.64	1.07[b]	−3.63	1.38[b]
Insured	−0.88	0.77	−0.53	0.79
Activity in tract	20.42	13.11	20.89	15.24
(Activity in tract)^2	−156.10	73.43[b]	181.30	88.85[b]
Front-end ratio	0.99	0.39[b]	0.92	0.45[b]
Tract population over 55 years	−0.03	0.01[b]	−0.03	0.02[a]
(TMS ≤ 600) * female	1.60	0.90[a]	2.07	1.18[a]
(600 < TMS ≤ 660) * female	0.31	0.81	0.58	1.10
(660 < TMS ≤ 720) * female	0.13	0.86	0.27	1.16
(TMS > 720) * female	−0.85	1.30	−0.13	1.46
(TMS ≤ 600) * male	2.02	0.82[b]	2.26	1.12[b]
(600 < TMS ≤ 660) * male	1.12	0.77	1.59	1.06
(660 < TMS ≤ 720) * male	1.49	0.78[a]	1.65	1.07
Relative Price	0.71	0.26[b]	0.89	0.30[b]
Loan-to-Value Ratio ≤ .80	−0.81	0.64	−0.90	0.77
Loan-to-Value Ratio > .90	1.37	1.01	1.22	1.33
N	916		916	
Number of delinquencies	90		64	

a. Significant at 10%.
b. Significant at 5%.
Note: Omitted category is male applicant with a coapplicant, a loan with a loan-to-value ratio between .80 and .90, and a TMS score of greater than 720. Regressions include separate dummy indicator variables for the first six months of 1990, 1991, 1992, and 1993, for the second six months of 1990 and 1991, and for the period of July, 1993, through September, 1994, (seven in total). The second six months of 1992 is the omitted category.

the imputation regression equation. As an additional test of the relationship between credit scores and likelihood of delinquency, observations with imputed scores were dropped. The gender differences observed above persisted when the "noisy" credit scores were used in place of the imputed scores and when observations with imputed credit scores were omitted.[17]

All of the robustness checks discussed above yielded similar results when ninety-day delinquency variable was used in place of the sixty-day delinquency measure as the dependent variable.

In spite of the observed gender-based differences in the credit score's quantification of risk, the estimates suggest that the credit-scoring model is generally effective at rank ordering borrowers according to their risk of default. The coefficient estimates, while not always significant, increase monotonically with credit score for female borrowers and generally increase with credit score for male borrowers.

9.6   Conclusion and Discussion

In many nations, personal privacy is a central aspect of citizenship and is protected by a diverse set of legal structures. These societies have made a determination that, in business matters, individuals should not be judged based on certain personal information. In some cases, this can enhance how markets function. For example, in the United States, the introduction of race-based privacy restrictions has helped to reduce the rationing of housing, employment, and credit that prevented high-quality minorities from participating in these markets.

This chapter, however, has focused on the potential for tension between notions of personal privacy and economic efficiency. Privacy restrictions can prevent the flow of potentially useful information that could be used to better discriminate between high- and low-quality applicants for homes, jobs, and credit. To demonstrate this, new research was presented based on loan performance data from a special mortgage lending program at one large depository institution in the United States. The results showed that the use of gender-specific credit scoring models, which is not permitted under United States law, may have enhanced program efficiency by allowing for increased credit allocation or a higher quality pool of borrowers.[18]

It is important to emphasize that this exercise was a thought experiment; the lender did not use credit scoring in making under-writing decisions. Given the increased prevalence of credit scoring in mortgage markets, however, it seems reasonable that similar issues may arise for lenders in other circumstances.

In balancing the sometimes conflicting objectives of privacy and efficiency, societal interests for economic efficiency must be weighed against interests of equity and equal access. In the United States, the U.S. Congress decided that the adverse effects of using prohibited bases and dated information were sufficiently contrary to societal notions of fairness that the potential losses in economic efficiency were justified. In determining privacy boundaries, each nation will have to conduct a similar benefit-cost analysis and assess whether the marginal benefits associated with imposing particular privacy restrictions outweigh the marginal efficiency costs each may entail. While this could result in a multiplicity of different privacy restrictions internationally, it will recognize the diversity of views about privacy that are held across nations.

In conclusion, it should be noted that privacy considerations are not the only factors that can reduce efficiencies associated with scoring models and the use of data stored at credit repositories. Avery et al. (2000) explore a number of potential statistical issues associated with scoring models and credit registry data and finds that several issues warrant attention. One of the most significant of these is whether the data used to develop scoring models has sufficient coverage; that is, whether it is sufficiently representative of the populations they are used to assess. If not, then underrepresented groups could be at a disadvantage and high quality applicants from these groups could be inappropriately denied access to credit.

Acknowledgments

The views expressed in this chapter do not necessarily represent those of the Board of Governors of the Federal Reserve System or its staff. The authors would like to thank Glenn Canner, Thomas Durkin, Jane Gell, David Stein, and Natalie Taylor for helpful comments. All errors are the authors'.

Notes

1. An historic example of a policy that had a disparate impact on blacks is the literacy requirement for voting that many U.S. jurisdictions imposed during the Reconstruction period.

2. Scoring-related impact issues can also be reasonably applied to other population classes. For example, concerns have been expressed about the effects of credit scoring on access to credit for disadvantaged populations, such as the poor and the poorly educated (see, e.g., Fishbein 1996). Some observers argue that, for a number of reasons, members of these groups should be assessed based on a different set of factors than the general population. Models developed based on these other factors, it is surmised, would be equally predictive while not raising disparate impact concerns. Hence, they argue, the use of standard scoring models "stacks the deck" against

members of these subpopulations. As a second example, previously self-employed individuals or those who once worked in volatile industries will likely have lower credit score distributions than others. If their employment status has changed, then the credit score might rate such individuals as riskier than they actually are.

3. The restrictions are waived if the consumer credit report is used to assist decision making in three areas: (1) the extension of credit involving, or reasonably expected to involve, a principal amount of $150,000 or more; (2) the underwriting of life insurance involving, or reasonably expected to involve, a face amount of $150,000 or more; or (3) the employment of any individual at an annual salary equaling, or reasonably expected to equal, $75,000 or more. In addition, the reporting periods have been lengthened for certain adverse information pertaining to U.S. government insured or guaranteed student loans, or pertaining to national direct student loans. See sections 430A(f) and 463(c)(3) of the Higher Education Act of 1965, 20 U.S.C. 1080a(f) and 20 U.S.C. 1087cc(c)(3), respectively.

4. See Avery et al. 2000.

5. Note that this is an example of disparate impact. Female applicants would have been adversely impacted by the uniform application of the credit-scoring system. The practical legal significance of this adverse impact would depend on the magnitude of this difference. Small, statistically insignificant differences would typically not be viewed as evidence of disparate impact. Further, an important feature of this example is that female performance exceeds male performance at all points along the distribution. This is a necessary condition to conclude that a lender's policy has a potentially disparate impact against females. If the performance relationship varied—that is, female performance exceeded male performance over some portions of the distribution and the opposite held for other portions—then the population affected by adverse impact would depend on the policy rule and which population had superior performance over the relevant range.

6. See Calem (1993) for details about the DVMP.

7. A few studies have focused on the relationships between gender and loan performance. Berkovec et al. (1998) find that female borrowers have a lower frequency of default on FHA-insured mortgages. By contrast, Peterson (1981) finds no statistical difference in the performance of males and females for various types of consumer credit. Neither of these studies, however, controlled for borrower credit history or credit score. Findings here are therefore more directly applicable to the question of how privacy restrictions on the use of gender information may affect the efficiency of scoring models.

8. Virtually no differences were observed in delinquency rates between the subsample with HMDA data and the original sample after controlling for differing distributions of loans by year of origination (by weighting the annual delinquency rates in the original sample). For instance, 9.2 percent of the loans in the subsample with HMDA data are delinquent sixty days or more. The corresponding, weighted average delinquency rate for the original sample is 9.4 percent. This implies that the reduction in the sample that arises from the use of HMDA data does not introduce significant selection bias.

9. Delinquent borrowers were allowed to resume making monthly loan payments and to defer past-due amounts until they become fully capable of making good on the missed payments. BANK reported that most often delinquencies were the result of a borrower becoming unemployed or becoming overextended as a result of excessive spending and / or unplanned expenses.

10. The Mortgage Score and TMS are service marks of Equifax Mortgage Services.

11. Scores were more frequently missing for loans originated in earlier years due to difficulties associated with retrieving archived credit records. In addition, scores were missing for male borrowers more frequently than for female borrowers. Once these factors are controlled for, delinquency rates do not differ between borrowers with and without scores.

12. For further details, see Calem and Wachter (1999).

13. One view is that the accuracy of property appraisals increases with neighborhood housing market activity (Lang and Nakamura 1993).

14. Substitution of other tract variables for these three, or inclusion of additional tract variables, does not substantially improve model performance.

15. The scales for TMS and generic credit history scores differ. In building the dataset, TMS scores were rescaled so that the two scales were identical.

16. The sample for the regressions contains 1,172 observations due to the loss of 50 observations because of missing data for some of the control variables.

17. When a random element was added, differences in male and female performance within credit ranges were statistically significant 97 percent of the time. Patterns of statistical significance were largely identical when observations with imputed scores were dropped.

18. Although the analysis does not address this directly, increased efficiency could also manifest itself through lower prices.

References

Avery, Robert B., Raphael W. Bostic, Paul S. Calem, and Glenn B. Canner. 2000. "Credit Scoring: Statistical Issues and Evidence from Credit-Bureau Files." *Real Estate Economics* 28 (3): 523–547.

Avery, Robert B., Raphael W. Bostic, Paul S. Calem, and Glenn B. Canner. 1996. "Credit Risk, Credit Scoring, and the Performance of Home Mortgages." *Federal Reserve Bulletin* 82 (7): 621–648.

Berkovec, James A., Glenn B. Canner, Stuart A. Gabriel, and Timothy H. Hannan. 1998. "Discrimination, Competition, and Loan Performance in FHA Mortgage Lending." *Review of Economics and Statistics* 80 (2): 241–250.

Calem, Paul S. 1996. "Patterns of Residential Mortgage Activity in Philadelphia's Low- and Moderate-Income Neighborhoods: 1990–1991." *Home Mortgage Lending and Discrimination: Research and Enforcement*, U.S. Department of Housing and Urban Development, 651–676.

Calem, Paul S. 1993. "The Delaware Valley Mortgage Plan: Extending the Reach of Mortgage Lenders." *Journal of Housing Research* 4: 337–358.

Calem, Paul S., and Susan M. Wachter. 1999. "Community Reinvestment and Credit Risk: Evidence from an Affordable Home Loan Program." *Real Estate Economics* 27 (1): 105–134.

Fishbein, Allen J. 1996. "Is Credit Scoring a Winner for Everyone?" *Stone Soup* (spring): 14–15.

Freddie Mac. 1996. "Automated Underwriting: Making Mortgage Lending Simpler and Fairer for America's Families." Freddie Mac report, September.

Lang, William W., and Leonard I. Nakamura. 1993. "A Model of Redlining." *Journal of Urban Economics* 33: 223–234.

Peterson, Richard L. 1981. "An Investigation of Sex Discrimination in Commercial Banks' Direct Consumer Lending." *Bell Journal of Economics* 12 (2): 547–561.

Pierzchalski, Lawrence J. 1996. "Guarding Against Risk." *Mortgage Banking* (June): 38–45.

10 Segmentation and the Use of Information in Brazilian Credit Markets

Armando Castelar Pinheiro
and Alkimar Moura

10.1 Introduction

Until 1994, when inflation was brought down from the sky-high levels that had prevailed since the mid-1970s, the financial system in Brazil was almost entirely geared toward maximizing nonlending operations income, which answered for almost half of the overall earnings of commercial banks. In that environment, being efficient in processing transactions, such as the payment of bills and checks, was paramount to banks, whereas credit-granting activities received much less attention, since little credit flowed to the private sector anyway.[1] Incentives for investing in proper credit analysis were further weakened by the fact that most medium and long-term credit to firms and households was provided by state banks, funded by specific taxes and government transfers. Political interference, soft budgets, and other distortions common to state-owned enterprises made the quality of credit analysis in those institutions particularly low (McKinsey 1998). Private banks, in turn, not only lent very little, but also concentrated their loan activities on short-term operations, such as overdraft facilities and working capital finance, for which borrowers' cash flows, managed by the same institution, worked as collateral. Entry deregulation in the late 1980s, although expanding the number of banks, did little to change this scenario.

The dramatic reduction in inflation rates after the introduction of Brazil's Real Plan produced many changes in the financial system. In particular, it reduced banks' income from nonlending operations, causing several of them to run into serious solvency problems. This was the case of most commercial state banks and also of many small and some large private ones. Some of the small banks were liquidated, while medium and large banks' distress was resolved mostly through purchase-and-assumption transactions, with the government assuming a large share of their bad loans.[2] In the case of *Banco do Brasil*, the country's largest bank, the government had to make a capital infusion of close to U.S. $8 billion to avoid bankruptcy. Other state banks were recapitalized and then privatized. Several of these failing banks were acquired by foreign institutions.

One could expect that the loss of income from nonlending operations, a more stable macroeconomic environment and the entry of foreign institutions, which command modern credit analysis technology, would lead to a substantial expansion in credit activities. Surprisingly, though, this did not occur, with the overall amount of credit extended to the private sector decreasing as a ratio of GDP (Pinheiro and Cabral 1998). The only segment of the credit market that showed a significant expansion was that of consumer and personal loans, which almost tripled as a proportion of GDP from 1993 to 1997. Banks were not prepared for this, with the boom in credit supply occurring with essentially no change in credit-granting practices, which continued to rely on old-fashioned methods for selecting borrowers. Other creditors, such as department stores and small retailers, were in a worse situation, since they lacked even this limited experience.

Not surprisingly, then, default rates increased dramatically in this market segment, causing the bankruptcy of creditors that just a few months before were posting record sales and interest income. This was the case of two of the country's largest department stores, *Arapuã* and *Mesbla*. Banks were not immune either. Public, national private, and foreign banks all experienced a surge in default rates in their loans to households. *Boavista*, one of Brazil's most traditional banks, went bankrupt a year after posting the industry's highest profit rate, which was almost entirely based on interest income due on loans to consumers.

Lenders were unprepared to use the available information to select good borrowers, but the quality and nature of that information may also be blamed for those poor results. Credit information registries (CIRs) have existed in Brazil for several decades, but they have traditionally maintained mostly negative information, obtained from judicial and security registries, chambers of commerce, and the Brazilian Central Bank's registry on returned checks. After the Real Plan many borrowers were accessing credit markets for the first time, thus the information available in those CIRs provided little guidance about the likelihood of borrowers' default. In addition, to some extent the function of CIRs was less to inform creditors than to encourage borrowers to pay, since a bad debtor's name is erased from those registries once payment is completed. That is, the emphasis was on enforcement rather than on building data banks on borrower's payment history.

The situation in Brazil's credit market in the immediate aftermath of the Real Plan was one in which bank supervision and prudential regulation had not been able to prevent the failure of a large number of financial institutions, banks had little expertise in providing credit, and CIRs were ill-equipped to provide the information necessary for adequate credit risk analysis. In sum, it was not an environment conducive to the sort of expansion in private sector credit that could help accelerate economic growth.[3]

Brazil's credit market has changed since then, with banks investing in improving their credit analysis, a renewed dynamism in the CIR industry and a substantial upgrade in the quality of bank regulation. The decline in real interest rates and in reserve requirements since the 1999 devaluation of the *real* have also contributed to stimulating credit activities. As argued in this chapter, however, one feature of Brazil's credit market should not change in the foreseeable future: its segmentation into different submarkets, with borrowers who pose equal risk to banks facing different loan conditions, depending on their size and the nature of their banking relationships. Segmentation, in turn, will limit the scope of CIR activities, which should continue to concentrate on collecting and disseminating negative information, largely with enforcement purposes. Further improvements in bank regulation should then take into account that a large share of the information necessary to assess credit risk will remain private to individual banks.

Taking the Brazilian case as an example, this chapter analyzes the consequences of interbank asymmetry of information for credit market operations and, in particular, for the role played by CIRs in disseminating information. Poor accounting and widespread tax evasion cause relationship banking to be a key source of information about a wide spectrum of borrowers, making much of the relevant information about creditworthiness private to individual banks. In this environment, credit markets tend to fragment into segments with different characteristics on interest rates and average loan size. The more pervasive is tax evasion and the more opaque is publicly available information, the larger the share of credit channeled through noncompetitive market segments, where banks exploit their information monopoly to extract rents from borrowers, charging interest rates above those that would prevail in the presence of symmetric information. In such a segmented credit market, the role of private CIRs is limited essentially to supplying negative information about borrowers, the main objective of which is to foster debt repayment. Although the analysis is centered on the Brazilian case, the authors believe that their results are relevant for other developing countries.

The chapter comprises three parts. Section 10.2 focuses on the use of credit information by banks in their loan operations, showing how interbank asymmetry of information resulting from relationship banking causes market segmentation. Section 10.3 argues that market segmentation helps to explain why CIRs in Brazil tend to collect and supply mostly negative information, and it explains why this situation is unlikely to change even if better mechanisms to screen borrower type become available. Section 10.4 looks at how market segmentation affects supervision and prudential regulation of the banking sector. A final section sums up the main conclusions and policy implications of this analysis.

10.2   Bank Lending to Private Parties in Brazil

10.2.1   The Credit Decision Process
Up to 1994, private Brazilian banks were not active in lending and therefore were not careful in implementing credit decision policies and processes. In the high inflation period, from 1974 to June 1994, with full indexation of wages, rents, contracts, foreign exchange, and financial assets, monetary policy was generally aimed at controlling the nominal interest rate, therefore providing liquidity to sustain increasing levels of aggregate demand. Default ratios by both firms and individuals were low, changes in loan-loss reserves were a small share of banks' total expenditures, and credit income answered for an equally small fraction of their overall revenue. Under those circumstances, credit information policies were almost nonexistent, being limited to maintaining internal customers' files (*cadastros*) to store mostly negative information. Banks exchanged information about their customers with other lenders (both banks and nonbanks) through a completely informal network of informers (the so-called

informantes) whose sole function was to crosscheck restrictive data about the bank's borrowers.

It was only after price stability in 1994 that financial institutions became keen on expanding their lending operations, particularly in financing the sale of durable consumer goods. In fact, there was an incipient credit bubble beginning with the stabilization plan in July 1994 and lasting up to March 1995. Expenses and income associated with credit activities began to account for a significant proportion of total bank expenditures and revenues. Both banks and borrowers, however, were not prepared to operate in the new environment of easy access to credit. The default ratio on bank loans increased faster than total performing loans during this period, which is, among other factors, an indication of the generally poor quality of credit management that prevailed in the country. In January 1995, on average, for each *real* of performing loans banks posted R$0.08 of nonperforming loans; in January 1997, the corresponding figure was R$0.18, a 125 percent increase. This unsuccessful experience prompted many banks to restructure their credit operations, trying to introduce new policies and procedures to cope with credit risk.

Six years after the burst of this credit bubble, there were still substantial cross-bank differences in the stage of their organizational development as far as the formulation, implementation, monitoring, controlling, and evaluation of credit policies, procedures, and practices. On the one hand, there were some banks with a relatively strong credit culture, which tend to make intensive use of internally generated information as well as external data (mainly data provided by the various CIRs) as inputs to their credit decision process. On the other hand, banks with a loose or ill-formulated credit policy in most cases did not make use of formal criteria to allocate credit (other than the traditional method of establishing fixed credit limits to customers) and therefore used information less intensively, including CIR data, to decide on lending operations. In between these two types, and this might be the case of most banks, there were many institutions trying to introduce formal policies, procedures, and practices of credit management, including purchase of foreign methods and models of credit analysis and scoring.

Procedures adopted in the credit decision process differ according to the type of bank and the characteristics of the loan/borrower. The general trend for loans to consumers and to small businesses is toward the introduction of a highly decentralized process of credit management. Accordingly, all loan requests are treated automatically by statistical methods (credit scoring, for instance), based on information supplied by the client and/or available from public records, with a decision rapidly reached at the branch level. Taking into consideration the borrower's characteristics, the statistical model assigns him or her a quantity of points and the corresponding automatic credit limit. Exceptions are dealt with at higher levels of the credit bureaucracy, generally by credit committees. This asset allocation process is mostly used in lending operations such as overdraft facilities, consumer installment credit, leasing, credit card loans, and secured or unsecured personal loans. That appears to be the most efficient way to guarantee speedy decisions in large retail banks, which can receive as much as 2,000 loan applications per day.[4] For loans to small business, typically for working capital needs (based on discounting of predated checks and *duplicatas*), the decision process is very similar, with branches having their own credit limits for secured operations.[5] This means that a large share of the total number of loans, as much as 80 percent in some banks, is decided at the branch level, based on automatic credit evaluation methods relying on statistical analysis.

For loans other than to the retail market, that is, consumers and small businesses, the traditional method of credit management is to establish credit limits per customer to restrain the lender's exposure to a particular borrower. A recent trend in the banking industry has been to transform the credit decision into a group decision made by formal credit committees that are generally organized according to such criteria as the value of the loan, the existence and kind of collateral, and the type of operation. Each application is treated on a case-by-case basis by the corresponding credit committee, taking into consideration variables such as the client's file (*cadastro*), its economic and financial situation, its relationship with the bank, its business tradition, and its industry's prospects. In some large banks, branches do not extend business loans (except to the small businesses mentioned earlier), with loan applications decided by these committees or by the bank's credit department. Some small wholesale banks with relatively large loan values per business customer have rather formalized rules for the credit committees' organization, including variables such as its composition, size of exposure, maximum and minimum loan maturity, types of collateral, rules for functioning and also for voting on loan requests.

Interviews with bank managers revealed substantial differences about the intensity with which financial institutions resort to CIR data—both negative and positive (see appendix 10A). As a general rule, it can be said that all banks use negative information provided by CIRs as a first filter in the credit decision-making process to decide whether or not to continue with the analysis of the credit application. Therefore, that type of information is the relevant barrier to discriminate between potential borrowers and applicants with no access to credit markets.[6] In the retail market, where a large number of low-value loans to small businesses and individuals takes place, the discriminating variable is the borrowers' credit records (*cadastro*), which is heavily biased towards weighing the importance of restrictive information. In this case, negative information provided by CIRs is probably the most relevant and possibly the only data used in the credit decision process.[7]

Once a credit relationship has been established, information provided by CIRs becomes useful for monitoring the borrower's financial situation, that is, to learn about the occurrence of events that might lead to default. In this way, both upgrades and downgrades in the borrower's creditworthiness can be anticipated by monitoring changes in his or her economic fortunes as recorded in those registries. This is not a trivial consideration, given that during the 1980s and 1990s the Brazilian economy was subjected to severe macroeconomic shocks, which deeply affected borrowers' ability to pay. High volatility in interest and exchange rates, varying restrictions on terms and conditions for lending, and trade liberalization are examples of macroeconomic outcomes that made banks face large swings in market as well as credit risks.

The importance of negative information in credit analysis decreases as the size and complexity of the loan operation increase. Its role is therefore less important in the middle market, which appears to be the most profitable business lending activity in Brazil. Banks use two types of information to make loan decisions in this credit segment: first, negative and positive information provided by CIRs and by other lenders and, second, data collected by the bank itself through balance-sheet analysis and on-site visits to firms. In most cases, lenders use the CIR information either to check or to complement their own private information and analysis. There are financial institutions that even maintain their own in-house credit rating facility. Some more aggressive banks in this market segment tend to disregard the usual published balance-sheet data due to their misrepresentation of the actual economic and financial situation of companies. Instead, they replace the formal accounting information with an internally created managerial information system to trace the actual changes in the company's financial conditions. One important part of such a system is to monitor the liquidity of the borrowers's receivables (mainly *duplicatas*), since the latter are the most commonly accepted collateral for business loans in Brazil. The data and analysis of borrowers' creditworthiness gathered by internally developed management information systems remain private to the bank and are not shared with credit bureaus.

In the case of loans to large firms (private corporations, Brazilian and multinational, and some state-owned firms), information provided by CIRs has a limited role in the credit analysis process, in comparison to the research and analysis conducted by the lender itself, coupled with whatever private information has been previously gathered by the financial intermediary. Audited balance sheets and other financial statements are also valuable in such cases because they are more reliable than for smaller firms. In particular, many of these borrowers, being public corporations (with shares quoted in domestic or U.S. stock markets, or having raised funds abroad through issuance of Euro bonds or through debt instruments in Brazilian markets, such as debentures and commercial papers), have to provide investors with a regular flow of information on their economic and financial conditions. The credit process takes longer and is obviously more costly, relative to other lending operations. Lending to the corporate sector accounts for a large proportion of the total credit portfolio of Brazilian retail banks, though its client-base is small. Spreads are also rather narrow in this type of credit operations.[8]

An important feature of the Brazilian credit market is its division into three segments, which differ with the typical loan size and the nature and amount of information on borrowers used by creditors. In the retail market, the number of loan applications is large, loan size is small, interest rates are high, and the credit-decision process is decentralized and automated, relying mostly on outsourced, negative information. In the middle market, banks tend to base their decisions on internally collected information, which is often obtained from a continued banking relationship with borrowers. This information remains private to the bank. The poor quality of the information contained in those borrowers' balance sheets, largely a result of pervasive tax evasion and poor accounting practices, makes information on the borrower's cash flows extremely valuable to assess actual creditworthiness. A third market segment comprises foreign and large national corporations that for various reasons keep much better accounting, which is largely public information. This market segment has fewer borrowers, but loans tend to be larger and interest rates lower than in the other segments.

Some of these features of the Brazilian credit market are evident in table 10.1, which shows the distribution of borrowers with total debts of R$20,000 or more in any single financial institution, according to loan size and number of institutions with which they contracted those loans.[9] On the whole, there were 1.1 million individual borrowers in this group on June 30, 2000, with outstanding debts of 65.0 billion *real*, each of them owing on average R$58,878. For the 178,800 firms in the same category, total debt added to 162.3 billion *real*, corresponding to an average loan of R$907,489 per firm.

Brazilian borrowers generally tend to prefer single-bank relationships. In the case of individual borrowers, only one in twenty owes money to more than one institution. This pattern is heavily influenced by the behavior of small debtors, that is, borrowers with total loans between R$20,000 and R$50,000, who account for 66 percent of all individuals with debts above R$20,000 *real*, and who only exceptionally (1% likelihood) borrow from more than one institution. Among mid-sized individual borrowers (R$50,000 < l ≤ R$200,000) single banking is also prevalent, with only 11.4 percent of them having debts with more than one institution. Even among large borrowers (l > R$200,000) single banking is common, although 52 percent of them have debts with two or more institutions.

Single banking is also dominant among firms; however, they tend to diversify their sources of loans more than individuals. Considering all firms with debts of R$20,000 or more, just 36.1 percent of them borrow from more than one bank. In the case of small debtors, single banking is more prevalent, with only one in every ten firms owing money to more than one institution. Mid-size commercial debtors tend to operate with more banks than small ones, but still 49.3 percent of them have debts with only one institution and 35.0 percent with just two institutions. For large commercial debtors, however, multiple-bank relationships are the norm, with only 23.8 percent of them operating with a single institution.

Table 10.1
Distribution of borrowers according to value of total loans (l) extended by the financial system and the number of institutions that have extended those loans, June 30, 2000

Sum of loans extended to each borrower (l) in 1000 R$	One institution		Two institutions		Three institutions		Four institutions		Five or more institutions		Total	
	Individuals	Firms	Individuals	Firms	Individuals	Firms	Individuals	Firms	Individuals	Firms	Individuals	Firms
20 ≤ l ≤ 35	503.118	55.372	2.450	1.690	135	342	26	113	4	105	505.733	57.622
35 < l ≤ 50	223.325	20.621	4.600	3.203	119	250	13	86	1	67	228.058	24.227
50 < l ≤ 100	246.001	21.005	20.458	13.030	1.187	2.242	83	258	11	224	267.740	36.759
100 < l ≤ 200	63.534	8.475	14.702	7.891	2.837	4.652	424	1.499	79	582	81.576	23.099
200 < l ≤ 1000	8.620	6.460	5.712	5.578	2.412	4.883	842	3.452	397	4.451	17.983	24.824
1000 < l ≤ 10000	1.021	2.032	504	1.514	266	1.324	170	1.128	172	4.234	2.133	10.232
10000 < l ≤ 50000	41	238	27	138	10	129	5	131	12	943	95	1.579
50000 < l ≤ 100000	5	47	—	13	—	18	—	20	—	165	5	263
>100000	3	42	1	13	1	11	—	8	—	153	5	227
Total	1.045.668	114.292	48.454	33.070	6.967	13.851	1.563	6.695	676	10.924	1.103.328	178.832

Source: Central Bank
Note: Includes only borrowers with debts of R$ 20,000 or more in any single financial institution. On June 30, 2000, 1 USD = R$ 1.769.

A simple model is presented here, with interbank asymmetry of information that produces the sort of market segmentation described above. Segmentation arises because good borrowers are "informationally captured" by the institution with which they bank, and as a consequence they end up paying higher interest rates than they would in the standard symmetric information case. The assumption that, in the context of interbank asymmetry of information, inside banks are able to extract rents from safe borrowers is standard in models that feature relationship banking.[10] Differently from those models, however, the authors assume that (1) even for the inside bank there is a cost to assess borrower type; and, (2) that a borrower can avoid this "information trap" by making its type known to outside banks, even if costly, which diminishes the monopoly power of the inside bank.[11] The model is then used to conduct some comparative statics exercises to see how this market structure changes with banks' borrowing rates and the cost of information.

10.2.2   The Model

The model has two types of borrowers, safe and risky, with probabilities of default $1 - q_s$ and $1 - q_r$ ($q_r < q_s$), respectively. When borrowers default, the bank receives nothing. Borrowers differ also on how much the loan is worth to them (v) and to the size of the loan (l) they seek, which is assumed to be independent of v. For consumers v may be interpreted as the rate of time preference and for firms as the rate of return they expect to obtain from investing the money they borrowed. Assume that v is uniformly distributed in $[0, V]$, while l has an exponential distribution with mean λ.[12] For all intervals $[V_0, V_1]x[L_0, L_1] \subset [0, V]x(0, \infty)$ there is a proportion p of safe borrowers. Borrowers' rate of return or time preference and the size of the loan they seek are private information, but their distributions are common knowledge. All banks and borrowers are assumed to be risk neutral.

At the beginning of each period, each borrower has a banking relationship with a single bank.[13] It is easier for this incumbent bank than for all other banks to ascertain this borrower's type, but this is not without cost.[14] To make her type known to outside banks, entering what is called the corporate market, a borrower has to spend C_C. Alternatively, she may decide to reveal her type to the incumbent bank at a cost C_M ($<C_C$).[15] Assume C_C and C_M to be public information. Finally, a borrower may opt not to reveal her type

and borrow in the retail market. There is no fixed cost in accessing the retail market.[16]

The credit market is then divided in three segments: corporate, middle, and retail. In the first, there is perfect symmetry of information and all banks know whether the potential borrower is safe or risky. In the retail market no bank knows a borrower's type, and complete asymmetry of information prevails between banks and borrowers. The number of banks is assumed to be sufficiently large for loans in the corporate and retail markets to be priced competitively. The middle market is characterized by a close banking relationship, so that only one bank knows whether the potential borrower is safe. This sort of interbank information asymmetry exists in all credit markets, but what is peculiar in Brazil and possibly in other developing countries is the magnifying effect of tax evasion and poor accounting practices, with only one bank being able to observe the actual cash flow, and indirectly the creditworthiness, of the borrower. Each bank is assumed to act as a monopolist in its middle market segment.[17]

The game is played as follows. Initially, banks set a menu of interest rates for the three market segments. Borrowers then decide whether or not to tap the market, and, if they decide to borrow, in which market segment to do so. A Nash equilibrium may then be derived by fixing the menu of interest rates so that banks maximize their expected profits conditional on borrowers' optimal reactions.

A safe borrower i will choose the corporate market if and only if

$$q_s(v_i - R_C^s)l_i > C_C \quad \text{and} \quad C_C - C_M < l_i(R_M^s - R_C^s)q_s$$

that is,

$$v_i > R_C^s + \frac{C_C}{l_i q_s} \tag{1}$$

and

$$l_i > \frac{(C_C - C_M)}{q_s(R_M^s - R_C^s)} = L_C \tag{2}$$

where R_C^s and R_M^s are the interest rates charged to safe borrowers in the corporate and middle markets, respectively. Competition in the corporate market ensures that $R_C^s = (1 + R)/q_s - 1$, where R is the banks' borrowing rate. Condition (1) states that a safe borrower will be interested in accessing the corporate market only if the expected net benefit of the loan exceeds the cost of informing the market about its type. Condition (2) says that a safe borrower will go to the corporate market if the savings from paying a lower rate of interest rate in this market segment more than compensate the additional cost of revealing her type to outside banks. These imply essentially that the corporate market is the best option for large safe borrowers.

Safe borrowers will choose the middle market if and only if

$$q_s(v_i - R_M^s)l_i > C_M, \quad C_C - C_M > l_i(R_M^s - R_C^s)q_s$$

and

$$C_M < l_i(R_T - R_M^s)q_s,$$

that is

$$v_i > R_M^s + \frac{C_M}{l_i q_s} \tag{3}$$

and

$$\frac{C_M}{q_s(R_T - R_M^s)} = L_M < l_i < L_C \tag{4}$$

where

$$R_T = \frac{1 + R}{p^T q_s + (1 - p^T)q_r} - 1$$

is the interest rate charged from borrowers in the retail market, with p^T being the proportion of credit extended to safe borrowers in that market segment.[18] L_M and L_C are, respectively, the lower and upper bounds of the middle market and, since they depend on the menu of interest rates, are determined endogenously.

Finally, a safe borrower will operate in the retail market if and only if

$$v_i > R_T \tag{5}$$

and

$$l_i > L_M \tag{6}$$

In equilibrium, all risky borrowers, independently of loan size and expected return, will be in the retail market, since it is always the case that

$$R_T \leq R_C^r = \frac{1+R}{q_r} - 1 \leq R_M^r$$

with R_T being strictly lower than R_C^r if $p^T > 0$.[19] Then, a risky firm or consumer will be willing to borrow if $v_i > R_T$. Therefore, the share of loans extended to safe borrowers in the retail market, p^T, is

$$p^T = \frac{p(1 - (1 + L_M/\lambda)e^{-L_M/\lambda})}{1 - p(1 + L_M/\lambda)e^{-L_M/\lambda}} \tag{7}$$

Under these assumptions, and considering a universe of N potential borrowers, the volume of credit extended in each of the three market segments is given by

corporate market:

$$VC_C = Npe^{-L_C/\lambda}\left[(L_C + \lambda)\frac{(V - R_C)}{V} - \frac{C_C}{Vq_s}\right]$$

middle market:

$$VC_M = Np\left\{\frac{(V - R_M)}{V}[(L_M + \lambda)e^{-L_M/\lambda} - (L_C + \lambda)e^{-L_C/\lambda}]\right.$$
$$\left. - \frac{C_M}{Vq_s}[e^{-L_M/\lambda} - e^{-L_C/\lambda}]\right\}$$

retail market:

$$VC_T = \frac{N(V - R_T)}{V}[\lambda - p(\lambda + L_M)e^{-L_M/\lambda}]$$

In equilibrium, banks make zero expected profit in the retail and corporate markets, which are actuarially balanced, and derive all their economic profits from the middle market, where they earn

$$(1 + R_M)q_s - 1 - R$$

for each dollar lent. Thus, total expected profit is given by

$$E(\Pi) = ((1 + R_M)q_s - (1 + R))VC_M \tag{8}$$

The only decision variable in this model is the interest rate charged by banks to their (safe) clients in the middle market. When fixing this rate, banks have to take two effects into account. On the one hand, the higher R_M, the more they earn from their middle-market clients. On the other hand, the more they raise this rate, the higher L^M and the lower L^C, so that less credit is extended through the middle market. Maximizing (8) with respect to R_M does not yield a closed form solution, but some exercises can be done on comparative statics using numerical maximization. Tables 10.2 to 10.5 display such an exercise, examining how the market behaves when changes are made in the banks' borrowing cost (R), the cost of accessing the corporate and middle markets $(C_C$ and $C_M)$, and borrower diversity $(q_s - q_r)$. In all cases, unless otherwise stated, we fix $R = 15\%$, $\lambda = \$1$, $N = 1,000$, $V = 0.8$, $C_C = \$0.1$, $C_M = \$0.01$, $p = 0.6$, $q_s = 0.98$, and $q_r = 0.8$.

To assess the impact of segmentation, the results of the model are compared with two benchmarks in which interbank asymmetry of information is not present. The first is the case in which borrower type is public information, so that the volume of credit (VC^*) extended to safe and risky borrowers and the corresponding market interest rates (R^*) are, respectively,

$$VC_j^* = p_j N\lambda (V - R_j)/V \tag{9}$$

and

$$R_j^* = (1 + R)/q_j - 1 \tag{10}$$

where $j = s$ and r stand for safe and risky borrowers, respectively, $p_s = p$ and $p_r = 1 - p$. With perfect information the average loan size would be λ for both safe and risky borrowers.

The other benchmark is given by a situation in which there is no way to determine borrower type, that is, there is interbank symmetry of information, but asymmetry between borrowers and banks. In this case the market interest rate and the volume of credit to safe and risky borrowers would be

$$R^{**} = (1 + R)/q^{**} - 1; \tag{11}$$

and

$$VC_j^{**} = p_j N\lambda (V - R^{**})/V \tag{12}$$

where $q^{**} = pq_s + (1 - p)q_r$.

It is immediate to verify that $q_s = q^C = q^M > q^{**} > q^T > q_r$, $R_s^* = R_C < R^{**} < R_T < R_r^*$, and that $R_C < R_M < R_T$. It follows that if borrower type is not known by any bank, safe (risky) borrowers are

Table 10.2
Credit market reaction to a reduction in the cost of funds to banks

Variables	Banks' cost of capital (R)				
	25.0%	20.0%	15.0%	10.0%	7.5%
With complete symmetry of information					
Interest rate					
Safe borrowers	27.6%	22.4%	17.3%	12.2%	9.7%
Risky borrowers	56.3%	50.0%	43.8%	37.5%	34.4%
Volume of credit ($)[a]	512.2	581.6	651.2	720.7	755.4
Safe borrowers	393.4	431.6	469.9	508.2	527.3
Risky borrowers	118.8	150.0	181.3	212.5	228.1
Market default rate	6.2%	6.6%	7.0%	7.3%	7.4%
Without interbank asymmetry of information					
Interest rate ($q^{**} = 9.2\%$ in all cases)	37.7%	32.2%	26.7%	21.1%	18.4%
Volume of credit ($)[a]	529.2	598.0	666.9	735.7	770.1
Safe borrowers	317.5	358.8	400.1	441.4	462.1
Risky borrowers	211.7	239.2	266.7	294.3	308.0
With interbank asymmetry of information					
Interest rates					
Corporate (R_C)	27.6%	22.4%	17.3%	12.2%	9.7%
Middle (R_M)	32.0%	27.0%	21.9%	16.8%	14.3%
Retail (R_T)	56.2%	50.0%	43.7%	37.4%	34.3%
Middle-market limits ($)					
Upper bound (L_C)	2.062	2.039	2.019	2.003	1.996
Lower bound (L_M)	0.042	0.044	0.047	0.049	0.051
Volume of Credit ($)					
All borrowers	475.7	545.0	614.3	683.7	718.4
Safe borrowers	356.7	394.8	432.8	470.9	490.0
Corporate (VC_C)	143.5	160.8	178.2	195.6	204.3
Middle (VC_M)	213.1	233.7	254.4	275.0	285.3
Retail (VC_T)	0.2	0.2	0.3	0.4	0.4
Risky borrowers (in retail market)	119.0	150.2	181.5	212.8	228.4
Number of borrowers					
Safe borrowers	336	373	410	448	467
Corporate	39	45	51	57	60
Middle	289	319	348	377	391
Retail	7	9	11	14	15

Table 10.2
(continued)

Variables	Banks' cost of capital (R)				
	25.0%	20.0%	15.0%	10.0%	7.5%
Avg loan size (safe borrowers, $)[b]					
Corporate	3.654	3.561	3.486	3.425	3.399
Middle	0.736	0.733	0.731	0.729	0.729
Retail	0.021	0.022	0.023	0.025	0.025
Market default rate[c]	6.50%	6.96%	7.32%	7.60%	7.72%
Banks' overall profit ($)	9.30	10.32	11.34	12.36	12.87

a. Without interbank asymmetry of information, the average loan size to both safe and risky borrowers is equal to $1, so that the number of borrowers in each case is equal to the volume of credit extended.
b. Average loan size for risky borrowers in retail market is $1 in all cases.
c. The default rate in the retail market declines very slightly, from 19.98% when R = 25.0% to 19.97% when R = 7.5%.

worse (better) off than if borrower type was known to all banks. The intermediate situation of a segmented credit market, as modeled above, produces losers and winners. Large borrowers will tend to gain, particularly if C_C and C_M are small, but risky and small safe borrowers will lose. Yet, even though default and interest rates are higher in the retail market than in the rest of the credit market, risky borrowers will be better off with market segmentation than if complete symmetry of information prevailed, and in this sense interbank asymmetry of information creates a cross subsidy from safe to risky borrowers in the retail market. This subsidy will increase with borrower diversity $(q_s - q_r)$ and decline with C_C and C_M.[20]

10.2.3 Comparative Statics
Compared to a situation of perfect symmetry of information, market segmentation penalizes safe borrowers in all three market segments (see table 10.2). Those in the corporate market pay the symmetric-information interest rate for safe borrowers, but have to spend C_C to reveal their type, which is equivalent to an additional 2.8 percent spread (considering the parameter values used in this exercise). Interest rates to borrowers in the middle market are 4.6 percentage points above the perfect information rate of interest, with borrowers incurring an information cost that is equivalent to a 1.4 percent spread. Safe borrowers in the retail market pay an interest rate markup that ranges between 24.6 and 28.6 percent depending on

Table 10.3
Reactions to changes in cost of access to corporate market (with interbank asymmetric information)

Variables	Cost of access to corporate market (C_C, in $)				
	0.015	0.040	0.080	0.100	0.150
Interest rate in middle market (R_M)	17.6%	19.0%	21.0%	21.9%	24.1%
Middle-market limits ($)					
Upper bound (L^C)	1.841	1.893	1.977	2.019	2.125
Lower bound (L^M)	0.039	0.041	0.045	0.047	0.052
Volume of credit ($)					
All borrowers	642.1	633.5	620.6	614.3	599.6
Safe borrowers	460.6	452.1	439.1	432.8	418.0
Corporate (VC_C)	210.0	200.1	185.2	178.2	161.6
Middle (VC_M)	250.5	251.8	253.6	254.4	256.1
Retail (VC_T)	0.2	0.2	0.3	0.3	0.4
Risky borrowers in retail market	181.4	181.5	181.5	181.5	181.6
Number of safe borrowers					
Corporate	72	66	56	51	41
Middle	365	360	352	348	339
Retail	9	11	11	12	14
Avg loan size (safe borrowers, $)[a]					
Corporate	2.896	3.051	3.329	3.486	3.943
Middle	0.686	0.699	0.720	0.731	0.756
Retail	0.019	0.020	0.022	0.023	0.026
Market default rate[b]	7.09%	7.16%	7.26%	7.32%	7.45%
Banks' overall profit ($)	0.68	3.99	8.98	11.34	16.87

a. Average loan size for risky borrowers in retail market is $1 in all cases.
b. The default rate in the retail market declines very slightly, from 19.98% when $C_C = \$0.015$ to 19.96% when $C_C = \$0.15$.

banks' borrowing rates. Risky borrowers pay an interest rate only marginally lower than they would if perfect information prevailed. These additional costs reduce the volume of credit extended to safe borrowers between 7 and 9 percent, compared to the amount that would have been extended in the case of perfect information symmetry. As a consequence, default rates are also higher than when borrower type is known to all banks.

Contrasted to a situation in which banks have equal ignorance about borrower type, market segmentation benefits borrowers in the corporate and middle markets, who are able to borrow at a

Table 10.4
Reactions to changes in cost of access to middle market (asymmetric information)

Variables	Cost of access to middle market (C_M)			
	0.020	0.010	0.005	0.001
Interest rates				
Middle (R^M)	21.3%	21.9%	22.2%	22.4%
Retail (R^T)	43.6%	43.7%	43.7%	43.7%
Middle-market limits ($)				
Upper bound (L^C)	2.041	2.019	2.009	2.002
Lower bound (L^M)	0.092	0.047	0.024	0.005
Volume of credit ($)				
All borrowers	611.4	614.3	616.1	617.7
Safe borrowers	429.2	432.8	434.8	436.4
Corporate (VC_C)	175.7	178.2	179.4	180.2
Middle (VC_M)	252.4	254.4	255.4	256.2
Retail (VC_T)	1.1	0.3	0.1	0.0
Risky borrowers in retail market	182.2	181.5	181.3	181.3
Number of safe borrowers	583	423	424	429
Corporate	50	51	52	52
Middle	326	348	360	371
Retail	206	24	12	6
Avg loan size (safe borrowers, $)[a]				
Corporate	3.512	3.486	3.475	3.466
Middle	0.774	0.731	0.709	0.691
Retail	0.045	0.023	0.012	0.002
Market default rate[b]	7.36%	7.32%	7.30%	7.28%
Overall credit market				
Banks' overall profit ($)	9.89	11.34	12.07	12.67

a. Average loan size for risky borrowers in retail market is $1 in all cases.
b. The default rate in the retail market rises very slightly, from 19.89% when $C_M = \$0.02$ to 20.00% when $C_M = \$0.001$.

Table 10.5
Reactions to changes in borrower diversity

Variables			
Default rates			
Safe borrowers $(1 - q_s)$	0.020	0.020	0.150
Risky borrowers $(1 - q_r)$	0.200	0.070	0.200
With complete information			
Interest rates			
Safe borrowers	17.3%	17.3%	35.3%
Risky borrowers	43.8%	23.7%	43.8%
Volume of credit ($)[a]			
Safe borrowers	469.9	469.9	335.3
Risky borrowers	181.3	281.7	181.3
Market default rate	7.0%	3.9%	16.8%
With asymmetric information			
Interest rates			
Corporate (R_C)	17.3%	17.3%	35.3%
Middle (R_M)	21.9%	20.6%	39.5%
Retail (R_T)	43.7%	23.1%	43.3%
Middle-market limits ($)			
Upper bound (L_C)	2.019	2.864	2.543
Lower bound (L_M)	0.047	0.402	0.310
Volume of credit ($)			
All borrowers	614.3	725.5	482.7
Safe borrowers	432.8	440.9	298.9
Corporate (VC_C)	178.2	99.2	86.5
Middle (VC_M)	254.4	315.2	201.7
Retail (VC_T)	0.3	26.5	10.8
Risky borrowers in retail market	181.5	284.5	183.7
Number of borrowers			
Safe borrowers	412	432	285
Corporate	51	22	19
Middle	348	269	193
Retail	12	141	73
Avg loan size (safe borrowers, $)[b]			
Corporate	3.486	4.479	4.581
Middle	0.731	1.174	1.045
Retail	0.023	0.188	0.147
Default rate			
Retail	19.97%	6.57%	19.72%
Overall credit market	7.32%	3.96%	16.90%
Banks' overall profit ($)	11.34	9.91	7.14

a. With perfect information, the average loan size to both safe and risky borrowers is equal to $1, so that the number of borrowers in each case is equal to the volume of credit extended.
b. Average loan size for risky borrowers in retail market is $1 in all cases.

lower cost, information costs included. Risky borrowers, in turn, are penalized with much higher rates of interest, as are small safe borrowers, for whom it is not worth paying to let the market know their type. As a consequence, although with market segmentation more credit flows to safe borrowers and less to risky ones than when borrower type may not be inferred by banks, and as consequence the market default rate is lower, credit becomes concentrated on large borrowers.

A decline in the cost of capital to banks lowers interest rates to both types of borrowers in all situations, but to a larger degree in the case of risky borrowers, when either market segmentation or perfect information prevail. In turn, a lower proportion of total credit goes to safe borrowers, raising the market default rate, which, however, stays below the rate observed when banks are equally ignorant about borrower type.[21] With market segmentation, all players benefit from a reduction in R, with a rise in borrower surplus and bank profits.[22]

An important conclusion that follows from these results is that market segmentation does not substantially affect the overall volume and the quality of credit. By treating debtors who do not want to pay to credibly reveal their type essentially as risky borrowers, banks limit the volume of bad credits and keep the market "relatively safe." The main negative consequence of market segmentation is then the high interest rates imposed on small safe borrowers.

With the parameter values used in table 10.2, approximately 30 percent of all credit is granted to borrowers in the corporate market, who represent less than 10 percent of the total number of borrowers (and between 4 and 6 percent of the universe of potential borrowers). Like corporate borrowers, all participants in the middle market are safe. But interest rates in this market segment are considerably higher, with $R_M - R_C$ giving the rent extracted by banks from middle-market borrowers. A remarkable result is that this rent rises when the cost of funds to banks declines, with spreads dropping less in the middle than in the corporate market. As a result, the range of loan values granted through the middle market (L_M, L_C) also contracts when R comes down, causing the expansion in the volume of credit to be particularly pronounced in the retail market. The increase in L_M leads to a rise in the average loan extended to safe borrowers in the retail market, but since most of the expansion in credit goes to risky borrowers, so does the cross subsidy provided by safe borrowers.

The average loan size extended to safe borrowers is different in the three market segments. A remarkable result is that the average loan extended to risky borrowers ($\lambda = \$1$), all in the retail market, is higher than that given to safe borrowers in the middle market, while forty to fifty times bigger than that granted to safe borrowers in the retail segment. To some extent, therefore, the difference between clients in the retail and middle-markets is more one of risk than of size. Also important is that, to disguise themselves, large risky borrowers will tend to spread their loan requests through various banks. This may help to explain why, as shown in table 10.1, many mid-sized individual and commercial borrowers operate with more than one bank.[23]

An important parameter in the model used here is the cost of informing outside banks about one's type (C_C). The higher the value of C_C, the more banks are able to extract rents from middle-market borrowers, and consequently the higher R_M and banks' profits (see table 10.3). An increase in C_C and in R_M, in turn, moves both L_M and L_C upward, reducing the volume of credit extended through the corporate market, but increasing lending in the middle and retail markets, even if the net effect is a decline in the total volume of lending. Since access to the corporate and middle markets becomes more expensive, proportionately more credit is extended to safe borrowers in the retail market, lowering R_T and attracting more risky borrowers, in the end raising the market default rate.

Therefore, although beneficial to banks, an increase in C_C harms almost all borrowers: (1) it moves borrowers in the lower end of the corporate market into the middle market, where they pay higher rates of interest; (2) it allows banks to extract more rents from borrowers in the middle market; and (3) it moves borrowers in the lower fringe of the middle market into the retail market, where interest rates are the highest. Still, safe borrowers already in the retail market and risky borrowers in general obtain a small gain from an increase in C_C, due to the marginal decline in R_T. It follows, conversely, that measures that contribute to reduce the cost for outside banks to infer borrower type, such as the adoption of better accounting practices, should help to reduce default rates, expand the volume of credit and benefit most borrowers. Still, inasmuch as this cost is due more to tax evasion than to poor accounting, the capacity of public policy to reduce the "information capture" of middle-market borrowers is in a sense rather limited.

A reduction in the value of C_M, the cost of informing the inside bank of one's type, attracts safe borrowers in the upper fringe of the retail market to the middle market, shifting upward the demand for middle-market loans, and consequently allowing for a rise in R_M and in profits (see table 10.4). Despite facing higher interest rates, most borrowers in the middle-market experience a net gain from this process, with the only losers being those in the upper end of this market segment, including those that as a consequence move to the corporate market. With fewer and only the small safe borrowers remaining in the retail market, R_T goes up, lowering the demand for credit of risky borrowers, which in turn causes the market default rate to decline. With a low C_M, the retail market will essentially serve only risky borrowers.

Table 10.5 shows that borrower diversity $(q_s - q_r)$ is good for banks. If risky borrowers become less so, as in the second column of table 10.5, banks have to bring spreads down in the middle market, and although this contributes to raise lending volumes, profits and especially profit rates come down. Interest rates drop substantially in the retail market, causing the number of borrowers and volume of credit to increase. If the decline in borrower diversity arises from growth in the default rate of safe borrowers (column 3), profits fall even more, as a result of lower spreads and volume of credit in the middle market. The retail market also becomes relatively more attractive in this case, with an increase in L_M and a decline in R_T.

Lower interest rates and more information on borrowers, due mainly to the decline in inflation, were the most important changes that took place in Brazilian credit markets in the late 1990s. The above exercises suggest that, although relevant, these changes should not eliminate or substantially alter market segmentation. The next section looks at another important change in Brazilian credit markets, the strengthening of the CIR industry, and examines its effect on credit market segmentation.

10.3   Credit Information

10.3.1   Implications of Market Segmentation to the CIR Industry

A credit market as featured in the model of section 10.2.2 implies a limited role for CIRs: essentially, maintaining negative information and providing good ratings for safe borrowers in the corporate sector. In particular, there are no incentives for banks to share positive information on borrowers, partly or completely, since by doing so they lose or at least reduce the rent they are able to extract from clients in the middle market (e.g., by lowering C_C), while gaining nothing in return, since banks make no profit in the retail and corporate markets.

Banks will be in general willing to share negative information. If such a borrower is in the retail market, the bank will not loose anything from not lending to her, while by blocking her access to credit it will make her more likely to settle her debts. Default and delinquency lists should be less effective in encouraging debt repayment in the middle market, since in this case the bank will have to weigh the expected gain from enforcement against the lost rent if it refuses to lend.[24] If the borrower is safe and sufficiently large to tap the corporate market, enforcement incentives will again be weak, since the borrower may negotiate a loan with another bank, allowing for a marginally positive profit to the lender. In these cases, the effectiveness of default and delinquency lists as an enforcement mechanism will depend on market structure and other incentives. Still, banks will have no incentive not to provide negative information (or at least threaten to) and will have some incentive to do so, even if access to credit is not entirely blocked. In the middle market, for instance, since outside banks cannot differentiate middle from retail market borrowers, inclusion of a defaulted safe borrower in a default and delinquency list will increase the bank's bargaining power and consequently the rent it is able to extract.

In a segmented credit market, the use of default and delinquency lists as an enforcement mechanism should extend to the willingness of lenders to drop borrowers from the list if they settle their debts. This will increase their incentives to repay, while doing little harm to creditors, since information in these lists is scarcely useful, even if borrower type is persistent through time. For the middle and corporate segments, these lists have little use. Whether a loan is granted or not depends on borrower type, and since in those market segments this is known for sure, there is little sense in trying to infer it from such lists. Default and delinquency lists are more useful for credit decisions in the retail market. Since borrowers who defaulted are more likely to be risky than those that did not or that had not been in the market before, and since on average banks lose money when they lend to risky borrowers, it makes sense to deny credit to firms and individuals on default and delinquency lists.[25] Considering that

Table 10.6
Probability of correctly inferring borrower type

Actual borrower type (X)	Inferred borrower type (Y)		
	Safe $(Y = 1)$	Risky $(Y = 0)$	
Safe $(X = 1)$	$P(X = 1, Y = 1)$ $= p\alpha(z)$	$P(X = 1, Y = 0)$ $= p(1 - \alpha(z))$	$P(X = 1) = p$
Risky $(X = 0)$	$P(X = 0, Y = 1)$ $= p(1 - \alpha(z))$	$P(X = 0, Y = 0)$ $= (1 - p) - p(1 - \alpha(z))$	$P(X = 0) = 1 - p$
	$P(Y = 1) = p$	$P(Y = 0) = 1 - p$	

where $\alpha(z) = p + z(\bar{\alpha} - p)$.
Note: Most of the following results would also apply if $\alpha(z) = p + F(z)(\bar{\alpha} - p)$, where $F(z)$ is any cumulative distribution function.

interest rates in the retail market are close to those that would be charged to risky borrowers if perfect information prevailed, recovering defaulted loans will likely be more important than the additional risk of extending a loan to a borrower who defaulted in the past, particularly if lenders are shortsighted (as they should be in an environment of high interest rates).

The role of credit bureaus in a segmented credit market may be more broadly assessed if one assumes that not all information relevant to predict borrower type is private to banks (as illustrated by the existence of default and delinquency lists). In this way, suppose that banks can improve their ability to infer borrower type by acquiring and processing information z $(0 \leq z \leq 1)$, at a cost $C(z) = c_0 + c_1 z N A_T$—where c_0 and $c_1 > 0$, and $N A_T$ is the number of loan applicants in the retail sector, as presented in table 10.6. The information cost $C(z)$ is charged on a pro rata basis to borrowers in the retail market, with each paying $C_T(z) = C(z)/N B_T(z)$, where $N B_T$ is the number of borrowers in the retail market.[26] In addition, banks charge an interest rate R_T to applicants who they consider to be safe; for reasons similar to those noted in section 10.2, loan applicants thought to be risky will not borrow in this market segment.

The use of the screening technology will further fragment the market, since it will allow for the creation of a new market segment, which can be called super-retail (ST), that operates in the same way as the retail segment did in section 10.2.2. No questions are asked, no initial fees charged, and all borrowers are charged the same (high) rate $R_{ST} \approx (1 + R)/q_r - 1$. In this sense, the technology should not change one main characteristic of the credit market: the negative correlation across market segments between average loan size on the one hand and spreads and default ratios on the other. Market segments will change, however, with their limits defined in table 10.7, which shows that:

1. The corporate market continues to operate as described in section 10.2.

2. The middle market now has borrowers of two types, both of them safe. The first are those discussed in section 10.2—not large enough to tap the corporate market, but sufficiently big to be willing to spend C_M to show that they are safe. The second are those who would prefer to borrow in the retail market, but because they were wrongly considered to be risky resort to the middle market.

3. The retail market continues to have safe and risky borrowers, but the latter in a lower proportion. All risky borrowers for whom $q_r l_i(v_i - R_T) > C_T$ and $l_i > L_T^R$ will apply for a loan in the retail market and borrow if (mistakenly) considered to be safe. Similarly, all safe borrowers for whom $L_T^S < l_i < L_M$ and $q_s l_i(v_i - R_T) > C_T$ will apply for a loan in the retail market. Those who are considered safe will go ahead and borrow in this market segment.

4. Small safe and risky borrowers (those who seek loans lower than L_T^S and L_T^R, respectively); safe borrowers who initially sought credit in the retail market but were wrongly considered to be risky, and for whom $l_i < L_M^R$; and all risky borrowers unable to access the retail market will go to the ST market segment, as long as they have $v_i > R_{ST}$.

Depending on the attributes of the screening technology, the model will generate a corner solution. If the technology is very efficient and cheap, it will cause market segmentation to disappear. If, on the other hand, it is inefficient and expensive, creditors will decline to use it. That is, for the technology to be attractive, and compatible with market segmentation, it can be neither too efficient and inexpensive nor too inefficient and costly. This translates to the following proposition: $\bar{\alpha} < 1$ or $C_T > C_M$. To see that, suppose the contrary, that for $z \geq \bar{z}$ $\alpha(z) = 1$ and that $C_T(\bar{z}) < C_M$. Then, for a sufficiently large z it would be possible to identify borrower type perfectly with the use of information accessible to all banks. Competition would then drive R_T down to R_C. Because $C_T(\bar{z}) < C_M$, all safe borrowers would go to the retail market and only this and the ST market segments would survive.[27] Therefore, segmentation of the

Table 10.7
Credit market segmentation with screening technology

Market segment	Loan range (A)	Willingness to contract loan (B)	Number of actual borrowers as proportion of number of borrowers satisfying conditions A and B
Corporate (all safe)	$l_i > (C_C - C_M)/((R_M - R_C)q_{fs}) = L_C$	$v_i > R_C + C_C/(q_s l_i)$	p
Middle—I (all safe)	$L_C > l_i > (C_M - C_T)/((R_T - R_M)q_s) = L_M$	$v_i > R_M + C_M/(q_s l_i)$	p
Middle—II (all safe)	$L_M^R = (C_M - C_T)/((R_{ST} - R_M)q_s) < l_i < L_M$	$v_i > R_M + C_M/(q_s l_i)$	$p(1 - \alpha(z))$
Retail—I: Safe and classified as safe	$L_T^S = C_T/((R_{ST} - R_T)q_s) < l_i < L_M$	$v_i > R_T + C_T/(q_s l_i)$	$p\alpha(z)$
Retail—II: Risky and classified as safe	$l_i > L_T^R = C_T/((R_{ST} - R_T)q_r)$	$v_i > R_T + C_T/(q_r l_i)$	$p(1 - \alpha(z))$
Super-retail—I: Very small safe	$l_i < L_T^S$	$v_i > R_{ST}$	p
Super-retail—II: Very small risky	$l_i < L_T^R$	$v_i > R_{ST}$	$(1 - p)$
Super-retail—III: Small safe	$L_T^S < l_i < L_M^R$	$v_i > R_{ST}$	$p(1 - \alpha(z))$
Super-retail—IV: Other risky	$l_i > L_T^R$	$v_i > R_{ST}$	$(1 - p) - p(1 - \alpha(z))$

credit market is not consistent with a technology that allows perfect screening at a low cost with the use of information that is publicly available.

On the other hand, the technology must be sufficiently cheap (low C_T) and accurate (low R_T) so as to make the retail market competitive vis-à-vis the middle and ST markets for at least some loan values. That is, the interest rate in the retail market must be sufficiently lower than in the ST market and not much higher than in the middle market so as to compensate, from the point of view of a sufficiently large number of safe borrowers, the fixed fee (C_T) they have to pay when contracting a loan in the retail market. That means that for at least some $z > 0$, $L_M > L_T^S$, which requires

$$\frac{C_M}{C_T} > \frac{R_{ST} - R_M}{R_{ST} - R_T} \tag{13}$$

Therefore, while, on the one hand, the screening technology may be unlikely to be used, for it will have to be reasonably cheap and efficient to be adopted; on the other hand, if introduced, it may completely change the nature of the credit market. In fact, one may verify that with competition in the retail segment and banks seeking to maximize profits, only two extreme possibilities exist: (1) banks do not use the technology and the retail and ST segments become the same, as was the case in section 10.2; (2) the polar situation ensues, with R_T arbitrarily close to R_M and L_M relatively large, so that almost all credit is channeled through the retail market.

The following three reasons explain why the no-technology equilibrium is the only feasible solution even for reasonably efficient and low-cost screening technologies.

First, due to economies of scale in the use of the screening technology, and the fact that all but the small risky borrowers want to borrow in the retail market, a separate retail market is feasible only if R_T is low enough to cause a substantial volume of safe credit to be extended through that market segment, in this way making the default rate and the borrowing fee (C_T) consistent with that demand. Even for rather cheap and moderately accurate screening technologies, it is not possible to generate such a solution unless R_M is relatively high.

Second, if the screening technology is sufficiently accurate and cheap as to satisfy (13), competition in the retail market will lead to a reduction in R_T such that the middle market will vanish, except for the provision of loans to safe borrowers who are mistakenly considered risky. This is possible because by lowering R_T down to R_M, banks are able to increase the volume of credit to safe borrowers in the retail segment by a larger extent than to risky borrowers, in this way lowering the default rate in a way consistent with the reduction in R_T.

Third, banks will react by making the middle market more attractive, however, deriving some profit by lowering R_M to a point where the technology is no longer able to generate a feasible solution to the retail market. Because banks can lower R_M to slightly more than R_C, and still make a profit, the technology will be used only if it is accurate and cheap. In this case the middle market will be eliminated.

The above argument is illustrated numerically in table 10.8, which shows how competition between the retail and middle markets works when the screening technology is available, in this case with $\bar{\alpha} = 0.97$, $c_0 = \$1$ and $c_1 = \$0.001$ (variables presented in table 10.8 are derived in appendix 10C). In columns A to E, banks' borrowing rate is fixed at 25 percent, and initially banks charge the profit maximizing rate $R_M = 32$ percent in the middle market. One of the possible ways the screening technology may be introduced is presented in column A, where $R_T = 32.5$ percent, substantially below the no-screening rate of 56.2 percent (see first column of table 10.2). In this case, the retail market takes up the lower half of what used to be the middle market, reducing the amount of credit extended through this market segment to about half its previous size, with banks' profits falling in tandem.

Despite the high efficiency of the technology, correctly predicting borrower type in 92.4 percent of the cases, about a fifth of all lending in the retail market goes to risky borrowers, causing the default rate in this segment, 5.7 percent, to be almost the triple of that observed in the middle and corporate markets (2%). The technology is made competitive by the lower cost of screening borrowers ($\$0.0044$ vs. $\$0.01$ in the middle market) and the relatively high rates of interest charged by banks in the middle market.

There are many feasible ways to use the technology in the retail market, for a given rate of interest in the middle market, but only one that maximizes the number of borrowers in this segment. This is the one presented in column B, where it can be seen that through a less intensive use of information (lower z) than in column A, banks are able to lower C_T, extend a larger volume of credit to safe

Table 10.8
Model solutions with screening technology

Case	A	B	C	D	E	F	G	H	I	J
Parameters	R = 0.25					R = 0.15				
c_0	1	1	1	1	0	1	1	1	1	0
R_M	0.320000	0.320000	0.290000	0.290000	0.288000	0.219000	0.219000	0.186000	0.186000	0.185000
Variables										
R_T	0.324962	0.320004	0.294644	0.290003	0.562144	0.225677	0.219003	0.188407	0.186003	0.437114
C_T	0.0044	0.0038	0.0039	0.0042	0.0000	0.0042	0.0032	0.0025	0.0037	0.0000
q_T	0.943	0.947	0.966	0.969	0.800	0.938	0.943	0.968	0.970	0.800
z	0.877	0.584	0.992	0.915	0.000	0.914	0.531	0.926	0.925	0.000
$\alpha(z)$	0.924	0.816	0.967	0.939	0.600	0.938	0.796	0.943	0.942	0.600
L_T^S	0.019	0.016	0.015	0.016	0.000	0.020	0.015	0.010	0.015	0.000
L_T^R	0.024	0.026	0.023	0.022	0.037	0.027	0.032	0.031	0.025	0.040
L_M^2	1.161	1734.740	1.347	1734.740	0.037	0.880	2531.229	3.195	2516.079	0.040
L_C	2.064	2.206	6.338	6.747	7.353	2.017	2.169	7.329	7.837	7.965
NA_T^S	231	354	268	377	7	236	429	432	454	11
NA_T^R	227	231	243	245	119	275	281	299	297	181
NB_T^S	213	289	260	353	4	221	342	407	427	6
NB_T^R	26	63	12	22	71	25	86	26	26	109
VC_T^S	104.3	291.5	140.7	356.1	0.1	87.2	345.1	356.4	431.3	0.1
VC_T^R	26.6	65.5	12.3	23.2	71.4	26.3	88.1	26.2	26.3	108.9
VC_M	110.6	41.6	231.2	22.8	374.3	168.4	55.2	97.8	26.0	452.1
Profit	4.82	1.81	3.28	0.32	4.58	7.51	2.46	1.20	0.32	5.11

Note: In all cases, the authors fix $\lambda = \$1$, $N = 1{,}000$, $V = 0.8$, $C_C = \$0.1$, $C_M = \$0.01$, $p = 0.6$, $q_s = 0.98$, and $q_r = 0.8$, $c_1 = \$0.001$ and $\bar{\alpha} = 0.97$. In columns B, D, G, and I, the upper end of the retail market is given by L_C.

borrowers, and reduce R_T to an extent that makes borrowing in the middle market completely unattractive, except for those safe borrowers who are mistakenly classified as risky by the technology, which occurs with a probability of 18.4 percent. As a result, banks' profits fall even more, to less than a fifth of what they used to be before the introduction of the technology.

Obviously, one should expect banks to react, lowering R_M to make the middle market more attractive to borrowers, in the process stealing some of the clients who used to go to the corporate market (as reflected in the rise in L_C). This will also lead to a reduction in R_T, to keep the technology viable, as shown in column C, but yet succeed in increasing profits, even if only to a third of the pretechnology level. Again, however, competition is not expected to leave things at that, and, as shown in column D, through a combination of lower interest rates and a less intensive use of information than in column C (although much higher than in column B), the retail market again wipes out the attractiveness of the middle market as a borrower's first option, with banks' profits coming down to almost nothing.

One should not expect banks to stand still, however, against this loss of profitability. In this way, note in column E that by marginally reducing R_M, to 28.8 percent, banks are able to make the screening technology not feasible—in the sense that it is not possible to attract to the retail market a sufficiently large volume of lending to safe borrowers to make R_T competitive (i.e., satisfy condition (13)). In this final outcome, profits are reduced to half their value in table 10.2, R_M is 3.2 percentage points below its profit-maximizing level (when the technology is not available), and the middle market covers a much wider range of the credit market, stealing the upper end of the retail market and a substantial part of the corporate segment.[28] R_T, however, is back to its previous level, so that existence of the technology, when it is not used, benefits most of all borrowers in the middle market, even if there are some positive spillovers to borrowers that used to be in the upper (lower) end of the retail (corporate) market.

Columns F to J repeat the previous exercise, while fixing R at 15 percent. The results are similar to the previous ones, with two important differences. First, maximization of the number of borrowers in columns G and I is carried out with less information per borrower (lower z) than in columns B and D, respectively, so that the probability of misclassification is higher than before. Second, the reduction in middle-market spreads and therefore in profits is also more significant. These two changes are the result of a higher number of safe borrowers seeking loans in the retail market when interest rates come down, making the screening technology more competitive.

Unless the screening technology generates feasible retail market configurations only for values of R_M above its profit-maximizing level, and/or if set-up costs are high and not recoverable, the mere existence of the technology should be sufficient to bring down interest rates in the middle market. If the costs of introducing the screening technology are low, and banks are slow to react to its use by a competitor, existence of the technology will pressure R_M down, much in the same way that contestability operates to keep profits low. As a consequence, a change in conditions that facilitate introduction of the technology will reflect on a lower R_M and a wider middle market. But two features of a segmented credit market derived in section 10.2 do not change. First, the retail/ST market is dominated by risky borrowers, which penalizes small safe borrowers. Second, despite the more intense use of information to assess borrower type—now banks keep records on a wider range of borrowers—positive information remains private to banks.

In practice, therefore, the use of the screening technology in the retail market presupposes limits to competition across the retail and middle-market segments. These could take several forms. For instance, banks may introduce the technology while capping the size of the loans extended through the retail market, since large loans in this market segment are more likely to go to risky borrowers than do small ones. This would make the screening technology more attractive if fixed costs are not high, but it would only be effective if banks could identify the overall debt exposure of borrowers in the financial system. A consequence of this strategy would be to secure a forced clientele for the middle market regardless of interest rates and costs in the retail segment. Alternatively, it may be the case that making sure that a borrower is safe becomes absurdly expensive for small loans and banks voluntarily limit the size of the middle market from below. Yet another possibility is that in the retail market banks have privileged access to some of the information relevant to infer borrow type or have some transaction cost advantage vis-à-vis other banks, so that they are able to make a nonzero economic profit from lending in that market segment. In this case they would weigh the gains made in the two market segments and possibly avoid corner solutions as those described above.

In any of these situations banks are not likely to provide the private positive information they have on middle-market borrowers to other lenders, for the reasons noted.[29] This contrasts with the results of Pagano and Japelli 1993, who found that under some circumstances banks might be willing to exchange positive information on borrowers, even if this reduces their ability to extract rents from them. The reason they reach a different result is that their model, distinct from ours, assumes that banks earn positive profits even if they have no information advantage, because they have a location advantage vis-à-vis other banks. So they will trade positive information, if by doing so they can increase location rents in excess of the loss in information rents. The existence of location rents appears unrealistic for the corporate and middle markets in Brazil, where all major banks operate nationwide, but it may be a reasonable assumption for the retail market, in this way helping to explain why banks could also extract rents in this market segment and would not want to make the screening technology unfeasible by lowering R_M too much.

10.3.2   The CIR Industry in Brazil

Traditionally, CIRs in Brazil have concentrated their activities on keeping default and delinquency lists on borrowers essentially for the purpose of enforcement.[30] Borrowers who settle their debts have their names cleared from those lists; CIRs have explicit rules requiring participants to drop debtor names from those registries upon repayment. Even if creditors do not strictly abide by those rules, CIRs are keen on providing debtors with facilities for them to do so.[31] And borrowers have strong incentives to repay, since inclusion of one's name in any of those lists is in general sufficient to exclude him or her from the credit market.

Although most CIRs emphasize negative information and share some of this information, they differ in their data sources, their clientele, and to how updated and encompassing their information is. The most traditional CIR is the Returned Check Register (*Cadastro de Cheque sem Fundos*), which is managed by the central bank and lists all people who issued unfunded checks, an information compulsorily supplied by banks.[32] Regularly updated copies of this register are made available to participants and clients of all CIRs in Brazil.

This is the case of the Credit Protection Service (SPC—*Serviço de Proteção ao Crédito*), a network of CIRs established at the municipal level and run by the local Associations of Retailers. The SPC not only facilitates the access of retailers to this data but it also collects and distributes among its members data on borrowers who have defaulted on their commercial or trading responsibilities with members of the association. These associations also keep a separate record for firms in default, but it is the SPC, which carries data on individuals only, that is the most used and best known of its default and delinquency lists.

SERASA, Brazil's largest profit-oriented CIR, was established in 1968 by three of Brazil's main national banks; currently all medium and large banks are shareholders in the company. As with the other CIRs, SERASA was created essentially to gather negative information. Although it also started to offer positive information since the Real Plan, several of its main products still focus on restrictive data. This is the case of *Achei* and *Recheque*, two related products that provide information on unfunded, canceled, stopped, stolen, and lost checks. A third product, *Concentre*, supplies information on *protestos*, checks with insufficient funds, bankruptcies, *concordatas*, judicial actions (executive actions, search and seizure actions, federal justice fiscal execution actions), tax debts (with *Secretaria da Receita Federal*, the Brazilian tax authority), and participation in bankruptcy processes.

A fourth important CIR in Brazil is Cadin (register of defaulters), which was originally created to block access to credit from public institutions to firms and individuals who were in default either with a public financial institution or in their tax obligations. For this reason, at first only public financial institutions could access the Cadin. With time, access was open to all public institutions in an attempt to enforce payment of all types of commercial obligations with public agencies, including state enterprises in many different sectors (e.g., public utilities, gas stations, etc.). It stayed out of reach, however, to private creditors. Soon the list of debtors in default increased so much that the law forbidding public banks to lend to firms in Cadin was revoked, so now public banks use Cadin as one more source of negative information on borrowers.

The growing demand for information on borrowers since the mid-1990s has attracted new players to the Brazilian CIR industry. Equifax, a large American company, bought SCI, a smaller competitor of

SERASA, and credit rating agencies such as S&P's established local offices. It has also encouraged existing CIRs to diversify their services toward the supply of positive information. This is the case of SERASA's *Fica*, *Relato*, and Credit Bureau.

Fica is a database that provides information on key determinants of a firm's performance and an indicative evaluation of its credit risk. Its data come mostly from banks; when a bank accepts a new business customer it is supposed to forward the data collected on the loan application to SERASA. Information can also be obtained from the firms themselves which usually respond to requests for information from SERASA. An offspring of *Fica* is *Fica Avançada*, which supplies the following information on a firm: (1) legal identification, addresses, and so forth; (2) balance sheets, income statements, and internal cash generation, including both current values and the position on December 31 of the two previous years; (3) working capital needs, its variation, cash balance, and operational cash flow; (4) sources and uses of funds; (5) main economic and financial indicators; and (6) a brief analysis of the recent performance of the firm, with an indicative evaluation of the credit risk.

Relato, in addition to the data provided by *Achei*/*Recheque* and *Concentre*, gives information on the payment history of the firm obtained from suppliers and banks. It includes the name and legal identification of the firm's five main suppliers, the total number of suppliers along with the length of their relationship with the firm, and the following information for the thirteen previous months: (1) the number of consultations about that firm, with information on the date and name of the firms responsible for the four last consultations; (2) information on due payment values classified as on time and by intervals of delay, together with the value of cash payments and total of payments for the month; (3) the evolution of the firm's debt to suppliers; (4) the date and value of the last purchase, of the largest invoice, and of the largest cumulate value of purchases; and (5) due and not paid financial obligations. It also gives the consolidated position of bank and supplier credit.

Credit Bureau includes positive information on individuals obtained from and used by credit card, financial, leasing, factoring, and insurance companies as well as other organizations related to individual credit. To receive the information, firms have to agree to provide feedback into the system (reciprocity regime). Credit Bureau includes the following information: (1) name, date, and place of birth, spouse's and parent's names, address, telephone, time at current address, if residence is owned or rented, main occupation, employer, and time at current job; (2) negative information such as delays in paying credit obligations, judicial actions, unfunded or irregular checks, and so forth; (3) number and dates of recent credit consultations; (4) occupation, professional address, schooling, other addresses and professional activities, existing financial obligations, and payment behavior; (5) outstanding credit obligations; and (6) credit scoring, calculated using risk predictive models.

Another important new development has been the creation of the Central Register of Credit Risk (CRC—*Central de Risco de Crédito*), a CIR managed by the Department of Bank Supervision (Departamento de Fiscalização) of the Brazilian Central Bank. Every month financial institutions must inform the CRC of the value of their loan exposures with all clients to whom they have extended credit (including guarantees and credit allowances) totaling R$20,000 or more (see table 10.1). For borrowers with total liabilities of more than R$50,000, they must also rate each loan operation according to a nine-tier rating system defined by the central bank. Each institution is free to use its own methods to assess the credit risk of each loan, but it must respect minimum standards established by the central bank.[33] To classify loans, banks are expected to take into account the economic and financial health of the debtor and of the loan's guarantor as well as characteristics of the loan itself. Financial institutions have up to the twentieth of the month to report balances at the end of the previous month.

Information in the CRC is made available at different levels to different customers, but not to the public at large, which the law does not allow. Financial institutions access the CRC through a computer system (Sisbacen), where they learn the consolidated value of the debt of firms and individuals and the number of institutions that reported credit operations with each debtor.[34] This information may be shared with other companies in the financial institution's conglomerate. To consult a client's record, the financial institution needs to obtain written authorization from the client, which is usually done when he or she applies for credit. The central bank charges a fee for access to the Sisbacen but not for the information in the CRC. Anyone can ask the central bank for information on all individual debts reported by financial institutions in his or her name, including the identification of the institutions and the value of the debts. If the debtor disagrees with the information in the CRC, however, it is up to him or her to go to the financial institution and ask for a correction.

10.4   Use of Credit Information in Bank Regulation and Supervision

The high inflation prevailing in Brazil until June 1994 made it more difficult for banks to accurately reflect the results of their operations in financial reports, which complicated bank supervision and regulation. At the same time, however, it made them less necessary by allowing even poorly run banks to be profitable. Moreover, inflation discouraged credit activity, particularly by private banks, so there was little credit risk. This situation encouraged a policy of regulatory forbearance, which was especially pronounced in the case of state-owned banks. When inflation came down, the inadequacy of those practices was seen in the insolvency of a number of banks. It was not by chance, therefore, that the reduction in inflation rates coincided with an effort to improve supervision and regulation.

Prudential bank regulation in Brazil relies on standard instruments. Entry is regulated through rules on minimum capital requirements and good reputation of owners and managers, and it is determined case by case by the central bank (and the president of the republic in the case of foreign banks). In recent years, decisions about entry have turned to facilitating the privatization of state banks and the purchase and assumption of banks with solvency problems. In this process, foreign banks were given greater access to the market.

Banks are also required to keep both minimum absolute levels of capital (that vary according to type, size, and region) and capital-asset ratios that follow the rules established by the Basle Accord (Cooke ratios), adopted in Brazil in August 1994 (Central Bank Resolution 2099). According to these, banks' own capital (net worth) has to be equal to or larger than 11 percent of their risk-weighted assets, plus 20 percent of the credit risk in swap operations. These values have been in place since November 27, 1997, when in the aftermath of the Asian crisis the central bank raised capital requirements.

Solvency regulations also include the requirement of minimum loan loss provisions. These reflect the credit risk of each loan, as classified in the nine categories (AA to H) used in the CRC (see section 10.3.2). These provisions, in the case of loans of R$50,000 and above, are of 0.5, 1, 3, 10, 30, 50, 70 and 100 percent for each category from A to H, respectively. For loans below R$50,000 similar provisions apply, but risk classification may reflect only the extent of payment delay, although banks are free to adopt more rigorous criteria at their discretion. These rules, introduced in 2000, are more stringent and detailed than the ones in place before.

The central bank also restricts the composition of banks' loan portfolios. These restrictions are intended both to guarantee a minimum level of diversification and to prevent relationship lending. A cap equivalent to 25 percent of the bank's net worth applies to all lending to individual borrowers. Lending to owners, managers, and their relatives is forbidden.

Deposit insurance, established after the post-Real Plan bank crisis, is managed by the Deposit Guarantee Fund (FGC—*Fundo Garantidor de Créditos*), a private nonprofit organization that guarantees deposits and certain financial investments up to R$20,000 per depositor in case of bankruptcy or closure by the central bank.[35] This insurance covers demand and term deposits, savings accounts, letters of exchange, real estate and mortgage letters (*letras imobiliárias* and *letras hipotecárias*) issued or guaranteed by the financial institution. All financial institutions, except for credit cooperatives, participate in the FGC, paying a monthly flat premium of 0.025 percent on the value of its outstanding balances on the accounts insured.

Although the rules are spelled out and relatively standard, their enforcement has not always been as strict as one might have wished, especially in the case of state banks, although that has begun to change in recent years. For instance, the closure of two state banks with a negative net worth—Banespa and Caixa Econômica Federal—was avoided through delaying the publication of their balance sheets until they could be restructured. The two largest federal commercial banks were given special grace periods to adjust their capital requirements to minimum regulatory standards. Another earlier example is provided by the lax application of the limits on relationship lending.[36] The resolution of some insolvent banks, prior to the creation of the FGC, also revealed a "too big to fail" policy, and a practice of de facto complete insurance by the government of all creditors of large banks.[37]

Although prudential regulation was changed in recent years to raise capital requirements and make them more sensitive to borrower and loan risk, these changes did not alter its almost exclusive reliance on past information, mostly obtained from banks' balance sheets and debtor performance. Therefore, even though provisions for loan losses are based on a rating system that in principle reflects lenders' forward expectations about the risk of each loan, it is not clear why banks should in practice be more conservative than required by the minimum standards imposed by the central bank, which depend only on the duration of defaults (section 10.3.2). On the contrary, banks will be subject to strategic biases and will tend to underestimate the probability of default, to lower their capital requirements and increase the goodwill of their clients, a behavior that probably explains why the CRC continues to be mainly seen as a source of negative information.

Little information outside that collected from balance sheets, supervision visits, or the CRC is used in bank regulation and supervision. In particular little use is made of credit information collected or generated by CIRs. The only noteworthy exception appears to be the use of negative information gathered by private CIRs (i.e., the borrowers' *cadastro*), which the central bank takes into consideration when analyzing a bank's credit portfolio in its on-site supervision.

Although on a par with the way prudential regulation works in most other countries, this situation contrasts with what the literature recommends, in particular with the need to make it more forward looking and risk sensitive.[38] Credit information can be used to adapt four of the above regulatory instruments in that way: reserves for loan losses, capital adequacy requirements, insurance premiums, and closure rules. Two of these instruments have received most of the attention in the literature: risk-adjusted deposit insurance premiums and capital adequacy ratios.

The idea of using risk-sensitive deposit insurance premiums goes back to the view that the main purpose of bank regulation is to protect small, largely unsophisticated depositors.[39] In the presence of limited liability, a bank's capital structure gives an incentive for owner-managers to follow an investment policy that carries more risk than its depositors would like to. This is explained by the fact that equity holders typically benefit more in favorable states (the project succeeds) than depositors, whereas the two groups share losses proportionately in bad states (the bank closes down). A flat rate deposit insurance premium, even if actuarially balanced, does not correct these perverse incentives. This could be done, however, under certain conditions, through risk-adjusted deposit insurance premiums. Rochet (1992) shows that if the objective of bank owners is to maximize the market value of their future profits, risk-based deposit insurance is the only way to prevent them from choosing risky portfolios. There are both conceptual and practical problems, however, in implementing fairly priced deposit insurance.[40] One of them is how to measure risk and determine risk premiums in an efficient and timely way.[41]

This perhaps explains the general preference of regulators to discourage excessive risk taking by banks through the use of minimum capital requirements. These not only provide a cushion for bank losses but also increase owners' stake when taking risk, encouraging more conservative decisions. For this regulation to be efficient, however, it is necessary that capital requirements be risk sensitive; that is, that the average cost of capital goes up when risk increases.[42] The best known effort to adapt capital adequacy rules to reflect credit risk is the Cooke ratio included in the Basle Accords of 1988. The Cooke ratio has been criticized, however, not only for disregarding other types of risk but also for not adequately weighting different types of credit risk (Dewatripont and Tirole 1994). A 1999 report of the Basle Committee on Banking Supervision, while reinforcing the view that minimum regulatory capital requirements, adjusted for credit risk, should remain the main approach to promote safety and soundness in the financial system, acknowledges that "[t]he current risk weighting of assets results, at best, in a crude measure of economic risk, primarily because degrees of credit risk exposure are not sufficiently calibrated as to adequately differentiate between borrowers' differing default risks" (BIS 1999, p. 9).[43] Feixas and Rochet (1997) suggest that a better way to make banks' capital-asset ratios dependent on their asset risk is to use borrowers' ratings, produced by independent agencies, to weight their assets. This idea is incorporated in the standardized approach included in the New Basel Capital Accord put forward by the Basle Committee on Banking Supervision (BIS 2001).

Some countries—New Zealand, Chile, and Argentina—also rely on credit ratings produced by government auditors and/or by private agencies to increase banks' sensitiveness to risk exposure, requiring the publication of their own credit ratings. The expectation is that this increases market discipline by making depositors and other creditors more aware of the risk carried out by their banks (see Goldstein and Turner 1996).[44]

Although the idea that prudential regulation can be improved by increasing the costs to banks of taking risk is well accepted, little in that direction has been done in practice.[45] The main reason for that is the difficulty of finding the adequate information to use for that purpose. Rochet (1992) argues that for capital-asset ratios to be effective in controlling excessive risk, the weights used in their computation have to be proportional to the systemic risk of the assets (their betas). But he remarks, in a later article (Rochet 1999), that "an important peculiarity of bank loans, which constitute the bulk of the assets of most banks, is that their true value is a private information of the bank that has granted the loan, that is, it is difficult for an outsider to assess how risky is the bank's loan portfolio." A second-best solution is then to weight loans using each borrower's credit-rating, but that leaves unanswered the question of how to deal with unrated borrowers. Moreover, the value of credit ratings as leading indicators of default are still a matter of controversy (see Goldstein and Turner 1996).

The Brazilian credit market illustrates the practical difficulties and limitations of these recommendations. As pointed out in section 10.2, for most borrowers, and a large share of the credit market, there is no public information to assess loan risk. The only exceptions are corporate borrowers, for which independent ratings are in general available. In fact, large firms are the prototype borrower addressed in the new BIS framework. They are rated by different institutions, including the most important credit rating agencies and possibly the large banks with which they operate, and these ratings can be used directly to weigh their loans when computing capital requirements. The problem in this case would be how to choose among different ratings, but the empirical evidence suggests that for large nonfinancial firms the divergence in independent ratings tend to be relatively small (Morgan 1997).

A more complicated issue is how to incorporate into prudential regulation the risk of loans to mid-sized companies for which there is no rating available. The problem is not only one of the quantity of firms, but that much of the relevant information for analyzing the credit risk of these borrowers arises from bilateral, long-term relationships that they keep with their banks, which is not disclosed either to the central bank or to private CIRs. In developing countries, balance sheets of many of these firms are utterly unreliable—even in some of the few cases in which they are audited by independent firms—and often do not reflect the financial health of the firm.[46]

Thus, one the most important features of the new Basel Capital Accord proposal is the relevance attributed to information private to banks to assess credit risk: "a key element of the proposed revisions to the 1988 Accord is a greater emphasis on banks' own assessment of the risks to which they are exposed in the calculation of regulatory capital charges" (BIS 2001, p. 1). In this way, the proposal advocates the adoption in bank regulation of an "evolutionary approach" in which more sophisticated banks would be given more responsibility in determining their own capital requirements. The main element of this approach would be the use of banks' internal ratings to assess the risk of their credit portfolios. This approach would be complemented by a strengthening of the supervisory authority and greater disclosure requirements "to ensure that market participants can better understand banks' risk profiles and the adequacy of their capital positions."

These recommendations are in line with the results of this chapter, in particular with the fact that in developing countries like Brazil banks have a monopoly over much of the information necessary to assess credit risk. Two other results of this analysis help to shed light on the issue of prudential regulation. First, as the cost of capital to banks (R) continues to decline (in December 2000 it was still 12 percent), market size will expand, but so will default ratios, signaling a deterioration in the quality of credit. Moreover, lower interest rates will not diminish the importance of market segmentation or the share of total credit channeled through the middle market. Bank profits will go up, with a higher volume of lending, but profit rates will come down, likely reducing the ratio of charter values to own capital.[47] Second, more access to credit information, through the CRC and the strengthening of the CIR industry, a continued upgrading of banks' credit decision process, and a more intense lending activity by foreign banks will make credit markets more competitive, or at least more constestable, significantly reducing bank profits, as shown in section 10.3.[48] Furthermore, more competition and the introduction of better screening mechanisms may lead to an expansion of the middle market, with banks reacting to competition by expanding the spectrum of borrowers on whom they keep their own information registers. Although more information on borrowers should be generated, the proportion of positive information that is private to banks should rise.

These results lead, in turn, to two conclusions. First, making prudential regulation more risk sensitive will depend on the regulator's ability to extract unbiased ratings from banks. The challenge, then, is for the central bank to introduce incentives that lead banks to improve the quality of their credit analysis process, to be able to correctly identify safe borrowers, and to correctly inform the central bank about their ratings for each loan. These could be done, for instance, by increasing capital requirements of banks that consistently underestimate the risk of their credit portfolios, as revealed by ex post debtor performance.[49]

Second, stiffer competition and lower profits will encourage banks to take higher risks, making the need for adequate prudential regulation even more necessary. As noted by Riordan (1993), selecting good projects depends on the probability of being chosen to finance the project and on the expected return from doing so. Both are reduced when competition increases, "so more competition might harm market performance, even as prices draw closer to marginal cost." Keeley (1990) argues that an increase in competition resulting from changes in the institutional environment explains the reduction in capital-asset ratios and the increase in asset risk that eventually led to the S&Ls and bank crises of the 1980s in the United States. Lower profits, in turn, cause charter values to decline, mitigating an endogenous deterrent to excessive risk taking. In this way, Weisbrod, Lee, and Rojas-Suarez (1992) show that a reduction in charter values has contributed to increased risk taking by banks in the United States and Japan. Besanko and Thakor (1993) use a similar argument that changes in the competition environment, by reducing the importance of relationship banking and of the valuable private information it generates, lower bank charter values and encourage risky lending.[50]

10.5 Final Remarks

The fact that the information generated by close banking relationships is valuable to creditors in assessing borrower risk has long been acknowledged in the literature. This chapter departed from this conclusion to argue that, in an institutional environment marked by poor accounting practices and pervasive tax evasion, the value of such information will be even higher, possibly to the point of segmenting the credit market. Segmentation causes banks to charge different interest rates and use different amounts of information when deciding whether or not to extend a loan to borrowers who pose the same risk. Segmentation is a reality in Brazil, where the loan market is divided into the retail (consumer credit and small business), middle, and corporate markets.

Comparative static exercises, based on a simple model with interbank asymmetry of information, showed that segmentation is robust to the sort of change that has characterized Brazilian credit markets in recent years, in particular to the lowering of interest rates, and therefore it is unlikely to go away in the near future. These exercises also showed, however, that market segmentation does not substantially affect the overall volume or the quality of credit. By treating debtors whose type is unknown to all banks essentially as risky borrowers, banks limit the volume of bad credits and keep the market relatively safe. Thus, the main negative consequences of market segmentation are the high interest rates imposed on small safe borrowers and the distorting effects of banks' monopoly power in the middle market, where borrowers are informationally captured. In this way, although participants in the middle and corporate markets tend to pose similar risks, the former pay higher interest rates, with the difference reflecting the rents extracted by banks for their information advantage.

Segmentation causes the credit decision process to differ considerably according to borrower type. For loans to consumers and to small business, the general trend since price stabilization has been toward the introduction of a highly decentralized process of credit management. According to this, all loan requests are treated automatically by statistical methods, based on information supplied by the client and/or available from public records, with a decision being rapidly reached at the branch level. The discriminating variable in these cases is the borrowers' credit records, which are heavily biased toward weighing the importance of restrictive information. Thus, negative information, provided mainly by CIRs, is probably the most relevant and often the only data used in the credit decision process in the retail market, which comprises as much as 80 percent of all loans in some banks.

The importance of negative information in credit analysis decreases as the size and complexity of the loan operation increase. Its role is therefore less important in the middle market, which appears to be the most profitable lending activity in Brazil. In this segment banks rely more on their own data collected through balance-sheet analysis and on-site visits to firms. Some financial institutions maintain their own in-house credit rating facility, with the more aggressive banks almost disregarding the usual published balance-sheet data because of their misrepresentation of the economic and financial situation of companies. Instead, they replace the formal accounting information with an internal information system, used to trace changes in companies' financial conditions. One important element of such a system is the monitoring of the liquidity of the borrowers's receivables, since the latter are the most commonly accepted collateral for business loans in Brazil.

In the case of loans to large firms, information provided by CIRs has a limited role in the credit decision process, which relies mainly on the research and analysis conducted by the lender itself. Audited balance sheets and other financial statements are more valuable in such cases because they are more reliable than for smaller firms. In particular, many of these borrowers, as public corporations with shares or bonds negotiated in domestic or international financial markets, provide investors with a regular flow of information on their economic and financial situation. Lending in the corporate market accounts for a large proportion of the total credit portfolio of Brazilian banks, though its client base is small and spreads rather narrow.

Since banks profit, on average, more from operations in the middle market than in the corporate and retail segments, and since these profits depend on their privileged access to information on borrower creditworthiness, they have no incentives to exchange positive information with other banks. That is the case, for instance, of the data and analysis of borrowers' creditworthiness gathered by internal information systems, which remain private to the bank and are not shared with credit bureaus. Therefore, segmentation implies a limited role for CIRs: maintaining negative information and providing good ratings for safe borrowers in the corporate sector.

Banks will be willing to share negative information, to a large extent for enforcement—that is, to increase the likelihood that defaulters settle their debts. The enforcement incentives of default and delinquency lists will be the strongest in the retail market, which is also the segment in which their information content will be the most valuable for the credit decision process. In a segmented credit market, the use of default and delinquency lists as an enforcement mechanism should extend to the willingness of lenders to exclude borrowers from these lists if they settle their debts, since this will increase their incentives to repay, while doing little harm to creditors, since the marginal gain from information in these lists is small, even if borrower type is persistent through time.

These results from the model used here are largely consistent with the way the CIR industry operates in Brazil. In this way, through its relatively long history, Brazilian CIRs have been characterized by the maintenance of default and delinquency lists, playing the dual role of informing creditors and encouraging defaulters to settle their debts to have their names removed from the list. Once a credit relationship has been established, information provided by CIRs becomes useful also for monitoring the borrower's financial situation, that is, to learn about the occurrence of events that might lead to default. In this way, both upgrades and downgrades in the borrower's creditworthiness can be anticipated by monitoring changes in his or her economic fortunes as recorded in those registries.

The introduction of better screening technologies or a greater availability of positive information in the retail market may change the credit market in one of two possible ways. If accurate and cheap, this technology will make the retail market more competitive, possibly to the extent that segmentation will be greatly reduced. But banks are expected to react to stiffer competition from the retail market by reducing interest rates in the middle market, in this way securing some profits. Because they have access to privileged information, arising from their banking relationship with borrowers, they will likely outcompete the screening technology. By making credit markets more contestable, however, an environment that facilitates introduction of credit information technologies will pressure interest rates downward and contribute to expansion of market size. Because segmentation will tend to slow down the expansion of private CIRs, public intervention may be necessary if possibilities in this area to be fully explored. Strengthening of the Central Register of Credit Risk (CRC) is likely to be an important step in that direction.

The end of the high inflation in mid-1994 exposed the deficiencies of bank supervision in Brazil and triggered a process of reform that has produced better and more stringent regulation, particularly on minimum capital requirements. But these changes did not alter the almost exclusive reliance of regulation on past information, mostly obtained from banks' balance sheets and debtor performance. This situation, although on a par with the way prudential regulation works in most other countries, contrasts with what the literature recommends, in particular with the need to make regulation more forward looking and risk sensitive. Credit information can be used to adapt four of the standard regulatory instruments in that way: reserves for loan losses, capital adequacy requirements, insurance premiums, and closure rules. Two of these instruments have received most of the attention in the literature: risk-adjusted deposit insurance premiums and capital adequacy ratios.

Although there are both conceptual and practical problems to implementing such policies, one of them being the difficulty of regulators to properly and timely measure risk, the Central Bank may wish to consider this alternative as a way to improve bank regulation. In particular, there is room to expand the amount of positive information available to banks and regulators to analyze credit risk. An effort to improve accounting practices appears especially worthwhile for its implications about market competition and greater access of regulators to information. CIRs may provide a useful way to organize this information, and regulators should consider the possibility of using CIRs more intensely. CIR ratings for corporate borrowers are a possible means to improve the quality of risk assessment in the CRC.

Risk measurement poses such difficulty to regulators because the true value of most of a bank's credits is private information for the bank itself. It makes sense, therefore, that the BIS proposal for reforming the 1988 Basel Capital Accord stresses the relevance of information private to banks to assess credit risk, advocating that more sophisticated banks should assume greater responsibility in determining their own capital requirements. The main element of this approach would be the use of banks' internal ratings to assess the risk of their credit portfolios.

These recommendations are in line with the results of this chapter, in particular with the fact that in developing countries like Brazil banks have a monopoly over much of the information necessary to assess credit risk. Two other results of the analysis here help to shed light on the issue of prudential regulation. First, as the cost of capital to banks continues to decline, market size will expand, but so will default ratios, signaling a deterioration in the quality of credit. Bank profits will go up, due to a higher volume of lending, but profit rates will come down, likely reducing the ratio of charter values to own capital. Second, more access to credit information, a continued upgrading of banks' credit decision process, and a rising participation of foreign banks in lending will make credit markets more competitive, or at least more contestable, thus reducing bank profits. Stiffer competition and lower profits will encourage banks to take higher risks, making the need for adequate prudential regulation even more necessary.

Second, the analysis here showed that if screening in the retail market is not sufficiently efficient to allow the retail segment to overtake the middle market, the result of competition may be less rather than more publicly available information. That is, financial institutions operating in the middle market may react to stiffer competition from the retail market by lowering spreads and in this way enlarging the coverage of the middle market. This would cause a large volume of the information generated by banks on borrowers creditworthiness to be kept private to them individually, making it more difficult for others, including the central bank, to assess credit risk. Since a major part of the overall credit in the economy is and will continue to be extended through the middle market, the central bank should devise mechanisms to encourage banks to improve their credit analysis and provide unbiased estimators of the credit risk associated with their loans. A possible means to do so would be through higher capital requirements or deposit insurance premiums for banks that consistently underestimate the risk of their loan portfolios.

Appendix 10A   Banking Expenditures with External Credit Information

This appendix presents empirical evidence on how much banks in Brazil spend to acquire external credit information on borrowers. Although the authors were not able to get data separated according to borrower type (corporate, middle, and retail), the figures presented below give an indication of the magnitudes involved.

Data cover a selected sample of 46 banks, out of a total of 220 banks operating in Brazil in December 1999. The sample is not random, in the sense that it was chosen to represent the banks most heavily engaged in credit granting activities. Forty-three out of those forty-six banks are privately owned, so the focus is on credit decisions by private institutions, but the two largest federal banks and one local state-owned bank are also in the sample. The sample comprises large, medium, and small retail banks, selected according to factors such as value of loans and number of branches; investment banks, for which credit is not the main operating activity; and financial institutions owned by automobile manufacturers, which basically finance the sale of vehicles assembled by their parent company. The sample includes domestic and foreign institutions.

For each of those banks, the authors collected data on monthly expenditures (in *real*) with credit information provided by SERASA, which is the most important CIR in Brazil. The time frame comprised the eighteen-month interval between January 1998 and June 1999. Table 10A.1 provides basic descriptive statistics on expenditures for each semester, showing that this variable presents a significant sample variance, as indicated by the difference between the maximum and the minimum expenditures per bank in each semester. The table also indicates that expenditures are relatively concentrated, with the five banks with largest expenditures (roughly 11 percent of the sample) answering for between 35 and 38 percent of the total.

Size is likely to be an important reason why some banks spend more on CIR services than others. To examine this possibility,

Table 10A.1
Total expenditures on Serasa credit information (monthly averages, in R$ thousand)

	1998-I	1998-II	1999-I
Monthly average	979.6	1,074.0	987.4
Standard-deviation	1,207.7	1,280.9	1,261.7
Coefficient of variation (%)	123.3	112.5	127.8
Minimum value	12.7	41.5	17.8
Maximum value	4,087.8	4,194.1	4,507.3
Share of the five largest (%)	38	35	38

Source: Based on data provided by SERASA.

Table 10A.2
Monthly expenditures on external information for each R$ 1,000 of credit balances (in R $)

	1998-I	1998-II	1999-I
Monthly average	0.82	0.82	0.76
Standard-deviation	1.07	1.21	1.12
Coefficient of variation	130.5	147.8	147.4
Minimum value	0.002	0.002	0.001
Maximum value	4.10	5.40	6.00
Number of observations	46	46	40

Source: Based on data provided by SERASA.

monthly average expenditures with SERASA's services were divided by the credit stock outstanding at the end of those three semesters. This ratio indicates the amount of money spent on buying external information for each *real* of the stock of loans prevailing at the end of the semester.[51] Table 10A.2 shows the data above normalized by the stock of credit outstanding at the end of each semester, except for the first period, in which the denominator is the total credit outstanding at the beginning of the period, December 1997. In general, banks spent less than R $1.00 in buying credit information for each R $1,000.00 of credit registered in their balance sheets. As shown in table 10C.1, there are large cross-bank differences in expenditures with CIR information, ranging from less than one cent of *real* to around R $5.00 for each R $1,000.00 of total credit.[52]

Is there a relationship between the amount of loans granted by each bank and its expenditure/credit ratio? Do banks with large stocks of loans spend more or less than small banks per unit of credit to buy information on their borrowers? A simple correlation test yields a negative, -0.170 and -0.179, respectively, for the first and second periods, but not a statistically significant coefficient. Therefore, for this sample there is no direct relationship between bank size and the ratio of expenditures with outside (SERASA) credit information to the stock of credit.

In addition to size, bank type may be another cause for the large dispersion in values shown in table 10A.2. To examine this possibility, the authors calculated the average and standard deviation of the ratio of expenditures with SERASA credit information to the stock of credit separately for five groups of banks. The first two are specialized banks associated with the car-assembly industry, the main

Table 10A.3
Monthly expenditures per R$1,000.00 of credit by groups of banks (in *real*)

Groups of banks	1998 (1)	1998 (2)	1999 (1)
Car-industry banks			
Average	0.136	0.106	0.080
Standard-deviation	0.105	0.034	0.032
Number	5	5	4
Investment banks			
Average	0.101	0.054	0.240
Standard-deviation	0.265	0.090	0.666
Number	12	12	9
Large retail			
Average	0.475	0.447	0.418
Standard-deviation	0.491	0.424	0.412
Number	7	7	7
Medium retail			
Average	1.38	1.30	1.154
Standard-deviation	1.23	0.87	0.826
Number	13	13	11
Small retail			
Average	1.47	1.97	1.37
Standard-deviation	1.34	1.94	1.85
Number	9	9	9
Total			
Average	0.82	0.82	0.76
Standard-deviation	1.07	1.21	1.12
Number	46	46	40

Source: Based on data provided by SERASA.

activity of which is financing the sale of motor vehicles, trucks, and motorcycles, either to dealers or to the final consumer; and multiple banks centered mostly on wholesale businesses typical of investment banks, which do not require large branch network and personnel, such as capital market operations, securities trading, and corporate finance. The last three groups are composed of retail banks, which in general are not specialized financial institutions, dealing with individuals and firms of all economic sizes. The latter differ according to their size, number and location of branches, and core business, and they are hence classified into three categories: large, medium, and small.

Table 10A.3 shows the ratio of expenditures with credit information to the stock of loans aggregated according to bank type. On average, retail banks spend more on collecting information on their borrowers, relative to the size of their credit balances, than either investment banks or specialized banks linked to the car-assembly industry. Considering only the retail banks, there appears to be a negative correlation between expenditures and bank size, with large retail banks spending less than either the medium or the small sized banks. Although within group standard deviations are high and sample sizes small, so that group averages are not statistically different, the data suggest that the latter is the group of banks with the largest expenditures per total credit outstanding in the sample. On average, they spend three to four times more than the large retail banks for external information to screen borrowers. Moreover, note that within group coefficients of variation are lower than for the complete sample, with the exception of investment banks, suggesting that bank type is a relevant explanation for cross-bank differences in expenditures with outside credit information.

The fact that small retail banks spend more, relative to credit balances, on buying CIR information than other types of retail banks may be due to three factors. First, this type of externally generated data may be the only informational input used by small banks to decide whether to grant credit, since their size might not justify incurring the costs of having a "proprietary" system of collecting and analyzing data on their customers, unlike the medium and large retail banks which maintain such facilities. Second, no matter how small, there is always a fixed cost component of assessing CIR information, which leads to a negative relation between loan size and costs of paying for external data. Therefore, there appears to be economies of scale not only in the information gathering process but also in its utilization by banks. Third, in pricing its products and services to banks, SERASA gives quantity discounts. Hence, the price of each additional unit of external data bought by any bank decreases as it buys more information from SERASA.

Appendix 10B   Empirical Distribution of Loan Values

Sections 10.2 and 10.3 assumed that loan values (l) were distributed exponentially, essentially out of easy mathematical manipulation. Data from the CRC, which became available to us afterwards, show that at least for loans above R$20,000, the exponential distribution is a good approximation for loans to individuals, but that it does not provide a good fit for the empirical distribution of loans to firms. The main problem in this case resides in the low probability ascribed

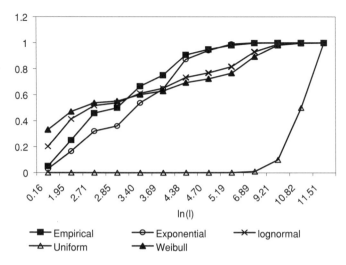

Figure 10B.1
Empirical, exponential, and other distributions of loan values for individuals

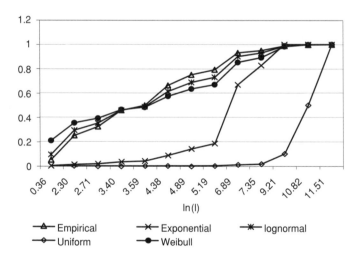

Figure 10B.2
Empirical, exponential, and other distributions for loan values extended to firms

by the exponential distribution for small loans, compared to what is observed empirically. Or, seen from the other side, the empirical distribution of loans to firms is much more positively skewed than the exponential distribution with the same mean. Although the authors do not have the necessary data to test this hypothesis, they believe that the exponential distribution may provide a good fit for loans to firms if the empirical distribution is truncated from above.

Figures 10B.1 and 10B.2 present the empirical, exponential, uniform, Weibull, and lognormal cumulative distribution functions of loan values for individuals and firms. In the last four cases, imposing the value of the distribution mean to be R$58,878 and R$907,489 for individuals and firms, respectively. In both cases the horizontal axis is in logarithmic scale $(\ln(l))$. The best fit, as measured by a MSE statistic calculated for the thirteen values for which information was available on the empirical distribution, is the exponential distribution in the case of individuals and the lognormal in the case of firms.

Appendix 10C The Retail and Middle Markets with the Use of the Screening Technology

With the use of the screening technology, the volume of credit, number of loan applicants and of borrowers, safe and risky, respectively, in the retail market are given by

Volume of Credit

$$
VC_T^S = Np\alpha(z) \int_{L_T^S}^{L_M} \left[\int_{R_T + C_T/(q_s l)}^{V} dv/V \right] \frac{1}{\lambda} e^{-l/\lambda} \, dl
$$

$$
= Np\alpha(z) \left\{ \frac{(V - R_T)}{V} d \, \exp(L_T^S, L_M) - \frac{C_T}{Vq_s} \Delta \, \exp(L_T^S, L_M) \right\}
$$

and

$$
VC_T^R = Np(1 - \alpha(z)) \int_{L_T^R}^{\infty} \left[\int_{R_T + C_T/(qrl)}^{V} dv/V \right] \frac{1}{\lambda} e^{-l/\lambda} \, dl
$$

$$
= Np(1 - \alpha(z)) e^{-L_T^R/\lambda} \left[(L_T^R + \lambda) \frac{(V - R_T)}{V} - \frac{C_T}{Vq_s} \right]
$$

number of loan applicants

$$NA_T^S = Np \int_{L_T^S}^{L_M} \left[\int_{R_T+C_T/(q_sl)}^{V} dv/V \right] \frac{e^{-1/\lambda}}{\lambda} dl$$

$$= Np \left\{ \frac{(V-R_T)}{V} \Delta \exp(L_T^S, L_M) - \frac{C_T}{Vq_s} \int_{L_T^S}^{L_M} \frac{e^{-1/\lambda}}{l\lambda} dl \right\}$$

$$NA_T^R = N(1-p) \int_{L_T^R}^{\infty} \left[\int_{R_T+C_T/(q_rl)}^{V} dv/V \right] \frac{e^{-1/\lambda}}{\lambda} dl$$

$$= N(1-p) \left\{ \frac{(V-R_T)}{V} e - L_T^R - \frac{C_T}{Vq_r} \int_{L_T^R}^{\infty} \frac{e^{-1/\lambda}}{l\lambda} dl \right\}$$

with $NA_T = NA_T^S + NA_T^R$

Number of Borrowers

$$NB_T^S = \alpha(z)NA_T^S$$

$$NB_T^R = p(1-\alpha(z))NA_T^R/(1-p)$$

with $NB_T = NB_T^S + NB_T^R$

In the middle market, in turn, the volume of credit is given by

$$VC_M = Np \left\{ \int_{L_M}^{L_C} \left[\int_{R_M+C_M/q_sl}^{V} dv/V \right] \frac{l}{\lambda} e^{-1/\lambda} dl \right\}$$

$$+ Np(1-\alpha(z)) \left\{ \int_{L_M^R}^{L_C} \left[\int_{R_M+C_M/q_sl}^{V} dv/V \right] \frac{l}{\lambda} e^{-1/\lambda} dl \right\}$$

$$= Np \left[\left(\frac{V-R_M}{V} \right) d \exp(\lambda, L_M, L_C) - \frac{C_M}{Vq_s} \Delta(L_M, L_C) \right]$$

$$+ Np(1-\alpha(z)) \left[\left(\frac{V-R_M}{V} \right) d \exp(\lambda, L_M^R, L_C) - \frac{C_M}{Vq_s} \Delta(L_M^R, L_C) \right]$$

where the first term in the expression above accounts for borrowers who originally looked for loans in this market segment and the second for safe borrowers wrongly classified as risky in the retail market. Competition in the retail market ensures that banks make no profit in this market segment, so that

$$R_T = (1+R)/q_T - 1, \quad \text{where}$$

$$q_T = (q_s VC_T^S + q_r VC_T^R)/(VC_T^S + VC_T^R)$$

Acknowledgments

The authors would like to thank Margaret Miller and an anonymous referee for comments to a previous version of the chapter.

Notes

1. In 1980–1991, the volume credit to the private sector in Brazil averaged 27 percent of GDP, against ratios several times larger in industrialized and Asian developing countries (Demirguç-Kunt and Makismovic 1996).

2. Since the Real Plan, 104 banks were resolved by different means: 42 were liquidated, 7 were incorporated in other institutions, 10 were transformed into non-financial institutions, 11 changed from universal banks to specialized financial institutions, and 34 went through purchase and assumption transactions.

3. For evidence on the positive impact of well functioning financial markets on economic growth, see King and Levine (1993) and Beck, Levine, and Loayza (1999).

4. In this type of retail operation, banks compete with each other on the speed with which they can decide on loan applications, with speed in being measured in number of seconds.

5. Given the precarious quality of accounting and other financial information on small businesses, where the firms' and the owners' banking accounts often mix together, lenders tend to consider them as a single entity for credit granting purposes.

6. The larger the geographical coverage of the CIR databases, the better the quality of the information. Banks also value two other aspects of the information supplied by CIRs. First, the timeliness and accuracy of the information, that is, the time lag between any event affecting borrowers' behavior and its transmission to the creditors' files. The shorter this time interval, the more rapidly the credit registry traces the changes in the borrower's economic and financial conditions. Second, the degree of completeness of the information in its market coverage, meaning the CIR's capacity to provide information on the borrower's behavior in other segments of the credit market, such as trade finance, consumer credit, real estate markets, capital markets, and so on.

7. Some of the large commercial banks have replaced their own business records by similar information gathered and processed by SERASA, Brazil's largest CIR.

8. They can vary from 0.5 to 5.0 percent p.a., with the lending rate closely following the changes in the basic domestic interest rate (Gazeta Mercantil, September 22, 1999). These contrast with much higher average spreads on commercial loans, which in September 1999 reached 36.9 percent (central bank).

9. Not shown in table 10.1 are the loans to borrowers with debts of less than 20,000 *real* in any single financial institution. Overall, these account for 30 percent of the total credit extended to individuals and firms in Brazil (R $325.0 billion on June 30, 2000), with R $53.0 billion lent to individuals and R $44.8 billion to firms.

10. See, for instance, Sharpe (1990), Besanko and Takor (1993), and Padilla and Pagano (2000).

11. There is also a difference of degree. The information advantage that the inside bank has vis à vis outside banks on being able to infer a borrower's shadow accounts is likely to be much larger than what it would be able to derive from a "normal" banking relationship.

12. Appendix 10B presents the empirical distributions of loan size for individuals and firms on June 30, 2000. Because these reflect the distribution of loans actually extended, they do not necessarily have to be exponentially distributed, even if the ex ante distribution is. Comparing the empirical distribution with the exponential, logonormal, uniform and Weibull distributions with the same mean, the exponential distribution is found to provide the best fit in the case of individual borrowers, but not for firms, for which the lognormal gives a closer approximation.

13. It is not necessary to assume that borrowers do not bank with other institutions, but simply that only one of these has sufficient information on the borrower's financial data to securely ascertain at a low cost whether she or he is safe or risky.

14. The cost to the incumbent bank stems from the need to process the relevant information and check creditworthiness in an environment of high market volatility, which causes borrower type to change frequently.

15. One way to interpret C_C is as being the cost to hire a rating agency. But in the Brazilian context a more relevant factor tends to be the cost of conducting business in a formal way, with proper accounting. In particular, because this makes tax evasion more difficult, it increases borrower's tax expenditures. Most of the difference between C_C and C_M can be attributed to the difficulty of borrowers who tap the corporate market to evade their taxes.

16. The results do not change if one assumes instead that it is the bank that initially incurs the cost C_C or C_M and later charges it to the borrower, as long as (1) the latter still incurs some upfront cost to apply for credit and (2) the mechanism to screen borrower type always correctly identifies her or his type and she or he knows that. The model would not change either if one assumed that banks pay for screening borrowers and afterward charge this cost to them by way of interest rate spread s so that $s(l) = Cj/l$, where $j = M$ or C for the middle and corporate markets, respectively.

17. The realization that a continuous financial contact between a bank and its clients generates valuable information dates back to Kane and Malkiel (1965) and Black (1975). Fama (1985) noted that this information is important for both screening and monitoring purposes. Lumer and McConnell (1989) present empirical evidence that the information generated by close bank relationships is well valued by market participants. Besanko and Thakor (1993) analyze the importance of relationship banking for both lenders and borrowers, and they argue that the rents earned by banks from that relationship may be an important incentive to avoid the moral hazard problems created by risk-insensitive deposit insurance. Boot (2000) reviews the recent literature on relationship banking and the empirical evidence on its value for borrowers and lenders.

18. Note that because the average loan size granted to risky borrowers in the retail market will be larger than the average loan size extended to safe borrowers, p^T will be smaller than the proportion of safe borrowers in the retail market.

19. Because only safe borrowers access the corporate and middle markets, from now on the superscript s is dropped from interest rates in these two market segments.

20. What is less intuitive is that safe borrowers in the retail segment also subsidize borrowers in the middle market by reducing R_T and in this way constraining the ability of the incumbent bank to extract rents.

21. Note that this exercise abstracts from the likely increase in q_s and q_r as a result of lower interest rates, which would contribute to reduce default rates.

22. Note, though, that since credit volumes rise more than profits, the rate of profit per dollar lent comes down.

23. This may also explain why, as shown by Cole (1998), borrowers who concentrate their financial transactions on a single bank are more likely to obtain credit than firms with multiple sources of financial services.

24. The fact that the bank knows that the borrower is safe, despite having defaulted in the past, weakens the enforcement incentive of default and delinquency lists. A comparable result was obtained by Padilla and Pagano (2000), who observed that a situation of complete information about borrower type may give borrowers weaker incentives to perform (i.e., strive to succeed with their projects) than one in which banks know only whether a borrower defaulted or not.

25.

$$P[risky \mid default] = \frac{(1 - q_r)(1 - p)}{[(1 - q_r)(1 - p) + p(1 - q_s)]} > \frac{(1 - q_r)(1 - p)}{[(1 - q_r)(1 - p) + p(1 - q_r)]}$$

$$= (1 - p) = P[risky]$$

$$= \frac{q_r(1 - p)}{[q_r(1 - p) + pq_r]} > \frac{q_r(1 - p)}{[q_r(1 - p) + pq_s]} = P[risky \mid no\ default], \quad for\ q_s > q_r.$$

26. This is equivalent to assuming that borrowers pay an interest rate spread to cover the cost banks incur when using the screening technology, which declines with loan size so that $s(l) = C_T/l$, where $s(l)$ is the spread charged for a loan of size l.

27. If $C_T(\bar{z}) > C_M$, then (1) if $C_T(\bar{z}) > C_C$, the technology, although precise, would not be used, at least with $z \geq \bar{z}$, since it would be too expensive and for that reason outcompeted by the technology used to identify borrowers in the corporate market; (2) if $C_T(\bar{z}) > C_C$, then the opposite would happen, and the technology would be the one used in the corporate market, with the situation returning otherwise to that described in section 10.2.

28. While price stability has made use of screening technologies more attractive, fostering demand for positive information, which private CIRs seek to supply and banks learn how to use, it has also been true that banks have started to expand their own information systems to absorb clients formerly in the retail segment into their middle-market clientele.

29. Although it would make sense for banks to share information voluntarily to learn the total lending extended by the financial system to each borrower, information that could be instrumental in identifying risky borrowers, nothing was done in that direction until mandated by the central bank (see section 10.3.2).

30. This section partly draws on Pinheiro and Cabral (1998).

31. For instance, SERASA has an agency in each state where borrowers can bring proof of debt settlement and get their names off of SERASA's listings. The Retailers

Associations also keep a window in their offices where borrowers can clear their names from the SPC listings.

32. The value of this register for credit analysis stems from the widespread use of checks in commercial transactions, a practice inherited from the high inflation period, which was sustained after stabilization by the use of predated checks as a major source of retail credit. It is estimated that about 60 percent of all checks issued in Brazil are predated.

33. The system created by the central bank has nine rating categories—AA, A, B, C, D, E, F, G, H. Loans with delays between 15 and 30 days can be rated at most a B, those between 31 and 60 days a C, and in this way successively until category H, which is mandatory for all loans with delays of more than 180 days. For loans with maturities of more than three years, the permissible delays are twice as large.

34. Even though the CRC allows banks to learn little more than the total debt of a loan applicant, the importance of the CRC to overcome interbank information asymmetries should not be overlooked. The simple fact that a firm has managed to secure credit is in itself revealing about its actual probability of default. As time passes by, financial institutions will also be able to learn about the payment history of these firms, further reducing information asymmetries. Moreover, the central bank is planning to increase the access of banks to information about borrowers. Yet, it is remarkable and telling about Brazil's CIRs that according to Brazil's central bank "today the *Central de Risco de Crédito* is mainly seen as a source of negative information" (Banco Central, "Nova Central de Risco de Crédito," presentation made at the Brazilian Federation of Banks, November 9, 2000).

35. The value of R$20,000 was applied in all cases of banks liquidated before the FGC was established.

36. A central bank document describing the Program for the Restructuring of the Public State Financial System (PROES) observes that "Like the private banks, official banks have also been forced to adjust to the new reality of a stable economy. In this case, however, their problems are more complex, not the least due to the excess of loans extended to controlling shareholders (here, the government of the respective state) and related firms, in disagreement with a basic prudential rule of the financial system."

37. State banks, in particular, are perceived as de facto fully insured by the public sector. This explains why, despite showing default rates much above the industry's average, state banks experience an increase in their shares of total deposits when depositors fear for the health of the financial system.

38. See, for instance, Dewatripont and Tirole (1994), Freixas and Rochet (1997), and BIS (1999, 2001). A possible reason for this contrast is the tendency noted by Rochet (1999) for "prudential authorities themselves (to) insist more on the prevention of systemic risk, a topic that has received so far less attention from theoreticians."

39. Dewatripont and Tirole (1994) call this justification for bank regulation the "representation hypothesis."

40. For a summary of the main issues see Freixas and Rochet (1997).

41. Commenting on proposals to reform the American deposit insurance system, Benston and Kaufaman (1997, pp. 143–144) go a step further to argue: "In theory, it is

clear that risk-based insurance premiums would, at least partially, discourage institutions from following a high-risk loan strategy. But as a practical matter, how the risks and premiums would be determined was unclear, and, by themselves, risk-based premiums did not address the problem of regulators who were often slow, whether because of personal inclination or institutional pressure, to take steps that would address financially troubled institutions."

42. Rochet (1992) shows that because of limited liability solvency, regulations should also require a minimum absolute level of own capital.

43. Moreover, risk weights also favor lending to the public sector.

44. In principle, credit information could also be used to inform the decision to close or intervene in a bank, allowing the central bank to resolve the bank while it is still moderately capitalized. In practice, however, it could be legally difficult to intervene in a bank that is economically insolvent but still has a positive net worth. Adopting such procedures would likely demand changes in the law, possibly making intervention less discretionary, along the lines of the rules-based intervention procedures of the SEIR (Structured Early Intervention and Resolution) proposal (see Benston and Kaufman 1997).

45. For instance, the risk-sensitive deposit insurance premiums adopted in the United States in 1991, when the Federal Deposit Insurance Improvement Act (FDICIA) was enacted, uses a bank's capital-asset ratio to measure its risk (Benston and Kaufman 1997).

46. The Argentine Central Bank tries to mitigate this problem using the interest rate charged by banks in individual operations as a proxy of credit risk, using these to generate an indicator of credit risk, used in computing minimum capital requirements. Escudé (1999) shows that under certain conditions interest rates are a good proxy to the systemic risk of loans. The shortcoming of this procedure is that it encourages banks to lower reported interest rates, using other means to remunerate their loans (e.g., minimum interest-free deposit balances).

47. This projection is consistent with Demirgüç-Kunt and Huizinga's (1999) empirical finding that a larger ratio of bank assets to GDP lead to lower bank profits and interest margins.

48. It is noteworthy that while the participation of foreign banks in total bank assets rose from 12.8 percent in 1997 to 27.5 percent in 2000, their share in total lending went from 11.7 to 17.8 percent (O Valor, February 13, 2001, p. C1).

49. It is less straightforward how to factor the available information about retail risks into prudential regulation, for which banks do not keep private information. The difficulty in this case is composed by the fact that only banks can truly differentiate between a middle and a retail market borrower. For outsiders the lack of information is the same in both cases, and only the value of their debts is indicative of which is which.

50. Some authors go as far as to advocate that prudential regulation should limit bank competition to discourage banks from investing in excessively risky assets (see, e.g., Matutes and Vives 2000; and Hellman, Murdock, and Stiglitz 2000).

51. Obviously, this indicator has all the shortcomings associated with a ratio between a flow and a stock variable. Since data on bank lending flows are not available in Brazil, the stock variable was used as a proxy for credit flows.

52. The number of observations drops from forty-six in the first two periods to forty in the last due to mergers/acquisitions in the private banking market, and to lack of information on credit figures for three institutions. The descriptive statistics for the last semester, rather similar to those for the two previous periods, suggest that this change in the sample did not compromise comparisons across semesters.

References

Beck, T., R. Levine, and N. Loayza. 1999. "Finance and the Sources of Growth." World Bank, mimeo.

Benston, G., and G. Kaufman. 1997. "FDICIA after Five Years." *Journal of Economic Perspectives* 11 (3): 139–158.

Besanko, D., and A. V. Thakor. 1993. "Relationship Banking, Deposit Insurance and Bank Portfolio Choice." In C. Mayer and X. Vives eds. *Capital Markets and Financial Intermediation*. Cambridge, UK: Cambridge University Press.

BIS. 1999. "A New Capital Adequacy Framework." Consultative paper issued by the Basle Committee on Banking Supervision. Mimeo.

BIS. 2001. "Overview of the New Basel Capital Accord." Consultative paper issued by the Basle Committee on Banking Supervision. Mimeo.

Black, F. 1975. "Bank Funds Management in an Efficient Market." *Journal of Financial Economics* 2: 323–339.

Boot, A. 2000. "Relationship Banking: What Do We Know?" *Journal of Financial Intermediation* 9 (1): 7–25.

Cole, R. 1998. "The Importance of Relationships To the Availability of Credit." *Journal of Banking and Finance* 22: 959–977.

Demirguç-Kunt, A., and V. Maksimovic. 1996. "Stock Market Development and Financing Choices of Firms." *World Bank Economic Review* 10 (2): 341–369.

Demirguç-Kunt, A., and H. Huizinga. 1999. "Determinants of Commercial Bank Interest Margins and Profitability: Some International Evidence." *World Bank Economic Review* 13 (2): 379–408.

Dewatripont, M., and J. Tirole. 1994. *The Prudential Regulation of Banks*. Cambridge, MA: MIT Press.

Escudé, G. 1999. "El Indicador de Riesgo Creditiício de Argentina Dentro de un Enfoque de Teoria de Carteras de la Exigencia de Capital por Riesgo Creditício." Banco Central de la Republica Argentina, working paper no. 8.

Fama, E. 1985. "What's Different about Banks?" *Journal of Monetary Economics* 15 (1): 29–39.

Freixas, X., and J-C Rochet. 1997. *Microeconomics of Banking*. Cambridge, MA: MIT Press.

Goldstein, M., and P. Turner. 1996. "Banking Crises in Emerging Economies: Origins and Policy Options." BIS economic papers, no. 46.

Hellman, T. F., K. C. Murdock, and J. E. Stiglitz. 2000. "Liberalization, Moral Hazard in Banking and Prudential Regulation: Are Capital Requirements Enough?" *American Economic Review* 90 (1): 147–165.

Kane, E., and B. Malkiel. 1965. "Bank Portfolio Allocation, Deposit Variability and the Availability Doctrine." *Quarterly Journal of Economics* 79: 113–134.

Keeley, M. C. 1990. "Deposit Insurance, Risk, and Market Power in Banking." *American Economic Review* 80 (5): 1183–1200.

King, R. G., and R. Levine. 1993. "Financial Intermediation and Economic Development." In C. Mayer and X. Vives eds. *Capital Markets and Financial Intermediation.* Cambridge, UK: Cambridge University Press.

Levine, R., N. Loayza, and T. Beck. "Financial Intermediation and Growth: Causality and Causes." World Bank. Mimeo.

Lumer, S., and J. McConnell. 1989. "Further Evidence on the Bank Lending Process and the Reaction of the Capital Market to Bank Loan Agreements." *Journal of Financial Economics* 25: 99–122.

Matutes, C., and X. Vives. 2000. "Imperfect Competition, Risk Taking, and Regulation in Banking." *European Economic Review* 44 (1): 1–34.

McKinsey & Company. 1998. "Productivity—the Key to an Accelerated Development Path for Brazil." Washington, DC: McKinsey & Company. Report.

Morgan, D. P. 1997. "Judging the Risk of Banks: What Makes Banks Opaque?" Federal Reserve Bank of New York. Mimeo.

Padilla, A., and M. Pagano. 2000. "Sharing Default Information as a Borrower Discipline Device." *European Economic Review* 44 (10): 1951–1980.

Pagano, M., and T. Jappelli. 1993. "Information Sharing in Credit Markets." *Journal of Finance* 48 (5): 1693–1718.

Pinheiro, A. C., and C. Cabral. 1998. "Credit Markets in Brazil: The Role of Judicial Enforcement and Other Institutions." *Ensaios BNDES*, no. 9. Available on-line at ⟨www.bndes.gov.br⟩.

Riordan, M. 1993. "Competition and Bank Performance." In C. Mayer and X. Vives, eds. *Capital Markets and Financial Intermediation.* Cambridge, UK: Cambridge University Press.

Rochet, J-C. 1992. "Capital Requirements and the Behaviour of Commercial Banks." *European Economic Journal* 36 (5): 1137–1178.

Rochet, J-C. 1999. "Solvency Regularions and the Management of Bank Risks." *European Economic Journal* 43 (4–6): 981–990.

Sharpe, S. 1990. "Asymmetric Information, Bank Lending, and Implicit Contracts: A Stylized Model of Customer Relationships." *Journal of Finance* 40 (2): 1069–1087.

Weisbrod, Steven R., H. Lee, and L. Rojas-Suarez. 1992. "Bank Risk and the Declining Franchise Value of the Banking Systems in the United States and Japan." Working paper no. 45. Washington, DC: FMI.

11

Regulation of Personal
Data Protection and of
Credit Reporting Firms: A
Comparison of Selected
Countries of Latin
America, the United States,
and the European Union

Rafael del Villar, Alejandro
Díaz de León, and Johanna
Gil Hubert

11.1 Introduction

A country's legal and regulatory framework for data protection and
credit reporting has an enormous impact on how, and even whether,
a credit reporting industry develops. This chapter compares the legal
and regulatory frameworks for six Latin American countries with
those of the United States and Europe. It begins with a discussion of
commonly held principles established by international guidelines for
data protection and distribution. The different laws and regulations
that govern data protection and the sharing of credit information in
six Latin American nations, the United States, and Europe are then
compared. What emerges from this discussion is that Latin American
countries are generally following international experience in the
development of new, specific laws for credit reporting, however,
concerns about bank secrecy laws and sector-specific regulations
continue to pose problems for the development of a credit reporting
industry in some countries. Latin American countries are found to
have significant weaknesses, especially in the institutional capacity
of supervisory authorities for data protection and credit reporting to
enforce laws and regulations.

At first glance, it may appear that data protection laws and credit
reporting activities pull in opposite directions, but that is not necessarily the case. When the role of personal data in an economy
is analyzed, two fundamental concerns must be considered and
balanced: privacy protections and access to information. Access to
information contributes to transparency and competition in an economy and may even be identified with basic rights, such as freedom

of speech and freedom of the press. At the same time, the constitutions of most nations recognize the individual's right to privacy. For a credit reporting industry to develop, consumers and businesses must be willing to share their data and participate in the system. Reasonable legal and regulatory safeguards on data sharing can help to strengthen consumer confidence in the system as well as help to maintain the integrity of private and public reporting activities.

The existence of and access to consumer information is an essential tool to:

1. Improve credit, and more broadly, business decision making

2. Encourage settling debts and complying with all kinds of obligations

3. Reduce transaction costs incurred by economic agents requiring consumer information; otherwise more expensive mechanisms must be used to obtain, verify, and analyze information

4. Encourage domestic and international trade

The importance of having access to reliable, timely, and accurate credit information is well understood by financial system regulators in Latin America. The poor quality of bank credit portfolios has been a contributing factor in financial crises in the region and lack of reliable information on borrowers is recognized as a key part of the problem. The importance attached to credit information by Latin American supervisors in the 1990s is evident in the policies followed, either to create public credit registries in the central bank and/or to support the development of a private credit reporting industry. The fact that public policies on credit reporting in Latin America have been closely tied to bank supervisors, however, has limited the vision of public authorities on the broader impact credit reporting can have in facilitating a variety of financial and nonfinancial commercial transactions in an economy.

This chapter focuses on personal data or data on individuals rather than on business data. In most countries with data protection laws, the focus is on the privacy rights of individuals, not firms, and usually there are greater restrictions on sharing data on individuals than data on firms. This is not always the case, however, since some laws, like those related to bank secrecy, do not usually distinguish between consumers and firms.

11.2   International Guidelines for Personal Data Protection

The importance of providing adequate legal protection for data about individuals has been recognized by international organizations for more than twenty years. In 1980, the Organization for Economic Cooperation and Development (OECD) issued a document "Guidelines for Privacy and Transborder Personal Data Flow Protection." This was followed by the Council of Europe's 1981 Convention on Personal Data Protection. In 1990 the United Nations extended these principles to the larger international community by adopting "Guidelines for Personal Data Automated Files." The OECD, Council of Europe, and UN guidelines share the same basic objectives. They cover information held by both the public and the private sector, and they are designed to protect individual rights and freedom, while at the same time preventing undue restrictions from being imposed on the transmission of data.

The basic rights established by these international guidelines include: (1) the individual's right to know, obtain, and dispute his or her personal information in the possession of data controllers; (2) limits on the collection, use, and withholding of data on individuals and; (3) the data controllers' obligation to specify the purpose of the data records, maintain high standards of information quality (accurate and updated), adopt measures to control inappropriate access or use of the data, and liability for the data they control. The guidelines are intended as a framework or set of common principles that countries can use to develop their own laws and regulations, including the establishment of enforcement mechanisms.

The international guidelines, referred to previously, are compared in table 11.1 which also includes a national example, the Canadian Standard Association Model Code for the Protection of Personal Information which has been adopted in the recent Electronic Commerce and Data Protection Act (2000). The different guidelines presented in table 11.1 share many similarities, beginning with a focus on data related to individuals or persons, not firms. All but the Canadian model relate to both public and private databases. All four sets of guidelines also have two central and complementary objectives: to protect the individual's privacy and liberty, while at the same time facilitating the flow of information necessary for commerce and other private and public transactions, whether within a country or across borders.

Table 11.1
International instruments for personal data protection

International instrument	September 1980 *OECD* Guidelines for privacy and trans-border personal data flow protection	1981 *Council of Europe* Convention for indi-viduals' pro-tection in relation to personal data auto-mated pro-cessing	December 1990 *United Nations Organization* Guidelines for per-sonal data automated files	March 1996 *Canadian Standard Association* Model code for personal data protection
Scope				
Personal data	X	X	X	X
Public sector	X	X	X	X
Private sector	X	X	X	X
Objectives				
Protect privacy and individual liberties	X	X	X	X
Facilitate transborder flow of personal data	X	X	X	X
Principles				
1. Consumer right to access and correction	X	X	X	X
2. Identifying purposes	X	X	X	X
3. Limiting collection	X	X	X	X
4. Limiting use	X	X	X	X
5. Limiting the withholding data	X	X	X	X
6. Data quality; accurate and up-to-date	X	X	X	X
7. Security measures	X	X	X	X
8. Sanctions and remedies in national laws	X	X	X	X
9. Data controllers' accountability	X			X
10. Opennes	X			X
11. Exceptions		X	X	

The guidelines also concur on the basic protections that should be afforded to individuals about the collection, distribution, and use of personal data. The first of these is the consumer's right to access his or her personal data and correct such information if it is erroneous. The guidelines also state that information collected should be limited to data relevant for the identified purpose for which the database was established, and that purpose should be specified before the data is assembled. Limits on the collection of information are also advised, including limits on potentially sensitive data such as race, religion, political affiliation, or sexual orientation. If possible, the guidelines suggest that individuals provide their consent to the distribution of the data, especially if the distribution differs from purposes for which it was originally obtained. The OECD guidelines and the Canadian Standard Association Model Code also discuss the accountability of data controllers for misuse of the data, as well as their responsibility to be open and transparent regarding the data they collect, their policies, and practices. Appendix 11A provides a more detailed discussion of the basic protections listed in table 11.1.

The United States has not adopted a similar set of guidelines in a general law, largely because the business community has successfully argued that some of the limits they would imply on the collection and distribution of data are onerous and would discourage economic activity. Section 11.3, on the legal framework for credit reporting, discusses the U.S. practice where access to data is determined by whether there is a "permissible purpose" which includes instances without the explicit permission of the individual. Businesses have also been given the responsibility to develop their own privacy policies, which are communicated to consumers and become binding on the use and distribution of personal data they collect.[1]

Privacy concerns in the United States are increasing, however, as leading firms take into account consumer preferences about the collection and distribution of personal data. At the same time, the sometimes severe restrictions on personal data in Europe are being questioned in the context of national security concerns as well as due to commercial pressures. It is likely that these different pressures may result in more similar data protection environments in the United States and Europe in the future.

11.3   The Legal Framework for Protection of Personal Data and Credit Reporting: A Comparison of Latin American, United States, and European Experience

This section compares the legal frameworks for protection of personal data and credit reporting in six Latin American countries (Argentina, Brazil, Chile, Colombia, Mexico, and Peru) with the United States and Europe. In some countries, rights about the collection and distribution of data on individuals are established in the constitution of the country. Specific laws may also have been passed to address issues related to the collection and distribution of personal information by credit reporting firms and other types of public and private databases. Laws on bank secrecy in Latin America are also discussed, since they can have a significant impact on the type of information that can be collected by credit reporting firms as well as the conditions and scope of the distribution of data.

11.3.1   Constitutional Laws Governing Credit Reporting and Protection of Personal Data

Constitutional laws about the protection of data on individuals relate to three basic rights: protection of privacy; the individual's right to access information on himself/herself, including the right to dispute incorrect information; and the right to speedy judicial redress when problems in the data or its use arise. Although data collected by credit reporting firms often include data on businesses as well as individuals, these protections usually extend only to individuals.

Table 11.2 compares the constitutional provisions for these rights in Latin American nations and the United States. The individual's right to privacy is the only principle common to all countries. The constitutions of Colombia and Peru further specify that the right to privacy extends to data or information on individuals.

In some Latin American countries, including Argentina, Brazil, Colombia, and Peru, constitutional law protects the individual's right to access and correct personal information collected by third parties. The most sweeping of these constitutional protections are found in Brazil and Colombia where individuals have the right to access, update, and correct personal information in any public or private database. The Argentine and Peruvian constitutions focus these protections on data held by the public sector, although the

Table 11.2
Constitutional protections on personal data

	Argentina	Brazil	Chile	Colombia	Mexico	Peru	United States
1. Right to privacy General principle of intimacy or privacy	yes article 19	yes article 5, X	yes article 19 paragraphs 4 and 5	yes article 15 and 21	yes article 7	yes article 2 paragraphs 5 and 7	yes first amendment
Specific reference to individual's data treatment and information	no	no	no	yes article 15	no	yes article 2 paragraph 6	no
2. Individual's right to access and correct information in the possession of any data controller	in any public data bank, and in private reporting banks. article 43	yes, public or private article 5, XIV and XXXIII	no	yes, public or private article 15	no	only in public data banks article 2 paragraph 5	no
3. Right to a judicial hearing on personal data (habeas data)	yes article 43	yes article 5, LXXII	yes article 20	yes article 15	no	yes article 200	no

Argentine law also extends these rights to private-sector databases that sell reports or other information services.

In all the Latin American countries studied here—with the exception of Mexico—the constitutions also include the right to bring disputes about personal data before the courts, in some cases with strict time frames for resolution of the dispute. Brazil and Colombia's constitutions provide the broadest protections in this context. For example, in Colombia, article 86 of the constitution states that individuals with disputes about personal data in either public or private agencies can seek a "guardianship," a preferential and summary proceeding that must be resolved within ten days of the court filing. In 2000, hundreds of cases involving disputes of personal data were filed under the guardianship clause of the constitution.

11.3.2   Specific Laws Governing Credit Reporting and Personal Data Protection

Many countries have a patchwork of laws that relate to issues of privacy and personal data protection. In recent years, some countries have attempted to develop more comprehensive laws in this sphere, the most noteworthy of these being the European Union's (EU) 1995 privacy directive which went into force in 1998. This directive is based on the Council of Europe resolution discussed in section 11.2, which establishes rigorous standards for the operation of databases in both the public and private sectors. The EU directive does not, however, specifically regulate credit reporting firms. As table 11.3 shows, of the six Latin American nations studied here, Argentina (2000) and Chile (1999) have developed data protection laws, while Peru (2001) and Mexico (2002) have enacted laws applicable to credit reporting agencies; the other Latin American nations do not have such laws. The data protection laws of Argentina and Chile, contain specific provisions governing credit reporting firms.

The EU's privacy directive has two complementary objectives: to safeguard the individual's right to privacy, and to support the flow of information necessary for commercial and financial transactions. The directive was intended, in particular, to create a common framework for privacy protections and database operations across the EU to stimulate sharing of information there. Other countries are also encouraged to adopt similar privacy protections under the EU directive to have access to the European market. This was a point of contention when the directive was first enacted, especially since the

Table 11.3
Specific laws related to credit reporting or protection of personal data

	Argentina	Brazil	Chile	Colombia	Mexico	Peru	United States
Data protection laws	personal data protection law 2000	no	natural person data protection law 1999	no	specific data protections in the Credit Bureau Law of 2002 and the Transparency and Access Law of 2002	specific data protections in the Law on Regulation of Private Credit Bureaus and the Protection of Personal Information	Gramm-Leach-Bliley Act 1999
Laws specifically related to the operation of credit reporting firms	specific provisions for RAs of the financial sector in the data protection law	no	specific provisions for RAs in the data protection law	no articles in Law 510 on credit reporting passed in 1999 found unconstitutional	Credit Bureau Law of 2002	statutes in Financial system Law 1996 and Law on Regulation of Private Credit Bureaus and the Protection of Personal Information	freedom of information Act (FOIA) and Fair Credit Reporting Act (FCRA)

United States has no general legal privacy protection. This issue was resolved by allowing U.S. corporations to adhere to standards accepted by the EU.

The United States has no comprehensive data protection law. Rather, the legal basis for privacy protections and the collection and distribution of personal data there has evolved through jurisprudence over many decades, which has been captured in separate laws about public and private-sector databases. The Freedom of Information Act (FOIA) sets forth the individual's right to access information collected by government entities. The Fair Credit Reporting Act provides the legal framework for private sector initiatives involving the collection and distribution of personal information, including specific attention to credit reporting firms. Although individuals do not have a universal right to access their personal data collected by third parties, they do have the right to access and correct data collected by consumer reporting firms, as defined by the law. Other recent sector-specific laws, especially in the financial sector, have also contributed to the legal framework in the United States for privacy and data protection.[2]

The data protection laws of Argentina and Chile focus on protection of privacy and do not explicitly address the role of information databases in supporting commerce, financial markets, and general economic development.[3] The scope of the Chilean Natural Person Data Protection Law of 1999[4] includes all public and private data controllers, while the Argentine law, enacted at the end of 2000[5], includes data controllers in the public sector and reporting firms in the private sector. Both laws have specific provisions for credit reporting firms in the financial sector. The Argentine and Chilean laws also provide a legal basis for the operation of public credit registries.

The rest of the analyzed Latin American countries—Brazil, Colombia, Mexico and Peru—do not have personal data protection laws. The legal framework in these countries varies considerably, involving laws for consumer protection as well as financial sector laws relevant for credit reporting.

In Brazil, law no. 9507 (published on November 11, 1997) regulates the consumer's right to access and correct personal information as well as the habeas data judicial proceeding. The legal environment for credit reporting in Brazil has also been affected by the Consumer Protection and Defense Code, articles 43 and 44, which describe consumer rights on information found in databanks or consumer records.[6] The consumer protection law states that individuals must be notified when their personal data are entered into a database. This law discouraged the development of credit reports with positive data in Brazil, since reporting firms were concerned that they would have to notify consumers every time a new piece of personal information was received, on a monthly or even more frequent basis. Although consumers can be asked to sign a waiver relieving the reporting firm of this obligation, this legal provision still contributes to an uncertain legal environment for credit reporting in Brazil.

In Mexico, the Credit Bureau Law, published in January 2002, and the Transparency and Access Law, published in May 2002, gave Mexican consumers the right to access and dispute personal data in credit bureaus and in public-sector databases and establish other principles included in the OECD and UN data protection guidelines. The protections on personal data collected in the private sector are scarce, fragmented, and inconsistent. Sector-specific regulations in Mexico, such as the long-distance rules in the telecommunications industry, are putting limits on the collection and distribution of personal data among sectors, adding to the fragmentation of payment data relevant for credit reporting. This situation may change as Congress is expected to discuss general data protection legislation in the fall of 2002.

In addition to the law that regulates credit reporting agencies and protects personal information in these databases, Peru has a law that regulates protection under habeas data and the 1996 general law for the financial system.[7] This law has specific provisions on the creation of a public credit registry and the legal requirement that supervised financial institutions provide data to the public registry. Statutes in the financial sector law also provide for a future transfer of the public credit registry to the private sector.

Colombia has a less well defined legal framework for credit reporting. In Colombia, jurisprudence from the Constitutional Court, resulting from litigation brought by consumers against private credit reporting firms, provides the legal context for this activity. Resolution SU-085/95, which regulates the habeas data protections in the law, has also unified the various court findings on credit reporting. An attempt to pass a law to govern credit reporting in 1999 was invalidated by the Constitutional Court.

11.3.3   Laws Pertaining to Bank Secrecy, Tax Secrecy, and Sensitive Information

Bank secrecy laws are among the most critical aspects of the legal framework for credit reporting since they place restrictions— sometimes bordering on outright prohibition—on the distribution of information in the financial system. In Latin America as well as in Eastern and Western Europe, Asia, and Africa, bank secrecy laws discourage the development of credit reporting. These laws are designed to reassure consumers that information gained through financial transactions will not be used for other purposes, including government functions such as tax collection.[8] At the same time, by reducing transparency in financial markets, these laws benefit large, established financial institutions that enjoy an information advantage over potential rivals. Growing concern over use of the international financial system for money laundering related to criminal activities, such as drug trafficking and terrorism, is prompting a reevaluation of these laws.

In Latin American countries, bank secrecy is usually part of the financial system laws. These laws often differentiate between information related to financial institutions' liabilities (deposits) and assets (credits), the latter typically having less protection. This distinction may not be useful in practice. For instance, the information about personal spending habits, which identifies the characteristics and preferences of an individual, should be highly protected independently of whether such information was generated through the issuance of checks or debit cards (liabilities) or credit cards (assets).

In all six Latin American countries studied here, the bank secrecy laws protect information on deposits. In Argentina[9] and Peru, credit information is not protected by bank secrecy and this information may be distributed without the borrower's consent or notification. In Chile, Brazil, Colombia, and Mexico[10] information on both deposits and credits is protected by the law on bank secrecy. In Chile, however, the data protection law permits negative credit information to be distributed without the borrower's consent, while reporting agencies are precluded from processing positive credit data. Nonetheless, positive credit information is shared among banks in an agreement approved by the bank regulator. In Brazil, the bank secrecy law has greatly limited the sharing of positive information, since the consumer's authorization in writing is viewed as a necessary prerequisite to share positive data. In Mexico, however, the bank secrecy law was amended in 1993 to allow credit reporting agencies to collect credit information, while distribution of such information still requires the borrower's prior authorization. In Colombia only data considered to be relevant to determining creditworthiness may be released, pursuant to article 15 of the constitution. In the past, this law has been used to discourage the distribution of information in the financial system, but now the Constitutional Court is reconsidering this interpretation.

11.3.3.1   Inclusion of Tax Information in Credit Reports. The information contained in tax returns is widely considered confidential; such confidentiality protections, however, do not typically extend to late or delinquent tax payments. In Latin America, where tax evasion continues to be a severe problem after years of reforms and heightened enforcement efforts, credit reporting is increasingly viewed as a valuable ally in the struggle for tax collection. In most of the Latin American countries in this study, legislation is being proposed, or has recently been passed, to reduce the confidentiality protections on tax information so that data on defaulting taxpayers can be provided to credit reporting firms.

In Peru, for example, the National Tax Administration Superintendent's Office (SUNAT) has entered into a cooperative agreement with credit bureaus whereby SUNAT provides credit bureaus with information on defaulting taxpayers and individuals who have not filed a tax return, in exchange for access to information from the credit bureaus on individuals and businesses with loans in default.[11] In Chile, the Internal Tax Service publishes information on taxpayers who have been identified as hard to audit or who have not responded to problems with their tax forms and payments, and these data are then included in reports provided by private credit bureaus.[12] In Mexico, the tax code was amended in December 2000 to permit information on delinquent taxes to be furnished to credit bureaus. The private credit bureau operating in Mexico is expected to include negative tax information in its database by the end of 2002. In Brazil the largest private credit reporting firm, SERASA, includes information on delinquent taxes provided by the Tax Administration (Secretaria da Receita Federal) in its reports.

Colombia is the only Latin American country in this study where credit reporting firms do not process any kind of taxpayer information. The Office of Tax Administration in Colombia is working on an agreement with reporting firms so that information on delinquent taxes can become part of the credit report.

While it clearly makes sense for information on taxpayers in default to be included in a credit report, the extent to which credit reporting should be used for aggressive pursuit of tax collection is not so easily defined. The main objective of credit reports should be to facilitate credit and other private, commercial transactions by encouraging transparency in markets and providing access to standardized, reliable, and timely information. If consumers perceive credit reporting as mainly a way for tax authorities to enforce obligations, this could have a depressing effect on credit markets and foster an increase in informal—and potentially less efficient—financial transactions that do not report.

11.3.3.2 Sensitive Information.   There is a broad international consensus that sensitive personal information requires extra protection. For instance, the EU directive states that personal data revealing racial or ethnic origin, political opinions, religious or philosophical beliefs, as well information on matters of health and sexual orientation, should be forbidden except upon the concerned party's explicit consent. While sensitive information is collected in the United States, it is often not allowed to be used in making credit decisions. The Equal Credit Opportunity Act, for example, does not allow creditors to deny credit application on the basis of gender or marital status.

In Latin America, sensitive data also receive special treatment in the law. In Argentina, sensitive data may be collected and analyzed only for issues of public security addressed in the law[13] or for statistical or scientific purposes provided individual data subjects are not identified. In Chile, sensitive data, including medical information, may only be collected if authorized by law or by the data subject, or required for the sake of the data subject's health, including the extension of medical benefits.

11.3.4 Consumer Rights Concerning Credit Reporting
Discussion of the legal framework for credit reporting so far has focused on laws that provide a context for banks and other lenders to share information or establish the responsibilities of supervisory authorities in the financial system on credit reporting. The consumer's rights and responsibilities in developing quality credit information are the focus of this section. Unfortunately, in many developing

countries, consumer concerns are not given the attention they deserve by the legal and regulatory framework, the supervisory agencies, or the private reporting industry. This is changing, however, as borrowers exert their rights and reporting firms recognize that individuals can help improve data quality by identifying errors in the data. As discussed by Miller (see chapter 1), public credit registries have been slower to enlist consumers as allies in efforts to improve data quality, with consumers still denied access to their own data in many public registries.

Table 11.4 compares the legal protections afforded consumers in the focus countries in Latin America, the United States, and Europe. In general, the EU has the strongest consumer protections, followed by the United States. Argentina, Chile, Mexico, and Peru provide the most extensive consumer protections in the region.

A fundamental aspect of data protection laws, and specific laws regulating credit reporting, concerns the individual's right to access his or her own data. Access to data in credit reports is important for three main reasons: (1) to contribute to consumer confidence in credit reporting; (2) to detect and correct errors; (3) to identify misuse of the data. Individuals are guaranteed access to their own data so that they may assist in creating and maintaining high quality databases, since they are in the best position—and have the greatest incentive—to recognize errors in the data and detect misuse of the information. Because of the use of credit information for important transactions, such as credit, employment, and property rentals, access to the information contained in credit reports is given special status in the laws of several countries in the sample here, including the United States and Argentina. All but one of the countries analyzed provide individuals with a legal right to access personal information held by credit reporting firms. In the case of Mexico, consumers may access the credit report through credit reporting firms and through firms that share data with the credit registry.

Several countries fail to provide a universal right to access data in any public or private database, including Argentina, Mexico, Peru, and the United States. In the United States, businesses are able to collect information on clients and are not obligated to provide access to this data, since they argue this could make the collection and analysis of information expensive, especially for small businesses. There are limits, however, on the type of information that can legitimately be collected, with sensitive information only collected with

Table 11.4
Consumer rights relative to personal data

	Argentina	Brazil	Chile	Colombia	Mexico	Peru	United States	European Union
Access to Information								
From credit bureaus	X	X	X	X	X	X	X	X
From any public or private data controller	X	X	X	X	—	X	—	X
The cost and time of delivery is regulated (at least from credit bureaus)	X	X	X	—	X	X	X	X
Demand correction of information								
From credit bureaus	X	X	X	X	X	X	X	X
From recipients of information or creditors	X	—	X	—	X	—	X	X
From public or private data controllers	X	X	X	X	X	X	X	X
Know recipients of reports with personal data (at least from credit bureaus)	X	—	X	X	X	X	X	X
Right to be excluded from lists used for marketing purposes	X	—	X	—	X	—	X	X
Regulation of consumer rights in the case of adverse actions	X	—	—	—	X	X	X	X

Comments on Table 11.4 (by country)

• Article 43 of the Constitution and the Data Protection Law of 2000 of Argentina grant every person the right to know and to correct or her personal data contained in public files and private RAs. Consequently, such rights may not be exercised with any private data controller.

• The Brazilian Constitution sets forth that the habeas data is a free right. The 9.507 law regulates the rights to access and correction and the habeas data proceeding.

• In the case of Chile, these rights are established in the Natural Person Data Protection Law of 1999.

• The Constitution of Colombia sets forth in article 15 people's right to know, up date, and correct their personal information.

• In Mexico the Federal Consumer Protection Law grants the right to access and correct data only with firms compiling information for marketing purposes. Consumers have direct access to their personal information from public data bases and from private credit bureaus.

• In Peru, the consumer may exercise such rights through the habeas data, the procedure of which is set forth in the 26301 Law and through Law 27489 on Regulation of Private Credit Bureaus and the Protection of Personal Information.

• Although the United States Constitution does not contain provisions on the subject and lacks a general personal data protection law, the consumer, through provisions in various laws, has the right to access and correct his or her personal information held by RAs, public sector databases, and financial institutions, among others. Through the Fair Credit Reporting Act, the right of access and correction of personal information includes all types of RAs as well. Access to the public sector databases are guaranteed by the Freedom of Information Act.

• The European Union directive sets forth that every individual has the right to demand anyone dealing either publicly or privately with personal data treatment, information on personal data, the origin and recipient thereof, the purpose of storing them, and the individualization of persons or organizations to whom data are regularly transferred. If the personal data are in a databank to which several organizations have lawful access, the data subject may request information to any of them. In the event personal data are mistaken, inaccurate, incorrect, or incomplete, and it is so proved, the consumer will have the right to modify them.

consent of the individual. Nonetheless the right to access personal data in any public or private data base is considered a right of the individual as noted in the international guidelines for personal data protection.

It is important to have access to one's own data in credit reports, but if access is not provided in a timely manner, or has a high cost, this weakens the effective exercise of this right. Although individuals are guaranteed access to their personal data in credit registries, in Colombia there are no rules about the timeliness or cost of such access.

Gaining access to the data is one step in securing consumer confidence, but it must be accompanied with legal and regulatory safeguards so that problems consumers detect in the data can be disputed and corrected in a timely and low-cost manner. Legal rights to dispute data and identify who is accessing the data are required. In all the countries studied here, consumers have the legal right to dispute data contained in a credit report with the credit reporting firm. The U.S. and EU laws provide dispute resolution clauses for consumers both on credit reporting firms and recipients of credit reports.

The laws of the United States, European Union, Argentina, Chile, and Mexico also provide consumers with the possibility of reviewing who has accessed their data from credit reports. Most countries place restrictions on access to the data in credit reports. Consumers know if they have initiated or authorized credit transactions or other commercial transactions that require a credit report, and thus they can identify instances where access has been obtained in violation of the law. The consumers' rights to review who has accessed their credit report are the most effective way to ensure that the confidentiality protections of the law are respected. A related matter is whether consumers can control the use of information in credit reports for marketing purposes. The laws of Argentina, Chile, Mexico, the United States, and Europe provide consumers with the right to be excluded from marketing lists.

The United States and Europe provide an important additional right to consumers still lacking in Latin America: to be notified when an "adverse action" is taken based on information received in a credit report. Such actions include denial of credit or employment. In the United States, the Fair Credit Reporting Act states that consumers who have been denied credit, employment, or other services because of their credit report are entitled to a free copy of the report, if requested within 60 days of the denial.

11.4 The Regulatory Framework for Credit Reporting

This section reviews the regulatory framework for credit reporting, including the supervisory and enforcement functions exercised by both public and private institutions. In many instances, these regulations apply not only to credit reporting firms but also to other types of databases that assemble nonfinancial information on consumers. While the laws in Latin America largely follow international norms, there are important weaknesses in the regulatory framework, especially in the institutional capacity of governments to monitor and enforce compliance with established laws and regulations.

11.4.1 Regulations Governing the Establishment of Credit Reporting Firms

From the time a credit reporting firm is established, the regulatory environment comes into play. In the United States as well as in Brazil, Peru, and Colombia, no registration or authorization is necessary to establish a credit reporting firm. In the European Union and Argentina, reporting firms must register with the national supervisory agency for data protection, as established in the respective protection laws. In Chile, reporting firms register with the Civil Registry Service. Mexico requires firms to obtain authorization form the Ministry of Finance to begin operations or change ownership.[14] The requirement that credit reporting firms obtain authorization to operate is not a substitute for a strong legal and regulatory framework, since revoking a firm's authorization to operate is such a severe penalty that it is unlikely to be used except in highly unusual circumstances.

11.4.2 Regulations on Data Collection and Distribution

A minimum level of protection on personal data is that they be obtained through legal and fair means. Argentina, Chile, and Colombia have regulations that set this minimum standard, but the other Latin American countries do not. European regulations stipulate what data can be collected lawfully and set additional requirements to be met by reporting firms, including notifying individuals that their data are being collected and for what purpose. The United

States regulations also specify what data can legally be collected, but they do not require notification of the consumer as a condition of including their information in a database. It is worth noting that Colombian law (law no. 510, article 114, 1999) required credit reporting firms to obtain the prior consent of borrowers as a condition for including them in a database, but that this provision was overturned in 2000 by the Constitutional Court which found that credit reporting was in the public interest.

The United States and the European Union have established the most comprehensive regulatory frameworks in this sample, which address the key aspects of data collection and transmission described in the international guidelines discussed previously. As was also the case in consumer protection, Argentina, Chile, Mexico and Peru—also have the most developed regulatory framework for credit reporting in Latin America. The regulations of these countries discuss what data can legally be collected as well as the conditions for the distribution of the data and the responsibilities of reporting firms vis-à-vis consumers. Brazil and Colombia have limited regulatory frameworks, covering only a few of the principles in the international guidelines. Table 11.5 compares the extent to which the regulatory frameworks in the countries in this study address the principles found in the international guidelines.

The U.S. regulations on distribution of data are based on industry self-regulation and the concept of a "permissible purpose" to access the data. Transactions initiated by the consumer, such as credit requests or insurance or job applications, are permissible purposes for which credit reports can legitimately be requested. The written authorization of the consumer is not required in such cases.

In the European Union the distribution of personal information, including data from credit reports, is the subject of detailed regulation. In many instances, consumers must provide written authorization for the release of their information. Nonetheless, the European Union data protection directive contemplates "exceptions" that permit the flow of personal data in other important circumstances. In addition, legislation at the national level may establish that personal credit information be distributed without restrictions. In Latin America, Colombia and Mexico require written authorization from the consumer to access personal data such as that found in a credit report. In contrast, Argentina, Brazil, Chile, and Peru do not require written authorization to distribute economic,

Table 11.5
Regulations for credit reporting agencies

	Argentina	Brazil	Chile	Colombia	Mexico	Peru	United States	European Union
Principles established in international instruments								
• Data collected should be obtained through lawful means	X	—	X		—	X	X	X
• Data transmitted should be authorized or a have a legal purpose								
a. Expressed in writing	—	—		X	X	—	X	X
b. Implied in transactions initiated by the consumer	—	—	—	—	—	—	X	X
c. Authorized purposes or lawful interest of the recipient of information	—	—		—	—	—	X	X
• Limiting data withholding period	X	X	X	—	X	X	X	X
• Data quality	X	X	X	X	X	X	X	X
• Security regulation	X	—	X	—	X	X		X
• Sanctions	X	—	X	—	X	—	X	X
• Openness and transparency	X	—	—	—	X	—	X	X

Note: The authors do not always mean data controllers in a broad sense. In Argentina they refer to public data banks and or private data banks aimed at furnishing reports; in Brazil, to consumer data banks or records, both public and private; in Chile and Europe, to all data controllers; in Colombia, Mexico, and Peru, they refer only to credit bureaus; in the United States, to consumer reporting agencies.

financial, banking, and business data so as to facilitate credit and commerce.[15, 16]

11.4.3   Regulating the Extent of Payment Histories

One of the most hotly debated aspects of the regulatory framework for credit reporting in many countries is the amount of time that data will be maintained. To provide people with the opportunity to rehabilitate poor credit histories, most countries place a limit on the number of years of historical data that is contained in standard credit reports. If negative data is omitted from credit reports after a relatively short period of time, however, such as one or two years, or if data on late payments or delinquent loans is erased when the loan is paid, this erodes the database and usefulness of credit reporting firms' information services and weakens the incentives for repayment a credit reporting system provides. Erasing negative data after a short time also provides perverse incentives to borrowers in the system, effectively helping people who are not honoring their obligations to the detriment of borrowers who are paying on time. Maintaining a more lengthy credit history on borrowers also can strengthen the "credit culture" or willingness to pay in the economy.

In the United States credit reporting firms may maintain data indefinitely, but they face restrictions on the data they can include in standard reports. Historical information on late payments and delinquencies is limited to seven years in the United States for a standard credit report, and information on bankruptcies has a ten year limit. In the case of credit or insurance transactions exceeding $150,000, or applications for employment with wages of more than $75,000 per year, there is no limit on the extent of historical information that can be included in the report. In Mexico, negative data can be maintained up to seven years after the loan has been settled. Data on loans in excess of $100,000 can be maintained indefinitely. The EU directive establishes as a general rule that data should be maintained for a period consistent with the purpose for which they were collected. In the case of Spain, for example, credit reporting agencies may register only historical information on late payments and delinquencies for six years.

In Latin American nations with the exception of Mexico, regulations limit the historical records in credit reports to a few years, especially if debts are cleared, thus weakening the role credit reporting systems can play in strengthening the credit culture in a region where informality, tax evasion, and avoidance of other obligations continues to be a problem. In Chile, information on economic, financial, banking, or business obligations can be maintained by reporting firms for seven years starting from the date payment was due. If the debt is paid, however, the negative information is erased after three years. Argentine regulations on historical records are modeled on those in Chile but are more restrictive; negative data can be maintained for only five years and if debts are cleared, the record is reduced to two years. In Brazil a five-year period has been established for personal data records, including credit reports. In Colombia there is currently no regulation on this subject.

Another troubling phenomena in Latin America concerns suggestions—and legal provisions in some cases—to provide "amnesty" for borrowers with negative information in their credit histories in new laws or as part of legal reforms for data protection or credit reporting. The data protection law of Argentina originally approved by Congress included a limited amnesty that would have erased negative information contained in credit reports, if the obligations had been paid when the law took effect. This article was vetoed by the president of the republic. In Colombia, a ten-month amnesty was provided to consumers beginning in August 1999[17]; negative information about obligations that were settled by June 2000 was omitted from credit histories.[18] Amnesty periods can significantly reduce the historical record available in a country, weakening the value of the credit reporting system for years, while benefiting those borrowers who have not met their obligations at the expense of those who have.

11.4.4   The Institutional Capacity to Regulate Credit Reporting

The weakest point of the legal and regulatory frameworks for credit reporting in Latin America is the limited institutional capacity that exists to enforce laws and regulations. In the absence of an effective regulatory body with enforcement capabilities, violations of the law and consumer rights must be addressed through the judicial system. The time, cost, and difficulty of going to court with a complaint discourages the effective exercise of rights provided in the laws.

Table 11.6 identifies the government agency or institution responsible for enforcing laws and regulations on personal data protection and credit reporting. The EU countries and Argentina have special-

Table 11.6
Institutional framework

	Independent data protection authority	Other authorities with competence on data protection and RAs matters	Judicial power habeas data proceeding
Argentina	Governing body	—	Local or federal court depending on the case[a]
Brazil	—	Consumer protection and defense department central bank	Civil Court depending on the defendant
Chile	—	—	Civil Court
Colombia	—	Banking superintendent's office	Civil Court
Mexico	Right of Access to Information Institute (public-sector databases)	Secretariat of Finance and Public Credit, Banco de Mexico, Banking and Securities Commission, National Commission for the Defense of Financial Services Users, Federal Consumer Attorney General's Office	Criminal or Civil Court
Peru	Consumer Protection Commission	Banking and insurance superintendent's office	Civil Court
United States[b]	—	Federal Trade Commission, financial and other sectorial authorities	District Court[c]
European Union	National control authorities		Judicial authority[d]

a. In Argentina, the habeas data proceeding is brought before a judge in the domicile of the plaintiff or defendant. Nevertheless, the federal jurisdiction shall govern records or public data files of national organizations or data banks interconnected to interjurisdictional networks.

b. For the United States, the authors refer to authorities set forth in the Fair Credit Reporting Act (section 621).

c. The U.S. District Court has jurisdiction over its district on federal laws.

d. Without prejudice of the administrative recourse that may be brought before the control authority, any person has a judicial remedy available in the event his or her rights are violated.

ized agencies to deal with data protection issues. In most of the Latin American countries studied here, however, it is the central bank or bank supervisor that bears the responsibility for overseeing data protection and credit reporting. In Mexico the situation is further complicated by the fact that four separate agencies or institutions responsible for oversight of the financial sector share oversight functions for data protection and credit reporting. Chile is the only country in the study that leaves all enforcement of laws for data protection and credit reporting with the judiciary, with no institution having an oversight or enforcement function. In the United States it is the Federal Trade Commission, not the central bank or bank supervisors, which is responsible for enforcing the Fair Credit Reporting Act, while specialized agencies may enforce other provisions of law about data protection.

The reliance on bank supervisors for enforcing data protection and credit reporting laws and regulations may have several undesirable consequences. Although banks are typically a primary source of information for credit reports, especially in the initial stages of development of a reporting industry, they should not be the only source. Bank regulators, concerned about the soundness of the banking system and more familiar with bankers than other credit providers or commercial firms, may make decisions that favor the development of a bank-centric credit reporting industry. This could contribute to the fragmentation of data in the economy, weakening the predictive power of credit reports and reducing their contribution to promoting competition in credit markets and other commercial markets. Another problem that central banks or bank supervisors may face in regulating and enforcing credit reporting legislation is their difficulty in dealing directly with the public. As discussed by Miller in this volume, central banks typically do not even provide direct support to the public on problems in public credit registries which they manage. Since reports are often decisive in key economic transactions, such as applications for mortgages or business credit, employment, and housing, it is important that consumers who feel they have been wronged by errors in their credit report bring their complaints to a government agency better suited to serve their needs.

The weaknesses in institutional capacity to regulate data protection and credit reporting in Latin America are described in detail in table 11.7. Institutional capacity is reviewed in three main

Table 11.7
Administrative authorities' responsibilities and powers relative to credit bureaus

	Argentina[a]	Brazil[b]	Chile	Colombia[c]	Mexico	Peru	United States	European Union
Regulatory powers								
Regulatory or advisory body	X	—	—	X	X	X	X	X
Examination or approval of industry codes of conduct or standards	X	—	—	—	—	—	—	X
Supervise regulation enforcement								
Receive and settle complaints	—	X	—	—	X	X	X	X
Access to data to verify compliance with data protection provisions	X	—	—	—	X	X	X	X
Conduct or cause audits to be conducted to data controllers	X	—	—	—	—	—	—	X
Bringing lawsuits	X	X	—	—	—	X	X	X
Sanctions and remedies	X	X	—	—	X	X	X	X
Diffusion, education	—	—	—	—	—	—	X	X
Bound to submit an activity report	—	—	—	—	—	—	—	X

a. The governing body advices people on the legal means of defending their rights. Complaints may be settled through the habeas data before courts. The governing body may request information on public and private institutions that shall furnish the records, documents, programs, or any other items relative to personal data treatment. The governing body may request judicial authorization to access data treatment premises, equipment, or programs to check for breaches of the relevant law. The Argentinean governing body may apply sanctions ranging from warning, suspension, a fine amounting from $ 1.000 to $ 100,000 to the closing or cancellation of the file, record or data bank.

b. In Brazil, the Consumer Protection and Defense Department of the Ministry of Justice Economic Law Secretariat is the authority in charge of settling complaints.

c. In Colombia there is no administrative authority liable for data protection. Individuals' complaints or actions against credit bureaus are brought through the habeas data before a court.

dimensions for the countries in the sample: (1) ability to issue regulations and review and approve industry self-regulation; (2) supervisory and enforcement powers; and (3) reporting (accountability) requirements.

The first row of data in table 11.7 concerns the ability of government agencies to issue secondary regulations related to data protection and credit reporting. It is quickly apparent that this is the institutional power most common to Latin American regulators, with four of the six Latin American nations in the sample providing this power as well as the United States and Europe. Unfortunately, supervisory and enforcement powers to ensure compliance with laws and regulations are much more restricted.

Most Latin American nations do not provide government agencies or institutions with the basic tools they need to effectively enforce laws and regulations concerning credit reporting, beginning with the ability to receive, and if possible, settle complaints. In the United States and Europe there are government bodies where consumers can lodge complaints about erroneous data or misuse of their credit report without turning to the court system. Only the Brazilian government offers this basic service among the Latin American nations in the sample. Although three of the Latin American countries in the sample—Argentina, Brazil, and Mexico—can apply sanctions and remedies as part of their enforcement of laws and regulations pertaining to data protection and credit reporting, only Argentina also provides the regulator with the complementary powers to investigate problems, such as the ability to require external audits. In the United States the main weapon of the Federal Trade Commission is the ability to bring lawsuits when they believe that the Fair Credit Reporting Act has been breached.[19] The EU's data protection authority can also engage firms in lawsuits, but in Latin America only Brazil has government bodies with this power.

Another important aspect of institutional capacity lacking in Latin America is the ability of government agencies to effectively interface with the broader public and the private sector. Both the United States and European systems require supervisory agencies to communicate with and educate the public about their rights and responsibilities under the law. Agencies there exercise a review function for codes of practice developed by private industry as part of self-regulation, and they provide periodic reports to the government and public about the performance of the supervisory agency. No countries in Latin America included dissemination of information to the public or education on data protection and credit reporting laws and regulations as part of the supervisory agency's mandate, nor did they require supervisors to submit activity reports. Only Argentina included review of industry self-regulation codes as part of the responsibilities of the supervisor, but it is not binding for the credit report agencies to register their self-regulation codes before the supervisory authority.

11.4.5   Difficulties in the Development of a Competitive Credit Information Market in Latin America

In contrast to the 170-year experience with private credit bureaus in the United States, Latin American countries' experience with private credit reporting agencies is generally only a few years, or at best a few decades, long. In these countries a competitive private credit reporting industry—as occurred in the United States—has often had difficulty developing because people tend to be less mobile and markets and industries are more concentrated. These factors reduce the need and, in the case of market concentration, even the willingness of market participants to share customer data with third parties. A common development in Latin America is that industry groups set up their own credit reporting agencies and restrict the distribution of this data to other sectors of the economy and other credit reporting firms. In Mexico, for instance, banks have established the only functioning credit bureau that operates in the country since other competing bureaus could not access the bank data. When banks own the credit reporting firm, they have the ability to control consumer credit information, which further strengthens their market power relative to other potential lenders and thus may dampen competition.

11.5   Conclusions

This chapter presented and analyzed the legal and regulatory frameworks for personal data protection and credit reporting in six Latin American countries, the United States, and Europe. It also discussed international guidelines that have been developed by the OECD and the United Nations for data protection. The United States experience is also discussed since it provides another model for regulation of this activity. In the United States there is more reliance on self-regulation of the private reporting industry, while restrictions are placed on government access to data. There is also relatively less weight given to privacy concerns in the United States than in Europe and relatively more weight to the role of information in encouraging credit and commerce.

The legal framework for data protection and credit reporting is comprised of a patchwork of laws in most countries, particularly in the United States. The European Union approved a comprehensive data protection law in the 1990s, and Argentina and Chile have since adopted similar laws. In general, Latin American laws designed specifically for credit reporting (Mexico and Peru) are in step with the U.S. Fair Credit Reporting Act. A greater problem concerns bank secrecy laws that may have been drafted for specific data protection issues, sometimes decades ago. Bank secrecy laws typically do not recognize the public good function that is served by credit reporting, but rather focus narrowly on protecting the confidentiality of data in banks. Sector-specific laws and the predominance of the banking sector also continue to pose problems, since they contribute to the fragmentation of databases and the failure to promote a competitive market for credit reporting. Consumer protection rights are another important aspect of the legal framework for credit reporting that are not adequately developed in Latin America.

The regulatory framework for data protection and credit reporting in Latin America is still underdeveloped and the institutional capacity is lacking in most countries to effectively enforce laws and regulations. Only half of the Latin American countries in this study have a regulatory environment that meets most of the objectives set in international guidelines. The institutional weaknesses of supervisory authorities in Latin America are even more pronounced. Here are some of the main institutional failings that need to be addressed:

1. Supervisory authority linked to only the banking sector, rather than an economy-wide focus, potentially leading to fragmentation of consumer credit data and lack of competition in credit reporting

2. Limited ability to receive and settle consumer complaints, and too much reliance on court remedies

3. Lack of attention to public outreach and education

4. Lack of engagement with the private-sector reporting firms to develop industry codes of conduct and strengthen self-regulation

5. Supervisory authorities not reporting on their performance and not adequately held accountable for enforcement of laws and regulations

Appendix 11A   Definition of Terms Used in Table 11.1 on International Guidelines

1. Consumer or Subject Rights
An individual must have the right to:

a. Obtain from a data controller, or his representative, the confirmation that he has data related to him

b. Be informed by the data controller of any personal data item in his possession, as follows:
1. Within a reasonable period of time
2. At a reasonable cost, if any
3. In a reasonable way
4. In a manner clearly intelligible for the individual

c. Be informed of the reasons why any of the requests made under paragraphs (a) and (b) are rejected and be able to dispute them

d. Dispute data related to him, and if such dispute is successful, erase, correct, complete, or modify such data.

Individuals' right to access and dispute personal data is one of the most important steps toward privacy protection. Data disputes may be settled with the data collector or brought before a court, an administrative or professional organization, or any other institution, pursuant to national regulations.

2. Identifying Purposes
The purposes for which personal data are collected must be specified at or before the time the information is assembled, and their subsequent use must be limited to achieve such purpose or any other that is not inconsistent with the former one, and every change in the purpose must also be specified. Furthermore, data must only include information required for the purposes for which the data will be used. No new purposes must be arbitrarily introduced; free-

dom to make changes must involve consistency with the original purposes.

3. Limiting Collection
Limits must be imposed on personal data collection; any item must be obtained by lawful and fair means and, when appropriate, with the previous knowledge or consent of the data subject. These collection limits apply particularly to specially sensitive data, such as personal data disclosing the individual's racial origin, political, religious opinions, or other beliefs as well as personal data on health or sexual life. These data may not be automatically processed unless the national law provides for the appropriate security measures.

4. Limiting Use and Transfer
Personal data must not be disclosed, made available, or used for purposes other than those specified, excluding (a) upon previous consent of the data subject; or (b) by operation of law.

5. Limiting Data Withholding
It may be required to erase data to protect the consumer or when the data are not suitable any more for the purposes for which they were collected.

6. Data Quality; Accurate, Complete and Up-to-date
Personal data must be accurate, complete, and up-to-date.

7. Security Measures
Reasonable security measures must be used to protect personal data against risks like loss, nonauthorized access, destruction, use, data modification, or disclosure. Safety measures may be physical (identification cards), organizational (different level access to data), or computational.

8. Sanctions and Remedies
Each country shall cause the appropriate sanctions and remedies to be established against any breach of the laws so that the basic data protection principles established herein are complied with.

9. Data Controller's Accountability

The data controller is accountable for the personal information he or she possesses and for the compliance with these principles and laws as well as decisions made for privacy protection. The data controller is not released from this responsibility upon transferring information for processing to a third party.[20]

10. Openness

The data controller must pursue a transparent policy by making specific information on the developments, policies, and practices relative to personal data management readily available to individuals. Devices for an individual to be aware of the existence and nature of the individual's personal data and the main purposes for which they will be used as well as the data controller's identity and address must be set up.

11. Exceptions

Exceptions to the implementation of these principles are authorized provided they are required to protect national security, public order, the morale, or public health.

Acknowledgments

We are highly indebted to Margaret Miller for her valuable comments, suggestions, and editing. We thank the valuable assistance of Clara de la Cerda and Luis Treviño, the many helpful comments from Alfredo Vicens, Natalia Tovar, and Norm Magnuson, and the participants of the International Conference on Credit Reporting Systems sponsored by the World Bank in June 2000. The authors work in the Economics Research Department of the Central Bank of Mexico and their views do not necessarily represent those of the central bank.

Notes

1. The importance of the privacy policy adopted by firms was tested in 2000 when an on-line toy retailer declared bankruptcy. It had developed an extensive database of information on children's toy preferences, which had been provided by parents with the clear understanding that only this toy retailer would ever have access or use of this information. In bankruptcy, this database was one of the most valuable assets of the

firm, but the courts found that this data could not be sold, even to pay debts, since it had been provided only for the use of the now-defunct firm.

2. The Gramm-Leach-Bliley Act (1999) regulates individuals' data protection in their transactions with financial institutions, banks, insurance companies, and other financial services firms. The law establishes the consumer's right to oppose, in certain circumstances, the disclosure of their nonpublic personal data by financial institutions and restrict the flow of information on individuals' consumption patterns. Financial institutions are largely expected to self-regulate adherence to these laws and must define and communicate to consumers their policy on the transmission of nonpublic customer information. Financial institutions are penalized if they do not comply with the policy they have defined.

3. The purpose of the Argentine law is the full protection of personal data recorded in files, records, data banks, or other technical media, public or private, to guarantee honor, privacy, and access to personal information in accordance with article 43, paragraph three of the national constitution (which refers to habeas data).

4. In Chile the Natural Person Data Protection Law (1999) proposed to adequately protect an individual's right to privacy by preventing eventual unlawful intromission that may affect them through the regulation of the use by third parties of their personal data. In the preliminary title, article 1 sets forth that "Any person may treat personal data . . . But in any case the full exercise of data owners fundamental rights must be respected."

5. The law was approved by the congress in October 2000. The law required the establishment of a control authority within 180 days (April 30, 2001). The government did not abide by this date, however, which delayed the law's coming into effect. The control authority was created in the second half of 2001.

6. The *Dispoe Sobre a Protecao do Consumidor e da Outras Providencias* of September 1990, article 43, sets forth:

• The consumer has the right to access information from real-estate official records, records, personal and consumer data on file, as well as on the respective sources thereof.

• Real-estate official records, records, personal and consumer data filed on individual must be objective, clear, and truthful and expressed in an easily comprehensible language, and negative information may not be maintained beyond five years.

• When real-estate official records, records, or personal or consumer data are released without the consumer's request, the individual must be notified in writing of the release.

• Whenever the consumer finds any inaccuracy on personal data and real-estate records, he or she may demand the immediate correction thereof, and the person in charge of the database must notify the individuals of the changes within five business days to the receivers of inaccurate data.

• Whenever the consumer finds any inaccuracy in data or real-estate records, he or she may demand the immediate correction thereof, the person in charge of the database must notify the individual of the changes within five business days to the receivers of inaccurate data.

• Data banks and consumer real-estate records or credit protection services are considered public entities; information related to debts that by law cannot be collected or have been dismissed may not be furnished to credit reporting firms.

7. General Financial and Insurance System Law and Organic Law of the Banking and Insurance Superintendent's Office, June 1996, art. 158–160.

8. In Switzerland, the country perhaps most identified with bank secrecy, the system of numbered accounts was initially developed to help Jews facing persecution by the Nazis protect their assets.

9. See for instance art. 26.2 of the Data Protection Law of Argentina.

10. The Credit Institutions Law, article 117, sets forth that credit institutions may only furnish news or information on deposits, services, or any kind of operation to the relevant consumer or beneficiary. The Credit Bureau Law (article 5) allows credit reporting firms to collect and furnish information on credit-related operations.

11. Only tax debt found in the coactive collection stage whose enforcement is not questioned is to be reported. The information to be furnished by the SUNAT to risk central offices includes:

• Sole taxpayer registration list (RUC)
• Last name, first name, firm name, registration, address, and so forth
• Legal representatives
• Tax debt
a. Amount of debt, debt tax period, date in which the coactive collection process begins, date of the last information processed
b. Persons failing to appear
c. Undeclared item(s), defaulting period(s), date of process

12. Included among services furnished by Dicom Chile is a report on the tax situation of individuals or corporations that may not stamp slips for any reason whatsoever. Tax information is released as well through a database containing information on state organizations with records of taxes for collection, real estate for collection, debts, defaulting persons (form 21), tax credit debtors, and other.

13. Personal data on health issues in Argentina may be released without authorization provided it is required for public health or emergency reasons or for the conduction of epidemiological research.

14. The central bank and the National Banking and Securities Commission also are involved in the authorization process for credit reporting firms.

15. The Data Protection Law (article 5) of Argentina sets forth that the data subject shall give consent in writing or by any other similar means, however article 26 exempts credit bureaus from requiring the consent to transfer or release data related to the transferees' business or credit activities.

16. In Chile the distribution of personal data from publicly available sources does not require any authorization, provided they are of an economic, financial, banking or business nature, or they are required for direct-reply business communications or direct marketing or sale of goods or services.

17. Article 76 of law 114/99 "on economic intervention" established the ten-month amnesty period in Colombia.

18. Another example of this kind of amnesty in Colombia is article 52, law 546 of 1999 "on the regulation of the housing financing system." This article sets forth that long-term individual housing credit debtors who restructure their mortgage loans or repay

with their house after January 1, 1997, will have the right to have their loans declared paid and their names withdrawn from risk central offices. In practice, the benefit is obtained after the first three restructured credit installments have been canceled and the obligation to withdraw information from defaulting debtors falls on the financial institution rather than on the credit bureau.

19. Federal financial authorities also are responsible for enforcing the FCRA, the Gramm-Leach-Bliley Act, and the Financial Information Privacy Protection Act, pursuant to the jurisdiction they have under the various financial system laws.

20. Outstanding among Canadian standards are:

• The data controller must designate one or more individuals to supervise the compliance with the principles within that organization.

• Upon express request, the identity of individuals appointed to supervise the compliance with the principles must be made publicly known.

Directory of Credit Reporting Firms around the World

Based on the World Bank Private Credit Registry survey responses

Latin America and the Caribbean

Argentina
Organización Veraz S.A.—
Equifax Argentina
Alfredo Vicens, General
Manager
Tacuari 202, 10° Floor,
(C1071AAF) Buenos Aires
Telephone: (54 11) 4348–4322
Fax: (54 11) 4348–4315
E-mail: avicens@veraz.com.ar
Website: ⟨www.veraz.com.ar⟩

Argentina
Experian
John Hadlow, Commercial
Manager
Talbot House, Talbot Street,
Nottingham, NG1 5HF
Telephone: (44 11) 5–976 8328
Fax: (44 11) 5–976 8328
E-mail: john.hadlow@uk.
experian.com
Website: ⟨www.experian.com⟩

Brazil
Associação Comercial De São
Paulo
Roberto Haidar, Services
Director
Rua Boa Vista, 51–4th Floor, São
Paulo (SP) 01014–911
Telephone: (55 11) 3244–3691
Fax: (55 11) 3244–3636
E-mail: rhaidar@acsp.com.br
President: Alencar Burti
General Manager: Luís Márcio
Domingues Aranha
Website: ⟨http://www.acsp.
com.br⟩

Brazil
Serasa S.A.
International Business
R. Líbero Badaró, 293-120 Andar,
Sao Paulo (SP) 01095-900
Phone: (55 11) 3150–0396
Fax: (55 11) 3242–3470
E-mail: internationalbusiness@
serasa.com
President: Elcio Anibal de Lucca
Website: ⟨www.serasa.com⟩

Brazil
Associação Comercial e
Industrial de Roraima
Paulo do Vale Pereira Filho,
Diretor
Av Jaime Brasil, 233-1° Andar
Centro, 69.301-350, Centro Boa
Vista, Roraima
Telephone: (55–95) 224–6164
Fax: (55–95) 224–6094
E-mail: acirr@osite.com.br
Diretor do SPC (Serviço de
Proteção ao Crédito): Edson
Araujo

Chile
Camara de Comercio De
Santiago
Claudio Ortiz Tello, Gerente
General
Monjitas 392, Comuna De
Santiago, Santiago
Telephone: (562) 360–7000
Fax: (562) 633–3395
E-mail: Cortiz@Ccs.Cl

Colombia
Computec-Datacrédito
Maria Olga Rehbein, Gerente
General
Cra 7 #76–35 Piso 11, Santa Fe
de Bogota
Telephone: (571) 640–5868
Fax: (571) 640–5867
E-mail: Mrehbein@Computec.
Com.Co

Chile
Asociacion de Bancos e
Instituciones Financieras de
Chile A.G.
Alejandro E. Alarcon, CEO
Ahumada 179, Piso 12, Santiago
Telephone: (56–2) 636–7100
Fax: (562) 698–8945
Website: ⟨www.abif.cl⟩

Chile
Dicom/Equifax S.A.
Marco Antonio Alvarez, General
Manager
Miraflores 353 Piso 8, Santiago
Telephone: (562) 631–5000
Fax: (562) 632–7879
E-mail: malvarez@dicom.cl
Website: ⟨www.dicom.cl⟩

Colombia
Covinoc S.A.
John Jairo Aristizabal Ramirez,
Gerente General
Calle 19 7–48 Piso 9, Bogota
Telephone: (571) 342–0011
Fax: (571) 286–2239
E-mail: Ggeneral@Covinoc.
Com.Co

Costa Rica
Promotora De Comercio Exterior
De Costa Rica (PROCOMER)
Ricardo Matarrita Venegas,
Gerente Estudios Econamicos e
Informacian Comercial
Avenida 3°, Calle 40, San José
Telephone: (506) 256–7111
Fax: (506) 233–5448
E-mail: Rmatarri@Procomer.
Go.Cr
Website: ⟨www.procomer.com⟩

El Salvador
Dicom Centroamerica / Equifax
El Salvador
Leonardo Jose Martinez Cañada,
Gerente General
Boulevard Del Hipodromo
#407 Co. San Benito, San
Salvador
Telephone: (503) 257–3636
Fax: (503) 243–3637
E-mail: ⟨leonardo.martinez@
equifax.com.sv⟩

Dominican Republic
Centro De Informacion
Crediticia de Las Americas, S.A.
(CICLA)
Marcelino San Miguel,
Presidente
1019 Ave. Abraham Lincoln,
Edif. Pages, 3Er. Piso, Santo
Domingo
Telephone: (809) 227–1888
Fax: (809) 549–7227
E-mail: M.SanMiguel@Cicla.
Com.Do
Website: ⟨http:// www.cicla.
com⟩

El Salvador
Procredito, Asociación
Protectora de Créditos de El
Salvador
Astrud Meléndez, Gerente
General
Urb. Jardines De La Libertad,
Calle Opico, Polig. "P," #14,
Cdad. Merliot
Telephone: PBX (503) 289–4840,
Consulta Crediticia Pbx
(503) 289–4811
Fax: (503) 278–0762
E-mail: info@procredito.com.sv
Website: ⟨www.procredito.
com.sv⟩

Guatemala
TransUnion Guatemala, S.A.
Gustavo Zachrisson, General
Director
Guillermo Montano, Executive
Director
Avenida Reforma 2-32 zona 9,
Guatemala, Guatemala
Telephone: (502) 361–7666
However, this phone number
will change in 2003 to (502) 474–
9999 and (502) 474–9800.
Fax: (502) 361–7663
E-mail: info@transunion.com.gt
Website: ⟨www.transunion.
com.gt⟩

México
Buro de Credito
Mauricio Gamboa, Director
General
Pico de Verapaz 435 6O Piso
Colonia Jardines En La
Montaña, Mex. D.F.
Telephone: (52–5) 449–4905
Fax: (52–5) 630–3920
E-mail: servicio.clientes@
burodecredito.com.mx
Website: ⟨www.burodecredito.
com.mx⟩

Guatemala
Protectora de Credito Comercial
Rodolfo Fuentes, General
Manger
7 Ave. 6-26 Z.9, Ofi. 6-82
Sotano, Edificio El Roble,
Guatemala City
Telephone: (502) 361–1033
Fax: (502) 261–0943
E-mail: rodfue@credomatic.
com.gt

Panamá
Asociación Panameña de
Crédito
Lizbeth G. Nieto de Ramsey,
Gerente General
Cl.50 y Ave. Aquilino de La
Guardia, Torre Banco
Continental, Piso 17,
Apartado 6852 Panamá 5
E-mail: gerencia@apc.com.pa
Website: ⟨www.apc.com.pa⟩

Perú
Centro de Riesgos Comerciales
SA—Certicom
Gino Zolezzi Möller, General
Manager
Parque Norte 710, San Isidro,
Lima, 27
Telephone: (511) 225–5119
Fax: (511) 475–2492
E-mail: gzolezzi@certicom.
com.pe
President of the Board:
Guillermo van Oordt

Perú
Infocorp
Julio Best, Gerente General
Las Camelias 780, Piso 8, Lima
27, Peru
Telephone: (51–1) 440–5270
Fax: (51–1) 422–9991
E-mail: Jbest@Infocorp.Com.Pe
Website: ⟨www.infocorp.
com.pe⟩

Uruguay
Clearing de Informes S.A.
Una empresa Equifax
Sra. Matilde Milicevic
Rincón 487, Piso 5, C.P. 11000
Telephone: (598–2) 916–2515/
6037 or (598–2) 915–2133
Fax: (598–2) 916–6400
E-mail: mmilicevic@clearing.
com.uy
Gerente General: José Luis Puig

Uruguay
Liga de Defensa Comercial
Marcos Dalla Rosa, Sub-Gerente
Julio Herrera Y Obes 1413,
Montevideo
Telephone: (598–2) 908–1636
Fax: (598–2) 902–2857
E-mail: marcos@Lideco.Com

Asia & the Pacific

Australia
Baycorp Advantage
Dr. David Grafton, CEO and
Director
90 Arthur Street, North Sydney,
NSW 2060
Tel: (61–2) 9464–6000
Fax: (61–2) 9951–7880
E-mail: assist.au@
baycorpadvantage.com
Website: ⟨www.
baycorpadvantage.com⟩

Australia
Tasmanian Collection Service
Peter Cretan, Managing Director
29 Argyle Street, Hobart,
Tasmania, Australia 7000
Ph: 61–3–62235599
Fax: 61–3–62342988
E-mail: pcretan@tascol.com.au
Website: ⟨http://www.tascol.
com.au/⟩

Hong Kong
Coface Frontline Credit
Management Services Ltd.
Grace Wong, General Manager
8th Floor, Sunning Plaza,
10 Hysan Avenue, Causeway
Bay, Hong Kong
Tel: (852) 2368–6965
Fax: (852) 2367–7275
E-mail: ⟨frontline@
frontlineinfo.com⟩

India
Mira Inform Private Limited
Minesh Gandhi
001-A Ground Floor, Neelambuj,
Shankar Lane, Kandivli (West),
Mumbai 400 067
Telephone: (91–22) 8081714/
8079467
Fax: (91–22) 8074108/8079691
E-mail: infomira@vsnl.com or
infomira@bol.net.in
Website: ⟨http://www.
mirainform.com⟩

Japan
Credit Information Center Corp.
(CIC)
Minoru Harada, Senior
Managing Director
Shinjyuku–Sankocho Bldg.,
5–15–5 Shinjyuku Shinjyuku–
Ku, Tokyo 160–0022
Telephone: (81–3) 3359–9221
Fax: (81–3) 3359–2492
President: Takumo Sato
Website: ⟨http://www.cic.co.jp⟩

Japan
Japan Information Center Corp
Kazuyoshi Takeya, Executive
41-1 kanda-higashimatsushita-
cho Chiyoda-ku Tokyo
Telephone: (81–3) 5294–7005
Fax: (81–3) 5294–7006
E-mail: takeya@zij.co.jp
President JIC: Masahito Hirano
Website: ⟨www.zij.co.jp⟩

Malaysia
Business & Search Information
Services Sdn Bhd
Francis Chan, Operation
Director
Suite 303, Wisma Singapore
Airlines, No. 2–4 Jalan Dang
Wangi, 50100 Kuala Lumpur
Telephone: (603) 26151128/
26151116
Fax: (603) 26915281/26989981
E-mail: Creditrpt@Basis.
Com.My

Philippines
BAP Credit Bureau, Inc.
Manuel R. Batallones, Manager
Ground Floor, Sagittarius
Building II, H.V. Dela Costa
Street, Salcedo Village, Makati
City
Telephone: (632) 813 6868
Fax: (632) 812 2870
E-mail: manuel.batallones@bap.
org.ph

Thailand
Central Credit Information
Services Co., Ltd.
Samma Kitsin, President
10th Floor SVOA Tower 900/7
Rama 3 Road, Yannawa District,
Bangkok 10120
Telephone: (66–2) 682–6404 to 8
Fax: (66–2) 682–6409
E-mail: samma@centralinfo.co.th

Thailand
Thai Credit Bureau, Co., Ltd.
Chom Sumanaseni, President
63 Rama 9 Road, 10th Fl. GHB
Building 2, Bangkok
Tel: (66–2) 643–1864
Fax: (66–2) 643–1266
E-mail: chom@tcb.co.th
Website: ⟨www.tcb.co.th⟩

Europe

Austria
Coface Intercredit Holding AG
Robert Kovacs, Manager Sales &
Marketing
Stubenring 24, A-1010 Vienna,
Austria
Telephone: (43–1) 51554–510
Fax: (43–1) 5335605
E-mail: robert.kovacs@
cofaceintercredit.at
Website: ⟨www.
cofaceintercredit.at⟩
or ⟨www.intercreditonline.com⟩

Austria
Kreditschutzverband von 1870
Harald Heschl
1010 Wien, Franz Josefs Kai 53
Telephone: (43–1) 534–94120
Fax: (43–1) 533–1440
E-mail: heschl.harald@ksv.at
Website: ⟨www.ksv.at⟩
Managing Director: Johannes
Nejedlik

Germany
Buergel
Wirtschaftsinformationen
GmbH + Co. KG
Sven Buckenberger, Vice
President
Gasstr. 18, 22761 Hamburg
Telephone: (49–40) 89803–140
Fax: (49–40) 89803–190
E-mail: sven.buckenberger@
buergel.de
International Director: Rainer
Holzwarth
Telephone: (49–40) 89803–700
Fax: (49–40) 89803–729
E-mail: rainer.holzwarth@
buergel.de
Website: ⟨www.buergel.de⟩

Greece
Tiresias SA
2 Alamanas and Ppemetis St.,
151 25 Maroussi, Athens
Telephone: (030–1) 6199335
Fax: (030–1) 6199910
E-mail: tiresias@tiresias.gr
Website: ⟨www.tiresias.gr⟩

Israel
B.D.I. Business Data Israel Ltd.
Daniel Singerman, Manager,
International Projects
11 Ben Gurion st. Bnei Brak
51260
Telephone: (972–3) 5770333
Fax: (972–3) 6160333

Germany
Creditreform Experian Gmbh
Werner Strahler, Managing
Director
Hellersbergstr. 14, 41460 Neuss
Telephone: (49–2131) 109–100
Fax: (49–2131) 109–215
E-mail: W.Strahler@Verband.
Creditreform.de

Ireland
Irish Credit Bureau Ltd.
Seamus O Tighearnaigh, Chief
Executive
ICB House, Newstead,
Clonskeagh Road, Dublin 14
Telephone: (353–1) 260–0388
Fax: (353–1) 260–0336
E-mail: seamus.otighearnaigh@
icb.ie

Italy
CRIF SPA.
Enrico Lodi, Director, Credit
Bureau Services, via Fantin,
1 / 3–40131 Bologna
Telephone: (39) 051–4176111
E-mail: info@crif.com or
creditbureauservices.
mark@crifgroup.com
Website: ⟨www.crif.com⟩
CEO: Carlo Gherardi

Italy
Experian
John Hadlow, Commercial
Manager
Talbot House, Talbot Street,
Nottingham NG1 5HF
Telephone: (44–115) 976–8328
Fax: (44–115) 976–8328
E-mail: john.hadlow@
uk.experian.com
Website: ⟨www.experian.com⟩

Netherlands
Experian
John Hadlow, Commercial
Manager
Talbot House, Talbot Street,
Nottingham NG1 5HF
Telephone: (44–115) 976–8328
Fax: (44–115) 976–8328
E-mail: john.hadlow@uk.
experian.com
Website: ⟨www.experian.com⟩

Sweden
UC AB
Tommy Bisander, Managing
Director
117 88 Stockholm
Telephone: (46–8) 670 90 00
Fax: (46–8) 670 90 20
E-mail: Mailbox@uc.se

Netherlands
Graydon
L. J. Quist, President
Hullenbergweg 260, Amsterdam
Telephone: (31–20) 567–9760
Fax: (31–20) 691–3520
E-mail: Lj.Quist@Graydon.Nl
Website: ⟨www.graydon.co.uk⟩
or ⟨www.graydon-group.com⟩

Spain
INFORMA S.A.
Marco Postigo, Deputy General
Manager
Avda. de la Industria, 32 28108,
Alcobendas, Madrid.
Telephone: (34–91) 661–71–19
Fax: (34–91) 661–46–96
E-mail: mpostigo@informasa.es
Website: ⟨www.informasa.net⟩

UK
Experian
Tony Leach, Managing Director
of Information Solutions
Talbot House, Talbot Street,
Nottingham NG1 5HF
Telephone: (44–115) 992–2400
Fax Number: (44–115) 992–2537
E-mail: tony.leach@experian.
com
Website: ⟨www.experian.com⟩

Eastern Europe and Central Asia

Croatian Banking Association
Zoran Bohacek
Centar Kaptol, Nova Ves 17,
Zagreb
Telephone: (01) 4860–080
Fax: (01) 4860–081
E-mail: hub@hub.hr
Website: ⟨www.hub.hr⟩

Czech Republic
Coface Intercredit Czechia, spol.
s r.o.
Roman Studnicny
Seifertova 9, 130 00 Praha 3
Telephone: (420) 2–21088–161
Fax: (420) 2–22540–446
E-mail: office@
cofaceintercredit.cz
Website: ⟨www.
cofaceintercredit.cz⟩

Czech Republic
Dun & Bradstreet, Ltd.
Martin Janak
Konevova 2747/99, 130 00
Praha 3
Telephone: (420) 2–71–03–15–00
Fax: (420) 2–71–03–15–30
E-mail: custserv@dbis.cz
Website: ⟨www.dbis.cz⟩

Estonia
Krediidiinfo AS
Veiko Meos
Pronksi 19, Tallinn 10124
Telephone: (372) 66–59–600
Fax: (372) 66–59–601
E-mail: Team@Kredinfo.Ee

Latvia
IGK-BALT
Galina Serjant, Managing
Director
Vilandes 13-9, Riga Lv-1010
Telephone: (371) 732–3460
Fax: (371) 782–0380
E-mail: Igk@Mailbox.Riga.Lv
Website: ⟨http://www.igk-
holding.de⟩
President: Hans Mund

Latvia
Balt Risk SIA
Vasilij Golda, Managing
Director
Vilandes 12-10, Riga LV-1010,
Latvia
Telephone: (371) 732–3470
Fax: (371) 750–8359
E-mail: risk@balt-risk.Lv
Website: ⟨http://www.balt-
risk.lv⟩
President: Hans Mund

Poland
Biuro Informacji Kredytowej
S.A.
Mr. Wyszogrodzki, President
ul. Jana Sengera "Cichego" 1,
02–790 Warszawa
Telephone: 48226457750
Fax: 48226457921
E-mail: biuro@bik.pl
Website: ⟨www.bik.pl⟩

Russia
Dun & Bradstreet Russia
Andrei Terebenin, Managing
Director
3-rd Khoroshevsky Proezd 1,
bld. 1, 123007
Telephone: (7–095) 940–1816
Fax: (7–095) 940–1702
E-mail: terebenin@dnb.ru
Website: ⟨www.dnb.ru⟩

Slovenia
Intercredit Ljubljana d.o.o.
Milos Varga, Managing Director
Cankarjeva 3, 1000 Ljubljana
Phone: (386–1) 425–90–65
Fax: (386–1) 425–91–30
E-mail: intercredit@intercredit.si
Website: ⟨http://www.
intercredit.si⟩

Romania
Coface Intercredit Romania
Teodor Gigea, Managing
Director
Str. Mihai Eminescu nr. 124, Sc.
C, Ap. 2, Sector 2, Bucharest
Telephone: (40–21) 212–1326 or
(40–21) 212–1327
Fax: (40–21) 212–1329
E-mail: office@
cofaceintercredit.ro
Website: ⟨www.
cofaceintercredit.ro⟩

Russia
RUSS-IGK
Igor Galperin, Managing
Director
Nahimovskij Prosp. 24b,
Moscow 117218
Telephone: (7–095) 785–57–10
Fax: (7–095) 129–52–11
E-mail: zinger@ftcenter.ru
Website: ⟨http://www.igk-
holding.de⟩ or
⟨www.igkgroup.ru⟩
President: Hans Mund

Turkey
Anorbis International Business
Information
Duygu Tufan, Asst. General
Manager
Akarsu Caddesi No. 32,
Cihangir, Taksim, 80060
Telephone: (212) 2528838
Fax: (212) 2936339
E-mail: Anorbis@
Superonline.Com

Turkey
KKB Kredi Kayit Burosu A.S.
Kazim Derman, IT, Project
Development & Operation
Manager
Gardenya 42 B Ofis Blok Kat:16
Atasehir Istanbul\
Telephone: (216) 455–45–45
Fax: (216) 455–45–36
E-mail: kazimderman@
kkb.com.tr
Website: ⟨www.kkb.com.tr⟩

Ukraine
IGK Ukraine
Ruslan Bernatski, Managing
Director
Turgenevskaya 71, Kiev 252050
Telephone: (380–44) 2165702,
2165804, 2191685
Fax: (380–44) 271–37–12 or
(380–44) 271–37–36
E-mail: Mail@Igk.Kiev.Ua
Website: ⟨http://www.igk-
holding.de⟩
President: Hans Mund

Other

South Aftrica
Experian
John Hadlow, Commercial
Manager
Talbot House, Talbot Street,
Nottingham NG1 5HF
Telephone: (44–115) 976 8328
Fax: (44–115) 976 8328
E-mail: john.hadlow@uk.
experian.com
Website: ⟨www.experian.com⟩

United States
Experian
Don Robert
President, Experian Information
Solutions
505 City Parkway West, Orange,
CA 92868
E-mail: don.robert@experian.
com
Website: ⟨www.experian.com⟩

United States
Dun & Bradstreet International
Ltd.
Frank E. De Risi, Vice President
8551 W. Sunrise Boulevard,
Hollywood, FL 33021
Telephone: (954) 577–4471
Fax: (954) 577–4548
E-mail: derisif@dnb.Com
Website: ⟨www.dnb.com⟩

Index